HANDBOOK ON MOBILE TECHNOLOGIES

HANDBOOK ON MOBILE TECHNOLOGIES

Tomas Kerepecky

Kruger Brentt
Publishers
2025

Kruger Brentt Publishers UK. LTD.
Company Number 9728962

Regd. Office: 68 St Margarets Road, Edgware, Middlesex HA8 9UU

ISBN: 978-1-78715-402-5

For information on all our publications visit our website at http://krugerbrentt.com/

PREFACE

Mobile technologies have revolutionized the way individuals and businesses interact, communicate, and access information globally. This overview explores the transformative impact of mobile technologies across various domains, from communication and entertainment to commerce and healthcare.

The evolution of mobile technologies began with the introduction of basic cellular networks in the 1980s, enabling voice communication over wireless networks. Over the decades, advancements in technology have led to the proliferation of smartphones and mobile devices equipped with robust computing capabilities, high-speed internet connectivity, and sophisticated applications. Today, mobile devices are ubiquitous, with billions of users worldwide relying on them for everyday tasks.

At its core, mobile technology facilitates instantaneous communication across vast distances through voice calls, messaging apps, and social media platforms. The shift from voice-centric to data-centric communication has enabled richer interactions, including video calls, multimedia messaging, and real-time collaboration tools. Mobile technologies have also bridged digital divides by providing internet access to remote and underserved regions, empowering communities with information and connectivity.

Mobile devices serve as portable entertainment hubs, offering access to a plethora of multimedia content such as streaming movies, music, games, and eBooks. The integration of high-definition displays, immersive audio technologies, and augmented reality (AR) capabilities has transformed how users consume and interact with entertainment content on the go. Mobile gaming, in particular, has emerged as a lucrative industry, catering to diverse demographics with engaging gameplay experiences.

Mobile technologies have reshaped commerce by facilitating seamless online shopping experiences, mobile payments, and digital banking services. E-commerce platforms optimized for mobile devices enable consumers to browse products, compare prices, and make purchases conveniently from their smartphones. Mobile wallets and payment apps provide secure transactions and financial management tools, driving the adoption of cashless economies globally.

In healthcare, mobile technologies have facilitated telemedicine and remote patient monitoring, expanding access to healthcare services beyond traditional clinics and hospitals. Mobile health apps enable individuals to track fitness metrics, monitor chronic conditions, and access medical information and resources in real time. Wearable devices integrated with mobile apps provide continuous health monitoring, promoting proactive wellness management and personalized healthcare solutions.

Looking ahead, mobile technologies are poised to continue driving innovation across industries with emerging trends such as 5G connectivity, Internet of Things (IoT) integration, artificial intelligence (AI) in mobile apps, and decentralized applications (DApps). These advancements promise to enhance connectivity speeds, enable real-time data processing, and unlock new possibilities for smart homes, autonomous vehicles, and industrial automation.

Tomas Kerepecky

CONTENTS

Part-VII: Emerging Trends in Mobile Technologies

PART I

INTRODUCTION TO MOBILE TECHNOLOGIES

CHAPTER 1
EVOLUTION OF MOBILE TECHNOLOGIES

1.1 HISTORICAL OVERVIEW OF MOBILE DEVICES

The evolution of mobile devices has been a remarkable journey that spans over several decades, transforming from simple communication tools to multifaceted gadgets integral to modern life. The history of mobile devices is a testament to human ingenuity and technological progress. From the early days of cumbersome two-way radios to the sleek, multifunctional smartphones of today, mobile devices have continually evolved to meet the changing needs and aspirations of society. As we move forward, the integration of cutting-edge technologies like 5G, AI, and flexible displays promises to shape the future of mobile communication, making it more interconnected, intelligent, and immersive than ever before.

1.1.1 Early Beginnings: The 1940s to 1960s

The concept of mobile communication dates back to the early 20th century, but it wasn't until the 1940s that the first practical devices emerged. In 1946, Bell Labs introduced the first commercial mobile telephone service in St. Louis, Missouri. These early mobile phones were essentially two-way radios, cumbersome and restricted to use in vehicles due to their large size and significant power requirements. In the 1960s, advances in transistor technology allowed for more compact and reliable mobile communication devices. The Improved Mobile Telephone Service (IMTS) introduced by Bell Labs in 1965 offered better call quality and more channels compared to its predecessors. However, these devices were still bulky and limited in functionality.

1.1.2 The Advent of Cellular Technology: The 1970s to 1980s

The 1970s marked a significant leap in mobile communication with the development of cellular technology. In 1973, Martin Cooper of Motorola made the first handheld mobile phone call using a prototype of the Motorola DynaTAC. This groundbreaking event signaled the beginning of a new era in mobile communication. The introduction of the Advanced Mobile Phone System (AMPS) in 1983, the first standardized cellular network, revolutionized mobile telephony. The Motorola DynaTAC 8000X, released in the same year, was the first commercially available handheld mobile phone. Despite its hefty price tag and considerable size, it marked a significant milestone, making mobile communication more accessible.

1.1.3 Digital Revolution: The 1990s

The 1990s saw the transition from analog to digital cellular networks, greatly enhancing the quality and capacity of mobile communication. The second-generation (2G) mobile networks, such as GSM (Global System for Mobile Communications), were introduced, offering better voice quality, text messaging (SMS), and increased security. In 1992, the first commercially available SMS was sent, heralding a new form of communication that quickly gained popularity. The Nokia 1011, released in 1992, was among the first GSM phones, compact, reliable, and capable of sending text messages. The late 1990s also witnessed the emergence of more sophisticated mobile devices. The Nokia 9000 Communicator, released in 1996, combined mobile telephony with PDA (Personal Digital Assistant) functionality, featuring email, fax, and internet access. This convergence of communication and computing capabilities foreshadowed the advent of smartphones.

1.1.4 The Rise of Smartphones: The 2000s

The early 2000s were marked by rapid advancements in mobile technology, leading to the rise of smartphones. These devices combined the functionality of PDAs with mobile phones, offering internet connectivity, multimedia capabilities, and extensive application support. In 2000, the Ericsson R380 was one of the first devices to be marketed as a "smartphone," featuring a touchscreen and the ability to run third-party applications. However, it was the launch of the BlackBerry 5810 in 2002 that truly popularized the concept of smartphones, particularly among business users. BlackBerry devices became renowned for their secure email and messaging capabilities. The release of Apple's iPhone in 2007 was a watershed moment in the history of mobile devices. The iPhone introduced a capacitive touchscreen interface, eschewing physical keyboards in favor of a virtual keyboard and a user-friendly operating system. The App Store, launched in 2008, revolutionized how applications were distributed and monetized, fostering a vast ecosystem of mobile apps.

1.1.5 Mobile Devices in the 2010s: The Era of Connectivity

The 2010s saw mobile devices become central to everyday life, driven by the proliferation of high-speed internet, powerful hardware, and versatile operating systems. Smartphones became ubiquitous, with major players like Apple, Samsung, and Google dominating the market. The introduction of 4G LTE networks significantly improved mobile internet speeds, enabling seamless streaming, gaming, and video conferencing on mobile devices. Smartphones also became essential tools for social media, transforming communication and information sharing.

In 2010, Apple introduced the iPad, ushering in the era of tablets. These larger devices offered enhanced multimedia experiences, productivity tools, and a more immersive interface for browsing and content consumption. Tablets became popular in both consumer and professional settings, complementing smartphones.

Android, developed by Google, emerged as a dominant mobile operating system, offering a more open and customizable alternative to iOS. The competition between Android and iOS spurred innovation, leading to rapid advancements in mobile hardware and software.

1.1.6 The Advent of 5G and Future Trends

As the 2020s unfold, the deployment of 5G networks promises to further revolutionize mobile communication. With significantly higher speeds, lower latency, and increased capacity, 5G is expected to enable new applications such as augmented reality (AR), virtual reality (VR), and the Internet of Things (IoT). Foldable smartphones, introduced by companies like Samsung and Huawei, represent another emerging trend, offering larger screens in more compact forms. These devices aim to combine the portability of smartphones with the expansive display of tablets.

Artificial intelligence (AI) and machine learning are becoming integral to mobile devices, enhancing user experiences through features like voice assistants, advanced photography, and personalized recommendations. Security and privacy continue to be paramount, with innovations such as biometric authentication and end-to-end encryption becoming standard.

1.2 MILESTONES IN MOBILE TECHNOLOGY ADVANCEMENTS

The evolution of mobile technology has been marked by several key milestones, each representing a significant leap in capability and functionality. These advancements have transformed mobile devices from basic communication tools into indispensable, multifunctional gadgets.

The history of mobile technology is a story of continuous innovation and transformation. From the early days of cumbersome two-way radios to the sophisticated, multifunctional smartphones of today, each milestone has brought us closer to a world where mobile devices are integral to our daily lives. As we look to the future, advancements in 5G, AI, and flexible displays promise to further revolutionize the mobile landscape, making these devices even more central to how we communicate, work, and entertain ourselves.

These milestones in mobile technology not only highlight the remarkable progress made over the past decades but also set the stage for future innovations that will continue to shape our connected world.

1.2.1 Early Mobile Communication: The 1940s to 1960s

The origins of mobile communication can be traced back to the 1940s with the advent of two-way radio systems. In 1946, Bell Labs introduced the first commercial mobile telephone service in St. Louis, Missouri. This system, known as the Mobile Telephone Service (MTS), allowed for the transmission of voice over radio waves, but the devices were large and cumbersome, limited to use in vehicles. In the 1960s, the Improved Mobile Telephone Service (IMTS) was launched, offering more channels and improved call quality. However, these systems still faced significant limitations, such as high costs, limited coverage, and the inability to handle a large number of users simultaneously.

1.2.2 The Birth of Cellular Technology: The 1970s

The 1970s marked the beginning of the cellular revolution. In 1973, Martin Cooper of Motorola made the first handheld mobile phone call using a prototype of the Motorola DynaTAC. This event is often considered the birth of mobile telephony as we know it. The DynaTAC 8000X, released commercially in 1983, was the first handheld mobile phone available to the public, despite its large size and high price. The development of cellular technology was a significant milestone. The concept of dividing a geographic area into "cells" and using low-power transmitters within each cell allowed for the efficient reuse of frequencies, significantly increasing the capacity of mobile networks. This technology laid the foundation for modern mobile communication systems.

1.2.3 The Digital Transition: The 1990s

The 1990s saw the transition from analog to digital cellular networks, a major advancement that improved call quality, security, and network capacity. The introduction of the second-generation (2G) networks, such as GSM (Global System for Mobile Communications) and CDMA (Code Division Multiple Access), marked this era.

One of the most notable milestones of the 1990s was the launch of SMS (Short Message Service). The first text message was sent in 1992, and SMS quickly became a popular means of communication due to its convenience and low cost. The Nokia 1011, released in 1992, was among the first GSM phones capable of sending and receiving text messages.

Another significant development was the integration of additional features into mobile phones. The IBM Simon, released in 1994, is considered the first smartphone, combining a mobile phone with a PDA (Personal Digital Assistant). It featured a touchscreen, email capability, and built-in apps, foreshadowing the multifunctional smartphones of today.

1.2.4 The Smartphone Revolution: The 2000s

The early 2000s witnessed the rapid evolution of mobile phones into smartphones. The release of the BlackBerry 5810 in 2002 was a pivotal moment, as BlackBerry devices became synonymous with mobile email and secure communication, particularly among business users.

The most transformative milestone of this era was the launch of the Apple iPhone in 2007. The iPhone introduced a capacitive touchscreen interface, replacing physical keyboards with a virtual keyboard and offering an intuitive user experience. Its operating system, iOS, supported third-party applications, leading to the creation of the App Store in 2008. This ecosystem of apps revolutionized how people used mobile devices, enabling a vast array of functionalities from gaming to productivity.

The emergence of Android, an open-source mobile operating system developed by Google, provided a robust alternative to iOS. The first Android phone, the HTC Dream (also known as the T-Mobile G1), was released in 2008. Android's open nature and extensive customization options contributed to its rapid adoption, fueling intense competition and innovation in the smartphone market.

1.2.5 The Era of Connectivity: The 2010s

The 2010s were characterized by the proliferation of smartphones and the advent of high-speed mobile internet. The introduction of 4G LTE networks significantly improved data speeds, enabling seamless streaming, gaming, and video conferencing on mobile devices.

The release of the Apple iPad in 2010 marked the beginning of the tablet era. Tablets offered a larger screen and enhanced multimedia capabilities, bridging the gap between smartphones and laptops. They quickly became popular for both personal and professional use, offering portability without sacrificing functionality.

The rise of mobile apps and social media platforms transformed smartphones into essential tools for communication, entertainment, and commerce. Applications like Facebook, Instagram, WhatsApp, and Snapchat became integral to daily life, fundamentally changing how people interacted and shared information.

1.2.6 The Advent of 5G and Emerging Technologies: The 2020s

As we entered the 2020s, the rollout of 5G networks began, promising even higher speeds, lower latency, and greater capacity. 5G technology is expected to enable a new wave of innovations, including the Internet of Things (IoT), augmented reality (AR), virtual reality (VR), and autonomous vehicles.

Foldable smartphones emerged as a new trend, with devices like the Samsung Galaxy Fold and Huawei Mate X offering larger, flexible displays that combine the portability of smartphones with the screen real estate of tablets. These devices represent the next evolution in mobile form factors, providing users with more versatility and enhanced multitasking capabilities.

Artificial intelligence (AI) and machine learning are increasingly integrated into mobile devices, enhancing user experiences through features like voice assistants (e.g., Siri, Google Assistant), advanced photography, and personalized recommendations. These technologies continue to push the boundaries of what mobile devices can do, making them smarter and more intuitive.

CHAPTER 2

MOBILE ECOSYSTEMS AND PLATFORMS

2.1 OVERVIEW OF IOS, ANDROID & OTHER MOBILE PLATFORMS

2.1.1 iOS

iOS (formerly iPhone OS) is a mobile operating system developed by Apple exclusively for its smartphones. It was unveiled in January 2007 for the first-generation iPhone, launched in June 2007.

It is the operating system that powers many of the company's mobile devices, including the iPhone. It was also used on iPads (introduced: January 2010; availability: April 2010) until iPadOS was introduced in 2019, and on the iPod Touch devices, which were discontinued in mid-2022. It is the world's second-most widely installed mobile operating system, after Android. It is the basis for three other operating systems made by Apple: iPadOS, tvOS, and watchOS.

As of December 2023, Apple's App Store contains more than 3.8 million iOS applications. These mobile apps have collectively been downloaded more than 130 billion times.

iOS is based on macOS. Like macOS, it includes components of the Mach microkernel and FreeBSD. It is a Unix-like operating system. Although some parts of iOS are open source under the Apple Public Source License and other licenses, iOS is proprietary software.

Major versions of iOS are released annually. The current stable version, iOS 17, was released to the public on September 18, 2023.

History

In 2005, when Steve Jobs began planning the iPhone, he had a choice to either "shrink the Mac, which would be an epic feat of engineering, or enlarge the iPod". Jobs favored the former approach but pitted the Macintosh and iPod teams, led by Scott Forstall and Tony Fadell, respectively, against each other in an internal competition, with Forstall winning by creating iPhone OS. The decision enabled the success of the iPhone as a platform for third-party developers: using a well-known desktop operating system as its basis allowed the many third-party Mac developers to write software for the iPhone with minimal retraining. Forstall was also responsible for creating a software development kit for programmers to build iPhone apps, as well as an App Store within iTunes.

The operating system was unveiled with the iPhone at the Macworld Conference & Expo on January 9, 2007, and released in June of that year. At the time of its unveiling in January, Steve Jobs claimed: "iPhone runs OS X" and runs "desktop class applications", but at the time of the iPhone's release, the operating system was renamed "iPhone OS". Initially, third-party native applications were not supported. Jobs' reasoning was that developers could build web applications through the Safari web browser that "would behave like native apps on the iPhone". In October 2007, Apple announced that a native Software Development Kit (SDK) was under development and that they planned to put it "in developers' hands in February". On March 6, 2008, Apple held a press event, announcing the iPhone SDK.

The iOS App Store was opened on July 10, 2008, with an initial 500 applications available. This quickly grew to 3,000 in September 2008, 15,000 in January 2009, 50,000 in June 2009, 100,000 in November 2009, 250,000 in August 2010, 650,000 in July 2012, 1 million in October 2013, 2 million in June 2016, and 2.2 million in January 2017.

As of March 2016, 1 million apps are natively compatible with the iPad tablet computer. These apps have collectively been downloaded more than 130 billion times. App intelligence firm Sensor Tower estimated that the App Store would reach 5 million apps by 2020.

In September 2007, Apple announced the iPod Touch, a redesigned iPod based on the iPhone form factor. On January 27, 2010, Apple introduced their much-anticipated media tablet, the iPad, featuring a larger screen than the iPhone and iPod Touch, and designed for web browsing, media consumption, and reading, and offering multi-touch interaction with multimedia formats including newspapers, e-books, photos, videos, music, word processing documents, video games, and most existing iPhone apps using a 9.7-inch (25 cm) screen. It also includes a mobile version of Safari for web browsing, as well as access to the App Store, iTunes Library, iBookstore, Contacts, and Notes. Content is downloadable via Wi-Fi and optional 3G service or synced through the user's computer. AT&T was initially the sole U.S. provider of 3G wireless access for the iPad.

In June 2010, Apple rebranded iPhone OS as "iOS". The trademark "IOS" had been used by Cisco for over a decade for its operating system, IOS, used on its routers. To avoid any potential lawsuit, Apple licensed the "IOS" trademark from Cisco.

The Apple Watch smartwatch was announced by Tim Cook on September 9, 2014, being introduced as a product with health and fitness-tracking. It was released on April 24, 2015. It uses watchOS as its operating system; watchOS is based on iOS, with new features created specially for the Apple Watch such as an activity tracking app.

In October 2016, Apple opened its first iOS Developer Academy in Naples inside University of Naples Federico II's new campus. The course is completely free, aimed at acquiring specific technical skills on the creation and management of applications for the Apple ecosystem platforms. At the academy there are also issues of business administration (business planning and business management with a focus on digital opportunities) and there is a path dedicated to the design of graphical interfaces. Students have the opportunity to participate in the "Enterprise Track", an in-depth training experience on the entire life cycle of an app, from design to implementation, to security, troubleshooting, data storage and cloud usage. As of 2020, the academy graduated almost a thousand students from all over the world, who have worked on 400 app ideas and have already published about 50 apps on the iOS App Store. In the 2018–2019 academic year, students from more than 30 countries arrived. 35 of these have been selected to attend the Worldwide Developer Conference, the annual Apple Developer Conference held annually in California in early June.

On June 3, 2019, iPadOS, the branded version of iOS for iPad, was announced at the 2019 WWDC; it was launched on September 25, 2019.

Features

Interface

The iOS user interface is based upon direct manipulation, using multi-touch gestures such as *swipe*, *tap*, *pinch*, and *reverse pinch*. Interface control elements include sliders, switches, and buttons. Internal accelerometers are used by some applications to respond to shaking the device (one common result is the undo command) or rotating it in three dimensions (one common result is switching between portrait and landscape mode). Various accessibility described in § Accessibility functions enable users with vision and hearing disabilities to properly use iOS.

iOS devices boot to the lock screen. The lock screen shows the time and a user's lock screen widgets, which display timely information from apps. Upon unlock, a user is directed to the home screen, which is the primary navigation and information "hub" on iOS devices, analogous to the desktop found on personal computers. iOS home screens are typically made up of app icons and widgets; app icons launch the associated app, whereas widgets display live, auto-updating content, such as a weather forecast, the user's email inbox, or a news ticker directly on the home screen. Along the top of the screen is a status bar, showing information about the device and its connectivity. The Control Center can be "pulled" down from the top right of the notch or Dynamic Island (on iPhones with Face ID) or can be "pulled" up from the bottom to top of the screen (on iPhones with Touch ID), giving access to various toggles to manage the device more quickly without having to open the Settings. It is possible to manage brightness, volume, wireless connections, music player, etc.

Scrolling from the top left to the bottom (or top to bottom on iPhones with Touch ID) will open the Notification Center, which in the latest versions of iOS is very similar to the lock screen. It displays notifications in chronological order and groups them by application. From the notifications of some apps it is possible to interact directly, for example by replying to a message directly from it. Notifications are sent in two modes, critical alerts that are displayed on the lock screen and signaled by a distinctive sound and vibration (e.g. emergency alerts or severe weather alerts), accompanied by a warning banner and the app badge icon, and standard alerts which use a default sound and vibration. Both can be found in the Notification Center, and show for a set amount of time on the lock screen (unless the user has Notification Center allowed when locked).

On iPhones with Touch ID, screenshots can be created with the simultaneous press of the home and power buttons. In comparison to Android, which requires the buttons to be held down, a short press does suffice on iOS. On iPhone with Face ID, screenshots are captured using the volume-up and power buttons instead.

The camera application used a skeuomorphic closing camera shutter animation prior to iOS 7. Since then, it uses a simple short blackout effect. Notable additions over time include HDR photography and the option to save both normal and high dynamic range photographs simultaneously where the former prevents ghosting effects from moving objects (since iPhone 5 on iOS 6), automatic HDR adjustment (since iOS 7.1), "live photo" with short video bundled to each photo if enabled (iPhone 6s, iOS 9), and a digital zoom shortcut (iPhone 7 Plus, iOS 10). Some camera settings such as video resolution and frame rate are not adjustable through the camera interface itself, but are outsourced to the system settings.

A new feature in iOS 13 called "context menus" shows related actions when you touch and hold an item. When the context menu is displayed, the background is blurred.

To choose from a few options, a selection control is used. Selectors can appear anchored at the bottom or in line with the content (called date selectors). Date selectors take on the appearance of any other selection control, but with a column for day, month, and optionally year.

Alerts appear in the center of the screen, but there are also alerts that scroll up from the bottom of the screen (called "action panels"). Destructive actions (such as eliminating any element) are colored red.

The official font of iOS is San Francisco. It is designed for small text readability, and is used throughout the operating system, including third-party apps.

The icons are 180x180px in size for iPhones with a larger screen, usually models over 6 inches, including iPhone 11 Pro and iPhone 8 Plus, while they are 120x120px on iPhones with smaller displays.

Home Screen

The home screen, rendered by SpringBoard, displays application icons and a dock at the bottom where users can pin their most frequently used apps. iOS home screens are typically made up of app icons and widgets; app icons launch the associated app, whereas widgets display live, auto-updating content, such as a weather forecast, the user's email inbox, or a news ticker directly on the home screen. The home screen appears whenever the user unlocks the device, presses the physical "Home" button while in an app, or swipes up from the bottom of the screen using the home bar. The screen has a status bar across the top to display data, such as time, battery level, and signal strength. The rest of the screen is devoted to the current application. When a passcode is set and a user switches on the device, the passcode must be entered at the Lock Screen before access to the Home screen is granted.

In iPhone OS 3, Spotlight was introduced, allowing users to search media, apps, emails, contacts, messages, reminders, calendar events, and similar content. In iOS 7 and later, Spotlight is accessed by pulling down anywhere on the home screen (except for the top and bottom edges that open Notification Center and Control Center). In iOS 9, there are two ways to access Spotlight. As with iOS 7 and 8, pulling down on any homescreen will show Spotlight. However, it can also be accessed as it was in iOS versions 3 through 6. This endows Spotlight with Siri suggestions, which include app suggestions, contact suggestions and news. In iOS 10, Spotlight is at the top of the now-dedicated "Today" panel.

Since iPhone OS 3.2, users are able to set a background image for the Home Screen. This feature is only available on third-generation devices—iPhone 3GS, third-generation iPod Touch (iOS 4.0 or newer), and all iPad models (since iPhone OS 3.2)—or newer.

iOS 7 introduced a parallax effect on the Home Screen, which shifts the device's wallpaper and icons in response to the movement of the device, creating a 3D effect and an illusion of floating icons. This effect is also visible in the tab view of Mail and Safari.

Researchers found that users organize icons on their homescreens based on usage frequency and relatedness of the applications, as well as for reasons of usability and aesthetics.

System Font

iOS originally used Helvetica as the system font. Apple switched to Helvetica Neue exclusively for the iPhone 4 and its Retina Display, and retained Helvetica as the system font for older iPhone devices on iOS 4. With iOS 7, Apple announced that they would change the system font to Helvetica Neue Light, a decision that sparked criticism for inappropriate usage of a light, thin typeface for low-resolution mobile screens. Apple eventually chose Helvetica Neue instead. The release of iOS 7 also introduced the ability to scale text or apply other forms of text accessibility changes through Settings. With iOS 9, Apple changed the font to San Francisco, an Apple-designed font aimed at maximum legibility and font consistency across its product lineup.

Folders

iOS 4 introduced folders, which can be created by dragging an application on top of another, and from then on, more items can be added to the folder using the same procedure. A title for the folder is automatically selected by the category of applications inside, but the name can also be edited by the user. When apps inside folders receive notification badges, the individual numbers of notifications are added up and the total number is displayed as a notification badge on the folder itself. Originally, folders on an iPhone could include up to 12 apps, while folders on iPad could include 20. With increasing display sizes on newer iPhone hardware, iOS 7 updated the folders with pages similar to the home screen layout, allowing for a significant expansion of folder functionality. Each page of a folder can contain up to nine apps, and there can be 15 pages in total, allowing for a total of 135 apps in a single folder. In iOS 9, Apple updated folder sizes for iPad hardware, allowing for 16 apps per page, still at 15 pages maximum, increasing the total to 240 apps.

Notification Center

Before iOS 5, notifications were delivered in a modal window and could not be viewed after being dismissed. In iOS 5, Apple introduced Notification Center, which allows users to view a history of notifications. The user can tap a notification to open its corresponding app, or clear it. Notifications are now delivered in banners that appear briefly at the top of the screen. If a user taps a received notification, the application that sent the notification will be opened. Users can also choose to view notifications in modal alert windows by adjusting the application's notification settings. Introduced with iOS 8, widgets are now accessible through the Notification Center, defined by 3rd parties.

When an app sends a notification while closed, a red badge appears on its icon. This badge tells the user, at a glance, how many notifications that app has sent. Opening the app clears the badge.

Applications

iOS devices come with preinstalled apps developed by Apple including Mail, Maps, TV, Music, FaceTime, Wallet, Health, and many more.

Applications ("apps") are the most general form of application software that can be installed on iOS. They are downloaded from the official catalog of the App Store digital store, where apps are subjected to security checks before being made available to users. In June 2017, Apple updated its guidelines to specify that app developers will no longer have the ability to use custom prompts for encouraging users to leave reviews for their apps. IOS applications can also be installed directly from an IPA file provided by the software distributor, via unofficial ways. They are written using iOS Software Development Kit (SDK) and, often, combined with Xcode, using officially supported programming languages, including Swift and Objective-C. Other companies have also created tools that allow for the development of native iOS apps using their respective programming languages.

Applications for iOS are mostly built using components of UIKit, a programming framework. It allows applications to have a consistent look and feel with the OS, nevertheless offering customization.

Elements automatically update along with iOS updates, automatically including new interface rules. UIKit elements are very adaptable, this allows developers to design a single app that looks the same on any iOS device. In addition to defining the iOS interface, UIKit defines the functionality of the application.

At first, Apple did not intend to release an SDK to developers, because they did not want third-party apps to be developed for iOS, building web apps instead. However, this technology never entered into common use, this led Apple to change its opinion, so in October 2007 the SDK for developers was announced, finally released on March 6, 2008.

The SDK includes an inclusive set of development tools, including an audio mixer and an iPhone simulator. It is a free download for Mac users. It is not available for Microsoft Windows PCs. To test the application, get technical support, and distribute applications through App Store, developers are required to subscribe to the Apple Developer Program.

Over the years, the Apple Store apps surpassed multiple major milestones, including 50,000, 100,000, 250,000, 500,000, 1 million, and 2 million apps. The billionth application was installed on April 24, 2009.

App Library

App Library automatically categorizes apps into folders based on their function or type and incluses an alphabetical list of all installed apps. For example, it might group all social media apps into one folder and productivity apps into another. Users can quickly find and access apps by using the search bar at the top of the App Library. Users can choose to hide specific app pages from the home screen, making it easier to focus on the apps they use most frequently.

Storage

iOS enforces strict sandboxing to maintain security and privacy. Apps are generally limited to accessing their own containers and specific system-provided directories, such as the Photos library. To access files outside of their sandbox, iOS uses mechanisms like document pickers, file providers, and app extensions.

iOS 8 introduced the Document Picker and Document Provider extensions as part of the document interaction controller. This allows apps to open, save, and interact with documents stored in a central location or cloud storage services.

With iOS 11, Apple introduced the Files app and the File Provider extension, providing a central location for users to manage and organize their files. Apps can integrate with the Files app to make their documents accessible and editable directly from the Files app.

The storage of iOS devices can be expanded through iCloud, the Apple's cloud-based storage solution that provides 5GB of storage for free to all users, while other plans require a paid subscription. iCloud Drive allows users to store various types of files, such as documents, presentations, and spreadsheets, in the cloud. These files can be accessed across multiple devices as long as the user is signed in with the same Apple ID.

Accessibility

iOS offers various accessibility features to help users with vision and hearing disabilities. One major feature, VoiceOver, provides a voice reading information on the screen, including contextual buttons, icons, links and other user interface elements, and allows the user to navigate the operating system through gestures. Any apps with default controls and developed with a UIKit framework gets VoiceOver functionality built in. One example includes holding up the iPhone to take a photo, with VoiceOver describing the photo scenery. As part of a "Made for iPhone" program, introduced with the release of iOS 7 in 2013, Apple has developed technology to use Bluetooth and a special technology protocol to let compatible third-party equipment connect with iPhones and iPads for streaming audio directly to a user's ears. Additional customization available for Made for iPhone products include battery tracking and adjustable sound settings for different environments. Apple made further efforts for accessibility for the release of iOS 10 in 2016, adding a new pronunciation editor to VoiceOver, adding a Magnifier setting to enlarge objects through the device's camera, software TTY support for deaf people to make phone calls from the iPhone, and giving tutorials and guidelines for third-party developers to incorporate proper accessibility functions into their apps.

In 2012, Liat Kornowski from *The Atlantic* wrote that "the iPhone has turned out to be one of the most revolutionary developments since the invention of Braille", and in 2016, Steven Aquino of *TechCrunch* described Apple as "leading the way in assistive technology", with Sarah Herrlinger, Senior Manager for Global Accessibility Policy and Initiatives at Apple, stating that "We see accessibility as a basic human right. Building into the core of our products supports a vision of an inclusive world where opportunity and access to information are barrier-free, empowering individuals with disabilities to achieve their goals".

Criticism has been aimed at iOS depending on both internet connection (either WiFi or through iTunes) and a working SIM card upon first activation. This restriction has been loosened in iOS 12, which no longer requires the latter.

Multitasking

Multitasking for iOS was first released in June 2010 along with the release of iOS 4. Only certain devices—iPhone 4, iPhone 3GS, and iPod Touch 3rd generation—were able to multitask. The iPad did not get multitasking until iOS 4.2.1 in that November.

The implementation of multitasking in iOS has been criticized for its approach, which limits the work that applications in the background can perform to a limited function set and requires application developers to add explicit support for it.

Before iOS 4, multitasking was limited to a selection of the applications Apple included on the device. Users could however "jailbreak" their device in order to unofficially multitask. Starting with iOS 4, on third-generation and newer iOS devices, multitasking is supported through seven background APIs:

- **Background Audio**—application continues to run in the background as long as it is playing audio or video content
- **Voice over IP**—application is suspended when a phone call is not in progress
- **Background Location**—application is notified of location changes

Push notifications

- **Local Notifications**—application schedules local notifications to be delivered at a predetermined time
- **Task Completion**—application asks the system for extra time to complete a given task
- **Fast App Switching**—application does not execute any code and may be removed from memory at any time

In iOS 5, three new background APIs were introduced:

- **Newsstand**—application can download content in the background to be ready for the user
- **External Accessory**—application communicates with an external accessory and shares data at regular intervals
- **Bluetooth Accessory**—application communicates with a bluetooth accessory and shares data at regular intervals

In iOS 7, Apple introduced a new multitasking feature, providing all apps with the ability to perform background updates. This feature prefers to update the user's most frequently used apps and prefers to use Wi-Fi networks over a cellular network, without markedly reducing the device's battery life.

Switching Applications

In iOS 4.0 to iOS 6.x, double-clicking the home button activates the application switcher. A scrollable dock-style interface appears from the bottom, moving the contents of the screen up. Choosing an icon switches to an application. To the far left are icons which function as music controls, a rotation lock, and on iOS 4.2 and above, a volume controller.

With the introduction of iOS 7, double-clicking the home button also activates the application switcher. However, unlike previous versions it displays screenshots of open applications on top of the icon and horizontal scrolling allows for browsing through previous apps, and it is possible to close applications by dragging them up, similar to how WebOS handled multiple cards.

With the introduction of iOS 9, the application switcher received a significant visual change; while still retaining the card metaphor introduced in iOS 7, the application icon is smaller, and appears above the screenshot (which is now larger, due to the removal of "Recent and Favorite Contacts"), and each application "card" overlaps the other, forming a rolodex effect as the user scrolls.

Now, instead of the home screen appearing at the leftmost of the application switcher, it appears rightmost. In iOS 11, the application switcher receives a major redesign. In the iPad, the Control Center and app switcher are combined. The app switcher in the iPad can also be accessed by swiping up from the bottom. In the iPhone, the app switcher cannot be accessed if there are no apps in the RAM.

Ending Tasks

In iOS 4.0 to iOS 6.x, briefly holding the icons in the application switcher makes them "jiggle" (similarly to the homescreen) and allows the user to *force* quit the applications by tapping the red minus circle that appears at the corner of the app's icon.

Clearing applications from multitasking stayed the same from iOS 4.0 through 6.1.6, the last version of iOS 6.

As of iOS 7, the process has become faster and easier. In iOS 7, instead of holding the icons to close them, they are closed by simply swiping them upwards off the screen. Up to three apps can be cleared at a time compared to one in versions up to iOS 6.1.6.

Task Completion

Task completion allows apps to continue a certain task after the app has been suspended. As of iOS 4.0, apps can request up to ten minutes to complete a task in the background.

This doesn't extend to background uploads and downloads though (e.g., if a user starts a download in one application, it won't finish if they switch away from the application).

Siri

Siri is a virtual assistant integrated into iOS. The assistant uses voice queries and a natural-language user interface to answer questions, make recommendations, and perform actions by delegating requests to a set of Internet services. The software adapts to users' individual language usages, searches, and preferences, with continuing use. Returned results are individualized.

Originally released as an app for iOS in February 2010, it was acquired by Apple two months later, and then integrated into iPhone 4S at its release in October 2011. At that time, the separate app was also removed from the iOS App Store.

Siri supports a wide range of user commands, including performing phone actions, checking basic information, scheduling events and reminders, handling device settings, searching the Internet, navigating areas, finding information on entertainment, and is able to engage with iOS-integrated apps.

With the release of iOS 10 in 2016, Apple opened up limited third-party access to Siri, including third-party messaging apps, as well as payments, ride-sharing, and Internet calling apps. With the release of iOS 11, Apple updated Siri's voices for more clear, human voices, it now supports follow-up questions and language translation, and additional third-party actions. iOS 17 enabled users to activate Siri by simply saying "Siri", while the previous command, "Hey Siri", is still supported.

Game Center

Game Center is an online multiplayer "social gaming network" released by Apple. It allows users to "invite friends to play a game, start a multiplayer game through matchmaking, track their achievements, and compare their high scores on a leaderboard." iOS 5 and above adds support for profile photos.

Game Center was announced during an iOS 4 preview event hosted by Apple on April 8, 2010. A preview was released to registered Apple developers in August. It was released on September 8, 2010, with iOS 4.1 on iPhone 4, iPhone 3GS, and iPod Touch 2nd generation through 4th generation. Game Center made its public debut on the iPad with iOS 4.2.1. There is no support for the iPhone 3G, original iPhone and the first-generation iPod Touch (the latter two devices did not have Game Center because they did not get iOS 4). However, Game Center is unofficially available on the iPhone 3G via a hack.

Hardware

The main hardware platform for iOS is the ARM architecture (the ARMv7, ARMv8-A, ARMv8.2-A, ARMv8.3-A). iOS releases before iOS 7 can only be run on iOS devices with 32-bit ARM processors (ARMv6 and ARMv7-A architectures). In 2013, iOS 7 was released with full 64-bit support (which includes a native 64-bit kernel, libraries, drivers as well as all built-in applications), after Apple announced that they were switching to 64-bit ARMv8-A processors with the introduction of the Apple A7 chip. 64-bit support was also enforced for all apps in the App Store; All new apps submitted to the App Store with a deadline of February 2015, and all app updates submitted to the App Store with a deadline of June 1, 2015. iOS 11 drops support for all iOS devices with 32-bit ARM processors as well as 32-bit applications, making iOS 64-bit only.

Development

The iOS SDK (Software development kit) allows for the development of mobile apps on iOS. While originally developing iPhone prior to its unveiling in 2007, Apple's then-CEO Steve Jobs did not intend to let third-party developers build native apps for iOS, instead directing them to make web applications for the Safari web browser. However, backlash from developers prompted the company to reconsider, with Jobs announcing in October 2007 that Apple would have a software development kit available for developers by February 2008. The SDK was released on March 6, 2008.

The SDK is a free download for users of Mac personal computers. It is not available for Microsoft Windows PCs. The SDK contains sets giving developers access to various functions and services of iOS devices, such as hardware and software attributes. It also contains an iPhone simulator to mimic the look and feel of the device on the computer while developing. New versions of the SDK accompany new versions of iOS. In order to test applications, get technical support, and distribute apps through App Store, developers are required to subscribe to the Apple Developer Program.

Combined with Xcode, the iOS SDK helps developers write iOS apps using officially supported programming languages, including Swift and Objective-C. Other companies have also created tools that allow for the development of native iOS apps using their respective programming languages.

Update History & Schedule

Apple provides major updates to the iOS operating system annually via iTunes and, since iOS 5, also over-the-air. The device checks an XML-based PLIST file on mesu.apple.com for updates. Updates are delivered as unencrypted ZIP files. Updates are checked for regularly, and are downloaded and installed automatically if enabled. Otherwise, the user can install them manually or are prompted to allow automatic installation overnight if plugged in and connected to Wi-Fi.

iPod Touch users originally had to pay for system software updates due to accounting rules that designated it not a "subscription device" like the iPhone or Apple TV, causing many iPod Touch owners not to update. In September 2009, a change in accounting rules won tentative approval, affecting Apple's earnings and stock price, and allowing iPod Touch updates to be delivered free of charge.

Apple significantly extended the cycle of updates for iOS-supported devices over the years. The iPhone (1st generation) and iPhone 3G only received two iOS updates, while later models had support for five, six, and seven years.

XNU Kernel

The iOS kernel is the XNU kernel of Darwin. The original iPhone OS (1.0) up to iPhone OS 3.1.3 used Darwin 9.0.0d1. iOS 4 was based on Darwin 10. iOS 5 was based on Darwin 11. iOS 6 was based on Darwin 13. iOS 7 and iOS 8 are based on Darwin 14. iOS 9 is based on Darwin 15. iOS 10 is based on Darwin 16. iOS 11 is based on Darwin 17. iOS 12 is based on Darwin 18. iOS 13 is based on Darwin 19. iOS 14 is based on Darwin 20. iOS 15 is based on Darwin 21. iOS 16 is based on Darwin 22.

In iOS 6 the kernel is subject to ASLR, similar to that of OS X Mountain Lion. This makes exploit possibilities more complex since it is not possible to know the location of kernel code.

Apple has made the XNU kernel open source. The source is under a 3-clause BSD license for the original BSD parts, with parts added by Apple under the Apple Public Source License. The versions contained in iOS are not available; only the versions used in macOS are available.

iOS does not have kernel extensions (kexts) in the file system, even if they are actually present. The kernel cache can be decompressed to show the correct kernel, along with the kexts (all packed in the __PRELINK_TEXT section) and their plists (in the __PRELINK_INFO section).

The kernel cache can also be directly decompressed (if decrypted) using third-party tools. With the advent of iOS 10 betas and default plain text kernelcaches, these tools can only be used after unpacking and applying lzssdec to unpack the kernel cache to its full size.

The kextstat provided by the Cydia alternative software does not work on iOS because the kextstat is based on kmod_get_info(...), which is a deprecated API in iOS 4 and Mac OS X Snow Leopard. There are other alternative software that can also dump raw XML data.

On developing devices, the kernel is always stored as a statically linked cache stored in /System/Library/Caches/com.apple.kernelcaches/kernelcache which is unpacked and executed at boot.

In the beginning, iOS had a kernel version usually higher than the corresponding version of macOS. Over time, the kernels of iOS and macOS have gotten closer. This is not surprising, considering that iOS introduced new features (such as the ASLR Kernel, the default freezer, and various security-strengthening features) that were first incorporated and subsequently arrived on macOS. It appears Apple is gradually merging the iOS and macOS kernels over time. The build date for each version varies slightly between processors. This is due to the fact that the builds are sequential.

Kernel Image

The kernel image base is randomized by the boot loader (iBoot). This is done by creating random data, doing a SHA-1 hash of it and then using a byte from the SHA-1 hash for the kernel slide. The slide is calculated with this formula:

*base = 0x01000000 + (slide_byte * 0x00200000)*

If the slide is 0, the static offset of 0x21000000 is used instead.

The adjusted base is passed to the kernel in the boot arguments structure at offset `0x04`, which is equivalent to gBootArgs->virtBase.

Kernel Map

The kernel map is used for kernel allocations of all types (kalloc(), kernel_memory_allocate(), etc.) and spans all of kernel space (0x80000000-0xFFFEFFFF). The kernel based maps are submaps of the *kernel_map*, for example *zone_map, ipc_kernel_map*, etc.

The strategy is to randomize the base of the *kernel_map*. A random 9-bit value is generated right after *kmem_init()* which establishes kernel_map, is multiplied by the page size. The resulting value is used as the size for the initial *kernel_map* allocation. Future *kernel_map* (and submap) allocations are pushed forward by a random amount. The allocation is silently removed after the first garbage collection and reused. This behaviour can be overridden with the "kmapoff" boot parameter.

Versions Codenames

Internally, iOS identifies each version by a codename, often used internally only, normally to maintain secrecy of the project. For example, the codename for iOS 17 is *Dawn.*

Jailbreaking

Since its initial release, iOS has been subject to a variety of different hacks centered around adding functionality not allowed by Apple. Prior to the 2008 debut of Apple's native iOS App Store, the primary motive for jailbreaking was to bypass Apple's purchase mechanism for installing the App Store's native applications. Apple claimed that it would not release iOS software updates designed specifically to break these tools (other than applications that perform SIM unlocking); however, with each subsequent iOS update, previously un-patched jailbreak exploits are usually patched.

When a device is booting, it loads Apple's own kernel initially, so a jailbroken device must be exploited and have the kernel patched each time it is booted up.

There are different types of jailbreak. An *untethered* jailbreak uses exploits that are powerful enough to allow the user to turn their device off and back on at will, with the device starting up completely, and the kernel will be patched without the help of a computer – in other words, it will be jailbroken even after each reboot.

However, some jailbreaks are tethered. A tethered jailbreak is only able to temporarily jailbreak the device during a single boot. If the user turns the device off and then boots it back up without the help of a jailbreak tool, the device will no longer be running a patched kernel, and it may get stuck in a partially started state, such as Recovery Mode.

In order for the device to start completely and with a patched kernel, it must be "re-jailbroken" with a computer (using the "boot tethered" feature of a tool) each time it is turned on.

All changes to the files on the device (such as installed package files or edited system files) will persist between reboots, including changes that can only function if the device is jailbroken (such as installed package files).

In more recent years, two other solutions have been created – *semi-tethered* and *semi-untethered.*

A semi-tethered solution is one where the device is able to start up on its own, but it will no longer have a patched kernel, and therefore will not be able to run modified code. It will, however, still be usable for normal functions, just like stock iOS. To start with a patched kernel, the user must start the device with the help of the jailbreak tool.

A semi-untethered jailbreak gives the ability to start the device on its own. On first boot, the device will not be running a patched kernel. However, rather than having to run a tool from a computer to apply the kernel patches, the user is able to re-jailbreak their device with the help of an app (usually sideloaded using Cydia Impactor) running on their device. In the case of the iOS 9.2-9.3.3 and 64-bit 10.x jailbreaks, Safari-based exploits were available, thereby meaning websites could be used to re-jailbreak.

In more detail: Each iOS device has a bootchain that tries to make sure only trusted/signed code is loaded. A device with a tethered jailbreak is able to boot up with the help of a jailbreaking tool because the tool executes exploits via USB that bypass parts of that "chain of trust", bootstrapping to a pwned (no signature check) iBEC, or iBoot to finish the boot process.

Since the arrival of Apple's native iOS App Store, and—along with it—third-party applications, the general motives for jailbreaking have changed. People jailbreak for many different reasons, including gaining filesystem access, installing custom device themes, and modifying SpringBoard. An additional motivation is that it may enable the installation of pirated apps. On some devices, jailbreaking also makes it possible to install alternative operating systems, such as Android and the Linux kernel. Primarily, users jailbreak their devices because of the limitations of iOS. Depending on the method used, the effects of jailbreaking may be permanent or temporary.

In 2010, the Electronic Frontier Foundation (EFF) successfully convinced the U.S. Copyright Office to allow an exemption to the general prohibition on circumvention of copyright protection systems under the Digital Millennium Copyright Act (DMCA). The exemption allows jailbreaking of iPhones for the sole purpose of allowing legally obtained applications to be added to the iPhone. The exemption does not affect the contractual relations between Apple and an iPhone owner, for example, jailbreaking voiding the iPhone warranty; however, it is solely based on Apple's discretion on whether they will fix jailbroken devices in the event that they need to be repaired. At the same time, the Copyright Office exempted unlocking an iPhone from DMCA's anticircumvention prohibitions. Unlocking an iPhone allows the iPhone to be used with any wireless carrier using the same GSM or CDMA technology for which the particular phone model was designed to operate.

Unlocking

Initially most wireless carriers in the US did not allow iPhone owners to unlock it for use with other carriers. However AT&T allowed iPhone owners who had satisfied contract requirements to unlock their iPhone. Instructions to unlock the device are available from Apple, but it is ultimately at the sole discretion of the carrier to authorize unlocking the device. This allows the use of a carrier-sourced iPhone on other networks. Modern versions of iOS and the iPhone fully support LTE across multiple carriers wherever the phone was purchased. Programs to remove SIM lock restrictions are available, but are not supported by Apple, and most often not a permanent unlock – a soft unlock, which modifies the iPhone so that the baseband will accept the SIM card of any GSM carrier. SIM unlocking is not jailbreaking, but a jailbreak is also required for these unofficial software unlocks.

The legality of software unlocking varies in each country; for example, in the US, there is a DMCA exemption for unofficial software unlocking of devices purchased before January 26, 2013.

Digital Rights Management

The closed and proprietary nature of iOS has garnered criticism, particularly by digital rights advocates such as the Electronic Frontier Foundation, computer engineer and activist Brewster Kahle, Internet-law specialist Jonathan Zittrain, and the Free Software Foundation who protested the iPad's introductory event and have targeted the iPad with their "Defective by Design" campaign. Competitor Microsoft, via a PR spokesman, criticized Apple's control over its platform.

At issue are restrictions imposed by the design of iOS, namely digital rights management (DRM) intended to lock purchased media to Apple's platform, the development model (requiring a yearly subscription to distribute apps developed for the iOS), the centralized approval process for apps, as well as Apple's general control and lockdown of the platform itself. Particularly at issue is the ability for Apple to remotely disable or delete apps at will.

Some in the tech community have expressed concern that the locked-down iOS represents a growing trend in Apple's approach to computing, particularly Apple's shift away from machines that hobbyists can "tinker with" and note the potential for such restrictions to stifle software innovation. Former Facebook developer Joe Hewitt protested against Apple's control over its hardware as a "horrible precedent" but praised iOS's sandboxing of apps.

Security and Privacy

The iOS operating system utilizes many security features in both hardware and software, from the boot process to biometrics.

Secure Boot

Before fully booting into iOS, there is low-level code that runs from the Boot ROM. Its task is to verify that the Low-Level Bootloader is signed by the Apple Root CA public key before running it. This process is to ensure that no malicious or otherwise unauthorized software can be run on an iOS device. After the Low-Level Bootloader finishes its tasks, it runs the higher level bootloader, known as iBoot.

If all goes well, iBoot will then proceed to load the iOS kernel as well as the rest of the operating system.

Secure Enclave

The Secure Enclave is a coprocessor found in iOS devices part of the A7 and newer chips used for data protection. It includes the user data pertaining to Touch ID, Face ID, and Apple Pay, among other sensitive data.

The purpose of the Secure Enclave is to handle keys and other info such as biometrics that is sensitive enough to not be handled by the Application Processor (AP). It is isolated with a hardware filter so the AP cannot access it. It shares RAM with the AP, but its portion of the RAM (known as TZ0) is encrypted.

The secure enclave itself is a flashable 4 MB AKF processor core called the secure enclave processor (SEP) as documented in Apple Patent Application 20130308838. The technology used is similar to ARM's TrustZone/SecurCore but contains proprietary code for Apple KF cores in general and SEP specifically. It is also responsible for generating the UID key on A9 or newer chips that protects user data at rest.

It has its own secure boot process to ensure that it is completely secure. A hardware random number generator is also included as a part of this coprocessor. Each device's Secure Enclave has a unique ID that is fused into the SoC at manufacturing time and cannot be changed. Starting with A9 devices, the unique ID is generated by the Secure Enclave's random number generator and is never exposed outside of the device. This identifier is used to create a temporary key that encrypts the memory in this portion of the system. The Secure Enclave also contains an anti-replay counter to prevent brute force attacks.

The SEP is located in the devicetree under IODeviceTree:/arm-io/sep and managed by the AppleSEPManager driver. In 2020, security flaws in the SEP were discovered, causing concerns about Apple devices such as iPhones.

Face ID

Face ID is a face scanner that is embedded in the notch on iPhone models X, XS, XS Max, XR, 11, 11 Pro, 11 Pro Max, 12, 12 Mini, 12 Pro, 12 Pro Max, 13, 13 Mini, 13 Pro, 13 Pro Max, 14, and the 14 Plus. On the iPhone 14 Pro, 14 Pro Max, IPhone 15, IPhone 15 Plus, IPhone 15 Pro, and IPhone 15 Pro Max, it is embedded in the Dynamic Island.

It can be used to unlock the device, make purchases, and log into applications among other functions. When used, Face ID only temporarily stores the face data in encrypted memory in the Secure Enclave, as described above. There is no way for the device's main processor or any other part of the system to access the raw data that is obtained from the Face ID sensor.

Passcode

iOS devices can have a passcode that is used to unlock the device, make changes to system settings, and encrypt the device's contents. Until recently, these were typically four numerical digits long. However, since unlocking the devices with a fingerprint by using Touch ID has become more widespread, six-digit passcodes are now the default on iOS with the option to switch back to four or use an alphanumeric passcode.

Touch ID

Touch ID is a fingerprint scanner that is embedded in the home button and can be used to unlock the device, make purchases, and log into applications among other functions. When used, Touch ID only temporarily stores the fingerprint data in encrypted memory in the Secure Enclave, as described above. Like Face ID, there is no way for the device's main processor or any other part of the system to access the raw fingerprint data that is obtained from the Touch ID sensor.

Address Space Layout Randomization

Address Space Layout Randomization (ASLR) is a low-level technique of preventing memory corruption attacks such as buffer overflows. It involves placing data in randomly selected locations in memory in order to make it more difficult to predict ways to corrupt the system and create exploits. ASLR makes app bugs more likely to crash the app than to silently overwrite memory, regardless of whether the behavior is accidental or malicious.

Non-Executable Memory

iOS utilizes the ARM architecture's Execute Never (XN) feature. This allows some portions of the memory to be marked as non-executable, working alongside ASLR to prevent buffer overflow attacks including return-to-libc attacks.

Encryption

As mentioned above, one use of encryption in iOS is in the memory of the Secure Enclave. When a passcode is utilized on an iOS device, the contents of the device are encrypted. This is done by using a hardware AES 256 implementation that is very efficient because it is placed directly between the flash storage and RAM. iOS, in combination with its specific hardware, uses crypto-shredding when erasing all content and settings by obliterating all the keys in 'effaceable storage'. This renders all user data on the device cryptographically inaccessible.

Keychain

The iOS keychain is a database of login information that can be shared across apps written by the same person or organization. This service is often used for storing passwords for web applications.

App Security

Third-party applications such as those distributed through the App Store must be code signed with an Apple-issued certificate. In principle, this continues the chain of trust all the way from the Secure Boot process as mentioned above to the actions of the applications installed on the device by users.

Applications are also sandboxed, meaning that they can only modify the data within their individual home directory unless explicitly given permission to do otherwise. For example, they cannot access data owned by other user-installed applications on the device. There is a very extensive set of privacy controls contained within iOS with options to control apps' ability to access a wide variety of permissions such as the camera, contacts, background app refresh, cellular data, and access to other data and services. Most of the code in iOS, including third-party applications, runs as the "mobile" user which does not have root privileges. This ensures that system files and other iOS system resources remain hidden and inaccessible to user-installed applications.

App Store Bypasses:

- Companies can apply to Apple for enterprise developer certificates. These can be used to sign apps such that iOS will install them directly (sometimes called "sideloading"), without the app needing to be distributed via the App Store. The terms under which they are granted make clear that they are only to be used for companies who wish to distribute apps directly to their employees.
- Circa January–February 2019, it emerged that a number of software developers were misusing enterprise developer certificates to distribute software directly to non-employees, thereby bypassing the App Store. Facebook was found to be abusing an Apple enterprise developer certificate to distribute an application to underage users that would give Facebook access to all private data on their devices. Google was abusing an Apple enterprise developer certificate to distribute an app to adults to collect data from their devices, including unencrypted data belonging to third parties. AltStore, AppValley, Panda Helper, TweakBox and TutuApp have all been abusing enterprise developer certificates to distribute apps that offer pirated software.

Network Security:

- iOS supports TLS with both low–and high-level APIs for developers. By default, the App Transport Security (ATS) framework requires that servers use at least TLS 1.2. However, developers are free to override this framework and utilize their own methods of communicating over networks. When Wi-Fi is enabled, iOS uses a randomized MAC address so that devices cannot be tracked by anyone sniffing wireless traffic.

Two-Factor Authentication

Two-factor authentication is an option in iOS to ensure that even if an unauthorized person knows an Apple ID and password combination, they cannot gain access to the account. It works by requiring not only the Apple ID and password, but also a verification code that is sent to an iDevice or mobile phone number that is already known to be trusted. If an unauthorized user attempts to sign in using another user's Apple ID, the owner of the Apple ID receives a notification that allows them to deny access to the unrecognized device.

Hardened Memory Allocation

iOS features a hardened memory allocator known as kalloc_type that was introduced in iOS 15. Since the XNU kernel is primarily written in memory unsafe languages such as C and C++, kalloc_type is designed to mitigate the large amount of vulnerabilities that result from the use of these languages in the kernel. In order to achieve this, kalloc_type implements mitigations such as type isolation in order to prevent type confusion and buffer overflow vulnerabilities. Ultimately, the prevention of privilege escalation is intended.

Reception

Market Share

iOS is the second most popular mobile operating system in the world, after Android. Sales of iPads in recent years are also behind Android, while, by web use (a proxy for all use), iPads (using iOS) are still the most popular.

At WWDC 2014, Tim Cook said 800 million devices had been sold by June 2014. During Apple's quarterly earnings call in January 2015, the company announced that they had sold over one billion iOS devices since 2007.

By February 2023, there were 2 billion devices activated, and 1.5 billion iPhones had been sold since 2007.

By late 2011, iOS accounted for 60% of the market share for smartphones and tablets. By the end of 2014, iOS accounted for 14.8% of the smartphone market and 27.6% of the tablet and two-in-one market. In May 2023, StatCounter reported iOS was used on 31.44% of smartphones and 55.75% of tablets worldwide, measured by internet usage instead of sales.

In the third quarter of 2015, research from Strategy Analytics showed that iOS adoption of the worldwide smartphone market was at a record low 12.1%, attributed to lackluster performance in China and Africa. Android accounted for 87.5% of the market, with Windows Phone and BlackBerry accounting for the rest.

2.1.2 Android

Android is a mobile operating system based on a modified version of the Linux kernel and other open-source software, designed primarily for touchscreen mobile devices such as smartphones and tablets. Android is developed by a consortium of developers known as the Open Handset Alliance, though its most widely used version is primarily developed by Google. It was unveiled in November 2007, with the first commercial Android device, the HTC Dream, being launched in September 2008.

At its core, the operating system is known as the Android Open Source Project (AOSP) and is free and open-source software (FOSS) primarily licensed under the Apache License. However, most devices run on the proprietary Android version developed by Google, which ships with additional proprietary closed-source software pre-installed, most notably Google Mobile Services (GMS) which includes core apps such as Google Chrome, the digital distribution platform Google Play, and the associated Google Play Services development platform. Firebase Cloud Messaging is used for push notifications. While AOSP is free, the "Android" name and logo are trademarks of Google, which imposes standards to restrict the use of Android branding by "uncertified" devices outside their ecosystem.

Over 70 percent of smartphones based on the Android Open Source Project run Google's ecosystem (which is known simply as Android), some with vendor-customized user interfaces and software suites, such as TouchWiz and later One UI by Samsung and HTC Sense. Competing ecosystems and forks of AOSP include Fire OS (developed by Amazon), ColorOS by Oppo, OriginOS by Vivo, MagicUI by Honor, or custom ROMs such as LineageOS.

The source code has been used to develop variants of Android on a range of other electronics, such as game consoles, digital cameras, portable media players, and PCs, each with a specialized user interface. Some well-known derivatives include Android TV for televisions and Wear OS for wearables, both developed by Google. Software packages on Android, which use the APK format, are generally distributed through proprietary application stores like Google Play Store, Amazon Appstore, Samsung Galaxy Store, Huawei AppGallery, Cafe Bazaar, GetJar, and Aptoide, or open source platforms like F-Droid.

Android has been the best-selling OS worldwide on smartphones since 2011 and on tablets since 2013. As of May 2021, it had over three billion monthly active users, the largest installed base of any operating system in the world, and as of January 2021, the Google Play Store featured over 3 million apps. Android 14, released on October 4, 2023, is the latest version, and the recently released Android 12.1/12L includes improvements specific to foldable phones, tablets, desktop-sized screens and Chromebooks.

History

Android Inc. was founded in Palo Alto, California, in October 2003 by Andy Rubin, Rich Miner, Nick Sears, and Chris White. Rubin described the Android project as having "tremendous potential in developing smarter mobile devices that are more aware of its owner's location and preferences". The early intentions of the company were to develop an advanced operating system for digital cameras, and this was the basis of its pitch to investors in April 2004. The company then decided that the market for cameras was not large enough for its goals, and five months later it had diverted its efforts and was pitching Android as a handset operating system that would rival Symbian and Microsoft Windows Mobile.

Rubin had difficulty attracting investors early on, and Android was facing eviction from its office space. Steve Perlman, a close friend of Rubin, brought him $10,000 in cash in an envelope, and shortly thereafter wired an undisclosed amount as seed funding. Perlman refused a stake in the company, and has stated "I did it because I believed in the thing, and I wanted to help Andy."

In 2005, Rubin tried to negotiate deals with Samsung and HTC. Shortly afterwards, Google acquired the company in July of that year for at least $50 million; this was Google's "best deal ever" according to Google's then-vice president of corporate development, David Lawee, in 2010. Android's key employees, including Rubin, Miner, Sears, and White, joined Google as part of the acquisition. Not much was known about the secretive Android Inc. at the time, with the company having provided few details other than that it was making software for mobile phones. At Google, the team led by Rubin developed a mobile device platform powered by the Linux kernel. Google marketed the platform to handset makers and carriers on the promise of providing a flexible, upgradeable system. Google had "lined up a series of hardware components and software partners and signaled to carriers that it was open to various degrees of cooperation".

Speculation about Google's intention to enter the mobile communications market continued to build through December 2006. An early prototype had a close resemblance to a BlackBerry phone, with no touchscreen and a physical QWERTY keyboard, but the arrival of 2007's Apple iPhone meant that Android "had to go back to the drawing board". Google later changed its Android specification documents to state that "Touchscreens will be supported", although "the Product was designed with the presence of discrete physical buttons as an assumption, therefore a touchscreen cannot completely replace physical buttons". By 2008, both Nokia and BlackBerry announced touch-based smartphones to rival the iPhone 3G, and Android's focus eventually switched to just touchscreens. The first commercially available smartphone running Android was the HTC Dream, also known as T-Mobile G1, announced on September 23, 2008.

On November 5, 2007, the Open Handset Alliance, a consortium of technology companies including Google, device manufacturers such as HTC, Motorola and Samsung, wireless carriers such as Sprint and T-Mobile, and chipset makers such as Qualcomm and Texas Instruments, unveiled itself, with a goal to develop "the first truly open and comprehensive platform for mobile devices". Within a year, the Open Handset Alliance faced two other open source competitors, the Symbian Foundation and the LiMo Foundation, the latter also developing a Linux-based mobile operating system like Google. In September 2007, *InformationWeek* covered an Evalueserve study reporting that Google had filed several patent applications in the area of mobile telephony.

On September 23, 2008, Android was introduced by Andy Rubin, Larry Page, Sergey Brin, Cole Brodman, Christopher Schlaeffer and Peter Chou at a press conference in a New York City subway station.

Since 2008, Android has seen numerous updates which have incrementally improved the operating system, adding new features and fixing bugs in previous releases. Each major release is named in alphabetical order after a dessert or sugary treat, with the first few Android versions being called "Cupcake", "Donut", "Eclair", and "Froyo", in that order. During its announcement of Android KitKat in 2013, Google explained that "Since these devices make our lives so sweet, each Android version is named after a dessert", although a Google spokesperson told CNN in an interview that "It's kind of like an internal team thing, and we prefer to be a little bit—how should I say—a bit inscrutable in the matter, I'll say".

In 2010, Google launched its Nexus series of devices, a lineup in which Google partnered with different device manufacturers to produce new devices and introduce new Android versions. The series was described as having "played a pivotal role in Android's history by introducing new software iterations and hardware standards across the board", and became known for its "bloat-free" software with "timely ... updates". At its developer conference in May 2013, Google announced a special version of the Samsung Galaxy S4, where, instead of using Samsung's own Android customization, the phone ran "stock Android" and was promised to receive new system updates fast. The device would become the start of the Google Play edition program, and was followed by other devices, including the HTC One Google Play edition, and Moto G Google Play edition. In 2015, *Ars Technica* wrote that "Earlier this week, the last of the Google Play edition Android phones in Google's online storefront were listed as "no longer available for sale" and that "Now they're all gone, and it looks a whole lot like the program has wrapped up".

From 2008 to 2013, Hugo Barra served as product spokesperson, representing Android at press conferences and Google I/O, Google's annual developer-focused conference. He left Google in August 2013 to join Chinese phone maker Xiaomi. Less than six months earlier, Google's then-CEO Larry Page announced in a blog post that Andy Rubin had moved from the Android division to take on new projects at Google, and that Sundar Pichai would become the new Android lead. Pichai himself would eventually switch positions, becoming the new CEO of Google in August 2015 following the company's restructure into the Alphabet conglomerate, making Hiroshi Lockheimer the new head of Android.

On Android 4.4 *KitKat*, shared writing access to MicroSD memory cards has been locked for user-installed applications, to which only the dedicated directories with respective package names, located inside `Android/data/`, remained writeable. Writing access has been reinstated with Android 5 *Lollipop* through the backwards-incompatible *Google Storage Access Framework* interface.

In June 2014, Google announced Android One, a set of "hardware reference models" that would "allow [device makers] to easily create high-quality phones at low costs", designed for consumers in developing countries. In September, Google announced the first set of Android One phones for release in India. However, *Recode* reported in June 2015 that the project was "a disappointment", citing "reluctant consumers and manufacturing partners" and "misfires from the search company that has never quite cracked hardware". Plans to relaunch Android One surfaced in August 2015, with Africa announced as the next location for the program a week later. A report from *The Information* in January 2017 stated that Google is expanding its low-cost Android One program into the United States, although *The Verge* notes that the company will presumably not produce the actual devices itself. Google introduced the Pixel and Pixel XL smartphones in October 2016, marketed as being the first phones made by Google, and exclusively featured certain software features, such as the Google Assistant, before wider rollout. The Pixel phones replaced the Nexus series, with a new generation of Pixel phones launched in October 2017.

In May 2019, the operating system became entangled in the trade war between China and the United States involving Huawei, which, like many other tech firms, had become dependent on access to the Android platform. In the summer of 2019, Huawei announced it would create an alternative operating system to Android known as Harmony OS, and has filed for intellectual property rights across major global markets. Under such sanctions Huawei has long-term plans to replace Android in 2022 with the new operating system, as Harmony OS was originally designed for internet of things devices, rather than for smartphones and tablets.

On August 22, 2019, it was announced that Android "Q" would officially be branded as Android 10, ending the historic practice of naming major versions after desserts. Google stated that these names were not "inclusive" to international users (due either to the aforementioned foods not being internationally known, or being difficult to pronounce in some languages). On the same day, *Android Police* reported that Google had commissioned a statue of a giant number "10" to be installed in the lobby of the developers' new office. Android 10 was released on September 3, 2019, to Google Pixel phones first.

In late 2021, some users reported that they were unable to dial emergency services. The problem was caused by a combination of bugs in Android and in the Microsoft Teams app; both companies released updates addressing the issue.

Features

Interface

Android's default user interface is mainly based on direct manipulation, using touch inputs that loosely correspond to real-world actions, like swiping, tapping, pinching, and reverse pinching to manipulate on-screen objects, along with a virtual keyboard. Game controllers and full-size physical keyboards are supported via Bluetooth or USB. The response to user input is designed to be immediate and provides a fluid touch interface, often using the vibration capabilities of the device to provide haptic feedback to the user. Internal hardware, such as accelerometers, gyroscopes and proximity sensors are used by some applications to respond to additional user actions, for example adjusting the screen from portrait to landscape depending on how the device is oriented, or allowing the user to steer a vehicle in a racing game by rotating the device, simulating control of a steering wheel.

Home Screen

Android devices boot to the home screen, the primary navigation and information "hub" on Android devices, analogous to the desktop found on personal computers. Android home screens are typically made up of app icons and widgets; app icons launch the associated app, whereas widgets display live, auto-updating content, such as a weather forecast, the user's email inbox, or a news ticker directly on the home screen. A home screen may be made up of several pages, between which the user can swipe back and forth. Third-party apps available on Google Play and other app stores can extensively re-theme the home screen, and even mimic the look of other operating systems, such as Windows Phone. Most manufacturers customize the look and features of their Android devices to differentiate themselves from their competitors.

Status Bar

Along the top of the screen is a status bar, showing information about the device and its connectivity. This status bar can be pulled (swiped) down from to reveal a notification screen where apps display important information or updates, as well as quick access to system controls and toggles such as display brightness, connectivity settings (WiFi, Bluetooth, cellular data), audio mode, and flashlight. Vendors may implement extended settings such as the ability to adjust the flashlight brightness.

Notifications

Notifications are "short, timely, and relevant information about your app when it's not in use", and when tapped, users are directed to a screen inside the app relating to the notification. Beginning with Android 4.1 "Jelly Bean", "expandable notifications" allow the user to tap an icon on the notification in order for it to expand and display more information and possible app actions right from the notification.

App Lists

An "All Apps" screen lists all installed applications, with the ability for users to drag an app from the list onto the home screen. The app list may be accessed using a gesture or a button, depending on the Android version. A "Recents" screen, also known as "Overview", lets users switch between recently used apps. The recent list may appear side-by-side or overlapping, depending on the Android version and manufacturer.

Navigation Buttons

Many early Android OS smartphones were equipped with a dedicated search button for quick access to a web search engine and individual apps' internal search feature. More recent devices typically allow the former through a long press or swipe away from the home button. The dedicated option key, also known as menu key, and its on-screen simulation, is no longer supported since Android version 10. Google recommends mobile application developers to locate menus within the user interface. On more recent phones, its place is occupied by a task key used to access the list of recently used apps when actuated. Depending on device, its long press may simulate a menu button press or engage split screen view, the latter of which is the default behaviour since stock Android version 7.

Split-Screen View

Native support for split screen view has been added in stock Android version 7.0 *Nougat*. The earliest vendor-customized Android-based smartphones known to have featured a split-screen view mode are the 2012 Samsung Galaxy S3 and Note 2, the former of which received this feature with the *premium suite* upgrade delivered in TouchWiz with Android 4.1 Jelly Bean.

Charging while Powered Off

When connecting or disconnecting charging power and when shortly actuating the power button or home button, all while the device is powered off, a visual battery meter whose appearance varies among vendors appears on the screen, allowing the user to quickly assess the charge status of a powered-off without having to boot it up first. Some display the battery percentage.

Applications

Most Android devices come with preinstalled Google apps including Gmail, Google Maps, Google Chrome, YouTube, Google Play Movies & TV, and others. Applications ("apps"), which extend the functionality of devices (and must be 64-bit), are written using the Android software development kit (SDK) and, often, Kotlin programming language, which replaced Java as Google's preferred language for Android app development in May 2019, and was originally announced in May 2017. Java is still supported (originally the only option for user-space programs, and is often mixed with Kotlin), as is C++. Java or other JVM languages, such as Kotlin, may be combined with C/C++, together with a choice of non-default runtimes that allow better C++ support.

The SDK includes a comprehensive set of development tools, including a debugger, software libraries, a handset emulator based on QEMU, documentation, sample code, and tutorials. Initially, Google's supported integrated development environment (IDE) was Eclipse using the Android Development Tools (ADT) plugin; in December 2014, Google released Android Studio, based on IntelliJ IDEA, as its primary IDE for Android application development.

Other development tools are available, including a native development kit (NDK) for applications or extensions in C or C++, Google App Inventor, a visual environment for novice programmers, and various cross platform mobile web applications frameworks. In January 2014, Google unveiled a framework based on Apache Cordova for porting Chrome HTML 5 web applications to Android, wrapped in a native application shell. Additionally, Firebase was acquired by Google in 2014 that provides helpful tools for app and web developers.

Android has a growing selection of third-party applications, which can be acquired by users by downloading and installing the application's APK (Android application package) file, or by downloading them using an application store program that allows users to install, update, and remove applications from their devices.

Google Play Store is the primary application store installed on Android devices that comply with Google's compatibility requirements and license the Google Mobile Services software. Google Play Store allows users to browse, download and update applications published by Google and third-party developers; as of January 2021, there are more than three million applications available for Android in Play Store.

As of July 2013, 50 billion application installations had been performed. Some carriers offer direct carrier billing for Google Play application purchases, where the cost of the application is added to the user's monthly bill. As of May 2017, there are over one billion active users a month for Gmail, Android, Chrome, Google Play and Maps.

Due to the open nature of Android, a number of third-party application marketplaces also exist for Android, either to provide a substitute for devices that are not allowed to ship with Google Play Store, provide applications that cannot be offered on Google Play Store due to policy violations, or for other reasons. Examples of these third-party stores have included the Amazon Appstore, GetJar, and SlideMe. F-Droid, another alternative marketplace, seeks to only provide applications that are distributed under free and open source licenses.

In October 2020, Google removed several Android applications from Play Store, as they were identified breaching its data collection rules. The firm was informed by International Digital Accountability Council (IDAC) that apps for children like *Number Coloring*, *Princess Salon* and *Cats & Cosplay*, with collective downloads of 20 million, were violating Google's policies.

At the Windows 11 announcement event in June 2021, Microsoft showcased the new Windows Subsystem for Android (WSA) to enable support for the Android Open Source Project (AOSP), but it has since been deprecated. It was meant to allow users running Android apps and games in Windows 11 on their Windows desktop. On March 5, 2024, Microsoft announced deprecation of WSA with support ending on March 5, 2025.

Storage

The storage of Android devices can be expanded using secondary devices such as SD cards. Android recognizes two types of secondary storage: *portable* storage (which is used by default), and *adoptable* storage. Portable storage is treated as an external storage device. Adoptable storage, introduced on Android 6.0, allows the internal storage of the device to be spanned with the SD card, treating it as an extension of the internal storage. This has the disadvantage of preventing the memory card from being used with another device unless it is reformatted.

Android 4.4 introduced the Storage Access Framework (SAF), a set of APIs for accessing files on the device's filesystem. As of Android 11, Android has required apps to conform to a data privacy policy known as *scoped storage*, under which apps may only automatically have access to certain directories (such as those for pictures, music, and video), and app-specific directories they have created themselves. Apps are required to use the SAF to access any other part of the filesystem.

Memory Management

Since Android devices are usually battery-powered, Android is designed to manage processes to keep power consumption at a minimum. When an application is not in use the system suspends its operation so that, while available for immediate use rather than closed, it does not use battery power or CPU resources. Android manages the applications stored in memory automatically: when memory is low, the system will begin invisibly and automatically closing inactive processes, starting with those that have been inactive for the longest amount of time. Lifehacker reported in 2011 that third-party task-killer applications were doing more harm than good.

Developer Options

Some settings for use by developers for debugging and power users are located in a "Developer options" sub menu, such as the ability to highlight updating parts of the display, show an overlay with the current status of the touch screen, show touching spots for possible use in screencasting, notify the user of unresponsive background processes with the option to end them ("Show all ANRs", i.e. "App's Not Responding"), prevent a Bluetooth audio client from controlling the system volume ("Disable absolute volume"), and adjust the duration of transition animations or deactivate them completely to speed up navigation.

Developer options are initially hidden since Android 4.2 "Jelly Bean", but can be enabled by actuating the operating system's build number in the device information seven times. Hiding developers options again requires deleting user data for the "Settings" app, possibly resetting some other preferences.

Hardware

The main hardware platform for Android is ARM (the ARMv7 and ARMv8-A architectures), with x86 and x86-64 architectures also officially supported in later versions of Android. The unofficial Android-x86 project provided support for x86 architectures ahead of the official support. Since 2012, Android devices with Intel processors began to appear, including phones and tablets. While gaining support for 64-bit platforms, Android was first made to run on 64-bit x86 and then on ARM64. An unofficial experimental port of the operating system to the RISC-V architecture was released in 2021.

Requirements for the minimum amount of RAM for devices running Android 7.1 range from in practice 2 GB for best hardware, down to 1 GB for the most common screen. Android supports all versions of OpenGL ES and Vulkan (and version 1.1 available for some devices).

Android devices incorporate many optional hardware components, including still or video cameras, GPS, orientation sensors, dedicated gaming controls, accelerometers, gyroscopes, barometers, magnetometers, proximity sensors, pressure sensors, thermometers, and touchscreens. Some hardware components are not required, but became standard in certain classes of devices, such as smartphones, and additional requirements apply if they are present. Some other hardware was initially required, but those requirements have been relaxed or eliminated altogether. For example, as Android was developed initially as a phone OS, hardware such as microphones were required, while over time the phone function became optional. Android used to require an autofocus camera, which was relaxed to a fixed-focus camera if present at all, since the camera was dropped as a requirement entirely when Android started to be used on set-top boxes.

In addition to running on smartphones and tablets, several vendors run Android natively on regular PC hardware with a keyboard and mouse. In addition to their availability on commercially available hardware, similar PC hardware-friendly versions of Android are freely available from the Android-x86 project, including customized Android 4.4. Using the Android emulator that is part of the Android SDK, or third-party emulators, Android can also run non-natively on x86 architectures. Chinese companies are building a PC and mobile operating system, based on Android, to "compete directly with Microsoft Windows and Google Android". The Chinese Academy of Engineering noted that "more than a dozen" companies were customizing Android following a Chinese ban on the use of Windows 8 on government PCs.

Development

Android is developed by Google until the latest changes and updates are ready to be released, at which point the source code is made available to the Android Open Source Project (AOSP), an open source initiative led by Google. The first source code release happened as part of the initial release in 2007. All releases are under the Apache License.

The AOSP code can be found with minimal modifications on select devices, mainly the former Nexus and current Android One series of devices. However, most original equipment manufacturers (OEMs) customize the source code to run on their hardware.

Android's source code does not contain the device drivers, often proprietary, that are needed for certain hardware components, and does not contain the source code of Google Play Services, which many apps depend on. As a result, most Android devices, including Google's own, ship with a combination of free and open source and proprietary software, with the software required for accessing Google services falling into the latter category. In response to this, there are some projects that build complete operating systems based on AOSP as free software, the first being CyanogenMod.

Update Schedule

Google provides annual Android releases, both for factory installation in new devices, and for over-the-air updates to existing devices. The latest major release is Android 14. The extensive variation of hardware in Android devices has caused significant delays for software upgrades and security patches. Each upgrade has had to be specifically tailored, a time- and resource-consuming process. Except for devices within the Google Nexus and Pixel brands, updates have often arrived months after the release of the new version, or not at all. Manufacturers often prioritize their newest devices and leave old ones behind. Additional delays can be introduced by wireless carriers who, after receiving updates from manufacturers, further customize Android to their needs and conduct extensive testing on their networks before sending out the upgrade. There are also situations in which upgrades are impossible due to a manufacturer not updating necessary drivers.

The lack of after-sale support from manufacturers and carriers has been widely criticized by consumer groups and the technology media. Some commentators have noted that the industry has a financial incentive not to upgrade their devices, as the lack of updates for existing devices fuels the purchase of newer ones, an attitude described as "insulting". *The Guardian* complained that the method of distribution for updates is complicated only because manufacturers and carriers have designed it that way. In 2011, Google partnered with a number of industry players to announce an "Android Update Alliance", pledging to deliver timely updates for every device for 18 months after its release; however, there has not been another official word about that alliance since its announcement.

In 2012, Google began de-coupling certain aspects of the operating system (particularly its central applications) so they could be updated through the Google Play store independently of the OS. One of those components, Google Play Services, is a closed-source system-level process providing APIs for Google services, installed automatically on nearly all devices running Android 2.2 "Froyo" and higher. With these changes, Google can add new system functions and update apps without having to distribute an upgrade to the operating system itself. As a result, Android 4.2 and 4.3 "Jelly Bean" contained relatively fewer user-facing changes, focusing more on minor changes and platform improvements.

HTC's then-executive Jason Mackenzie called monthly security updates "unrealistic" in 2015, and Google was trying to persuade carriers to exclude security patches from the full testing procedures. In May 2016, Bloomberg Businessweek reported that Google was making efforts to keep Android more up-to-date, including accelerated rates of security updates, rolling out technological workarounds, reducing requirements for phone testing, and ranking phone makers in an attempt to "shame" them into better behavior. As stated by *Bloomberg*: "As smartphones get more capable, complex and hackable, having the latest software work closely with the hardware is increasingly important". Hiroshi Lockheimer, the Android lead, admitted that "It's not an ideal situation", further commenting that the lack of updates is "the weakest link on security on Android". Wireless carriers were described in the report as the "most challenging discussions", due to their slow approval time while testing on their networks, despite some carriers, including

Verizon Wireless and Sprint Corporation, already shortening their approval times. In a further effort for persuasion, Google shared a list of top phone makers measured by updated devices with its Android partners, and is considering making the list public. Mike Chan, co-founder of phone maker Nextbit and former Android developer, said that "The best way to solve this problem is a massive re-architecture of the operating system", "or Google could invest in training manufacturers and carriers 'to be good Android citizens'".

In May 2017, with the announcement of Android 8.0, Google introduced Project Treble, a major re-architect of the Android OS framework designed to make it easier, faster, and less costly for manufacturers to update devices to newer versions of Android. Project Treble separates the vendor implementation (device-specific, lower-level software written by silicon manufacturers) from the Android OS framework via a new "vendor interface". In Android 7.0 and earlier, no formal vendor interface exists, so device makers must update large portions of the Android code to move a device to a newer version of the operating system. With Treble, the new stable vendor interface provides access to the hardware-specific parts of Android, enabling device makers to deliver new Android releases simply by updating the Android OS framework, "without any additional work required from the silicon manufacturers."

In September 2017, Google's Project Treble team revealed that, as part of their efforts to improve the security lifecycle of Android devices, Google had managed to get the Linux Foundation to agree to extend the support lifecycle of the Linux Long-Term Support (LTS) kernel branch from the 2 years that it has historically lasted to 6 years for future versions of the LTS kernel, starting with Linux kernel 4.4.

In May 2019, with the announcement of Android 10, Google introduced Project Mainline to simplify and expedite delivery of updates to the Android ecosystem. Project Mainline enables updates to core OS components through the Google Play Store. As a result, important security and performance improvements that previously needed to be part of full OS updates can be downloaded and installed as easily as an app update.

Google reported rolling out new amendments in Android 12 aimed at making the use of third-party application stores easier. This announcement rectified the concerns reported regarding the development of Android apps, including a fight over an alternative in-app payment system and difficulties faced by businesses moving online because of COVID-19.

Linux Kernel

Android's kernel is based on the Linux kernel's long-term support (LTS) branches.

As of 2024, Android (14) uses versions 6.1 or 5.15 (for "Feature kernels", can be older for "Launch kernels", e.g. android12-5.10, android11-5.4, depending on Android version down to e.g. android11-5.4, android-4.14-stable, android-4.9-q), and older Android versions, use version 5.15 or a number of older kernels. The actual kernel depends on the individual device.

Android's variant of the Linux kernel has further architectural changes that are implemented by Google outside the typical Linux kernel development cycle, such as the inclusion of components like device trees, ashmem, ION, and different out of memory (OOM) handling. Certain features that Google contributed back to the Linux kernel, notably a power management feature called "wakelocks", were initially rejected by mainline kernel developers partly because they felt that Google did not show any intent to maintain its own code. Google announced in April 2010 that they would hire two employees to work with the Linux kernel community, but Greg Kroah-Hartman, the current Linux kernel maintainer for the stable branch, said in December 2010 that he was concerned that Google was no longer trying to get their code changes included in mainstream Linux. Google engineer Patrick Brady once stated in the company's developer conference that "Android is not Linux", with *Computerworld* adding that "Let me make it simple for you, without Linux, there is no Android". *Ars Technica* wrote that "Although Android is built on top of the Linux kernel, the platform has very little in common with the conventional desktop Linux stack".

In August 2011, Linus Torvalds said that "eventually Android and Linux would come back to a common kernel, but it will probably not be for four to five years". (that has not happened yet, while some code has been upstreamed, not all of it has, so modified kernels keep being used). In December 2011, Greg Kroah-Hartman announced the start of Android Mainlining Project, which aims to put some Android drivers, patches and features back into the Linux kernel, starting in Linux 3.3. Linux included the autosleep and wakelocks capabilities in the 3.5 kernel, after many previous attempts at a merger. The interfaces are the same but the upstream Linux implementation allows for two different suspend modes: to memory (the traditional suspend that Android uses), and to disk (hibernate, as it is known on the desktop). Google maintains a public code repository that contains their experimental work to re-base Android off the latest stable Linux versions.

Android is a Linux distribution according to the Linux Foundation, Google's open-source chief Chris DiBona, and several journalists. Others, such as Google engineer Patrick Brady, say that Android is not Linux in the traditional Unix-like Linux distribution sense; Android does not include the GNU C Library (it uses Bionic as an alternative C library) and some other components typically found in Linux distributions.

With the release of Android Oreo in 2017, Google began to require that devices shipped with new SoCs had Linux kernel version 4.4 or newer, for security reasons. Existing devices upgraded to Oreo, and new products launched with older SoCs, were exempt from this rule.

Rooting

The flash storage on Android devices is split into several partitions, such as /system/ for the operating system itself, and `/data/` for user data and application installations. In contrast to typical desktop Linux distributions, Android device owners are not given root access to the operating system and sensitive partitions such as /system/ are partially read-only. However, root access can be obtained by exploiting security flaws in Android, which is used frequently by the open-source community to enhance the capabilities and customizability of their devices, but also by malicious parties to install viruses and malware. Root access can also be obtained by unlocking the bootloader which is available on most Android devices, for example on most Google Pixel, OnePlus and Nothing models OEM Unlocking option in the developer settings allows Fastboot to unlock the bootloader. But most OEMs have their own methods. The unlocking process resets the system to factory state, erasing all user data.

Software Stack

On top of the Linux kernel, there are the middleware, libraries and APIs written in C, and application software running on an application framework which includes Java-compatible libraries. Development of the Linux kernel continues independently of Android's other source code projects.

Android uses Android Runtime (ART) as its runtime environment (introduced in version 4.4), which uses ahead-of-time (AOT) compilation to entirely compile the application bytecode into machine code upon the installation of an application. In Android 4.4, ART was an experimental feature and not enabled by default; it became the only runtime option in the next major version of Android, 5.0. In versions no longer supported, until version 5.0 when ART took over, Android previously used Dalvik as a process virtual machine with trace-based just-in-time (JIT) compilation to run Dalvik "dex-code" (Dalvik Executable), which is usually translated from the Java bytecode. Following the trace-based JIT principle, in addition to interpreting the majority of application code, Dalvik performs the compilation and native execution of select frequently executed code segments ("traces") each time an application is launched. For its Java library, the Android platform uses a subset of the now discontinued Apache Harmony project. In December 2015, Google announced that the next version of Android would switch to a Java implementation based on the OpenJDK project.

Android's standard C library, Bionic, was developed by Google specifically for Android, as a derivation of the BSD's standard C library code. Bionic itself has been designed with several major features specific to the Linux kernel. The main benefits of using Bionic instead of the GNU C Library (glibc) or uClibc are its smaller runtime footprint, and optimization for low-frequency CPUs. At the same time, Bionic is licensed under the terms of the BSD licence, which Google finds more suitable for the Android's overall licensing model.

Aiming for a different licensing model, toward the end of 2012, Google switched the Bluetooth stack in Android from the GPL-licensed BlueZ to the Apache-licensed BlueDroid. A new Bluetooth stack, called Gabeldorsche, was developed to try to fix the bugs in the BlueDroid implementation.

Android does not have a native X Window System by default, nor does it support the full set of standard GNU libraries. This made it difficult to port existing Linux applications or libraries to Android, until version r5 of the Android Native Development Kit brought support for applications written completely in C or C++. Libraries written in C may also be used in applications by injection of a small shim and usage of the JNI.

In current versions of Android, "Toybox", a collection of command-line utilities (mostly for use by apps, as Android does not provide a command-line interface by default), is used (since the release of Marshmallow) replacing a similar "Toolbox" collection found in previous Android versions.

Android has another operating system, Trusty OS, within it, as a part of "Trusty" "software components supporting a Trusted Execution Environment (TEE) on mobile devices." "Trusty and the Trusty API are subject to change. [..] Applications for the Trusty OS can be written in C/C++ (C++ support is limited), and they have access to a small C library. [..] All Trusty applications are single-threaded; multithreading in Trusty userspace currently is unsupported. [..] Third-party application development is not supported in" the current version, and software running on the OS and processor for it, run the "DRM framework for protected content. [..] There are many other uses for a TEE such as mobile payments, secure banking, full-disk encryption, multi-factor authentication, device reset protection, replay-protected persistent storage, wireless display ("cast") of protected content, secure PIN and fingerprint processing, and even malware detection."

Open-Source Community

Android's source code is released by Google under an open-source license, and its open nature has encouraged a large community of developers and enthusiasts to use the open-source code as a foundation for community-driven projects, which deliver updates to older devices, add new features for advanced users or bring Android to devices originally shipped with other operating systems. These community-developed releases often bring new features and updates to devices faster than through the official manufacturer/carrier channels, with a comparable level of quality; provide continued support for older devices that no longer receive official updates; or bring Android to devices that were officially released running other operating systems, such as the HP TouchPad. Community releases often come pre-rooted and contain modifications not provided by the original vendor, such as the ability to overclock or over/undervolt the device's processor. CyanogenMod was the most widely used community firmware, now discontinued and succeeded by LineageOS.

There are, as of August 2019, a handful of notable custom Android distributions (ROMs) of Android version 9.0 Pie, which was released publicly in August 2018. Historically, device manufacturers and mobile carriers have typically been unsupportive of third-party firmware development. Manufacturers express concern about improper functioning of devices running unofficial software and the support costs resulting from this. Moreover, modified firmware such as CyanogenMod sometimes offer features, such as tethering, for which carriers would otherwise charge a premium. As a result, technical obstacles including locked bootloaders and restricted access to root permissions are common in many devices. However, as community-developed software has grown more popular, and following a statement by the Librarian of Congress in the United States that permits the "jailbreaking" of mobile devices, manufacturers and carriers have softened their position regarding third party development, with some, including HTC, Motorola, Samsung and Sony, providing support and encouraging development. As a result of this, over time the need to circumvent hardware restrictions to install unofficial firmware has lessened as an increasing number of devices are shipped with unlocked or unlockable bootloaders, similar to Nexus series of phones, although usually requiring that users waive their devices' warranties to do so. However, despite manufacturer acceptance, some carriers in the US still require that phones are locked down.

Device Codenames

Internally, Android identifies each supported device by its device codename, a short string, which may or may not be similar to the model name used in marketing the device. For example, the device codename of the Pixel smartphone is *sailfish*. The device codename is usually not visible to the end user, but is important for determining compatibility with modified Android versions. It is sometimes also mentioned in articles discussing a device, because it allows to distinguish different hardware variants of a device, even if the manufacturer offers them under the same name. The device codename is available to running applications under `android.` os.Build.DEVICE.

Security and Privacy

In 2020, Google launched the Android Partner Vulnerability Initiative to improve the security of Android. They also formed an Android security team.

Common Security Threats

Research from security company Trend Micro lists premium service abuse as the most common type of Android malware, where text messages are sent from infected phones to premium-rate telephone numbers without the consent or even knowledge of the user. Other malware displays unwanted and intrusive advertisements on the device, or sends personal information to unauthorised third parties. Security threats on Android are reportedly growing exponentially; however, Google engineers have argued that the malware and virus threat on Android is being exaggerated by security companies for commercial reasons, and have accused the security industry of playing on fears to sell virus protection software to users. Google maintains that dangerous malware is actually extremely rare, and a survey conducted by F-Secure showed that only 0.5% of Android malware reported had come from the Google Play store.

In 2021, journalists and researchers reported the discovery of spyware, called Pegasus, developed and distributed by a private company which can and has been used to infect both iOS and Android smartphones often – partly via use of 0-day exploits – without the need for any user-interaction or significant clues to the user and then be used to exfiltrate data, track user locations, capture film through its camera, and activate the microphone at any time. Analysis of data traffic by popular smartphones running variants of Android found substantial by-default data collection and sharing with no opt-out by this pre-installed software. Both of these issues are not addressed or cannot be addressed by security patches.

Scope of Surveillance by Public Institutions

As part of the broader 2013 mass surveillance disclosures it was revealed in September 2013 that the American and British intelligence agencies, the National Security Agency (NSA) and Government Communications Headquarters (GCHQ), respectively, have access to the user data on iPhone, BlackBerry, and Android devices. They are reportedly able to read almost all smartphone information, including SMS, location, emails, and notes. In January 2014, further reports revealed the intelligence agencies' capabilities to intercept the personal information transmitted across the Internet by social networks and other popular applications such as *Angry Birds*, which collect personal information of their users for advertising and other commercial reasons. GCHQ has, according to *The Guardian*, a wiki-style guide of different apps and advertising networks, and the different data that can be siphoned from each. Later that week, the Finnish Angry Birds developer Rovio announced that it was reconsidering its relationships with its advertising platforms in the light of these revelations, and called upon the wider industry to do the same.

The documents revealed a further effort by the intelligence agencies to intercept Google Maps searches and queries submitted from Android and other smartphones to collect location information in bulk. The NSA and GCHQ insist their activities comply with all relevant domestic and international laws, although the Guardian stated "the latest disclosures could also add to mounting public concern about how the technology sector collects and uses information, especially for those outside the US, who enjoy fewer privacy protections than Americans."

Leaked documents codenamed Vault 7 and dated from 2013 to 2016, detail the capabilities of the Central Intelligence Agency (CIA) to perform electronic surveillance and cyber warfare, including the ability to compromise the operating systems of most smartphones (including Android).

Security Patches

In August 2015, Google announced that devices in the Google Nexus series would begin to receive monthly security patches. Google also wrote that "Nexus devices will continue to receive major updates for at least two years and security patches for the longer of three years from initial availability or 18 months from last sale of the device via the Google Store." The following October, researchers at the University of Cambridge concluded that 87.7% of Android phones in use had known but unpatched security vulnerabilities due to lack of updates and support. Ron Amadeo of *Ars Technica* wrote also in August 2015 that "Android was originally designed, above all else, to be widely adopted. Google was starting from scratch with zero percent market share, so it was happy to give up control and give everyone a seat at the table in exchange for adoption. [...] Now, though, Android has around 75–80 percent of the worldwide smartphone market—making it not just the world's most popular mobile operating system but arguably the most popular operating system, period. As such, security has become a big issue. Android still uses a software update chain-of-command designed back when the Android ecosystem had zero devices to update, and it just doesn't work". Following news of Google's monthly schedule, some manufacturers, including Samsung and LG, promised to issue monthly security updates, but, as noted by Jerry Hildenbrand in *Android Central* in February 2016, "instead we got a few updates on specific versions of a small handful of models. And a bunch of broken promises".

In a March 2017 post on Google's Security Blog, Android security leads Adrian Ludwig and Mel Miller wrote that "More than 735 million devices from 200+ manufacturers received a platform security update in 2016" and that "Our carrier and hardware partners helped expand deployment of these updates, releasing updates for over half of the top 50 devices worldwide in the last quarter of 2016". They also wrote that "About half of devices in use at the end of 2016 had not received a platform security update in the previous year", stating that their work would continue to focus on streamlining the security updates program for easier deployment by manufacturers. Furthermore, in a comment to *TechCrunch*, Ludwig stated that the wait time for security updates had been reduced from "six to nine weeks down to just a few days", with 78% of flagship devices in North America being up-to-date on security at the end of 2016.

Patches to bugs found in the core operating system often do not reach users of older and lower-priced devices. However, the open-source nature of Android allows security contractors to take existing devices and adapt them for highly secure uses. For example, Samsung has worked with General Dynamics through their Open Kernel Labs acquisition to rebuild *Jelly Bean* on top of their hardened microvisor for the "Knox" project.

Location-Tracking

Android smartphones have the ability to report the location of Wi-Fi access points, encountered as phone users move around, to build databases containing the physical locations of hundreds of millions of such access points. These databases form electronic maps to locate smartphones, allowing them to run apps like Foursquare, Google Latitude, Facebook Places, and to deliver location-based ads. Third party monitoring software such as TaintDroid, an academic research-funded project, can, in some cases, detect when personal information is being sent from applications to remote servers.

Further Notable Exploits

In 2018, Norwegian security firm Promon has unearthed a serious Android security hole which can be exploited to steal login credentials, access messages, and track location, which could be found in all versions of Android, including Android 10. The vulnerability came by exploiting a bug in the multitasking system enabling a malicious app to overlay legitimate apps with fake login screens that users are not aware of when handing in security credentials. Users can also be tricked into granting additional permissions to the malicious apps, which later enable them to perform various nefarious activities, including intercepting texts or calls and stealing banking credentials. *Avast Threat Labs* also discovered that many pre-installed apps on several hundred new Android devices contain dangerous malware and adware. Some of the preinstalled malware can commit ad fraud or even take over its host device.

In 2020, the Which? watchdog reported that more than a billion Android devices released in 2012 or earlier, which was 40% of Android devices worldwide, were at risk of being hacked. This conclusion stemmed from the fact that no security updates were issued for the Android versions below 7.0 in 2019. Which? collaborated with the AV Comparatives anti-virus lab to infect five phone models with malware, and it succeeded in each case. Google refused to comment on the watchdog's speculations.

On August 5, 2020, Twitter published a blog urging its users to update their applications to the latest version with regards to a security concern that allowed others to access direct messages. A hacker could easily use the "Android system permissions" to fetch the account credentials in order to do so. The security issue is only with Android 8 (Android Oreo) and Android 9 (Android Pie). Twitter confirmed that updating the app will restrict such practices.

Technical Security Features

Android applications run in a sandbox, an isolated area of the system that does not have access to the rest of the system's resources, unless access permissions are explicitly granted by the user when the application is installed, however this may not be possible for pre-installed apps. It is not possible, for example, to turn off the microphone access of the pre-installed camera app without disabling the camera completely. This is valid also in Android versions 7 and 8.

Since February 2012, Google has used its Google Bouncer malware scanner to watch over and scan apps available in the Google Play store. A "Verify Apps" feature was introduced in November 2012, as part of the Android 4.2 "Jelly Bean" operating system version, to scan all apps, both from Google Play and from third-party sources, for malicious behaviour. Originally only doing so during installation, Verify Apps received an update in 2014 to "constantly" scan apps, and in 2017 the feature was made visible to users through a menu in Settings.

Before installing an application, the Google Play store displays a list of the requirements an app needs to function. After reviewing these permissions, the user can choose to accept or refuse them, installing the application only if they accept. In Android 6.0 "Marshmallow", the permissions system was changed; apps are no longer automatically granted all of their specified permissions at installation time. An opt-in system is used instead, in which users are prompted to grant or deny individual permissions to an app when they are needed for the first time. Applications remember the grants, which can be revoked by the user at any time. Pre-installed apps, however, are not always part of this approach. In some cases it may not be possible to deny certain permissions to pre-installed apps, nor be possible to disable them. The Google Play Services app cannot be uninstalled, nor disabled. Any force stop attempt, result in the app restarting itself. The new permissions model is used only by applications developed for Marshmallow using its software development kit (SDK), and older apps will continue to use the previous all-or-nothing approach. Permissions can still be revoked for those apps, though this might prevent them from working properly, and a warning is displayed to that effect.

In September 2014, Jason Nova of *Android Authority* reported on a study by the German security company Fraunhofer AISEC in antivirus software and malware threats on Android. Nova wrote that "The Android operating system deals with software packages by sandboxing them; this does not allow applications to list the directory contents of other apps to keep the system safe. By not allowing the antivirus to list the directories of other apps after installation, applications that show no inherent suspicious behavior when downloaded are cleared as safe. If then later on parts of the app are activated that turn out to be malicious, the antivirus will have no way to know since it is inside the app and out of the antivirus' jurisdiction". The study by Fraunhofer AISEC, examining antivirus software from Avast, AVG, Bitdefender, ESET, F-Secure, Kaspersky, Lookout, McAfee (formerly Intel Security), Norton, Sophos, and Trend Micro, revealed that "the tested antivirus apps do not provide protection against customized malware or targeted attacks", and that "the tested antivirus apps were also not able to detect malware which is completely unknown to date but does not make any efforts to hide its malignity".

In August 2013, Google announced Android Device Manager (renamed Find My Device in May 2017), a service that allows users to remotely track, locate, and wipe their Android device, with an Android app for the service released in December. In December 2016, Google introduced a Trusted Contacts app, letting users request location-tracking of loved ones during emergencies. In 2020, Trusted Contacts was shut down and the location-sharing feature rolled into Google Maps.

On October 8, 2018, Google announced new Google Play store requirements to combat over-sharing of potentially sensitive information, including call and text logs. The issue stems from the fact that many apps request permissions to access users' personal information (even if this information is not needed for the app to function) and some users unquestionably grant these permissions. Alternatively, a permission might be listed in the app manifest as required (as opposed to optional) and the app would not install unless user grants the permission; users can withdraw any, even required, permissions from any app in the device settings after app installation, but few users do this.

Google promised to work with developers and create exceptions if their apps require Phone or SMS permissions for "core app functionality". The new policies enforcement started on January 6, 2019, 90 days after policy announcement on October 8, 2018. Furthermore, Google announced a new "target API level requirement" (targetSdkVersion in manifest) at least Android 8.0 (API level 26) for all new apps and app updates. The API level requirement might combat the practice of app developers bypassing some permission screens by specifying early Android versions that had a coarser permission model.

Verified Boot

The Android Open Source Project implements a verified boot chain with intentions to verify that executed code, such as the kernel or bootloader, comes from an official source instead of a malicious actor. This implementation establishes a full chain of trust, as it initially starts at a hardware level. Subsequently, the boot loader is verified and system partitions such as system and vendor are checked for integrity. Furthermore, this process verifies that a previous version of Android has not been installed. This effectively provides rollback protection, which mitigates exploits that are similar to a downgrade attack.

Dm-Verity

Android (all supported versions, as far back as version 4.4 of the Android Open Source Project) has the option to provide a verified boot chain with `dm-verity`. This is a feature in the Linux kernel that allows for transparent integrity checking of block devices. This feature is designed to mitigate persistent rootkits.

Google Play Services and Vendor Changes

Dependence on proprietary Google Play Services and customizations added on top of the operating system by vendors who license Android from Google is causing privacy concerns.

Licensing

The source code for Android is open-source: it is developed in private by Google, with the source code released publicly when a new version of Android is released. Google publishes most of the code (including network and telephony stacks) under the non-copyleft Apache License version 2.0. which allows modification and redistribution.

The license does not grant rights to the "Android" trademark, so device manufacturers and wireless carriers have to license it from Google under individual contracts. Associated Linux kernel changes are released under the copyleft GNU General Public License version 2, developed by the Open Handset Alliance, with the source code publicly available at all times.

The only Android release which was not immediately made available as source code was the tablet-only 3.0 *Honeycomb* release. The reason, according to Andy Rubin in an official Android blog post, was because *Honeycomb* was rushed for production of the Motorola Xoom, and they did not want third parties creating a "really bad user experience" by attempting to put onto smartphones a version of Android intended for tablets.

Only the base Android operating system (including some applications) is open-source software, whereas most Android devices ship with a substantial amount of proprietary software, such as Google Mobile Services, which includes applications such as Google Play Store, Google Search, and Google Play Services – a software layer that provides APIs for the integration with Google-provided services, among others. These applications must be licensed from Google by device makers, and can only be shipped on devices which meet its compatibility guidelines and other requirements. Custom, certified distributions of Android produced by manufacturers (such as Samsung Experience) may also replace certain stock Android apps with their own proprietary variants and add additional software not included in the stock Android operating system. With the advent of the Google Pixel line of devices, Google itself has also made specific Android features timed or permanent exclusives to the Pixel series. There may also be "binary blob" drivers required for certain hardware components in the device. The best known fully open source Android services are the LineageOS distribution and MicroG which acts as an open source replacement of Google Play Services.

Richard Stallman and the Free Software Foundation have been critical of Android and have recommended the usage of alternatives such as Replicant, because drivers and firmware vital for the proper functioning of Android devices are usually proprietary, and because the Google Play Store application can forcibly install or uninstall applications and, as a result, invite non-free software. In both cases, the use of closed-source software causes the system to become vulnerable to backdoors.

It has been argued that because developers are often required to purchase the Google-branded Android license, this has turned the theoretically open system into a freemium service.

Leverage Over Manufacturers

Google licenses their Google Mobile Services software, along with the Android trademarks, only to hardware manufacturers for devices that meet Google's compatibility standards specified in the Android Compatibility Program document. Thus, forks of Android that make major changes to the operating system itself do not include any of Google's non-free components, stay incompatible with applications that require them, and must ship with an alternative software marketplace in lieu of Google Play Store.

A prominent example of such an Android fork is Amazon's Fire OS, which is used on the Kindle Fire line of tablets, and oriented toward Amazon services. The shipment of Android devices without GMS is also common in mainland China, as Google does not do business there.

In 2014, Google also began to require that all Android devices which license the Google Mobile Services software display a prominent "Powered by Android" logo on their boot screens. Google has also enforced preferential bundling and placement of Google Mobile Services on devices, including mandated bundling of the entire main suite of Google applications, mandatory placement of shortcuts to Google Search and the Play Store app on or near the main home screen page in its default configuration, and granting a larger share of search revenue to OEMs who agree to not include third-party app stores on their devices. In March 2018, it was reported that Google had begun to block "uncertified" Android devices from using Google Mobile Services software, and display a warning indicating that "the device manufacturer has preloaded Google apps and services without certification from Google". Users of custom ROMs can register their device ID to their Google account to remove this block.

Some stock applications and components in AOSP code that were formerly used by earlier versions of Android, such as Search, Music, Calendar, and the location API, were abandoned by Google in favor of non-free replacements distributed through Play Store (Google Search, YouTube Music, and Google Calendar) and Google Play Services, which are no longer open-source. Moreover, open-source variants of some applications also exclude functions that are present in their non-free versions. These measures are likely intended to discourage forks and encourage commercial licensing in line with Google requirements, as the majority of the operating system's core functionality is dependent on proprietary components licensed exclusively by Google, and it would take significant development resources to develop an alternative suite of software and APIs to replicate or replace them. Apps that do not use Google components would also be at a functional disadvantage, as they can only use APIs contained within the OS itself. In turn, third-party apps may have dependencies on Google Play Services.

Members of the Open Handset Alliance, which include the majority of Android OEMs, are also contractually forbidden from producing Android devices based on forks of the OS; in 2012, Acer Inc. was forced by Google to halt production on a device powered by Alibaba Group's Aliyun OS with threats of removal from the OHA, as Google deemed the platform to be an incompatible version of Android. Alibaba Group defended the allegations, arguing that the OS was a distinct platform from Android (primarily using HTML5 apps), but incorporated portions of Android's platform to allow backwards compatibility with third-party Android software. Indeed, the devices did ship with an application store which offered Android apps; however, the majority of them were pirated.

Reception

Android received a lukewarm reaction when it was unveiled in 2007. Although analysts were impressed with the respected technology companies that had partnered with Google to form the Open Handset Alliance, it was unclear whether mobile phone manufacturers would be willing to replace their existing operating systems with Android. The idea of an open-source, Linux-based development platform sparked interest, but there were additional worries about Android facing strong competition from established players in the smartphone market, such as Nokia and Microsoft, and rival Linux mobile operating systems that were in development. These established players were skeptical: Nokia was quoted as saying "we don't see this as a threat", and a member of Microsoft's Windows Mobile team stated "I don't understand the impact that they are going to have."

Since then Android has grown to become the most widely used smartphone operating system and "one of the fastest mobile experiences available". Reviewers have highlighted the open-source nature of the operating system as one of its defining strengths, allowing companies such as Nokia (Nokia X family), Amazon (Kindle Fire), Barnes & Noble (Nook), Ouya, Baidu and others to fork the software and release hardware running their own customised version of Android. As a result, it has been described by technology website *Ars Technica* as "practically the default operating system for launching new hardware" for companies without their own mobile platforms. This openness and flexibility is also present at the level of the end user: Android allows extensive customisation of devices by their owners and apps are freely available from non-Google app stores and third party websites. These have been cited as among the main advantages of Android phones over others.

Despite Android's popularity, including an activation rate three times that of iOS, there have been reports that Google has not been able to leverage their other products and web services successfully to turn Android into the money maker that analysts had expected. *The Verge* suggested that Google is losing control of Android due to the extensive customization and proliferation of non-Google apps and services – Amazon's Kindle Fire line uses Fire OS, a heavily modified fork of Android which does not include or support any of Google's proprietary components, and requires that users obtain software from its competing Amazon Appstore instead of Play Store. In 2014, in an effort to improve prominence of the Android brand, Google began to require that devices featuring its proprietary components display an Android logo on the boot screen.

Android has suffered from "fragmentation", a situation where the variety of Android devices, in terms of both hardware variations and differences in the software running on them, makes the task of developing applications that work consistently across the ecosystem harder than rival platforms such as iOS where hardware and software varies less. For example, according to data from OpenSignal in July 2013, there were 11,868 models of Android devices, numerous screen sizes and eight Android OS versions simultaneously in use, while the large majority of iOS users have upgraded to the latest iteration of that OS. Critics such as *Apple Insider* have asserted that fragmentation via hardware and software pushed Android's growth through large volumes of low end, budget-priced devices running older versions of Android. They maintain this forces Android developers to write for the "lowest common denominator" to reach as many users as possible, who have too little incentive to make use of the latest hardware or software features only available on a smaller percentage of devices. However, OpenSignal, who develops both Android and iOS apps, concluded that although fragmentation can make development trickier, Android's wider global reach also increases the potential reward.

Market Share

Android is the most used operating system on phones in virtually all countries, with some countries, such as India, having over 96% market share. On tablets, usage is more even, as iOS is a bit more popular globally.

Research company Canalys estimated in the second quarter of 2009, that Android had a 2.8% share of worldwide smartphone shipments. By May 2010, Android had a 10% worldwide smartphone market share, overtaking Windows Mobile, whilst in the US Android held a 28% share, overtaking iPhone OS. By the fourth quarter of 2010, its worldwide share had grown to 33% of the market becoming the top-selling smartphone platform, overtaking Symbian. In the US it became the top-selling platform in April 2011, overtaking BlackBerry OS with a 31.2% smartphone share, according to *comScore*.

By the third quarter of 2011, Gartner estimated that more than half (52.5%) of the smartphone sales belonged to Android. By the third quarter of 2012 Android had a 75% share of the global smartphone market according to the research firm IDC.

In July 2011, Google said that 550,000 Android devices were being activated every day, up from 400,000 per day in May, and more than 100 million devices had been activated with 4.4% growth per week. In September 2012, 500 million devices had been activated with 1.3 million activations per day. In May 2013, at Google I/O, Sundar Pichai announced that 900 million Android devices had been activated.

Android market share varies by location. In July 2012, "mobile subscribers aged 13+" in the United States using Android were up to 52%, and rose to 90% in China. During the third quarter of 2012, Android's worldwide smartphone shipment market share was 75%, with 750 million devices activated in total. In April 2013, Android had 1.5 million activations per day. As of May 2013, 48 billion application ("app") installation have been performed from the Google Play store, and by September 2013, one billion Android devices had been activated.

As of August 2020, the Google Play store had over 3 million Android applications published, and as of May 2016, apps had been downloaded more than 65 billion times. The operating system's success has made it a target for patent litigation as part of the so-called "smartphone wars" between technology companies.

Android devices account for more than half of smartphone sales in most markets, including the US, while "only in Japan was Apple on top" (September–November 2013 numbers). At the end of 2013, over 1.5 billion Android smartphones had been sold in the four years since 2010, making Android the most sold phone and tablet OS. Three billion Android smartphones were estimated to be sold by the end of 2014 (including previous years). According to Gartner research company, Android-based devices outsold all contenders, every year since 2012. In 2013, it outsold Windows 2.8:1 or by 573 million. As of 2015, Android has the largest installed base of all operating systems; Since 2013, devices running it also sell more than Windows, iOS and Mac OS X devices combined.

According to StatCounter, which tracks only the use for browsing the web, Android is the most popular mobile operating system since August 2013. Android is the most popular operating system for web browsing in India and several other countries (e.g. virtually all of Asia, with Japan and North Korea exceptions). According to StatCounter, Android is most used on phones in all African countries, and it stated "mobile usage has already overtaken desktop in several countries including India, South Africa and Saudi Arabia", with all countries in Africa having done so already in which mobile (including tablets) usage is at 90.46% (Android only, accounts for 75.81% of all use there).

While Android phones in the Western world almost always include Google's proprietary code (such as Google Play) in the otherwise open-source operating system, Google's proprietary code and trademark is increasingly not used in emerging markets; "The growth of AOSP Android devices goes way beyond just China [..] ABI Research claims that 65 million devices shipped globally with open-source Android in the second quarter of [2014], up from 54 million in the first quarter"; depending on country, percent of phones estimated to be based only on AOSP source code, forgoing the Android trademark: Thailand (44%), Philippines (38%), Indonesia (31%), India (21%), Malaysia (24%), Mexico (18%), Brazil (9%).

According to a January 2015 Gartner report, "Android surpassed a billion shipments of devices in 2014, and will continue to grow at a double-digit pace in 2015, with a 26 percent increase year over year." This made it the first time that any general-purpose operating system has reached more than one billion end users within a year: by reaching close to 1.16 billion end users in 2014, Android shipped over four times more than iOS and OS X combined, and over three times more than Microsoft Windows. Gartner expected the whole mobile phone market to "reach two billion units in 2016", including Android. Describing the statistics, Farhad Manjoo wrote in *The New York Times* that "About one of every two computers sold today is running Android. [It] has become Earth's dominant computing platform."

According to a Statistica's estimate, Android smartphones had an installed base of 1.8 billion units in 2015, which was 76% of the estimated total number of smartphones worldwide. Android has the largest installed base of any mobile operating system and, since 2013, the highest-selling operating system overall with sales in 2012, 2013 and 2014 close to the installed base of all PCs.

In the second quarter of 2014, Android's share of the global smartphone shipment market was 84.7%, a new record. This had grown to 87.5% worldwide market share by the third quarter of 2016, leaving main competitor iOS with 12.1% market share.

According to an April 2017 StatCounter report, Android overtook Microsoft Windows to become the most popular operating system for total Internet usage. It has maintained the plurality since then. In September 2015, Google announced that Android had 1.4 billion monthly active users. This changed to 2 billion monthly active users in May 2017.

Adoption on Tablets

Despite its success on smartphones, initially Android tablet adoption was slow, then later caught up with the iPad, in most countries. One of the main causes was the chicken or the egg situation where consumers were hesitant to buy an Android tablet due to a lack of high quality tablet applications, but developers were hesitant to spend time and resources developing tablet applications until there was a significant market for them. The content and app "ecosystem" proved more important than hardware specs as the selling point for tablets. Due to the lack of Android tablet-specific applications in 2011, early Android tablets had to make do with existing smartphone applications that were ill-suited to larger screen sizes, whereas the dominance of Apple's iPad was reinforced by the large number of tablet-specific iOS applications.

Despite app support in its infancy, a considerable number of Android tablets, like the Barnes & Noble Nook (alongside those using other operating systems, such as the HP TouchPad and BlackBerry PlayBook) were rushed out to market in an attempt to capitalize on the success of the iPad. *InfoWorld* has suggested that some Android manufacturers initially treated their first tablets as a "Frankenphone business", a short-term low-investment opportunity by placing a smartphone-optimized Android OS (before Android 3.0 *Honeycomb* for tablets was available) on a device while neglecting user interface. This approach, such as with the Dell Streak, failed to gain market traction with consumers as well as damaging the early reputation of Android tablets. Furthermore, several Android tablets such as the

Motorola Xoom were priced the same or higher than the iPad, which hurt sales. An exception was the Amazon Kindle Fire, which relied upon lower pricing as well as access to Amazon's ecosystem of applications and content.

This began to change in 2012, with the release of the affordable Nexus 7 and a push by Google for developers to write better tablet applications. According to International Data Corporation, shipments of Android-powered tablets surpassed iPads in Q3 2012.

As of the end of 2013, over 191.6 million Android tablets had sold in three years since 2011. This made Android tablets the most-sold type of tablet in 2013, surpassing iPads in the second quarter of 2013.

According to StatCounter's web use statistics, as of 2020, Android tablets represent the majority of tablet devices used in Africa (70%), South America (65%), while less than half elsewhere, e.g. Europe (44%), Asia (44%), North America (34%) and Oceania/Australia (18%). There are countries on all continents where Android tablets are the majority, for example, Mexico.

In March 2016, Galen Gruman of *InfoWorld* stated that Android devices could be a "real part of your business [..] there's no longer a reason to keep Android at arm's length. It can now be as integral to your mobile portfolio as Apple's iOS devices are". A year earlier, Gruman had stated that Microsoft's own mobile Office apps were "better on iOS and Android" than on Microsoft's own Windows 10 devices.

Platform Information

Android has 71% market share vs Apple's iOS/iPadOS at 29% (on tablets alone Apple is slightly ahead, i.e. 45% vs 55%, though Android is ahead in virtually all countries). The recently released Android 13 is the most popular Android version on smartphones and tablets combined. Usage is at 75% for all supported versions of Android combined, i.e. Android 11 and newer.

As of 2024, Android 13 is most popular single Android version on smartphones at 29%, followed by Android 12, 11 and then Android 14 at 13%. Latest Android 14 is though most used single version in several countries e.g. the US, Canada and Nordic countries, with over a third of the share in those countries. Usage of Android 11 and newer, i.e. supported versions, is at 75%, the rest of users are not supported with security updates. Android 13 is most popular version in many countries such as India, most European, and Brazil and Australia.

Application Piracy

Paid Android applications in the past were simple to pirate. In a May 2012 interview with Eurogamer, the developers of *Football Manager* stated that the ratio of pirated players vs legitimate players was 9:1 for their game *Football Manager Handheld*.

However, not every developer agreed that piracy rates were an issue; for example, in July 2012 the developers of the game *Wind-up Knight* said that piracy levels of their game were only 12%, and most of the piracy came from China, where people cannot purchase apps from Google Play.

In 2010, Google released a tool for validating authorized purchases for use within apps, but developers complained that this was insufficient and trivial to crack. Google responded that the tool, especially its initial release, was intended as a sample framework for developers to modify and build upon depending on their needs, not as a finished piracy solution. Android "Jelly Bean" introduced the ability for paid applications to be encrypted, so that they may work only on the device for which they were purchased.

Legal Issues

The success of Android has made it a target for patent and copyright litigation between technology companies, both Android and Android phone manufacturers having been involved in numerous patent lawsuits and other legal challenges.

Patent Lawsuit with Oracle

On August 12, 2010, Oracle sued Google over claimed infringement of copyrights and patents related to the Java programming language. Oracle originally sought damages up to $6.1 billion, but this valuation was rejected by a United States federal judge who asked Oracle to revise the estimate. In response, Google submitted multiple lines of defense, counterclaiming that Android did not infringe on Oracle's patents or copyright, that Oracle's patents were invalid, and several other defenses. They said that Android's Java runtime environment is based on Apache Harmony, a clean room implementation of the Java class libraries, and an independently developed virtual machine called Dalvik. In May 2012, the jury in this case found that Google did not infringe on Oracle's patents, and the trial judge ruled that the structure of the Java APIs used by Google was not copyrightable. The parties agreed to zero dollars in statutory damages for a small amount of copied code. On May 9, 2014, the Federal Circuit partially reversed the district court ruling, ruling in Oracle's favor on the copyrightability issue, and remanding the issue of fair use to the district court.

In December 2015, Google announced that the next major release of Android (Android Nougat) would switch to OpenJDK, which is the official open-source implementation of the Java platform, instead of using the now-discontinued Apache Harmony project as its runtime. Code reflecting this change was also posted to the AOSP source repository. In its announcement, Google claimed this was part of an effort to create a "common code base" between Java on Android and other platforms. Google later admitted in a court filing that this was part of an effort to address the disputes with Oracle, as its use of OpenJDK code is governed under the GNU General Public License (GPL) with a linking exception, and that "any damages claim associated with the new versions expressly licensed by Oracle under OpenJDK would require a separate analysis of damages from earlier releases". In June 2016, a United States federal court ruled in favor of Google, stating that its use of the APIs was fair use.

In April 2021, the Supreme Court of the United States ruled that Google's use of the Java APIs was within the bounds of fair use, reversing the Federal Circuit Appeals Court ruling and remanding the case for further hearing. The majority opinion began with the assumption that the APIs may be copyrightable, and thus proceeded with a review of the factors that contributed to fair use.

Anti-Competitive Challenges in Europe

In 2013, FairSearch, a lobbying organization supported by Microsoft, Oracle and others, filed a complaint regarding Android with the European Commission, alleging that its free-of-charge distribution model constituted anti-competitive predatory pricing. The Free Software Foundation Europe, whose donors include Google, disputed the Fairsearch allegations. On April 20, 2016, the EU filed a formal antitrust complaint against Google based upon the FairSearch allegations, arguing that its leverage over Android vendors, including the mandatory bundling of the entire suite of proprietary Google software, hindering the ability for competing search providers to be integrated into Android, and barring vendors from producing devices running forks of Android, constituted anti-competitive practices. In August 2016, Google was fined US$6.75 million by the Russian Federal Antimonopoly Service (FAS) under similar allegations by Yandex. The European Commission issued its decision on July 18, 2018, determining that Google had conducted three operations related to Android that were in violation of antitrust regulations: bundling Google's search and Chrome as part of Android, blocking phone manufacturers from using forked versions of Android, and establishing deals with phone manufacturers and network providers to exclusively bundle the Google search application on handsets (a practice Google ended by 2014). The EU fined Google for €4.3 billion (about US$5 billion) and required the company to end this conduct within 90 days. Google filed its appeal of the ruling in October 2018, though will not ask for any interim measures to delay the onset of conduct requirements.

On October 16, 2018, Google announced that it would change its distribution model for Google Mobile Services in the EU, since part of its revenues streams for Android which came through use of Google Search and Chrome were now prohibited by the EU's ruling. While the core Android system remains free, OEMs in Europe would be required to purchase a paid license to the core suite of Google applications, such as Gmail, Google Maps and the Google Play Store. Google Search will be licensed separately, with an option to include Google Chrome at no additional cost atop Search. European OEMs can bundle third-party alternatives on phones and devices sold to customers, if they so choose. OEMs will no longer be barred from selling any device running incompatible versions of Android in Europe.

Others

In addition to lawsuits against Google directly, various proxy wars have been waged against Android indirectly by targeting manufacturers of Android devices, with the effect of discouraging manufacturers from adopting the platform by increasing the costs of bringing an Android device to market. Both Apple and Microsoft have sued several manufacturers for patent infringement, with Apple's legal action against Samsung being a particularly high-profile case.

In January 2012, Microsoft said they had signed patent license agreements with eleven Android device manufacturers, whose products account for "70 percent of all Android smartphones" sold in the US and 55% of the worldwide revenue for Android devices. These include Samsung and HTC. Samsung's patent settlement with Microsoft included an agreement to allocate more resources to developing and marketing phones running Microsoft's Windows Phone operating system. Microsoft has also tied its own Android software to patent licenses, requiring the bundling of Microsoft Office Mobile and Skype applications on Android devices to subsidize the licensing fees, while at the same time helping to promote its software lines.

Google has publicly expressed its frustration for the current patent landscape in the United States, accusing Apple, Oracle and Microsoft of trying to take down Android through patent litigation, rather than innovating and competing with better products and services. In August 2011, Google purchased Motorola Mobility for US$12.5 billion, which was viewed in part as a defensive measure to protect Android, since Motorola Mobility held more than 17,000 patents. In December 2011, Google bought over a thousand patents from IBM.

Turkey's competition authority investigations about the default search engine in Android, started in 2017, led to a US$17.4 million fine in September 2018 and a fine of 0.05 percent of Google's revenue per day in November 2019 when Google did not meet the requirements. In December 2019, Google stopped issuing licenses for new Android phone models sold in Turkey.

2.1.3 Windows Phone

Windows Phone (WP) is a discontinued mobile operating system developed by Microsoft for smartphones as the replacement successor to Windows Mobile and Zune. Windows Phone featured a new user interface derived from the Metro design language. Unlike Windows Mobile, it was primarily aimed at the consumer market rather than the enterprise market.

It was first launched in October 2010 with Windows Phone 7. Windows Phone 8 succeeded it in 2012, replacing the Windows CE-based kernel of Windows Phone 7 with the Windows NT kernel used by the PC versions of Windows (and, in particular, a large amount of internal components from Windows 8). Due to these changes, the OS was incompatible with all existing Windows Phone 7 devices, although it still supported apps originally developed for Windows Phone 7. In 2014, Microsoft released the Windows Phone 8.1 update, which introduced the Cortana virtual assistant, and Windows Runtime platform support to create cross-platform apps between Windows PCs and Windows Phone.

In 2015, Microsoft released Windows 10 Mobile, which promoted increased integration and unification with its PC counterpart, including the ability to connect devices to an external display or docking station to display a PC-like interface. Although Microsoft dropped the Windows Phone brand at this time in order to focus more on synergies with Windows 10 for PCs, it was still a continuation of the Windows Phone line from a technical standpoint, and updates were issued for selected Windows Phone 8.1 devices.

While Microsoft's investments in the platform were headlined by a major partnership with Nokia (whose Lumia series of smartphones, including the Lumia 520 in particular, would represent the majority of Windows Phone devices sold by 2013) and Microsoft's eventual acquisition of the company's mobile device business for just over US$7 billion (which included Nokia's then-CEO Stephen Elop joining Microsoft to lead its in-house mobile division), the duopoly of Android and iPhone remained the dominant platforms for smartphones, and interest in Windows Phone from app developers began to diminish by mid-decade. Microsoft laid off the Microsoft Mobile staff in 2016, after having taken a write-off of $7.6 billion on the acquired Nokia hardware assets, while market share sank to 1% that year. Microsoft began to prioritize software development and integrations with Android and iOS instead, and ceased active development of Windows 10 Mobile in 2017.

History

Development

Work on a major Windows Mobile update may have begun as early as 2004 under the codename "Photon", but work moved slowly and the project was ultimately cancelled. In 2008, Microsoft reorganized the Windows Mobile group and started work on a new mobile operating system. The product was to be released in 2009 as Windows Phone, but several delays prompted Microsoft to develop Windows Mobile 6.5 as an interim release.

Following this, Windows Phone was developed quickly. One result was that the new OS would not be compatible with Windows Mobile applications. Larry Lieberman, senior product manager for Microsoft's Mobile Developer Experience, told eWeek: "If we'd had more time and resources, we may have been able to do something in terms of backward compatibility." Lieberman said that Microsoft was attempting to look at the mobile phone market in a new way, with the end user in mind as well as the enterprise network. Terry Myerson, corporate VP of Windows Phone engineering, said, "With the move to capacitive touch screens, away from the stylus, and the moves to some of the hardware choices we made for the Windows Phone 7 experience, we had to break application compatibility with Windows Mobile 6.5." From the beginning of Windows Phone until at least 2015, Joe Belfiore was the head of development and the face of the platform's initiatives.

Partnership with Nokia

On February 11, 2011, at a press event in London, Microsoft CEO Steve Ballmer and Nokia CEO Stephen Elop announced a partnership between their companies in which Windows Phone would become the primary smartphone operating-system for Nokia, replacing Symbian. The event focused largely on setting up "a new global mobile ecosystem", suggesting competition with Android and iOS with the words "It is now a three horse race".

Elop stated the reason for choosing Windows Phone over Android, saying: "the single most important word is 'differentiation'. Entering the Android environment late, we knew we would have a hard time differentiating." While Nokia would have had more long-term creative control with Android (MeeGo as used by Nokia resembles Android more than it does Windows Phone 7 as both Android and MeeGo are based on the Linux kernel), Elop enjoyed familiarity with his past company where he had been a top executive.

The pair announced integration of Microsoft services with Nokia's own services; specifically:

- Bing would power search across Nokia devices
- Integration of Nokia Maps with Bing Maps
- Integration of Nokia's Ovi store with the Windows Phone Store

The partnership involves "funds changing hands for royalties, marketing and ad-revenue sharing", which Microsoft later announced as "measured in billions of dollars".

Jo Harlow, whom Elop tapped to run Nokia's smartphone business, rearranged her team to match the structure led by Microsoft's VP of Windows Phone, Terry Myerson. Myerson was quoted as saying, "I can trust her with what she tells me. She uses that same direct and genuine communication to motivate her team."

The first Nokia Lumia Windows Phones, the Lumia 800 and Lumia 710, were announced in October 2011 at Nokia World 2011.

At the Consumer Electronics Show in 2012 Nokia announced the Lumia 900, featuring a 4.3-inch AMOLED ClearBlack display, a 1.4 GHz processor and 16 GB of storage. The Lumia 900 was one of the first Windows Phones to support LTE and was released on AT&T on April 8, 2012. An international version launched in Q2 2012, with a UK launch on May 11, 2012. The Lumia 610 was the first Nokia Windows Phone to run the Tango Variant (Windows Phone 7.5 Refresh) and was aimed at emerging markets.

On September 2, 2013, Microsoft announced a deal to acquire Nokia's mobile phone division outright, retaining former CEO Stephen Elop as the head of Microsoft's devices operation. The merger was completed after regulatory approval in all major markets in April 2014. As a result, Nokia's hardware division became a subsidiary of Microsoft operating under the name Microsoft Mobile.

In February 2014, Nokia released the Nokia X series of smartphones (later discontinued) using a version of Android forked from the Android Open Source Project. The operating system was modified; Google's software was not included in favour of competing applications and services from Microsoft and Nokia, and with a user interface highly modified to resemble Windows Phone.

Versions

Windows Phone 7

Windows Phone 7 was announced at Mobile World Congress in Barcelona, Catalonia, Spain, on February 15, 2010, and released publicly on November 8, 2010 in the United States. In 2011, Microsoft released Windows Phone 7.5 *Mango*. The update included a mobile version of Internet Explorer 9 that supports the same web standards and graphical capability as the desktop version, multi-tasking of third-party apps, Twitter integration for the People Hub, and Windows Live SkyDrive access. A minor update released in 2012 known as "Tango", along with other bug fixes, lowered the hardware requirements to allow for devices with 800 MHz CPUs and 256 MB of RAM to run Windows Phone. Windows Phone 7 devices can not be upgraded to Windows Phone 8 due to hardware limitations. Windows Phone 7.8 was released as a stopgap update in 2013 to include some of the user interface features from Windows Phone 8.

Windows Phone 8

On October 29, 2012, Microsoft released Windows Phone 8, a new generation of the operating system. Windows Phone 8 replaced its previously Windows CE-based architecture with one based on the Windows NT kernel with many components shared with Windows 8.

Windows Phone 8.1

Windows Phone 8.1 was announced on April 2, 2014, after being released in preview form to developers on April 10, 2014. New features added include a notification center, support for the Internet Explorer 11 web browser, with tab syncing among Windows 8.1 devices, separate volume controls, and the option to skin and add a third column of live tiles to the Start Screen. Starting with this release, Microsoft dropped the requirement that all Windows Phone OEMs include a camera button and physical buttons for back, Start, and Search. Windows Phone 8.1 introduced Cortana, a voice assistant similar to Siri and Google Now. Cortana replaced the previous Bing search feature, and was released as a beta in the United States in the first half of 2014, before expanding to other countries in early 2015.

Windows 10 Mobile

Windows 10 Mobile was announced on January 21, 2015, as a mobile operating system for smartphones and tablets running on ARM architecture. Its primary focus is unification with Windows 10, its PC counterpart, in software and services; in accordance with this strategy, the Windows Phone name has been phased out in favor of branding the platform as an edition of Windows 10, although it is still a continuation of Windows Phone, and most Windows Phone 8.1 devices can be upgraded to the platform.

Windows 10 Mobile emphasized software using the Universal Windows Platform (UWP), which allowed apps to be designed for use across multiple Windows 10-based product families with nearly identical code, functionality, and adaptations for available input methods. When connected to an external display, devices could also render a stripped-down desktop interface similar to Windows on PCs, with support for keyboard and mouse input. Windows 10 Mobile featured Skype message integration, updated Office Mobile apps, notification syncing with other Windows 10 devices, support for the Microsoft Edge web browser, and other user interface improvements. Microsoft developed a middleware known as Windows Bridge to allow iOS Objective-C and Android C++ or Java software to be ported to run on Windows 10 Mobile with limited changes to code. With the diminishing interest and application development for the platform, Microsoft discontinued active development of Windows 10 Mobile in 2017, and the platform was declared end of life on January 14, 2020.

Features

User Interface

Windows Phone features a user interface based on Microsoft's "Metro" design language, and was inspired by the user interface in the Zune HD. The home screen, called the "Start screen", is made up of "Live Tiles", which have been the inspiration for the Windows 8 live tiles. Tiles are links to applications, features, functions and individual items (such as contacts, web pages, applications or media items). Users can add, rearrange, or remove tiles. Tiles are dynamic and update in real time – for example, the tile for an email account would display the number of unread messages or a tile could display a live update of the weather. Since Windows Phone 8, live tiles can also be resized to either a small, medium, or large appearance.

Several features of Windows Phone are organized into "hubs", which combine local and online content via Windows Phone's integration with popular social networks such as Facebook, Windows Live, and Twitter. For example, the Pictures hub shows photos captured with the device's camera and the user's Facebook photo albums, and the People hub shows contacts aggregated from multiple sources including Windows Live, Facebook, and Gmail. From the hub, users can directly comment and 'like' on social network updates. The other built-in hubs are Xbox Music and Video, Xbox Live Games, Windows Phone Store, and Microsoft Office.

Windows Phone uses multi-touch technology. The default Windows Phone user interface has a dark theme that prolongs battery life on OLED screens as fully black pixels do not emit light.

Alternatively, users may choose a light theme in their phone's settings menu. The user may also choose from several accent colors. User interface elements such as links, buttons and tiles are shown in the user's chosen accent color.

Third-party applications can be automatically themed with these colors. Windows Phone 8.1 introduces transparent tiles and a customizable background image for the Start screen. The image is visible through the transparent area of the tiles and features a parallax effect when scrolling which gives an illusion of depth. If the user does not pick a background image the tiles render with the accent color of the theme.

Text Input

Users input text by using an on-screen virtual keyboard, which has a dedicated key for inserting emoticons, and features spell checking and word prediction. App developers (both inhouse and ISV) may specify different versions of the virtual keyboard in order to limit users to certain character sets, such as numeric characters alone. Users may change a word after it has been typed by tapping the word, which will invoke a list of similar words. Pressing and holding certain keys will reveal similar characters. The keys are somewhat larger and spaced farther apart when in landscape mode. Phones may also be made with a hardware keyboard for text input. Users can also add accents to letters by holding on an individual letter. Windows Phone 8.1 introduces a new method of typing by swiping through the keyboard without lifting the finger, in a manner similar to Swype and SwiftKey.

Web Browser

Internet Explorer on Windows Phone allows the user to maintain a list of favorite web pages and tiles linking to web pages on the Start screen. The browser supports up to 6 tabs, which can all load in parallel. Other features include multi-touch gestures, smooth zoom in/out animations, the ability to save pictures that are on web pages, share web pages via email, and support for inline search which allows the user to search for a word or phrase in a web page by typing it. Tabs are synced with Windows 8.1 devices using Internet Explorer 11.

Contacts

Contacts are organized via the "People hub", and can be manually entered into contacts or imported from Facebook, Windows Live Contacts, Twitter, LinkedIn, Google, and Outlook. A "What's New" section shows a user's Facebook news feed and a "Pictures" section show pictures from those social networks, while a "Me" section within the "People" hub shows a user's own social network status and wall and allows them to view social network updates. Contacts can also be pinned to the Start Screen. The contact's "Live Tile" displays their social network status and profile picture on the homescreen. Clicking on a contact's tile or accessing their card within the "People" hub will reveal their recent social network activity as well as the rest of their contact information. If a contact has information stored on multiple networks, users can link the two separate contact accounts, allowing the information to be viewed and accessed from a single card. As of Windows Phone 7.5, contacts can also be sorted into "Groups". Here, information from each of the contacts is combined into a single page which can be accessed directly from the Hub or pinned to the Start screen.

Email

Windows Phone supports Outlook.com, Exchange, Yahoo! Mail and Gmail natively and supports many other services via the POP and IMAP protocols. Updates added support for more services such as iCloud and IBM Notes Traveler. Contacts and calendars may be synced from these services as well. Users can also search through their email by searching in the subject, body, senders, and receivers. Emails are shown with threads, and multiple email inboxes can be combined into a single view (a feature commonly referred to as "combined inbox") or can viewed separately.

Multimedia

Xbox Music and Xbox Video are built-in multimedia hubs providing entertainment and synchronization capabilities between PC, Windows Phone, and other Microsoft products. The two hubs were previously combined until standalone apps were released in late 2013, shortly before Windows Phone 8.1 debuted. The hubs allow users to access music, videos, and podcasts stored on the device, and links directly to the "Xbox Music Store" to buy or rent music and the "Xbox Video Store" to purchase movies and TV episodes. Xbox Music also allows the user to stream music with an Xbox Music Pass. When browsing the music by a particular artist, users are able to view artist biographies and photos. The Xbox Music hub also integrates with many other apps that provide video and music services, including, but not limited to, iHeartRadio, YouTube, and Vevo. This hub also includes Smart DJ which compiles a playlist of songs stored on the phone similar to the song or artist selected.

The Pictures hub displays the user's Facebook and OneDrive photo albums, as well as photos taken with the phone's built-in camera. Users can also upload photos to social networks, comment on photos uploaded by other people, and tag photos posted to social networks. Multi-touch gestures permit zooming in and out of photos. An official file manager app called Files, which is available for download from the Windows Phone Store, enables users to move and rearrange documents, videos, music and other files within their device's hard drive or to an external SD card.

Media Support

Windows Phone supports WAV, MP3, WMA, AMR, AAC/MP4/M4A/M4B and 3GP/3G2 standards. The video file formats supported on WP include WMV, AVI, MP4/M4V, 3GP/3G2 and MOV (QuickTime) standards. These supported audio and video formats would be dependent on the codecs contained inside them. It has also been previously reported that the DivX and Xvid codecs within the AVI file format are also playable on WP devices.

Windows Phone does not support DRM protected media files that are obtained from services other than Xbox Music Pass. The image file formats that are supported include JPG/JPEG, PNG, GIF, TIF and Bitmap (BMP). Users can also add custom ringtones which are less than 1MB in size and less than 40 seconds long. DLNA streaming and stereoscopic 3D are also supported.

Games

The "Games hub" provides access to games on a phone along with Xbox Live functionality, including the ability for a user to interact with their avatar, view and edit their profile, see their achievements and view leaderboards, and send messages to friends on Xbox Live. The hub also features an area for managing invitations and turn notifications in turn-based multiplayer games. Games are downloaded from Windows Phone Store.

Search

Bing is the default search engine on Windows Phone handsets because its functions are deeply integrated in the OS (which also include the utilization of its map service for location-based searches and queries). However, Microsoft has stated that other search engine applications can be used.

In the area of location-based searches, Bing Maps (which is powered by Nokia's location services) provides turn-by-turn navigation service to Windows Phone users, and Local Scout shows interest points such as attractions and restaurants in the nearby area. On Nokia devices, Nokia's Here Maps is preinstalled in place of Bing Maps. Furthermore, Bing Audio allows the user to match a song with its name, and Bing Vision allows the user to scan barcodes, QR codes, and other types of tags.

Cortana

Every Windows Phone has either a dedicated physical Search button or an on-screen Search button, which was previously reserved for a Bing Search app, but has been replaced on Windows Phone 8.1 devices and later in the United Kingdom and United States by Cortana, a digital personal assistant which can also double as an app for basic searches. Cortana allows users to do tasks such as set calendar reminders and alarms, and recognizes a user's natural voice, and can be used to answer questions (like current weather conditions, sports scores, and biographies). The app also keeps a "Notebook" to learn a user's behavior over time and tailor reminders for them. Users can edit the "Notebook" to keep information from Cortana or reveal more about themselves.

Office Suite

All Windows Phones come preinstalled with Microsoft Office Mobile, which provides interoperability between Windows Phone and the desktop version of Microsoft Office. Word Mobile, Excel Mobile, PowerPoint Mobile, and SharePoint Workspace Mobile apps are accessible through a single "Office Hub", and allow most Microsoft Office file formats to be viewed and edited directly on a Windows Phone device. The "Office Hub" can access files from OneDrive and Office 365, as well as files which are stored locally on the device's hard drive. Although they are not preinstalled in Windows Phone's "Office Hub", OneNote Mobile, Lync Mobile, and OneDrive for Business can be downloaded separately as standalone applications from the Windows Phone Store.

Multitasking

Multitasking in Windows Phone is invoked through long pressing the "back" arrow, which is present on all Windows Phones. Windows Phone 7 uses a card-based task switcher, whereas later versions of Windows Phone utilize true background multitasking.

Sync

- **Windows Phone 7:** Zune Software manages the contents on Windows

Phone 7 devices and Windows Phone can wirelessly sync with Zune Software.

- **Later Versions:** Syncing content between Windows Phone 8 and 8.1 and Windows PCs or Macs is provided through the Windows Phone App, which is available for both Windows and Mac OS X. It is the official successor to Zune software only for Windows Phone 8 and Windows Phone 8.1, and allows users to transfer content such as music, videos, and documents. Users also have the ability to use a "Tap and Send" feature that allows for file transfer between Windows phones, and NFC-compatible devices through NFC.

Updates

Software updates are delivered to Windows Phone users via Microsoft Update, as is the case with other Windows operating systems. Microsoft initially had the intention to directly update any phone running Windows Phone instead of relying on OEMs or wireless carriers, but on January 6, 2012, Microsoft changed their policy to let carriers decide if an update will be delivered.

While Windows Phone 7 users were required to attach their phones to a PC to install updates, starting with Windows Phone 8, all updates are done via over-the-air downloads. Since Windows Phone 8, Microsoft has also begun releasing minor updates that add features to a current OS release throughout the year. These updates were first labeled "General Distribution releases" (or GDRs), but were later rebranded simply as "Updates". All third-party applications can be updated automatically from the Windows Phone Store.

Advertising platform

Microsoft has also launched an advertising platform for the Windows Phone platform. Microsoft's General Manager for Strategy and Business Development, Kostas Mallios, said that Windows Phone will be an "ad-serving machine", pushing advertising and brand-related content to the user. The platform will feature advertising tiles near applications and toast notifications, which will bring updating advertising notifications. Mallios said that Windows Phone will be able to "preserve the brand experience by going directly from the web site right to the application", and that Windows Phone "enables advertisers to connect with consumers over time". Mallios continued: "you're now able to push information as an advertiser, and stay in touch with your customer. It's a dynamic relationship that is created and provides for an ongoing dialog with the consumer."

Bluetooth

Windows Phone supports the following Bluetooth profiles:

- Advanced Audio Distribution Profile (A2DP 1.2)
- Audio/Video Remote Control Profile (AVRCP 1.3)
- Hands Free Profile (HFP 1.5)
- Headset Profile (HSP 1.1)
- Phone Book Access Profile (PBAP 1.1)
- Bluetooth File Transfer (OBEX) (from Windows Phone 7.8)

Windows Phone BTF support is available from Windows Phone 7.8, but is limited to the transferring of pictures, music and videos via a 'Bluetooth Share' app.

Feature Additions

Microsoft keeps a site where people can submit and vote on features they would like to see added to Windows Phone.

Store

The Windows Phone Store was used to digitally distribute music, video content, podcasts, and third-party applications to Windows Phone handsets. The store was accessible using the Zune Software client or the Windows Phone Store hub on devices (though videos were not downloadable through the store hub and must be downloaded and synced through the Zune software). The Store was managed by Microsoft, which included an approval process. As of March 2012, the Windows Phone Store was available in 54 countries.

Music and Videos

Xbox Music offered approximately 50 million songs up to 320 kbit/s in DRM-free MP3 format from the big four music groups (EMI, Warner Music Group, Sony BMG and Universal Music Group), as well as smaller music labels. Xbox Video offered HD movies from Paramount, Universal, Warner Brothers, and other studios and plus television shows from popular television networks. Microsoft offered the *Xbox Music Pass* music subscription service, which allowed subscribers to download an unlimited number of songs for as long as their subscription was active and play them on current Microsoft devices.

Applications and Games

Development:

- Third-party applications and games for Windows Phone can be based on XNA, a Windows Phone-specific version of Silverlight, the GUI-based Windows Phone App Studio, or the Windows Runtime, which allows developers to develop an app for both the Windows Store and Windows Phone Store simultaneously. App developers can develop apps using C# / Visual Basic.NET (.NET), C++ (CX) or HTML5/JavaScript.

- For Windows Phone apps to be designed and tested within Visual Studio or Visual Studio Express, Microsoft offers Windows Phone Developer Tools, which run only on Windows Vista SP2 and later, as an extension Microsoft also offers Expression Blend for Windows Phone for free. On November 29, 2009, Microsoft announced the Release-to-web (RTW) version of its Visual Basic .NET Developer Tool, to aid development of Windows Phone apps in Visual Basic.
- Later versions of Windows Phone support the running of managed code through a Common Language Runtime similar to that of the Windows operating system itself, as opposed to the .NET Compact Framework. This, along with support for native C and C++ libraries, allows some traditional Windows desktop programs to be easily ported to Windows Phone.

Submission:

- Registered Windows Phone and Xbox Live developers can submit and manage their third-party applications for the platforms through the App Hub web applications. The App Hub provides development tools and support for third-party application developers. The submitted applications undergo an approval process for verifications and validations to check if they qualify the applications standardization criteria set by Microsoft. The cost of the applications that are approved is up to the developer, but Microsoft will take 20% of the revenue (the other 80% goes to the developer). Microsoft will only pay developers once they reach a set sales figure, and will withhold 30% tax from non-US developers, unless they first register with the United States Government's Internal Revenue Service. Microsoft only pays developers from a list of thirty countries. A yearly fee is also payable for developers wishing to submit apps.
- In order to get an application to appear in the Windows Phone Store, the application must be submitted to Microsoft for approval. Microsoft has outlined the content that it will not allow in the applications, which includes content that, among other things, advocates discrimination or hate, promotes usage of drugs, alcohol or tobacco, or includes sexually suggestive material.

Hardware

Windows Phone 7 devices were first produced by HTC, LG and Samsung. These hardware partners were later joined by Acer, Alcatel, Fujitsu, Toshiba, Nokia, and Chinese OEM ZTE. Windows Phone 8 devices were being produced by HTC, Huawei, Nokia, and Samsung.

At the 2014 Mobile World Congress, Microsoft announced that upcoming Windows Phone 8.1 devices would be manufactured by Celkon, Gionee, HTC, Huawei, JSR, Karbonn, LG, Lenovo, Longcheer, Micromax, Microsoft Mobile, Samsung, Xolo, and ZTE among others. Sony (under the Xperia or Vaio brand) had also stated its intention to produce Windows Phone devices in the near future. Yezz announced two smartphones in May, and at Computex 2014 BYD, Compal, Pegatron, Quanta and Wistron were also named as new Windows Phone OEMs. In August 2014, Huawei said it was dropping support for Windows Phone due to low sales.

Reception

User Interface

The Metro UI and overall interface of the OS were highly praised for their style, with ZDNet noting their originality and fresh, clean look. Engadget and ZDNet applauded the integration of Facebook into the People Hub as well as other built-in capabilities, such as Windows Live, etc. However, in version 8.1, the once tight Facebook and Twitter integration was removed, so updates from those social media sites had to be accessed via their respective apps.

2.1.4 BlackBerry OS

BlackBerry OS is a discontinued proprietary mobile operating system developed by Canadian company BlackBerry Limited for its BlackBerry line of smartphone handheld devices. The operating system provides multitasking and supports specialized input devices adopted by BlackBerry for use in its handhelds, particularly the trackwheel, trackball, and most recently, the trackpad and touchscreen.

The BlackBerry platform natively supports corporate email, through Java Micro Edition MIDP 1.0 and, more recently, a subset of MIDP 2.0, which allows complete wireless activation and synchronization with Microsoft Exchange, Lotus Domino, or Novell GroupWise email, calendar, tasks, notes and contacts, when used with BlackBerry Enterprise Server. The operating system also supports WAP 2.0.

Updates to the operating system were automatically available from wireless carriers that supported the BlackBerry over the air software loading (OTASL) service. Third-party developers wrote software using the available BlackBerry API classes, although applications that made use of certain functionality needed to be digitally signed. Research from June 2011 indicated that approximately 45% of mobile developers were using the platform. BlackBerry OS was discontinued after the release of BlackBerry 10 in January 2013, and support for it ceased on January 4, 2022.

2.1.5 Symbian OS

Symbian is a discontinued mobile operating system (OS) and computing platform designed for smartphones. It was originally developed as a proprietary software OS for personal digital assistants in 1998 by the Symbian Ltd. consortium. Symbian OS is a descendant of Psion's EPOC, and was released exclusively on ARM processors, although an unreleased x86 port existed. Symbian was used by many major mobile phone brands, like Samsung, Motorola, Sony Ericsson, and above all by Nokia. It was also prevalent in Japan by brands including Fujitsu, Sharp and Mitsubishi. As a pioneer that established the smartphone industry, it was the most popular smartphone OS on a worldwide average until the end of 2010, at a time when smartphones were in limited use, when it was overtaken by iOS and Android. It was notably less popular in North America.

The Symbian OS platform is formed of two components: one being the microkernel-based operating system with its associated libraries, and the other being the user interface (as middleware), which provides the graphical shell atop the OS. The most prominent user interface was the S60 (formerly Series 60) platform built by Nokia, first released in 2002 and powering most Nokia Symbian devices. UIQ was a competing user interface mostly used by Motorola and Sony Ericsson that focused on pen-based devices, rather than a traditional keyboard interface from S60. Another interface was the MOAP(S) platform from carrier NTT DoCoMo in the Japanese market. Applications for these different interfaces were not compatible with each other, despite each being built atop Symbian OS. Nokia became the largest shareholder of Symbian Ltd. in 2004 and purchased the entire company in 2008. The non-profit Symbian Foundation was then created to make a royalty-free successor to Symbian OS. Seeking to unify the platform, S60 became the Foundation's favoured interface and UIQ stopped development. The touchscreen-focused Symbian^1 (or S60 5th Edition) was created as a result in 2009. Symbian^2 (based on MOAP) was used by NTT DoCoMo, one of the members of the Foundation, for the Japanese market. Symbian^3 was released in 2010 as the successor to S60 5th Edition, by which time it became fully free software. The transition from a proprietary operating system to a free software project is believed to be one of the largest in history. Symbian^3 received the Anna and Belle updates in 2011.

The Symbian Foundation disintegrated in late 2010 and Nokia took back control of the OS development. In February 2011, Nokia, by then the only remaining company still supporting Symbian outside Japan, announced that it would use Microsoft's Windows Phone 7 as its primary smartphone platform, while Symbian would be gradually wound down. Two months later, Nokia moved the OS to proprietary licensing, only collaborating with the Japanese OEMs and later outsourced Symbian development to Accenture. Although support was promised until 2016, including two major planned updates, by 2012 Nokia had mostly abandoned development and most Symbian developers had already left Accenture, and in January 2014 Nokia stopped accepting new or changed Symbian software from developers. The Nokia

808 PureView in 2012 was officially the last Symbian smartphone from Nokia. NTT DoCoMo continued releasing OPP(S) (Operator Pack Symbian, successor of MOAP) devices in Japan, which still act as middleware on top of Symbian. Phones running this include the F-07F [ja] from Fujitsu and SH-07F [ja] from Sharp in 2014.

2.1.6 Tizen OS

Tizen is a Linux-based mobile operating system backed by the Linux Foundation, developed and used primarily by Samsung Electronics. The project was originally conceived as an HTML5-based platform for mobile devices to succeed MeeGo. Samsung merged its previous Linux-based OS effort, Bada, into Tizen and has since used it primarily on platforms such as wearable devices and smart TVs.

Much of Tizen is open source software, although the software development kit contains proprietary components owned by Samsung, and portions of the OS are licensed under the Flora License, a derivative of the Apache License 2.0 that grants a patent license only to "Tizen-certified platforms".

In May 2021, Google announced that Samsung would partner with the company on integrating Tizen features into Google's Android-derived Wear OS and committed to using it on future wearables, leaving Tizen to be mainly developed for Samsung Smart TVs.

2.1.7 Firefox OS

Firefox OS is a discontinued open-source operating system – made for smartphones, tablet computers, smart TVs, and dongles designed by Mozilla and external contributors. It is based on the rendering engine of the Firefox web browser, Gecko, and on the Linux kernel. It was first commercially released in 2014. Firefox OS was designed to provide a complete, community-based alternative operating system, for running web applications directly or those installed from an application marketplace. The applications use open standards and approaches such as JavaScript and HTML5, a robust privilege model, and open web APIs that can communicate directly with hardware, e.g. cellphone hardware. As such, Mozilla with Firefox OS competed with commercially developed operating systems such as Apple's iOS, Google's Android, Microsoft's Windows Phone, BlackBerry's BlackBerry 10, Samsung's/Linux Foundation's Tizen, and Jolla's Sailfish OS. In December 2015, Mozilla announced it would stop development of new Firefox OS smartphones and, in September 2016, announced the end of development. Successors to Firefox OS include the discontinued B2G OS and Acadine Technologies' H5OS as well as KaiOS Technologies' KaiOS and Panasonic's My Home Screen.

2.1.8 Sailfish OS

Sailfish OS is a Linux-based operating system based on free software, and open source projects such as Mer as well as including a closed source UI. The project is being developed by the Finnish company Jolla. The OS first shipped with the original Jolla Phone in 2013; while its sale stopped in 2016, it was supplied with software updates until the end of 2020. It also shipped with Jolla Tablet in 2015 and from other vendors licensing the OS. The OS is ported by community enthusiasts to third-party mobile devices including smartphones and tablet computers. Sailfish OS can be used for many kinds of devices.

2.2 UNDERSTANDING THE MOBILE APP ECOSYSTEM

The mobile app ecosystem has revolutionized how people interact with technology, providing a vast array of functionalities and services at their fingertips. This ecosystem comprises various stakeholders, technologies, and processes that collectively enable the creation, distribution, and use of mobile applications.

The mobile app ecosystem is a vibrant and dynamic network that continues to shape how we interact with technology. With key players like Apple and Google driving innovation, and emerging trends such as AI, 5G, and IoT expanding possibilities, the future of mobile apps looks promising.

However, developers and stakeholders must navigate challenges related to security, market saturation, and monetization to succeed in this competitive landscape. As the ecosystem evolves, the integration of new technologies and the continuous improvement of user experiences will remain central to its growth and sustainability.

2.2.1 The Structure of the Mobile App Ecosystem

The mobile app ecosystem is a complex and dynamic network that includes app developers, platform providers, app stores, and end-users. Understanding the interplay between these elements is crucial to grasping how the ecosystem functions.

2.2.2 App Developers

App developers are the creators of mobile applications. They range from individual hobbyists to large software development companies. Developers use a variety of tools and programming languages, such as Swift and Objective-C for iOS, and Java and Kotlin for Android. Development environments like Xcode for iOS and Android Studio for Android provide the necessary frameworks and libraries to build robust applications.

2.2.3 Platform Providers

The primary platform providers, Apple and Google, offer the operating systems (iOS and Android) that power the majority of mobile devices. These platforms provide the underlying infrastructure and services that enable apps to function. They also offer development tools, documentation, and support to help developers create high-quality applications.

2.2.4 App Stores

App stores are digital distribution platforms where users can download and install mobile applications. The Apple App Store and Google Play Store are the dominant players in this space.

These stores handle app distribution, payment processing, and user reviews, providing a centralized marketplace for both developers and consumers. App stores also enforce policies and guidelines to ensure app quality and security.

2.2.5 End-Users

End-users are the consumers who download and use mobile applications. Their preferences, feedback, and behaviors significantly influence the app ecosystem. Users access apps for various purposes, including communication, entertainment, productivity, and health. The user experience and satisfaction are crucial for the success of any mobile application.

2.2.6 Apple and iOS

Apple's iOS platform is known for its high standards of quality, security, and user experience. The Apple App Store, launched in 2008, was the first major app marketplace and set the standard for app distribution.

Apple's ecosystem includes a range of devices like iPhones, iPads, and Apple Watches, all of which are tightly integrated, offering a seamless user experience.

2.2.7 Google and Android

Google's Android platform is characterized by its openness and flexibility. The Google Play Store, also launched in 2008, offers a vast selection of apps and has a broader reach due to the wide variety of devices that run Android.

Google's ecosystem includes services like Google Play Services, which provide essential APIs for app functionality and user engagement.

2.2.8 Third-Party App Stores

While the Apple App Store and Google Play Store dominate, there are other significant players in the app distribution landscape. Amazon Appstore, Samsung Galaxy Store, and Huawei AppGallery are examples of third-party app stores that offer alternative platforms for app distribution.

These stores often cater to specific devices or markets and provide additional opportunities for developers.

2.2.9 Mobile App Development Frameworks

Frameworks and tools such as React Native, Flutter, Xamarin, and Unity play a vital role in the mobile app ecosystem. These frameworks enable developers to create cross-platform applications that run on both iOS and Android, reducing development time and costs. They offer pre-built components, real-time testing, and other features that streamline the development process.

2.2.10 Artificial Intelligence and Machine Learning

AI and machine learning are becoming integral to mobile apps, enhancing functionality and user experience. AI-powered features like personalized recommendations, voice assistants, and image recognition are increasingly common. Machine learning algorithms help apps to learn from user behavior and improve over time, providing more relevant and engaging experiences.

2.2.11 5G Technology

The rollout of 5G networks is set to revolutionize the mobile app ecosystem by providing faster data speeds, lower latency, and increased connectivity. This technology will enable new applications and services, such as augmented reality (AR), virtual reality (VR), and real-time gaming. Developers will be able to create more immersive and responsive apps, expanding the possibilities of mobile technology.

2.2.12 Internet of Things (IoT)

The integration of IoT with mobile apps is creating new opportunities for connected devices and smart homes. Mobile apps serve as control hubs for IoT devices, allowing users to monitor and manage their environments remotely. The growing adoption of IoT devices is driving the development of apps that offer seamless interaction and integration with these technologies.

2.2.13 Mobile Payments and Fintech

The rise of mobile payments and financial technology (fintech) is transforming how users conduct transactions and manage their finances. Apps like Apple Pay, Google Wallet, and various banking apps provide secure and convenient ways to make payments, transfer money, and track expenses. The integration of blockchain and cryptocurrency into mobile apps is also gaining traction, offering new avenues for financial services.

2.2.14 Health and Wellness Apps

Health and wellness apps are increasingly popular, driven by a growing focus on personal health and fitness. These apps offer features like fitness tracking, diet management, mental health support, and telemedicine. The integration of wearable devices with health apps provides users with real-time data and insights into their health, promoting healthier lifestyles.

2.2.15 Augmented Reality (AR) and Virtual Reality (VR)

AR and VR technologies are creating new experiences in mobile apps, from gaming and entertainment to education and retail. Apps like Pokémon GO and IKEA Place demonstrate the potential of AR in enhancing user engagement and providing practical solutions. VR apps offer immersive experiences in gaming, training, and virtual tours, pushing the boundaries of what mobile devices can achieve.

2.2.16 Security and Privacy Concerns

As mobile apps handle increasing amounts of personal data, security and privacy have become major concerns. Developers must implement robust security measures to protect user data and comply with regulations like GDPR and CCPA. App stores also play a crucial role in ensuring that apps meet security standards before they are published.

2.2.17 Market Saturation

The sheer number of apps available on major app stores makes it challenging for new apps to gain visibility and traction. Developers need effective marketing strategies and unique value propositions to stand out in a crowded market. User retention is also a critical issue, as users have many options and can easily switch to competing apps.

2.2.18 Platform Fragmentation

The diversity of devices and operating system versions in the Android ecosystem can lead to fragmentation, making it difficult for developers to ensure consistent performance and compatibility across all devices. This challenge requires extensive testing and optimization efforts.

2.2.19 Monetization Strategies

Finding sustainable monetization strategies remains a key challenge for app developers. While in-app purchases, subscriptions, and advertising are common revenue models, developers must balance monetization with providing a positive user experience. Understanding user behavior and preferences is crucial for optimizing monetization efforts.

CHAPTER 3

MOBILE HARDWARE AND COMPONENTS

3.1 SMARTPHONE ARCHITECTURE AND COMPONENTS

Smartphones have become an integral part of modern life, thanks to their sophisticated architecture and components that enable a wide range of functionalities. Understanding the internal workings of these devices involves exploring the various hardware and software elements that work together seamlessly.

Smartphone architecture and components are the foundation of the advanced functionalities and seamless user experiences that define modern mobile devices. From the powerful SoC integrating the CPU, GPU, DSP, and NPU, to the diverse sensors and connectivity modules, each component plays a crucial role. Coupled with sophisticated software architecture, smartphones continue to evolve, driven by innovations in technology and user demand. Understanding these elements provides insight into the intricate design and engineering that make smartphones indispensable tools in today's digital world.

3.1.1 Overview of Smartphone Architecture

Smartphone architecture is a complex interplay of hardware and software designed to provide efficient performance, connectivity, and user experience. The main components include the system-on-chip (SoC), memory, storage, display, battery, sensors, connectivity modules, and software layers that manage these hardware elements.

- **System-on-Chip (SoC):** The System-on-Chip (SoC) is the heart of the smartphone, integrating multiple components into a single chip to optimize performance and power efficiency.
- **Central Processing Unit (CPU):** The CPU is responsible for executing instructions and performing calculations. Modern smartphones typically use multi-core processors, which can handle multiple tasks simultaneously, enhancing performance and efficiency. Leading manufacturers like Qualcomm (Snapdragon), Apple (A-series), and Samsung (Exynos) produce powerful CPUs that drive smartphone capabilities.

- **Graphics Processing Unit (GPU):** The GPU handles rendering images, videos, and animations. It is crucial for gaming, video playback, and graphical user interfaces. High-performance GPUs, such as those from ARM's Mali series, Qualcomm's Adreno series, and Apple's custom GPUs, ensure smooth visual experiences.
- **Digital Signal Processor (DSP):** The DSP processes real-time signals such as audio, video, and sensor data. It offloads these tasks from the CPU, improving efficiency and performance for specific applications like voice recognition and camera processing.
- **Neural Processing Unit (NPU):** The NPU, or AI accelerator, is dedicated to handling artificial intelligence and machine learning tasks. It enables features like facial recognition, image processing, and augmented reality by performing complex computations more efficiently than general-purpose CPUs.

3.1.2 Memory and Storage

- **Random Access Memory (RAM):** RAM is used for temporary data storage while the smartphone is running. It allows for quick access to data and applications, ensuring smooth multitasking and performance. Smartphones typically come with varying amounts of RAM, from 4GB to 16GB or more, depending on the model and intended use.
- **Internal Storage:** Internal storage is used to store the operating system, applications, and user data. Flash memory technologies like NAND are commonly used for internal storage due to their speed and durability. Storage capacities range from 32GB to 1TB, with higher capacities supporting more apps, media files, and other data.

3.1.3 Display

The display is one of the most critical components of a smartphone, affecting both user experience and device aesthetics.

- **Types of Displays:** Smartphones use various types of displays, including Liquid Crystal Displays (LCD) and Organic Light Emitting Diode (OLED) displays. OLED displays, including variations like AMOLED and Super AMOLED, offer better color accuracy, contrast, and energy efficiency compared to LCDs.
- **Touchscreen Technology:** Touchscreens use capacitive or resistive technology to detect user inputs. Capacitive touchscreens are more common in modern smartphones due to their responsiveness and multi-touch capabilities. These screens are layered with conductive materials that detect touch through changes in the electrostatic field.

3.1.4 Battery

The battery powers all the components of a smartphone. Lithium-ion (Li-ion) and lithium-polymer (Li-poly) batteries are the most commonly used types due to their high energy density and longevity.

- **Battery Capacity:** Battery capacity is measured in milliampere-hours (mAh) and indicates how much charge the battery can hold. Higher capacity batteries provide longer usage times between charges. Advances in battery technology and energy-efficient components have led to improvements in battery life.
- **Charging Technologies:** Fast charging technologies, such as Qualcomm's Quick Charge, USB Power Delivery (USB-PD), and proprietary solutions like Apple's MagSafe, have become standard. These technologies reduce charging times significantly. Wireless charging, based on the Qi standard, is also widely adopted, offering convenient charging without cables.

3.1.5 Sensors

Sensors are integral to the functionality and interactivity of smartphones, enabling a range of features.

- **Accelerometer and Gyroscope:** These sensors detect motion and orientation. The accelerometer measures linear acceleration, while the gyroscope measures rotational movement. Together, they enable functionalities like screen rotation, gesture control, and augmented reality.
- **Proximity Sensor:** The proximity sensor detects the presence of nearby objects without physical contact. It is commonly used to turn off the display during calls when the phone is near the user's ear, conserving battery and preventing accidental touches.
- **Ambient Light Sensor:** The ambient light sensor adjusts the screen brightness based on the surrounding light conditions, enhancing visibility and reducing eye strain.
- **Biometric Sensors:** Biometric sensors, such as fingerprint scanners and facial recognition systems, provide secure and convenient authentication methods. Fingerprint sensors can be located on the front, back, or integrated into the display. Facial recognition systems use infrared and depth sensors to map the user's face and unlock the device securely.

- **Other Sensors:** Additional sensors include barometers (for altitude detection), magnetometers (compass functionality), and infrared sensors (for remote control applications).

3.1.6 Connectivity Modules

Smartphones incorporate various connectivity modules to facilitate communication and data transfer.

- **Cellular Modem:** The cellular modem connects the smartphone to mobile networks, enabling voice calls, text messaging, and data services. Modern smartphones support multiple generations of mobile networks, from 2G to 5G, with 5G providing significantly faster data speeds and lower latency.
- **Wi-Fi and Bluetooth:** Wi-Fi modules connect smartphones to wireless local area networks (WLANs), enabling high-speed internet access. Bluetooth modules facilitate short-range wireless communication with other devices, such as headphones, smartwatches, and car systems.
- **Global Positioning System (GPS):** The GPS module provides location-based services by receiving signals from satellites. It enables navigation, location tracking, and geo-tagging functionalities in various apps.

3.1.7 Software Architecture

The software architecture of smartphones is layered, with each layer interacting closely with the hardware to provide a cohesive user experience.

- **Operating System (OS):** The OS is the core software that manages hardware resources and provides common services for applications. The two dominant mobile operating systems are iOS and Android. Both systems offer robust development environments, extensive APIs, and a wide range of functionalities to support diverse applications.
- **Middleware:** Middleware consists of software that sits between the OS and applications, providing additional services such as data management, authentication, and communication. It includes libraries and frameworks that simplify app development and enhance functionality.
- **Applications:** Applications, or apps, are software programs designed to perform specific tasks for the user. They range from system apps, like phone dialers and web browsers, to third-party apps available on app stores. Apps are developed using SDKs (Software Development Kits) provided by the OS vendors, which include tools, libraries, and documentation.

3.2 EMERGING TECHNOLOGIES IN MOBILE HARDWARE

The relentless pace of technological advancement in mobile hardware is transforming smartphones and other mobile devices, making them more powerful, efficient, and feature-rich. From foldable displays to advanced AI processors, the latest innovations are pushing the boundaries of what mobile hardware can achieve.

The mobile hardware landscape is undergoing rapid and exciting transformations, driven by innovations in displays, processors, connectivity, security, cameras, AR/VR, and battery technology. These emerging technologies are not only enhancing the capabilities and performance of mobile devices but also redefining user experiences and opening up new possibilities for mobile applications. As these technologies continue to evolve, they will shape the future of mobile devices, making them more powerful, versatile, and indispensable in our daily lives.

3.2.1 Foldable and Flexible Displays

A flexible display or rollable display is an electronic visual display which is flexible in nature, as opposed to the traditional flat screen displays used in most electronic devices. In recent years there has been a growing interest from numerous consumer electronics manufacturers to apply this display technology in e-readers, mobile phones and other consumer electronics. Such screens can be rolled up like a scroll without the image or text being distorted. Technologies involved in building a rollable display include electronic ink, Gyricon, Organic LCD, and OLED.

Electronic paper displays which can be rolled up have been developed by E Ink. At CES 2006, Philips showed a rollable display prototype, with a screen capable of retaining an image for several months without electricity. In 2007, Philips launched a 5-inch, 320 x 240-pixel rollable display based on E Ink's electrophoretic technology. Some flexible organic light-emitting diode displays have been demonstrated.The first commercially sold flexible display was an electronic paper wristwatch. A rollable display is an important part of the development of the roll-away computer.

Applications

With the flat panel display having already been widely used more than 40 years, there have been many desired changes in the display technology, focusing on developing a lighter, thinner product that was easier to carry and store. Through the development of rollable displays in recent years, scientists and engineers agree that flexible flat panel display technology has huge market potential in the future.

Rollable displays can be used in many places:

- Mobile devices.
- Laptops and PDAs.

- A permanently conformed display that securely fits around the wrists.
- A child's mask for Halloween and other uses.
- An odd-shaped display integrated in a steering wheel or automobile.

History

Flexible Electronic Paper based Displays

Flexible electronic paper (e-paper) based displays were the first flexible displays conceptualized and prototyped. While the idea for this type of display is not recent and had been attempted by several companies in the past, only recently has mass production of this technology begun for implementation in consumer electronic devices.

Xerox PARC

The concept of developing a flexible display was first put forth by Xerox PARC (Palo Alto Research Company). In 1974, Nicholas K. Sheridon, a PARC employee, made a major breakthrough in flexible display technology and produced the first flexible e-paper display. Dubbed Gyricon, this new display technology was designed to mimic the properties of paper, but married with the capacity to display dynamic digital images. Sheridon envisioned the advent of paperless offices and sought commercial applications for Gyricon. In 2003 Gyricon LLC was formed as a direct subsidiary of Xerox to commercialize the electronic paper technology developed at Xerox PARC. Gyricon LLC's operations were short lived and in December 2005 Xerox closed the subsidiary company in a move to focus on licensing the technology instead.

HP and ASU

In 2005, Arizona State University (ASU) opened a 250,000 square foot facility dedicated to flexible display research named the ASU Flexible Display Center (FDC). ASU received $43.7 million from the U.S. Army Research Laboratory (ARL) towards the development of this research facility in February 2004. A planned prototype device was slated for public demonstration later that year. However, the project met a series of delays. In December 2008, ASU in partnership with Hewlett Packard demonstrated a prototype flexible e-paper from the Flexible Display Center at the university. HP continued on with the research, and in 2010, showcased another demonstration. However, due to limitations in technology, HP stated "[our company] doesn't actually see these panels being used in truly flexible or rollable displays, but instead sees them being used to simply make displays thinner and lighter."

Between 2004–2008, ASU developed its first small-scale flexible displays. Between 2008–2012, ARL committed to further sponsorship of ASU's Flexible Display Center, which included an additional $50 million in research funding. Although the U.S. Army funds ASU's development of the flexible display, the center's focus is on commercial applications.

Plastic Logic

Plastic Logic is a company that develops and manufactures monochrome plastic flexible displays in various sizes based on its proprietary organic thin film transistor (OTFT) technology. They have also demonstrated their ability to produce colour displays with this technology, however they are currently not capable of manufacturing them on a large scale. The displays are manufactured in the company's purpose-built factory in Dresden, Germany, which was the first factory of its kind to be built – dedicated to the high volume manufacture of organic electronics. These flexible displays are cited as being "unbreakable", because they are made completely of plastic and do not contain glass. They are also lighter and thinner than glass-based displays and low-power. Applications of this flexible display technology include signage, wristwatches and wearable devices as well as automotive and mobile devices.

Organic User Interfaces and the Human Media Lab

In 2004, a team led by Prof. Roel Vertegaal at Queen's University's Human Media Lab in Canada developed PaperWindows, the first prototype bendable paper computer and first Organic User Interface. Since full-colour, US Letter-sized displays were not available at the time, PaperWindows deployed a form of active projection mapping of computer windows on real paper documents that worked together as one computer through 3D tracking. At a lecture to the Gyricon and Human-Computer Interaction teams at Xerox PARC on 4 May 2007, Prof. Vertegaal publicly introduced the term Organic User Interface (OUI) as a means of describing the implications of non-flat display technologies on user interfaces of the future: paper computers, flexible form factors for computing devices, but also encompassing rigid display objects of any shape, with wrap-around, skin-like displays. The lecture was published a year later as part of a special issue on Organic User Interfaces in the Communications of the ACM. In May 2010, the Human Media Lab partnered with ASU's Flexible Display Center to produce PaperPhone, the first flexible smartphone with a flexible electrophoretic display. PaperPhone used bend gestures for navigating contents. Since then, the Human Media Lab has partnered with Plastic Logic and Intel to introduce the first flexible tablet PC and multi-display e-paper computer, PaperTab, at CES 2013, debuting the world's first actuated flexible smartphone prototype, MorePhone in April 2013.

Others

Since 2010, Sony Electronics, AU Optronics and LG Electronics have all expressed interest in developing flexible e-paper displays. However, only LG have formally announced plans for mass production of flexible e-paper displays.

Flexible OLED-Based Displays

Research and development into flexible OLED displays largely began in the late 2000s with the main intentions of implementing this technology in mobile devices. However, this technology has recently made an appearance, to a moderate extent, in consumer television displays as well.

Nokia Morph and Kinetic concepts

Nokia first conceptualized the application of flexible OLED displays in mobile phone with the Nokia Morph concept mobile phone. Released to the press in February 2008, the Morph concept was project Nokia had co-developed with the University of Cambridge. With the Morph, Nokia intended to demonstrate their vision of future mobile devices to incorporate flexible and polymorphic designs; allowing the device to seamlessly change and match a variety of needs by the user within various environments. Though the focus of the Morph was to demonstrate the potential of nanotechnology, it pioneered the concept of utilizing a flexible video display in a consumer electronics device. Nokia renewed their interest in flexible mobile devices again in 2011 with the Nokia Kinetic concept. Nokia unveiled the Kinetic flexible phone prototype at Nokia World 2011 in London, alongside Nokia's new range of Windows Phone 7 devices. The Kinetic proved to be a large departure from the Morph physically, but it still incorporated Nokia's vision of polymorphism in mobile devices.

Sony

Sony Electronics has expressed interest for research and development towards a flexible display video display since 2005. In partnership with RIKEN (the Institute of Physical and Chemical Research), Sony promised to commercialize this technology in TVs and cellphones sometime around 2010. In May 2010 Sony showcased a rollable TFT-driven OLED display.

Samsung

In late 2010, Samsung Electronics announced the development of a prototype 4.5 inch flexible AMOLED display. The prototype device was then showcased at Consumer Electronics Show 2011. During the 2011 Q3 quarterly earnings call, Samsung's vice president of investor relations, Robert Yi, confirmed the company's intentions of applying the technology and releasing products utilizing it by early 2012. In January 2012 Samsung acquired Liquavista, a company with expertise in manufacturing flexible displays, and announced plans to begin mass production by Q2 2012.

In January 2013, Samsung exposed its brand new, unnamed product during the company's keynote address at CES in Las Vegas. Brian Berkeley, the senior vice president of Samsung's display lab in San Jose, California had announced the development of flexible displays. He said "the technology will let the company's partners make bendable, rollable, and foldable displays," and he demonstrated how the new phone can be rollable and flexible during his speech.

During Samsung's CES 2013 keynote presentation, two prototype mobile devices codenamed "Youm" that incorporated the flexible AMOLED display technology were shown to the public. "Youm" has curved display screen, the use of OLED screen giving this phone deeper blacks and a higher overall contrast ratio with better power efficiency than traditional LCD displays. Also this phone has the advantages of a rollable display; it is lighter, thinner, and more durable than LCD displays. Samsung stated that "Youm" panels will be seen in the market in a short time and production will commence in 2013.

Samsung subsequently released the Galaxy Round, a smartphone with an inward curving screen and body, in October 2013. One of the Youm concepts, which featured a curved screen edge used as a secondary area for notifications and shortcuts, was developed into the Galaxy Note Edge released in 2014. In 2015, Samsung applied the technology to its flagship Galaxy S series with the release of the Galaxy S6 Edge, a variant of the S6 model with a screen sloped over both sides of the device. During a developer conference in 2018, Samsung showed a foldable smartphone prototype, which was subsequently revealed in February 2019 as the Galaxy Fold.

ASU

The Flexible Display Center (FDC) at Arizona State University announced a continued effort in forwarding flexible displays in 2012. On 30 May, in partnership with Army Research Lab scientists, ASU announced that it has successfully manufactured the world's largest flexible OLED display using thin-film transistor (TFTs) technology. ASU intends the display to be used in "thin, lightweight, bendable and highly rugged devices."

Xiaomi

In January 2019, Chinese manufacturer Xiaomi showed a foldable smartphone prototype. CEO Lin Bin of Xiaomi demoed the device in a video on the Weibo social network. The device features a large foldable display that curves 180 degrees inwards on two sides. The tablet turns into a smartphone, with a screen diagonal of 4,5 inch, adjusting the user interface on the fly.

- **Advantages:** Flexible displays have many advantages over glass: better durability, lighter weight, thinner as plastic, and can be perfectly curved and used in many devices. Moreover, the major difference between glass and rollable display is that the display area of a rollable display can be bigger than the device itself; If a flexible device measuring, for example, 5 inches in diagonal and a roll of 7.5mm, it can be stored in a device smaller than the screen itself and close to 15mm in thickness.

- **Authentication Methods:** Flexible screens can open the doors to novel and alternative authentication schemes by emphasizing the interaction between the user and the touch screen. In "Bend Passwords: Using Gestures to Authenticate on Flexible Devices," the authors introduce a new method called Bend Passwords where users perform bending gestures and deform the touch screen to unlock the phone. Their work and research points to Bend Passwords possibly becoming a new way to keep smartphones secure alongside the popularization of flexible displays.

Electronic Paper

Flexible displays that use electronic paper technology commonly use Electrophoretic or Electrowetting technologies. However, each type of flexible electronic paper varies in specification due to different implementation techniques by different companies.

HP and ASU e-paper

The flexible electronic paper display technology co-developed by Arizona State University and HP employs a manufacturing process developed by HP Labs called Self-Aligned Imprint Lithography (SAIL). The screens are made by layering stacks of semi-conductor materials and metals between pliable plastic sheets. The stacks need to be perfectly aligned and stay that way. Alignment proves difficult during manufacturing when heat during manufacturing can deform the materials and when the resulting screen also needs to remain flexible. The SAIL process gets around this by 'printing' the semiconductor pattern on a fully composed substrate, so that the layers always remain in perfect alignment. The limitation of the material the screen is based on allows only a finite amount of full rolls, hence limiting its commercial application as a flexible display. Specifications provided regarding the prototype display are as follows:

- flexible and rollable up to "about half a dozen times"; and
- unbreakable.

Asu e-paper

The flexible electronic paper display announced by AUO is unique as it is the only solar powered variant. A separate rechargeable battery is also attached when solar charging is unavailable. Specifications

- 6-inch diagonal display size.
- Radius of curvature can reach 100mm.
- 9:1 high contrast ratio.
- Reflectance of 33%.
- 16 gray levels.
- Solar powered.
- unbreakable.

LG e-paper

Specifications:

- 6-inch diagonal display size.
- 1024x768 (XGA) resolution.
- 4:3 aspect ratio.
- TFT based electronic display.
- allows bending at a range of 40 degrees from the center of the screen.
- 0.7mm thickness from the side,
- 14g weight.
- can drop from 1.5m above ground with no resultant damage.
- unbreakable (from tests with a small urethane hammer).

OLED

Many of the e-paper based flexible displays are based on OLED technology and its variants. Though this technology is relatively new in comparison with e-paper based flexible displays, implementation of OLED flexible displays saw considerable growth in the last few years.

ASU

Specifications:

- 6-inch diagonal display size.
- 480x360 4k resolution.
- 4:3 aspect ratio.
- OLED display technology with a TFT back plane.

Samsung

Specifications:

- 4.5-inch diagonal display size.

- 800x480 WVGA, 1280x720 WXGA and WQXGA (2560×1600) resolutions.
- AMOLED display technology.
- unbreakable.

Mobile Devices

In May 2011, Human Media Lab at Queen's University in Canada introduced PaperPhone, the first flexible smartphone, in partnership with the Arizona State University Flexible Display Center. PaperPhone used 5 bend sensors to implement navigation of the user interface through bend gestures of corners and sides of the display. In January 2013, the Human Media Lab introduced the first flexible tablet PC, PaperTab, in collaboration with Plastic Logic and Intel Labs, at CES. PaperTab is a multi-display environment in which each display represents a window, app or computer document. Displays are tracked in 3D to allow multidisplay operations, such as collate to enlarge the display space, or pointing with one display onto another to pull open a document file. In April 2013 in Paris, the Human Media Lab, in collaboration with Plastic Logic, unveiled the world's first actuated flexible smartphone prototype, MorePhone. MorePhone actuates its body to notify users upon receiving a phone call or message.

Nokia introduced the Kinetic concept phone at Nokia World 2011 in London. The flexible OLED display allows users to interact with the phone by twisting, bending, squeezing and folding in different manners across both the vertical and horizontal planes. The technology journalist website Engadget described interactions such as "[when] bend the screen towards yourself, [the device] acts as a selection function, or zooms in on any pictures you're viewing." Nokia envisioned this type of device to be available to consumers in "as little as three years", and claimed to already possess "the technology to produce it."

At CES 2013, Samsung showcased the two handsets which incorporates AMOLED flexible display technology during its keynote presentation, the Youm and an unnamed Windows Phone 8 prototype device. The Youm possessed a static implementation of flexible AMOLED display technology, as its screen has a set curvature along one of its edges. The benefit of the curvature allows users "to read text messages, stock tickers, and other notifications from the side of the device even if [the user] have a case covering the screen." The unnamed Windows Phone 8 prototype device was composed of a solid base from that extends a flexible AMOLED display. The AMOLED display itself bends and was described as "virtually unbreakable even when dropped" according to Samsung representatives. Brian Berkeley, the senior vice president of Samsung Display, believes that this flexible form factor "will really begin to change how people interact with their devices, opening up new lifestyle possibilities ... [and] allow our partners to create a whole new ecosystem of devices." The Youm's form factor was ultimately utilized on the Galaxy Note Edge, and future Samsung Galaxy S series devices. ReFlex is a flexible smartphone created by Queen's University's Human Media Lab.

Curved OLED TVs

LG Electronics and Samsung Electronics both introduced curved OLED televisions with a curved display at CES 2013 hours apart from each other. Both companies recognized their respective curved OLED prototype television as a first-of-its-kind due to its flexed OLED display. The technology journalist website The Verge noted the subtle curve on 55" Samsung OLED TV allowed it to have a "more panoramic, more immersive viewing experience, and actually improves viewing angles from the side." The experience was also shared viewing the curved 55" LG OLED TV. The LG set is also 3D capable, in addition to the curvature.

3.2.2 Advanced AI Processors

Role of AI in Mobile Devices

Artificial Intelligence (AI) is becoming integral to mobile devices, enhancing functionalities such as photography, voice recognition, and personalized user experiences. AI processors, or neural processing units (NPUs), are specialized hardware designed to handle AI tasks efficiently.

Technological Developments

Leading smartphone manufacturers are integrating powerful AI processors into their devices. For instance, Apple's A14 Bionic chip and Qualcomm's Snapdragon 888 feature dedicated NPUs that perform trillions of operations per second. These processors enable real-time AI applications, such as augmented reality, computational photography, and natural language processing.

Impact on User Experience

AI processors significantly enhance the user experience by providing smarter, faster, and more responsive interactions. They enable features like real-time translation, advanced camera capabilities, and intelligent battery management. As AI technology advances, we can expect even more sophisticated and context-aware functionalities in mobile devices.

3.2.3 Enhanced Biometric Security

Evolution of Biometric Security

Biometric security features, such as fingerprint scanners and facial recognition, have become standard in modern smartphones. These technologies offer convenient and secure ways to unlock devices and authenticate users.

Recent Innovations

Recent advancements in biometric security include in-display fingerprint sensors and 3D facial recognition. Companies like Apple have pioneered Face ID, which uses infrared sensors and machine learning to create a detailed 3D map of the user's face. Qualcomm's 3D Sonic Sensor employs ultrasonic waves to capture a high-resolution image of the fingerprint, even through glass and metal.

Future Trends

Emerging biometric technologies aim to provide even higher levels of security and convenience. Iris recognition, vein pattern recognition, and voice authentication are potential future developments. Additionally, multi-modal biometric systems that combine several biometric methods could offer enhanced security by ensuring accurate and reliable authentication.

3.2.4 5G Connectivity

Introduction to 5G

5G is the fifth generation of mobile network technology, promising significantly faster data speeds, lower latency, and improved connectivity compared to 4G. It is set to revolutionize mobile communication and enable new applications and services.

Technological Capabilities

5G technology operates on a range of frequency bands, including low-band, mid-band, and high-band (millimeter wave). It supports peak data rates of up to 10 Gbps and latency as low as 1 millisecond. These capabilities enable seamless streaming of high-definition content, real-time gaming, and enhanced augmented reality experiences.

Impact on Mobile Hardware

To leverage 5G, mobile devices require advanced modem chips and antenna designs. Companies like Qualcomm, MediaTek, and Samsung are at the forefront of developing 5G-enabled chipsets. These advancements ensure that smartphones and other mobile devices can fully exploit the potential of 5G networks, providing users with faster and more reliable connections.

3.2.5 Advanced Camera Technologies

Importance of Camera Technology

Camera quality has become a critical differentiator in smartphones, with manufacturers continuously innovating to enhance photography and videography capabilities.

Recent Innovations

Recent camera technologies include multi-lens setups, periscope zoom lenses, and advanced image sensors. Computational photography, powered by AI, allows for features like night mode, portrait mode, and enhanced image stabilization. Companies like Apple, Google, and Huawei are leading the charge in integrating these advanced camera technologies into their flagship devices.

Future Directions

Future advancements in camera technology may include even higher resolution sensors, improved optical zoom capabilities, and enhanced low-light performance. Innovations like under-display cameras and advanced sensor-shift stabilization are also on the horizon, promising to further elevate the quality of mobile photography and videography.

3.2.6 Augmented Reality (AR) and Virtual Reality (VR)

Role of AR and VR in Mobile Devices

AR and VR technologies are transforming how users interact with their environment and digital content. These technologies overlay digital information onto the real world (AR) or create immersive virtual environments (VR).

Technological Advancements

Modern smartphones are equipped with powerful processors and advanced sensors, making them capable platforms for AR and VR applications. Apple's ARKit and Google's ARCore provide robust frameworks for developing AR experiences. Devices like the Samsung Gear VR and Google Daydream View have popularized mobile VR.

Potential Applications

AR and VR have vast potential across various sectors, including gaming, education, healthcare, and retail. Future advancements could lead to more immersive and interactive experiences, with better hardware integration and more sophisticated software capabilities, making AR and VR an integral part of everyday mobile interactions.

3.2.7 Battery and Charging Innovations

Challenges in Battery Technology

Battery life remains a crucial aspect of mobile device performance. Users demand longer battery life and faster charging times to keep up with their active lifestyles.

Recent Innovations

Recent advancements in battery technology include higher capacity batteries, more efficient power management systems, and fast charging technologies. Lithium-polymer batteries offer improved energy density and safety. Fast charging technologies like Qualcomm's Quick Charge, USB Power Delivery, and proprietary solutions from manufacturers enable rapid charging times.

Future Trends

Emerging technologies such as solid-state batteries promise significant improvements in energy density, safety, and charging speed. Wireless charging advancements, including longer-range wireless power transfer, could eliminate the need for physical connectors, providing more convenience for users.

PART II

MOBILE APP DEVELOPMENT

CHAPTER 4

INTRODUCTION TO MOBILE APP DEVELOPMENT

4.1 BASICS OF MOBILE APP ARCHITECTURE

Mobile app architecture refers to the set of techniques and patterns used to design and build mobile applications. A well-thought-out architecture is crucial for creating scalable, maintainable, and robust mobile apps. A well-designed mobile app architecture is the foundation for building high-quality, scalable, and maintainable applications. By adhering to key principles, choosing the right architecture pattern, considering platform-specific requirements, and focusing on security, data management, and user experience, developers can create apps that meet user expectations and stand the test of time. Continuous testing, deployment, and performance monitoring further ensure that the app remains robust and reliable throughout its lifecycle.

4.1.1 Introduction to Mobile App Architecture

Mobile app architecture is the blueprint that defines the structure and interactions of components within a mobile application. It addresses key aspects like the choice of platforms (iOS, Android), design patterns, and technology stack. The goal is to ensure optimal performance, user experience, and ease of maintenance.

4.1.2 Key Principles of Mobile App Architecture

Effective mobile app architecture is guided by several principles:

- **Separation of Concerns:** Different components of the app should handle distinct concerns. This makes the app easier to develop, test, and maintain.
- **Reusability:** Components should be designed to be reusable to reduce redundancy and increase efficiency.
- **Scalability:** The architecture should support the app's growth, accommodating more features and higher user loads.
- **Maintainability:** Code should be easy to understand, update, and debug.
- **Performance:** The architecture must ensure the app runs efficiently, utilizing resources optimally.

4.1.3 Layers of Mobile App Architecture

Mobile app architecture typically consists of three main layers:

- **Presentation Layer:** This layer includes the UI components and handles the presentation logic. It interacts with users and displays data received from the business layer.
- **Business Layer:** This layer contains the domain logic, application-specific business rules, and workflows. It processes data and performs operations required by the presentation layer.
- **Data Layer:** This layer manages data persistence and network operations. It includes local storage (like databases) and remote servers (APIs).

4.1.4 Choosing the Right Architecture Pattern

Selecting the right architecture pattern is crucial for the app's success. Common architecture patterns include:

- **MVC (Model-View-Controller):** Separates the app into three interconnected components. The model represents the data, the view displays the data, and the controller handles input and updates the model.
- **MVVM (Model-View-ViewModel):** Similar to MVC but introduces a ViewModel to handle the presentation logic, making the view more passive.
- **MVP (Model-View-Presenter):** The presenter handles all the presentation logic, interacting with both the model and the view, which only handles UI updates.
- **Clean Architecture:** Emphasizes separation of concerns through layers that define clear boundaries, making the app more maintainable and testable.

4.1.5 Platform Considerations

Choosing the platform(s) for your mobile app influences its architecture:

- **iOS:** Uses Swift or Objective-C. iOS apps typically follow the MVC or MVVM pattern. Apple's frameworks like UIKit and SwiftUI guide the architecture.
- **Android:** Uses Java or Kotlin. Android apps often use MVVM or MVP patterns. Google's architecture components, such as LiveData and ViewModel, support these patterns.
- **Cross-Platform:** Technologies like Flutter, React Native, and Xamarin

allow building apps for both iOS and Android from a single codebase. They require architecture patterns that support platform-specific features.

4.1.6 Designing for User Experience

User experience (UX) is a critical aspect of mobile app architecture:

- **Responsive Design:** Ensure the app works well on various screen sizes and orientations.
- **Navigation:** Implement intuitive navigation patterns to enhance usability.
- **Performance Optimization:** Minimize loading times and ensure smooth transitions.
- **Accessibility:** Design with accessibility in mind to accommodate all users, including those with disabilities.

4.1.7 Data Management

Efficient data management is crucial for mobile apps:

- **Local Storage:** Use databases like SQLite or Realm for storing data locally. Shared preferences or key-value storage can be used for small amounts of data.
- **Remote Data:** RESTful APIs or GraphQL are commonly used for fetching data from servers. Proper error handling and caching mechanisms are important for reliability.
- **Synchronization:** Ensure data synchronization between local storage and remote servers to handle offline scenarios gracefully.

4.1.8 Security Considerations

Security is paramount in mobile app development:

- **Authentication:** Implement secure user authentication methods, such as OAuth or JWT.
- **Data Encryption:** Encrypt sensitive data both in transit and at rest to prevent unauthorized access.
- **Secure Coding Practices:** Follow best practices to avoid common vulnerabilities like SQL injection, cross-site scripting (XSS), and insecure data storage.

4.1.9 Testing and Debugging

A robust testing strategy ensures the app's reliability and performance:

- **Unit Testing:** Test individual components to ensure they function correctly.
- **Integration Testing:** Verify that different parts of the app work together seamlessly.
- **UI Testing:** Automate testing of user interface interactions to catch visual or functional bugs.
- **Beta Testing:** Release beta versions to a group of users to gather feedback and identify issues before the public release.

4.1.10 Continuous Integration and Deployment

Implementing CI/CD pipelines enhances development efficiency and product quality:

- **Continuous Integration (CI):** Automatically build and test the app whenever code changes are committed.
- **Continuous Deployment (CD):** Automate the release process to ensure timely updates and fixes.

4.1.11 Performance Monitoring

Regularly monitor the app's performance to identify and address issues:

- **Analytics:** Use tools like Google Analytics or Firebase to track user behavior and app usage.
- **Crash Reporting:** Integrate crash reporting tools to get detailed reports on app crashes and errors.
- **Performance Metrics:** Monitor metrics like load times, memory usage, and battery consumption to optimize performance.

4.2 CHOOSING THE RIGHT DEVELOPMENT FRAMEWORKS

Selecting the appropriate development framework is a crucial decision in mobile app architecture. The right framework can streamline the development process, enhance performance, and ensure a consistent user experience across different devices.

Choosing the right development framework is a pivotal decision in mobile app architecture. It involves evaluating project requirements, performance needs, user experience goals, community support, scalability, and integration capabilities. Native frameworks offer optimal performance and deep platform integration, making them ideal for high-performance, platform-specific apps. Cross-platform frameworks like Flutter and React Native provide a balance between performance and development efficiency, enabling the creation of apps for multiple platforms from a single codebase. Hybrid frameworks offer quick development cycles and ease of learning, but may face limitations in performance and user experience. By carefully considering these factors, developers can select the framework that best aligns with their project goals and delivers a high-quality mobile app.

4.2.1 Understanding Mobile App Frameworks

Mobile app frameworks provide the foundational structure for building applications. They offer pre-written code, tools, and libraries that simplify development tasks, such as user interface design, database management, and network communication. Frameworks can be categorized into three main types:

- **Native Frameworks:** These frameworks are platform-specific, designed for building apps on a single operating system like iOS or Android.
- **Cross-Platform Frameworks:** These frameworks enable the development of apps that run on multiple platforms (iOS, Android, etc.) from a single codebase.
- **Hybrid Frameworks:** These frameworks combine elements of native and web apps, often using web technologies within a native shell.

4.2.2 Factors to Consider When Choosing a Framework

Selecting the right framework involves evaluating various factors to ensure it aligns with your project requirements and goals:

- **Project Requirements:** Understand the specific needs of your project, including features, performance expectations, and target audience.
- **Development Time:** Consider the framework's impact on development speed. Some frameworks enable rapid prototyping, while others may require more time for development and debugging.
- **Performance:** Evaluate the performance capabilities of the framework. Native frameworks typically offer better performance, while cross-platform and hybrid frameworks may introduce performance trade-offs.
- **User Experience:** Ensure the framework supports the creation of a smooth and responsive user experience.
- **Community and Support:** A strong community and robust support can be invaluable for troubleshooting and accessing resources.
- **Scalability:** Consider the framework's ability to support future growth and new features.
- **Integration with Existing Systems:** Ensure the framework can integrate seamlessly with your existing tools and systems.

4.2.3 Popular Native Frameworks

Native frameworks are tailored to specific platforms, providing optimal performance and access to all native features:

- **iOS (Swift and Objective-C):**
  - *Swift:* Apple's modern programming language designed for iOS development. It offers safety features, performance optimizations, and a concise syntax.
  - *Objective-C:* An older language still used in many legacy iOS applications. It provides deep integration with Apple's frameworks.
- **Android (Kotlin and Java):**
  - *Kotlin:* A modern, concise, and safe programming language officially supported by Google for Android development. It offers improved syntax and null safety compared to Java.
  - *Java:* The traditional language for Android development, known for its robustness and extensive libraries.

4.2.4 Popular Cross-Platform Frameworks

Cross-platform frameworks enable the development of apps for multiple platforms from a single codebase, reducing development time and costs:

Flutter

Developed by Google, Flutter uses the Dart language and offers a rich set of predesigned widgets. It allows for highly customizable and responsive UI development.

- **Advantages:** High performance, single codebase for both iOS and Android, hot-reload feature for rapid development.
- **Considerations:** Larger app size, relatively new with evolving community support.

React Native

Maintained by Facebook, React Native uses JavaScript and React for building native-like apps. It enables code sharing between web and mobile apps.

- **Advantages:** Strong community support, reusable components, efficient performance.
- **Considerations:** Performance can be an issue for complex animations and heavy computations, requires bridging to access some native features.

Xamarin

Owned by Microsoft, Xamarin uses C# and .NET to build cross-platform apps. It provides access to native APIs through a single codebase.

- **Advantages:** Shared codebase, deep integration with Visual Studio, access to native features.
- **Considerations:** Larger app size, potential for higher memory usage, licensing costs for enterprise features.

4.2.5 Popular Hybrid Frameworks

Hybrid frameworks leverage web technologies (HTML, CSS, JavaScript) to build apps that run inside a native container, allowing access to device features:

Ionic

Built on Angular and Apache Cordova, Ionic enables the creation of hybrid apps with a native look and feel.

- **Advantages:** Wide range of pre-designed components, strong community, ease of learning.
- **Considerations:** Performance may not match fully native apps, dependency on web technologies.

Cordova

Formerly known as PhoneGap, Cordova allows building hybrid apps using web technologies and deploying them in a native wrapper.

- **Advantages:** Quick development cycle, access to device APIs via plugins.
- **Considerations:** Performance limitations, less native-like experience.

4.2.6 Performance Considerations

Performance is a critical factor in mobile app development. Native frameworks typically offer the best performance as they are optimized for their respective platforms. Cross-platform frameworks like Flutter and React Native have made significant strides in performance, but they may still lag behind fully native solutions in certain scenarios, such as complex animations or heavy computational tasks. Hybrid frameworks tend to offer lower performance compared to native and cross-platform frameworks due to their reliance on web technologies.

4.2.7 User Experience and UI Design

The ability to create a seamless user experience is another vital consideration. Native frameworks offer the most control over UI components and behaviors, ensuring a consistent and responsive user experience. Cross-platform frameworks like Flutter provide a rich set of widgets and tools for creating highly customizable UIs, while React Native allows for the reuse of web-based UI components. Hybrid frameworks often face challenges in delivering a truly native-like experience, as they depend on web technologies.

4.2.8 Community and Support

A strong community and robust support are essential for successful mobile app development. Frameworks with active communities provide a wealth of resources, including tutorials, documentation, plugins, and libraries. Native frameworks benefit from official support and extensive documentation provided by Apple and Google. Cross-platform frameworks like React Native and Flutter have rapidly growing communities and comprehensive support from their respective maintainers. Hybrid frameworks also have dedicated communities, but their support may not be as extensive as native or cross-platform solutions.

4.2.9 Scalability and Future Growth

When choosing a framework, consider its ability to support future growth and scalability. Native frameworks are well-suited for scalable apps as they are built with platform-specific optimizations. Cross-platform frameworks like Flutter and React Native are designed to handle scaling effectively, allowing for the addition of new features and performance enhancements. Hybrid frameworks may face limitations in scalability due to their reliance on web technologies, which can impact performance as the app grows in complexity.

4.2.10 Integration with Existing Systems

Seamless integration with existing tools and systems is crucial for efficient development workflows. Native frameworks offer deep integration with platform-specific tools, such as Xcode for iOS and Android Studio for Android. Cross-platform frameworks like Xamarin integrate well with tools like Visual Studio, providing a cohesive development environment. Hybrid frameworks can integrate with various tools through plugins and APIs, but may require additional effort to achieve seamless integration.

CHAPTER 5
PROGRAMMING LANGUAGES FOR MOBILE APPS

5.1 OVERVIEW OF LANGUAGES: JAVA, SWIFT, KOTLIN, ETC.

Choosing the right programming language is fundamental to mobile app development. The language not only influences the ease and speed of development but also affects app performance, maintainability, and scalability.

Choosing the right programming language for mobile app development depends on various factors, including the target platform, performance requirements, development speed, and existing codebases. Java and Kotlin are the primary choices for Android development, while Swift is preferred for iOS. For cross-platform development, languages like JavaScript, TypeScript, Dart, and C# offer compelling frameworks that allow a single codebase to serve multiple platforms. Understanding the strengths and use cases of each language can help developers make informed decisions and create high-quality, efficient mobile applications.

5.1.1 Java

Java is a high-level, class-based, object-oriented programming language that is designed to have as few implementation dependencies as possible. It is a general-purpose programming language intended to let programmers *write once, run anywhere* (WORA), meaning that compiled Java code can run on all platforms that support Java without the need to recompile. Java applications are typically compiled to bytecode that can run on any Java virtual machine (JVM) regardless of the underlying computer architecture.

Although its syntax is similar to that of C and C++, the Java language has fewer low-level facilities than either of them. The Java runtime provides dynamic capabilities (such as reflection and runtime code modification) that are typically not available in traditional compiled languages.

Java gained popularity shortly after its release, and has been a very popular programming language since then. Java was the third most popular programming language in 2022 according to GitHub. Although still widely popular, there has been a gradual decline in use of Java in recent years with other languages using JVM gaining popularity.

Java was originally developed by James Gosling at Sun Microsystems. It was released in May 1995 as a core component of Sun's Java platform. The original and reference implementation Java compilers, virtual machines, and class libraries were originally released by Sun under proprietary licenses. As of May 2007, in compliance with the specifications of the Java Community Process, Sun had relicensed most of its Java technologies under the GPL-2.0-only license. Oracle offers its own HotSpot Java Virtual Machine, however the official reference implementation is the OpenJDK JVM which is free open-source software and used by most developers and is the default JVM for almost all Linux distributions.

As of March 2024, Java 22 is the latest version. Java 8, 11, 17, and 21 are previous LTS versions still officially supported.

History

James Gosling, Mike Sheridan, and Patrick Naughton initiated the Java language project in June 1991. Java was originally designed for interactive television, but it was too advanced for the digital cable television industry at the time. The language was initially called *Oak* after an oak tree that stood outside Gosling's office. Later the project went by the name *Green* and was finally renamed *Java*, from Java coffee, a type of coffee from Indonesia. Gosling designed Java with a C/C++-style syntax that system and application programmers would find familiar.

Sun Microsystems released the first public implementation as Java 1.0 in 1996. It promised write once, run anywhere (WORA) functionality, providing no-cost run-times on popular platforms. Fairly secure and featuring configurable security, it allowed network- and file-access restrictions. Major web browsers soon incorporated the ability to run Java applets within web pages, and Java quickly became popular. The Java 1.0 compiler was re-written in Java by Arthur van Hoff to comply strictly with the Java 1.0 language specification. With the advent of Java 2 (released initially as J2SE 1.2 in December 1998 – 1999), new versions had multiple configurations built for different types of platforms. J2EE included technologies and APIs for enterprise applications typically run in server environments, while J2ME featured APIs optimized for mobile applications. The desktop version was renamed J2SE. In 2006, for marketing purposes, Sun renamed new J2 versions as *Java EE*, *Java ME*, and *Java SE*, respectively.

In 1997, Sun Microsystems approached the ISO/IEC JTC 1 standards body and later the Ecma International to formalize Java, but it soon withdrew from the process. Java remains a *de facto* standard, controlled through the Java Community Process. At one time, Sun made most of its Java implementations available without charge, despite their proprietary software status. Sun generated revenue from Java through the selling of licenses for specialized products such as the Java Enterprise System.

On November 13, 2006, Sun released much of its Java virtual machine (JVM) as free and open-source software (FOSS), under the terms of the GPL-2.0-only license. On May 8, 2007, Sun finished the process, making all of its JVM's core code available under free software/open-source distribution terms, aside from a small portion of code to which Sun did not hold the copyright.

Sun's vice-president Rich Green said that Sun's ideal role with regard to Java was as an *evangelist*. Following Oracle Corporation's acquisition of Sun Microsystems in 2009–10, Oracle has described itself as the steward of Java technology with a relentless commitment to fostering a community of participation and transparency. This did not prevent Oracle from filing a lawsuit against Google shortly after that for using Java inside the Android SDK.

On April 2, 2010, James Gosling resigned from Oracle. In January 2016, Oracle announced that Java run-time environments based on JDK 9 will discontinue the browser plugin. Java software runs on everything from laptops to data centers, game consoles to scientific supercomputers. Oracle (and others) highly recommend uninstalling outdated and unsupported versions of Java, due to unresolved security issues in older versions.

There were five primary goals in the creation of the Java language:

- It must be simple, object-oriented, and familiar.
- It must be robust and secure.
- It must be architecture-neutral and portable.
- It must execute with high performance.
- It must be interpreted, threaded, and dynamic.

As of September 2023, Java 8, 11, 17 and 21 are supported as Long-Term Support (LTS) versions. Oracle released the last zero-cost public update for the legacy version Java 8 LTS in January 2019 for commercial use, although it will otherwise still support Java 8 with public updates for personal use indefinitely. Other vendors such as Adoptium continue to offer free builds of OpenJDK's Long-Term Support (LTS) versions. These builds may include additional security patches and bug fixes.

Editions

Sun has defined and supports four editions of Java targeting different application environments and segmented many of its APIs so that they belong to one of the platforms. The platforms are:

- Java Card for smart-cards.
- Java Platform, Micro Edition (Java ME)—targeting environments with limited resources.

- Java Platform, Standard Edition (Java SE)—targeting workstation environments.
- Java Platform, Enterprise Edition (Java EE)—targeting large distributed enterprise or Internet environments.

The classes in the Java APIs are organized into separate groups called packages. Each package contains a set of related interfaces, classes, subpackages and exceptions.

Sun also provided an edition called Personal Java that has been superseded by later, standards-based Java ME configuration-profile pairings.

Java JVM and Bytecode

One design goal of Java is portability, which means that programs written for the Java platform must run similarly on any combination of hardware and operating system with adequate run time support. This is achieved by compiling the Java language code to an intermediate representation called Java bytecode, instead of directly to architecture-specific machine code. Java bytecode instructions are analogous to machine code, but they are intended to be executed by a virtual machine (VM) written specifically for the host hardware. End-users commonly use a Java Runtime Environment (JRE) installed on their device for standalone Java applications or a web browser for Java applets.

Standard libraries provide a generic way to access host-specific features such as graphics, threading, and networking.

The use of universal bytecode makes porting simple. However, the overhead of interpreting bytecode into machine instructions made interpreted programs almost always run more slowly than native executables. Just-in-time (JIT) compilers that compile byte-codes to machine code during runtime were introduced from an early stage. Java's Hotspot compiler is actually two compilers in one; and with GraalVM (included in e.g. Java 11, but removed as of Java 16) allowing tiered compilation. Java itself is platform-independent and is adapted to the particular platform it is to run on by a Java virtual machine (JVM), which translates the Java bytecode into the platform's machine language.

Performance

Programs written in Java have a reputation for being slower and requiring more memory than those written in C++. However, Java programs' execution speed improved significantly with the introduction of just-in-time compilation in 1997/1998 for Java 1.1, the addition of language features supporting better code analysis (such as inner classes, the StringBuilder class, optional assertions, etc.), and optimizations in the Java virtual machine, such as HotSpot becoming Sun's default JVM in 2000. With Java 1.5, the performance was improved with the addition of the java.util.concurrent package, including lock-free implementations of the ConcurrentMaps and other multi-core collections, and it was improved further with Java 1.6.

Non-JVM

Some platforms offer direct hardware support for Java; there are micro controllers that can run Java bytecode in hardware instead of a software Java virtual machine, and some ARM-based processors could have hardware support for executing Java bytecode through their Jazelle option, though support has mostly been dropped in current implementations of ARM.

Automatic Memory Management

Java uses an automatic garbage collector to manage memory in the object lifecycle. The programmer determines when objects are created, and the Java runtime is responsible for recovering the memory once objects are no longer in use. Once no references to an object remain, the unreachable memory becomes eligible to be freed automatically by the garbage collector. Something similar to a memory leak may still occur if a programmer's code holds a reference to an object that is no longer needed, typically when objects that are no longer needed are stored in containers that are still in use. If methods for a non-existent object are called, a null pointer exception is thrown.

One of the ideas behind Java's automatic memory management model is that programmers can be spared the burden of having to perform manual memory management. In some languages, memory for the creation of objects is implicitly allocated on the stack or explicitly allocated and deallocated from the heap. In the latter case, the responsibility of managing memory resides with the programmer. If the program does not deallocate an object, a memory leak occurs. If the program attempts to access or deallocate memory that has already been deallocated, the result is undefined and difficult to predict, and the program is likely to become unstable or crash. This can be partially remedied by the use of smart pointers, but these add overhead and complexity. Garbage collection does not prevent logical memory leaks, i.e. those where the memory is still referenced but never used.

Garbage collection in Java can occur at any moment, though it ideally runs when the program is idle. However, if the heap lacks sufficient free memory for a new object, garbage collection is guaranteed to trigger, which may cause the program to pause briefly. It's important to note that Java does not allow for explicit memory management by the programmer. Java does not support C/C++ style pointer arithmetic, where object addresses can be arithmetically manipulated (e.g. by adding or subtracting an offset). This allows the garbage collector to relocate referenced objects and ensures type safety and security.

As in C++ and some other object-oriented languages, variables of Java's primitive data types are either stored directly in fields (for objects) or on the stack (for methods) rather than on the heap, as is commonly true for non-primitive data types. This was a conscious decision by Java's designers for performance reasons.

Java contains multiple types of garbage collectors. Since Java 9, HotSpot uses the Garbage First Garbage Collector (G1GC) as the default. However, there are also several other garbage collectors that can be used to manage the heap. For most applications in Java, G1GC is sufficient. Previously, the Parallel Garbage Collector was used in Java 8.

Having solved the memory management problem does not relieve the programmer of the burden of handling properly other kinds of resources, like network or database connections, file handles, etc., especially in the presence of exceptions.

Syntax

The syntax of Java is largely influenced by C++ and C. Unlike C++, which combines the syntax for structured, generic, and object-oriented programming, Java was built almost exclusively as an object-oriented language. All code is written inside classes, and every data item is an object, with the exception of the primitive data types, (i.e. integers, floating-point numbers, boolean values, and characters), which are not objects for performance reasons. Java reuses some popular aspects of C++ (such as the printf method).

Unlike C++, Java does not support operator overloading or multiple inheritance for classes, though multiple inheritance is supported for interfaces.

Java uses comments similar to those of C++. There are three different styles of comments: a single line style marked with two slashes (//), a multiple line style opened with /* and closed with */, and the Javadoc commenting style opened with /** and closed with */. The Javadoc style of commenting allows the user to run the Javadoc executable to create documentation for the program and can be read by some integrated development environments (IDEs) such as Eclipse to allow developers to access documentation within the IDE.

Implementations

Oracle Corporation owns the official implementation of the Java SE platform, due to its acquisition of Sun Microsystems on January 27, 2010. This implementation is based on the original implementation of Java by Sun.

The Oracle implementation is available for Windows, macOS, Linux, and Solaris. Because Java lacks any formal standardization recognized by Ecma International, ISO/IEC, ANSI, or other third-party standards organizations, the Oracle implementation is the de facto standard.

The Oracle implementation is packaged into two different distributions: The Java Runtime Environment (JRE) which contains the parts of the Java SE platform required to run Java programs and is intended for end users, and the Java Development Kit (JDK), which is intended for software developers and includes development tools such as the Java compiler, Javadoc, Jar, and a debugger. Oracle has also released GraalVM, a high performance Java dynamic compiler and interpreter.

OpenJDK is another Java SE implementation that is licensed under the GNU GPL. The implementation started when Sun began releasing the Java source code under the GPL. As of Java SE 7, OpenJDK is the official Java reference implementation.

The goal of Java is to make all implementations of Java compatible. Historically, Sun's trademark license for usage of the Java brand insists that all implementations be *compatible*. This resulted in a legal dispute with Microsoft after Sun claimed that the Microsoft implementation did not support Java remote method invocation (RMI) or Java Native Interface (JNI) and had added platform-specific features of their own. Sun sued in 1997, and, in 2001, won a settlement of US$20 million, as well as a court order enforcing the terms of the license from Sun. As a result, Microsoft no longer ships Java with Windows.

Platform-independent Java is essential to Java EE, and an even more rigorous validation is required to certify an implementation. This environment enables portable server-side applications.

5.1.2 Swift

Swift is a high-level general-purpose, multi-paradigm, compiled programming language created by Chris Lattner in 2010 for Apple Inc. and maintained by the open-source community. Swift compiles to machine code, as it is an LLVM-based compiler. Swift was first released in June 2014, and the Swift toolchain has shipped in Xcode since version 6, released in 2014.

Apple intended Swift to support many core concepts associated with Objective-C, notably dynamic dispatch, widespread late binding, extensible programming, and similar features, but in a "safer" way, making it easier to catch software bugs; Swift has features addressing some common programming errors like null pointer dereferencing and provides syntactic sugar to help avoid the pyramid of doom. Swift supports the concept of protocol extensibility, an extensibility system that can be applied to types, structs and classes, which Apple promotes as a real change in programming paradigms they term "protocol-oriented programming" (similar to traits and type classes).

Swift was introduced at Apple's 2014 Worldwide Developers Conference (WWDC). It underwent an upgrade to version 1.2 during 2014 and a major upgrade to Swift 2 at WWDC 2015. It was initially a proprietary language, but version 2.2 was made open-source software under the Apache License 2.0 on December 3, 2015, for Apple's platforms and Linux.

Through version 3.0 the syntax of Swift went through significant evolution, with the core team making source stability a focus in later versions. In the first quarter of 2018 Swift surpassed Objective-C in measured popularity.

Swift 4.0, released in 2017, introduced several changes to some built-in classes and structures. Code written with previous versions of Swift can be updated using the migration functionality built into Xcode. Swift 5, released in March 2019, introduced a stable binary interface on Apple platforms, allowing the Swift runtime to be incorporated into Apple operating systems. It is source compatible with Swift 4.

Swift 5.1 was officially released in September 2019. Swift 5.1 builds on the previous version of Swift 5 by extending the stable features of the language to compile-time with the introduction of module stability. The introduction of module stability makes it possible to create and share binary frameworks that will work with future releases of Swift.

Swift 5.5, officially announced by Apple at the 2021 WWDC, significantly expands language support for concurrency and asynchronous code, notably introducing a unique version of the actor model.

Swift 5.9, was released in September 2023 and includes a macro system, generic parameter packs, and ownership features like the new consume operator.

The current version, Swift 5.10, was released in March 2024. This version improves the language's concurrency model, allowing for full data isolation to prevent data races. It is also the last release before Swift 6. Version 5.10 is currently available for macOS, Windows and, in experimental use, for Linux.

History

Development of Swift started in July 2010 by Chris Lattner, with the eventual collaboration of many other programmers at Apple. Swift was motivated by the need for a replacement for Apple's earlier programming language Objective-C, which had been largely unchanged since the early 1980s and lacked modern language features. Swift took language ideas "from Objective-C, Rust, Haskell, Ruby, Python, C#, CLU, and far too many others to list". On June 2, 2014, the Apple Worldwide Developers Conference (WWDC) application became the first publicly released app written with Swift.

A beta version of the programming language was released to registered Apple developers at the conference, but the company did not promise that the final version of Swift would be source code compatible with the test version. Apple planned to make source code converters available if needed for the full release.

The Swift Programming Language, a free 500-page manual, was also released at WWDC, and is available on the Apple Books Store and the official website.

Swift reached the 1.0 milestone on September 9, 2014, with the *Gold Master* of Xcode 6.0 for iOS. Swift 1.1 was released on October 22, 2014, alongside the launch of Xcode 6.1. Swift 1.2 was released on April 8, 2015, along with Xcode 6.3. Swift 2.0 was announced at WWDC 2015, and was made available for publishing apps in the App Store on September 21, 2015. Swift 3.0 was released on September 13, 2016. Swift 4.0 was released on September 19, 2017. Swift 4.1 was released on March 29, 2018.

Swift won first place for *Most Loved Programming Language* in the Stack Overflow Developer Survey 2015 and second place in 2016.

On December 3, 2015, the Swift language, supporting libraries, debugger, and package manager were open-sourced under the Apache 2.0 license with a Runtime Library Exception, and Swift.org was created to host the project. The source code is hosted on GitHub, where it is easy for anyone to get the code, build it themselves, and even create pull requests to contribute code back to the project.

In December 2015, IBM announced its Swift Sandbox website, which allows developers to write Swift code in one pane and display output in another. The Swift Sandbox was deprecated in January 2018.

During the WWDC 2016, Apple announced an iPad exclusive app, named Swift Playgrounds, intended to teach people how to code in Swift. The app is presented in a 3D video game-like interface which provides feedback when lines of code are placed in a certain order and executed.

In January 2017, Chris Lattner announced his departure from Apple for a new position with Tesla Motors, with the Swift project lead role going to team veteran Ted Kremenek. During WWDC 2019, Apple announced SwiftUI with Xcode 11, which provides a framework for declarative UI structure design across all Apple platforms. Official downloads for the Ubuntu distribution of Linux have been available since Swift 2.2, with more distros added since Swift 5.2.4, CentOS and Amazon Linux. There is an unofficial SDK and native toolchain package for Android too.

Platforms

The platforms Swift supports are Apple's operating systems (Darwin, iOS, iPadOS, macOS, tvOS, watchOS), Linux, Windows, and Android. A key aspect of Swift's design is its ability to interoperate with the huge body of existing Objective-C code developed for Apple products over the previous decades, such as Cocoa and the Cocoa Touch frameworks. On Apple platforms, it links with the Objective-C runtime library, which allows C, Objective-C, C++ and Swift code to run within one program.

Features

Swift is a general purpose programming language that employs modern programming-language theory concepts and strives to present a simple, yet powerful syntax. Swift incorporates innovations and conventions from various programming languages, with notable inspiration from Objective-C, which it replaced as the primary development language on Apple Platforms.

Swift was designed to be safe and friendly to new programmers while not sacrificing speed. By default Swift manages all memory automatically and ensures variables are always initialized before use. Array accesses are checked for out-of-bounds errors and integer operations are checked for overflow. Parameter names allow creating clear APIs. Protocols define interfaces that types may adopt, while extensions allow developers to add more function to existing types. Swift enables object-oriented programming with the support for classes, subtyping, and method overriding. Optionals allow nil values to be handled explicitly and safely. Concurrent programs can be written using async/await syntax and actors isolate shared mutable state in order to eliminate data races.

Basic Syntax

Swift's syntax is similar to C-style languages. Code begins executing in the global scope by default. Alternatively, the `@main` attribute can be applied a structure, class, or enumeration declaration to indicate that it contains the program's entry point.

Swift's "Hello, World!" program is:

print("Hello, world!")

The print(_:separator:terminator:) function used here is included in Swift's standard library, which is available to all programs without the need to import external modules. Statements in Swift don't have to end with a semicolon, however semicolons are required to separate multiple statements written on the same line. Single-line comments begin with // and continue until the end of the current line. Multiline comments are contained by /* and */ characters. Constants are declared with the let keyword and variables with the var keyword. Values must be initialized before they are read. Values may infer their type based on the type of the provided initial value. If the initial value is set after the value's declaration, a type must be declared explicitly.

let highScoreThreshold = 1000 // A constant with type Int. The type was inferred based on the provided value.

var currentScore = 980 // A variable with type Int.

currentScore = 1200 // The value of variables can change over time.

```
let playerMessage: String // A constant with explicit type String.
if currentScore > highScoreThreshold {
  playerMessage = "You are a top player!"
} else {
  playerMessage = "Better luck next time."
}
print(playerMessage) // Prints "You are a top player!"
```

Control flow in Swift is managed with if-else, guard, and switch statements, along with while and for-in loops.

If statements take a boolean parameter and execute the body of the if statement if the condition is true, otherwise it executes the optional else body. if-let syntax provides syntactic sugar for checking for the existence of an optional value and unwrapping it at the same time.

```
let someNumber = 42
if someNumber % 2 == 0 { // Use the remainder operator to find the remainder of someNumber divided
by 2.
  print("\(someNumber) is even.")
} else {
  print("\(someNumber) is odd.")
}

// Prints "42 is even."
```

Functions are defined with the func keyword. Function parameters may have names which allow function calls to read like phrases. An underscore before the parameter name allows the argument label to be omitted from the call site. Tuples can be used by functions to return multiple pieces of data at once.

```
func constructGreeting(for name: String) -> String {
  return "Hello \(name)!"
}

let greeting = constructGreeting(for: "Craig")

print(greeting) // Prints "Hello Craig!"
```

Functions, and anonymous functions known as closures, can be assigned to properties and passed around the program like any other value.

```
func divideByTwo(_ aNum: Int) -> Int {
   return aNum / 2
}
func multiplyByTwo(_ aNum: Int) -> Int {
   return aNum * 2
}
let mathOperation = multiplyByTwo
print(mathOperation(21)) // Prints "42"
```

Guard statements require that the given condition is true before continuing on past the guard statement, otherwise the body of the provided else clause is run. The else clause must exit control of the code block in which the guard statement appears. guard statements are useful for ensuring that certain requirements are met before continuing on with program execution. In particular they can be used to create an unwrapped version of an optional value that is guaranteed to be non-nil for the remainder of the enclosing scope.

```
func divide(numerator: Int?, byDenominator denominator: Int) -> Int? {
   guard denominator != 0 else {
      print("Can't divide by 0.")
      return nil
   }
  guard let numerator else {
      print("The provided numerator is nil.")
      return nil
   }

   return numerator / denominator
}

let result = divide(numerator: 3, byDenominator: 0)
print("Division result is: \(result)")
// Prints:
```

```
// "Can't divide by 0."
// "Division result is: nil."
```

Switch statements compare a value with multiple potential values and then executes an associated code block. switch statements must be made exhaustive, either by including cases for all possible values or by including a default case which is run when the provided value doesn't match any of the other cases. switch cases do not implicitly fall through, although they may explicitly do so with the fallthrough keyword. Pattern matching can be used in various ways inside switch statements. Here is an example of an integer being matched against a number of potential ranges:

```
let someNumber = 42
switch someNumber {
case ..<0:
  print("\(someNumber) negative.")
case 0:
  print("\(someNumber) is 0.")
case 1...9:
  print("\(someNumber) greater than 0, but less than 10.")
default:
  print("\(someNumber) is greater than 9.")
}
// Prints "42 is greater than 9."
```

For-in loops iterate over a sequence of values:

```
let names = ["Will", "Anna", "Bart"]
for name in names {
  print(name)
}
// Prints:
// Will
// Anna
// Bart
```

While loops iterate as long as the given boolean condition evaluates to true:

```
// Add together all the numbers from 1 to 5.
```

```
var i = 1
var result = 0
while i <= 5 { // The loop performs its body as long as i is less than or equal to 5.
  result += i // Add i to the current result.
  i += 1 // Increment i by 1.
}
print(result) // Prints "15"
```

Closure Support

Swift supports closures, which are self-contained blocks of functionality that can be passed around and used in code, and can also be used as anonymous functions. Here are some examples:

```
// Closure type, defined by its input and output values, can be specified outside the closure:
let closure1: (Int, Int) -> Int = { arg1, arg2 in
  return arg1 + arg2
}
// ...or inside it:
let closure2 = { (arg1: Int, arg2: Int) -> Int in
  return arg1 + arg2
}
// In most cases, closure's return type can be inferred automatically by the compiler.
let closure3 = { arg1: Int, arg2: Int in
  return arg1 + arg2
}
```

Closures can be assigned to variables and constants, and can be passed into other functions or closures as parameters. Single-expression closures may drop the return keyword.

Swift also has a trailing closure syntax, which allows the closure to be written after the end of the function call instead of within the function's parameter list. Parentheses can be omitted altogether if the closure is the function's only parameter:

```
// This function takes a closure which receives no input parameters and returns an integer,
// evaluates it, and uses the closure's return value (an Int) as the function's return value.
func foo(closure bar: () -> Int) -> Int {
```

```
    return bar()
}
// Without trailing closure syntax:
foo(closure: { return 1 })
// With trailing closure syntax, and implicit return:
foo { 1 }
```

Starting from version 5.3, Swift supports multiple trailing closures:

```
// This function passes the return of the first closure as the parameter of the second,
// and returns the second closure's result:
func foo(bar: () -> Int, baz: (Int) -> Int) -> Int {
    return baz(bar())
}
// With no trailing closures:
foo(bar: { return 1 }, baz: { x in return x + 1 })
// With 1 trailing closure:
foo(bar: { return 1 }) { x in return x + 1 }
// With 2 trailing closures (only the first closure's argument name is omitted):
foo { return 1 } baz: { x in return x + 1 }
```

Swift will provide shorthand argument names for inline closures, removing the need to explicitly name all of the closures parameters. Arguments can be referred to with the names $0, $1, $2, and so on:

```
let names = ["Josephine", "Steve", "Chris", "Barbara"]
// filter calls the given closure for each value in names.
// Values with a character count less than 6 are kept, the others are dropped.
let shortNames = names.filter { $0.count < 6 }
print(shortNames) // Prints "["Steve", "Chris"]"
```

Closures may capture values from their surrounding scope. The closure will refer to this captured value for as long as the closure exists:

```
func makeMultiplier(withMultiple multiple: Int) -> (Int) -> (Int) {
    // Create and return a closure that takes in an Int and returns the input multiplied by the value of
  multiple.
    return {
```

```
        $0 * multiple
    }
}
let multiplier = makeMultiplier(withMultiple: 3)
print(multiplier(3)) // Prints "9"
print(multiplier(10)) // Prints "30"
```

String Support

The Swift standard library includes unicode-compliant String and Character types. String values can be initialized with a String literal, a sequence of characters surrounded by double quotation marks. Strings can be concatenated with the + operator:

```
var someString = "Hello,"
someString += " world!"
```

String interpolation allows for the creation of a new string from other values and expressions. Values written between parentheses preceded by a \ will be inserted into the enclosing string literal:

```
var currentScore = 980
print("Your score is \(currentScore).")
// Prints "Your score is 980."
```

A for-in loop can be used to iterate over the characters contained in a string:

```
for character in "Swift" {
    print(character)
}
// S
// w
// i
// f
// t
```

When the Foundation framework is imported Swift invisibly bridges the String type to NSString, the String class commonly used in Objective-C.

Callable Objects

In Swift, callable objects are defined using callAsFunction.

```
struct CallableStruct {
  var value: Int
  func callAsFunction(_ number: Int, scale: Int) {
    print(scale * (number + value))
  }
}
let callable = CallableStruct(value: 100)
callable(4, scale: 2)
callable.callAsFunction(4, scale: 2)
// Both function calls print 208.
```

Access Control

Swift supports five access control levels for symbols: open, public, internal, fileprivate, and private. Unlike many object-oriented languages, these access controls ignore inheritance hierarchies: private indicates that a symbol is accessible only in the immediate scope, fileprivate indicates it is accessible only from within the file, internal indicates it is accessible within the containing module, public indicates it is accessible from any module, and open (only for classes and their methods) indicates that the class may be subclassed outside of the module.

Optionals and Chaining

An important feature in Swift is option types, which allow references or values to operate in a manner similar to the common pattern in C, where a pointer may either refer to a specific value or no value at all. This implies that non-optional types cannot result in a null-pointer error; the compiler can ensure this is not possible.

Optional types are created with the Optional enum. To make an Integer that is nullable, one would use a declaration similar to var optionalInteger: Optional<Int>. As in C#, Swift also includes syntactic sugar for this, allowing one to indicate a variable is optional by placing a question mark after the type name, var optionalInteger: Int?. Variables or constants that are marked optional either have a value of the underlying type or are nil. Optional types wrap the base type, resulting in a different instance. String and String? are fundamentally different types, the former is of type String while the latter is an Optional that may be holding some String value.

To access the value inside, assuming it is not nil, it must be unwrapped to expose the instance inside. This is performed with the ! operator:

```
let myValue = anOptionalInstance!.someMethod()
```

In this case, the ! operator unwraps an optional instance to expose the instance inside, allowing the method call to be made on it. If anOptionalInstance is nil, a null-pointer error occurs, terminating the program. This is known as force unwrapping. Optionals may be safely unwrapped using optional chaining which first tests whether the instance is nil, and then unwrap it if it is non-null:

let myValue = anOptionalInstance?.someMethod()

In this case the runtime calls someMethod only if anOptionalInstance is not nil, suppressing the error. A ? must be placed after every optional property. If any of these properties are nil the entire expression evaluates as nil. The origin of the term chaining comes from the more common case where several method calls/ getters are chained together. For instance:

let aTenant = aBuilding.tenantList[5]

let theirLease = aTenant.leaseDetails

let leaseStart = theirLease?.startDate

can be reduced to:

let leaseStart = aBuilding.tenantList[5].leaseDetails?.startDate

Swift's use of optionals allows the compiler to use static dispatch because the unwrapping action is called on a defined instance (the wrapper), versus occurring in a runtime dispatch system.

Value Types

In many object-oriented languages, objects are represented internally in two parts. The object is stored as a block of data placed on the heap, while the name (or "handle") to that object is represented by a pointer. Objects are passed between methods by copying the value of the pointer, allowing the same underlying data on the heap to be accessed by anyone with a copy.

In contrast, basic types like integers and floating-point values are represented directly; the handle contains the data, not a pointer to it, and that data is passed directly to methods by copying. These styles of access are termed pass-by-reference in the case of objects, and pass-by-value for basic types.

Both concepts have their advantages and disadvantages. Objects are useful when the data is large, like the description of a window or the contents of a document. In these cases, access to that data is provided by copying a 32- or 64-bit value, versus copying an entire data structure.

However, smaller values like integers are the same size as pointers (typically both are one word), so there is no advantage to passing a pointer, versus passing the value.

Swift offers built-in support for objects using either pass-by-reference or pass-by-value semantics, the former using the class declaration and the latter using struct. Structs in Swift have almost all the same features as classes: methods, implementing protocols and using the extension mechanisms. For this reason, Apple terms all data generically as instances, versus objects or values. Structs do not support inheritance, however.

The programmer is free to choose which semantics are more appropriate for each data structure in the application. Larger structures like windows would be defined as classes, allowing them to be passed around as pointers. Smaller structures, like a 2D point, can be defined as structs, which will be pass-by-value and allow direct access to their internal data with no indirection or reference counting. The performance improvement inherent to the pass-by-value concept is such that Swift uses these types for almost all common data types, including Int and Double, and types normally represented by objects, like String and Array. Using value types can result in significant performance improvements in user applications as well.

Array, Dictionary, and Set all utilize copy on write so that their data are copied only if and when the program attempts to change a value in them. This means that the various accessors have what is in effect a pointer to the same data storage. So while the data is physically stored as one instance in memory, at the level of the application, these values are separate and physical separation is enforced by copy on write only if needed.

Extensions

Extensions add new functionality to an existing type, without the need to subclass or even have access to the original source code. Extensions can add new methods, initializers, computed properties, subscripts, and protocol conformances. An example might be to add a spell checker to the base String type, which means all instances of String in the program gain the ability to spell-check.

The system is also widely used as an organizational technique, allowing related code to be gathered into library-like extensions.

Extensions are declared with the extension keyword.

```
struct Rectangle {
  let width: Double
  let height: Double
}
extension Rectangle {
  var area: Double {
```

```
        return height * width
    }
}
```

Protocol-Oriented Programming

Protocols promise that a particular type implements a set of methods or properties, meaning that other instances in the system can call those methods on any instance implementing that protocol. This is often used in modern object-oriented languages as a substitute for multiple inheritance, although the feature sets are not entirely similar.

In Objective-C, and most other languages implementing the protocol concept, it is up to the programmer to ensure that the required methods are implemented in each class. Swift adds the ability to add these methods using extensions, and to use generic programming (generics) to implement them. Combined, these allow protocols to be written once and support a wide variety of instances. Also, the extension mechanism can be used to add protocol conformance to an object that does not list that protocol in its definition.

For example, a protocol might be declared called Printable, which ensures that instances that conform to the protocol implement a description property and a printDetails() method requirement:

```
// Define a protocol named Printable
protocol Printable {
    var description: String { get } // A read-only property requirement
    func printDetails() // A method requirement
}
```

This protocol can now be adopted by other types:

```
// Adopt the Printable protocol in a class
class MyClass: Printable {
    var description: String {
        return "An instance of MyClass"
    }
    func printDetails() {
        print(description)
    }
}
```

Extensions can be used to add protocol conformance to types. Protocols themselves can also be extended to provide default implementations of their requirements. Adopters may define their own implementations, or they may use the default implementation:

```
extension Printable { // All Printable instances will receive this implementation, or they may define their own.
    func printDetails() {
        print(description)
    }
}
// Bool now conforms to Printable, and inherits the printDetails() implementation above.
extension Bool: Printable {
    var description: String {
        return "An instance of Bool with value: \(self)"
    }
}
```

In Swift, like many modern languages supporting interfaces, protocols can be used as types, which means variables and methods can be defined by protocol instead of their specific type:

```
func getSomethingPrintable() -> any Printable {
    return true
}
var someSortOfPrintableInstance = getSomethingPrintable()
print(someSortOfPrintableInstance.description)
// Prints "An instance of Bool with value: true"
```

It does not matter what concrete type of someSortOfPrintableInstance is, the compiler will ensure that it conforms to the protocol and thus this code is safe. This syntax also means that collections can be based on protocols also, like let printableArray = [any Printable].

Both extensions and protocols are used extensively in Swift's standard library; in Swift 5.9, approximately 1.2 percent of all symbols within the standard library were protocols, and another 12.3 percent were protocol requirements or default implementations. For instance, Swift uses extensions to add the Equatable protocol to many of their basic types, like Strings and Arrays, allowing them to be compared with the == operator. The Equatable protocol also defines this default implementation:

```
func !=<T : Equatable>(lhs: T, rhs: T) -> Bool
```

This function defines a method that works on any instance conforming to Equatable, providing a not equals operator. Any instance, class or struct, automatically gains this implementation simply by conforming to Equatable.

Protocols, extensions, and generics can be combined to create sophisticated APIs. For example, constraints allow types to conditionally adopt protocols or methods based on the characteristics of the adopting type. A common use case may be adding a method on collection types only when the elements contained within the collection are Equatable:

```
extension Array where Element: Equatable {
  // allEqual will be available only on instances of Array that contain Equatable elements.
  func allEqual() -> Bool {
    for element in self {
      if element != self.first {
        return false
      }
    }
    return true
  }
}
```

Concurrency

Swift 5.5 introduced structured concurrency into the language. Structured concurrency uses Async/await syntax similar to Kotlin, JavaScript, and Rust. An async function is defined with the async keyword after the parameter list. When calling an async function the await keyword must be written before the function to indicate that execution will potentially suspend while calling function. While a function is suspended the program may run some other concurrent function in the same program. This syntax allows programs to clearly call out potential suspension points and avoid a version of the Pyramid of doom (programming) caused by the previously widespread use of closure callbacks.

```
func downloadText(name: String) async -> String {
  let result = // ... some asynchronous downloading code ...
  return result
```

```
}
let text = await downloadText("text1")
```

The async let syntax allows multiple functions to run in parallel. await is again used to mark the point at which the program will suspend to wait for the completion of the async functions called earlier.

```
// Each of these calls to downloadText will run in parallel.
async let text1 = downloadText(name: "text1")
async let text2 = downloadText(name: "text2")
async let text3 = downloadText(name: "text3")
let textToPrint = await [text1, text2, text3] // Suspends until all three downloadText calls have returned.
print(textToPrint)
```

Tasks and TaskGroups can be created explicitly to create a dynamic number of child tasks during runtime:

```
let taskHandle = Task {
  await downloadText(name: "someText")
}
let result = await taskHandle.value
```

Swift uses the Actor model to isolate mutable state, allowing different tasks to mutate shared state in a safe manner. Actors are declared with the actor keyword and are reference types, like classes. Only one task may access the mutable state of an actor at the same time. Actors may access and mutate their own internal state freely, but code running in separate tasks must mark each access with the await keyword to indicate that the code may suspend until other tasks finish accessing the actor's state.

```
actor Directory {
  var names: [String] = []

  func add(name: String) {
    names.append(name)
  }
}
let directory = Directory()
// Code suspends until other tasks finish accessing the actor.
```

await directory.add(name: "Tucker")

print(await directory.names)

Libraries, Runtime, Development

On Apple systems, Swift uses the same runtime as the extant Objective-C system, but requires iOS 7 or macOS 10.9 or higher. It also depends on Grand Central Dispatch. Swift and Objective-C code can be used in one program, and by extension, C and C++ also.

Beginning in Swift 5.9, C++ code can be used directly from Swift code. In the case of Objective-C, Swift has considerable access to the object model, and can be used to subclass, extend and use Objective-C code to provide protocol support. The converse is not true: a Swift class cannot be subclassed in Objective-C.

To aid development of such programs, and the re-use of extant code, Xcode 6 and higher offers a semi-automated system that builds and maintains a bridging header to expose Objective-C code to Swift. This takes the form of an additional header file that simply defines or imports all of the Objective-C symbols that are needed by the project's Swift code. At that point, Swift can refer to the types, functions, and variables declared in those imports as though they were written in Swift. Objective-C code can also use Swift code directly, by importing an automatically maintained header file with Objective-C declarations of the project's Swift symbols. For instance, an Objective-C file in a mixed project called "MyApp" could access Swift classes or functions with the code #import "MyApp-Swift.h". Not all symbols are available through this mechanism, however—use of Swift-specific features like generic types, non-object optional types, sophisticated enums, or even Unicode identifiers may render a symbol inaccessible from Objective-C.

Swift also has limited support for attributes, metadata that is read by the development environment, and is not necessarily part of the compiled code. Like Objective-C, attributes use the @ syntax, but the currently available set is small. One example is the @IBOutlet attribute, which marks a given value in the code as an outlet, available for use within Interface Builder (IB). An outlet is a device that binds the value of the on-screen display to an object in code.

On non-Apple systems, Swift does not depend on an Objective-C runtime or other Apple system libraries; a set of Swift "Corelib" implementations replace them. These include a "swift-corelibs-foundation" to stand in for the Foundation Kit, a "swift-corelibs-libdispatch" to stand in for the Grand Central Dispatch, and an "swift-corelibs-xctest" to stand in for the XCTest APIs from Xcode.

As of 2019, with Xcode 11, Apple has also added a major new UI paradigm called SwiftUI. SwiftUI replaces the older Interface Builder paradigm with a new declarative development paradigm.

Memory Management

Swift uses Automatic Reference Counting (ARC) to manage memory. Every instance of a class or closure maintains a reference count which keeps a running tally of the number of references the program is holding for on to. When this count reaches 0 the instance is deallocated. This automatic deallocation removes the need for a garbage collector as instances are deallocated as soon as they are no longer needed.

A strong reference cycle can occur if two instances each strongly reference each other. Since neither instances reference count can ever reach zero neither is ever deallocated, resulting in a memory leak. Swift provides the keywords weak and unowned to prevent strong reference cycles. These keywords allow an instance to be referenced without incrementing its reference count. weak references must be optional variables, since they can change and become nil. Attempting to access an unowned value that has already been deallocated results in a runtime error.

A closure within a class can also create a strong reference cycle by capturing self references. Self references to be treated as weak or unowned can be indicated using a capture list.

```
class Person {
  let name: String
   weak var home: Home? // Defined as a weak reference in order to break the reference cycle. weak
references do not increment the reference count of the instance that they refer to.

  init(name: String) {
    self.name = name
  }

  deinit { print("De-initialized \(name)") }
}
class Home {
  let address: String
  var owner: Person?

  init(address: String, owner: Person?) {
    self.address = address
    self.owner = owner
```

```
    }

    deinit { print("De-initialized \(address)") }
  }
  var stacy: Person? = Person(name: "Stacy")
  var house21b: Home? = Home(address: "21b Baker Street", owner: stacy)
  stacy?.home = house21b // stacy and house42b now refer to each other.
  stacy = nil // The reference count for stacy is now 1, because house21b is still holding a reference to it.
  house21b = nil // house21b's reference count drops to 0, which in turn drops stacy's count to 0 because house21b was the last instance holding a strong reference to stacy.
  // Prints:
  // De-initialized 21b Baker Street
  // De-initialized Stacy
```

Debugging

A key element of the Swift system is its ability to be cleanly debugged and run within the development environment, using a read–eval–print loop (REPL), giving it interactive properties more in common with the scripting abilities of Python than traditional system programming languages.

The REPL is further enhanced with playgrounds, interactive views running within the Xcode environment or Playgrounds app that respond to code or debugger changes on-the-fly. Playgrounds allow programmers to add in Swift code along with markdown documentation. Programmers can step through code and add breakpoints using LLDB either in a console or an IDE like Xcode.

Comparisons to Other Languages

Swift is considered a C family programming language and is similar to C in various ways:

- Most operators in C also appear in Swift, although some operators such as + have slightly different behavior. For example, in Swift, + traps on overflow, whereas &+ is used to denote the C-like behavior of wrapping on overflow.
- Curly braces are used to group statements.
- Variables are assigned using an equals sign, but compared using two consecutive equals signs. A new identity operator, ===, is provided to check if two data elements refer to the same object.

- Control statements while, if, and switch are similar, but have extended functions, e.g., a switch that takes non-integer cases, while and if supporting pattern matching and conditionally unwrapping optionals, for uses the for i in 1...10 syntax.
- Square brackets are used with arrays, both to declare them and to get a value at a given index in one of them.

It also has similarities to Objective-C:

- Basic numeric types: Int, UInt, Float, Double
- Class methods are inherited, like instance methods; self in class methods is the class the method was called on.
- Similar for...in enumeration syntax.

Differences from Objective-C include:

- Statements need not end with semicolons (;), though these must be used to allow more than one statement on one line.
- No header files.
- Uses type inference.
- Generic programming.
- Functions are first-class objects.
- Enumeration cases can have associated data (algebraic data types).
- Operators can be redefined for classes (operator overloading), and new operators can be defined.
- Strings fully support Unicode. Most Unicode characters can be used in either identifiers or operators.
- No exception handling. Swift 2 introduces a different and incompatible error-handling model.
- Several features of earlier C-family languages that are easy to misuse have been removed:
  - Pointers are not exposed by default. There is no need for the programmer to keep track of and mark names for referencing or dereferencing.
  - Assignments return no value. This prevents the common error of writing i = 0 instead of i == 0 by throwing a compile-time error.
  - No need to use break statements in switch blocks. Individual cases do not fall through to the next case unless the fallthrough statement is used.
  - Variables and constants are always initialized and array bounds are always checked.

- Integer overflows, which result in undefined behavior for signed integers in C, are trapped as a run-time error in Swift. Programmers can choose to allow overflows by using the special arithmetical operators &+, &-, &*, &/ and &%. The properties min and max are defined in Swift for all integer types and can be used to safely check for potential overflows, versus relying on constants defined for each type in external libraries.
- The one-statement form of if and while, which allows for the omission of braces around the statement, is unsupported.
- C-style enumeration for (int i = 0; i < c; i++), which is prone to off-by-one errors, is unsupported (from Swift 3 onward).
- The pre- and post- increment and decrement operators (i++, --i ...) are unsupported (from Swift 3 onward), more so since C-style for statements are also unsupported from Swift 3 onward.

Development and Other Implementations

Because Swift can run on Linux, it is sometimes also used as a server-side language. Some web frameworks have already been developed, such as IBM's Kitura (now discontinued), Perfect and Vapor. An official "Server APIs" work group has also been started by Apple, with members of the Swift developer community playing a central role.

A second free implementation of Swift that targets Cocoa, Microsoft's Common Language Infrastructure (.NET Framework, now .NET), and the Java and Android platform exists as part of the *Elements Compiler* from RemObjects Software. Subsets of Swift have been ported to additional platforms, such as Arduino and Mac OS 9.

5.1.3 Kotlin

Kotlin is a cross-platform, statically typed, general-purpose high-level programming language with type inference. Kotlin is designed to interoperate fully with Java, and the JVM version of Kotlin's standard library depends on the Java Class Library, but type inference allows its syntax to be more concise. Kotlin mainly targets the JVM, but also compiles to JavaScript (e.g., for frontend web applications using React) or native code via LLVM (e.g., for native iOS apps sharing business logic with Android apps). Language development costs are borne by JetBrains, while the Kotlin Foundation protects the Kotlin trademark.

On 7 May 2019, Google announced that the Kotlin programming language was now its preferred language for Android app developers. Since the release of Android Studio 3.0 in October 2017, Kotlin has been included as an alternative to the standard Java compiler. The Android Kotlin compiler produces Java 8 bytecode by default (which runs in any later JVM), but lets the programmer choose to target Java 9 up to 20, for optimization, or allows for more features; has bidirectional record class interoperability support for JVM, introduced in Java 16, considered stable as of Kotlin 1.5.

Kotlin has support for the web with Kotlin/JS, either through a classic interpreter-based backend which has been declared stable since version 1.3, or an intermediate representation-based backend which has been declared stable since version 1.8. Kotlin/Native (for e.g. Apple silicon support) is considered beta since version 1.3.

History

The name is derived from Kotlin Island, a Russian island in the Gulf of Finland, near St. Petersburg. Andrey Breslav, Kotlin's former lead designer, mentioned that the team decided to name it after an island, just like the programming language Java was named after the Indonesian island of Java (though the language's name is said to have been inspired by "java" the American slang term for coffee, which itself is derived from the island name).

- In July 2011, JetBrains unveiled Project Kotlin, a new language for the JVM, which had been under development for a year. JetBrains lead Dmitry Jemerov said that most languages did not have the features they were looking for, with the exception of Scala. However, he cited the slow compilation time of Scala as a deficiency. One of the stated goals of Kotlin is to compile as quickly as Java. In February 2012, JetBrains open sourced the project under the Apache 2 license.
- JetBrains hoped that the new language would drive IntelliJ IDEA sales.
- The first commit to the Kotlin Git repository was on November 8, 2010.
- Kotlin 1.0 was released on February 15, 2016. This is considered to be the first officially stable release and JetBrains has committed to long-term backwards compatibility starting with this version.
- At Google I/O 2017, Google announced first-class support for Kotlin on Android.
- Kotlin 1.2 was released on November 28, 2017. Sharing code between JVM and JavaScript platforms feature was newly added to this release (multiplatform programming is by now a beta feature upgraded from "experimental"). A full-stack demo has been made with the new Kotlin/JS Gradle Plugin.
- Kotlin 1.3 was released on 29 October 2018, adding support for coroutines for use with asynchronous programming.
- On 7 May 2019, Google announced that the Kotlin programming language is now its preferred language for Android app developers.

- Kotlin 1.4 was released in August 2020, with e.g. some slight changes to the support for Apple's platforms, i.e. to the Objective-C/Swift interop.
- Kotlin 1.5 was released in May 2021.
- Kotlin 1.6 was released in November 2021.
- Kotlin 1.7 was released in June 2022, including the alpha version of the new Kotlin K2 compiler.
- Kotlin 1.8 was released in December 2022, 1.8.0 was released on January 11, 2023.
- Kotlin 1.9 was released in July 2023, 1.9.0 was released on July 6, 2023.
- Kotlin 2.0 was released in May 2024, 2.0.0 was released on May 21, 2024.

Design

Development lead Andrey Breslav has said that Kotlin is designed to be an industrial-strength object-oriented language, and a "better language" than Java, but still be fully interoperable with Java code, allowing companies to make a gradual migration from Java to Kotlin.

Semicolons are optional as a statement terminator; in most cases a newline is sufficient for the compiler to deduce that the statement has ended.

Kotlin variable declarations and parameter lists have the data type come after the variable name (and with a colon separator), similar to Ada, BASIC, Pascal, TypeScript and Rust. This, according to an article from Roman Elizarov, current project lead, results in alignment of variable names and is more pleasing to eyes, especially when there are a few variable declarations in succession, and one or more of the types is too complex for type inference, or needs to be declared explicitly for human readers to understand.

Variables in Kotlin can be read-only, declared with the val keyword, or mutable, declared with the var keyword.

Class members are public by default, and classes themselves are final by default, meaning that creating a derived class is disabled unless the base class is declared with the open keyword.

In addition to the classes and member functions (which are equivalent to methods) of object-oriented programming, Kotlin also supports procedural programming with the use of functions. Kotlin functions and constructors support default arguments, variable-length argument lists, named arguments, and overloading by unique signature. Class member functions are virtual, i.e. dispatched based on the runtime type of the object they are called on. Kotlin 1.3 added support for contracts, which are stable for the standard library declarations, but still experimental for user-defined declarations. Contracts are inspired by Eiffel's design by contract programming paradigm.

Kotlin code may be compiled to JavaScript, allowing for interoperability between code written in the two languages. This can be used either to write full web applications in Kotlin, or to share code between a Kotlin backend and a JavaScript frontend.

Syntax

Procedural Programming Style

Kotlin relaxes Java's restriction of allowing static methods and variables to exist only within a class body. Static objects and functions can be defined at the top level of the package without needing a redundant class level. For compatibility with Java, Kotlin provides a JvmName annotation which specifies a class name used when the package is viewed from a Java project.

Main Entry Point

As in C, C++, C#, Java, and Go, the entry point to a Kotlin program is a function named "main", which may be passed an array containing any command-line arguments. This is optional since Kotlin 1.3. Perl, PHP, and Unix shell–style string interpolation is supported. Type inference is also supported.

```
// Hello, World! example
fun main() {
  val scope = "World"
  println("Hello, $scope!")
}
fun main(args: Array<String>) {
  for (arg in args)
    println(arg)
}
```

Extension Functions

Similar to C#, Kotlin allows adding an extension function to any class without the formalities of creating a derived class with new functions. An extension function has access to all the public interface of a class, which it can use to create a new function interface to a target class. An extension function will appear exactly like a function of the class and will be shown in code completion inspection of class functions. For example:

```
package MyStringExtensions

fun String.lastChar(): Char = get(length - 1)

>>> println("Kotlin".lastChar())
```

By placing the preceding code in the top-level of a package, the String class is extended to include a lastChar function that was not included in the original definition of the String class.

```
// Overloading '+' operator using an extension function

operator fun Point.plus(other: Point): Point {
   return Point(x + other.x, y + other.y)
}

>>> val p1 = Point(10, 20)

>>> val p2 = Point(30, 40)

>>> println(p1 + p2)

Point(x=40, y=60)
```

Unpack Arguments with Spread Operator

Similar to Python, the spread operator asterisk (*) unpacks an array's contents as individual arguments to a function, e.g:

```
fun main(args: Array<String>) {
   val list = listOf("args: ", *args)
   println(list)
}
```

Destructuring Declarations

Not to be confused with the destructor method common in object-oriented languages.

Destructuring declarations decompose an object into multiple variables at once, e.g. a 2D coordinate object might be destructured into two integers, x and y.

For example, the Map.Entry object supports destructuring to simplify access to its key and value fields:

```
for ((key, value) in map)
   println("$key: $value")
```

Nested Functions

Kotlin allows local functions to be declared inside of other functions or methods.

```
class User(val id: Int, val name: String, val address: String)
```

```
fun saveUserToDb(user: User) {
  fun validate(user: User, value: String, fieldName: String) {
    require(value.isNotEmpty()) { "Can't save user ${user.id}: empty $fieldName" }
  }

  validate(user, user.name, "Name")
  validate(user, user.address, "Address")
  // Save user to the database
  ...
}
```

Classes are Final by Default

In Kotlin, to derive a new class from a base class type, the base class needs to be explicitly marked as "open". This is in contrast to most object-oriented languages such as Java where classes are open by default.

Example of a base class that is open to deriving a new subclass from it:

```
// open on the class means this class will allow derived classes
open class MegaButton {
  // no-open on a function means that
  //   polymorphic behavior disabled if function overridden in derived class
  fun disable() { ... }
  // open on a function means that
  //   polymorphic behavior allowed if function is overridden in derived class
  open fun animate() { ... }
}
class GigaButton: MegaButton() {
  // Explicit use of override keyword required to override a function in derived class
  override fun animate() { println("Giga Click!") }
}
```

Abstract Classes are Open by Default

Abstract classes define abstract or "pure virtual" placeholder functions that will be defined in a derived class. Abstract classes are open by default.

```
// No need for the open keyword here, it's already open by default
abstract class Animated {
  // This virtual function is already open by default as well
  abstract fun animate()

  open fun stopAnimating() { }
  fun animateTwice() { }
}
```

Primary Constructor vs. Secondary Constructors

Kotlin supports the specification of a "primary constructor" as part of the class definition itself, consisting of an argument list following the class name. This argument list supports an expanded syntax on Kotlin's standard function argument lists that enables declaration of class properties in the primary constructor, including visibility, extensibility, and mutability attributes. Additionally, when defining a subclass, properties in super-interfaces and super-classes can be overridden in the primary constructor.

```
// Example of class using primary constructor syntax
// (Only one constructor required for this class)
open class BaseUser(open var isSubscribed: Boolean)
open class PowerUser(protected val nickname: String, final override var isSubscribed: Boolean =
true):BaseUser(isSubscribed) { }
```

However, in cases where more than one constructor is needed for a class, a more general constructor can be defined using secondary constructor syntax, which closely resembles the constructor syntax used in most object-oriented languages like C++, C#, and Java.

```
// Example of class using secondary constructor syntax
// (more than one constructor required for this class)
class Context
class AttributeSet
open class View(ctx:Context) {
  constructor(ctx: Context, attr: AttributeSet): this(ctx)
}
class MyButton : View {
  // Constructor #1
```

```
    constructor(ctx: Context) : super(ctx) {
    }
    // Constructor #2
    constructor(ctx: Context, attr: AttributeSet) : super(ctx, attr) {
      // ...
    }
}
```

Sealed Classes

Sealed classes and interfaces restrict subclass hierarchies, meaning more control over the inheritance hierarchy.

Declaration of sealed interface and class:

```
sealed interface Expr
sealed class Job
```

All the subclasses of the sealed class are defined at compile time. No new subclasses can be added to it after the compilation of the module having the sealed class. For example, a sealed class in a compiled jar file cannot be subclassed.

```
sealed class Vehicle
data class Car(val brandName: String, val owner: String, val color: String): Vehicle()
class Bike(val brandName: String, val owner: String, val color: String): Vehicle()
class Tractor(val brandName: String, val owner: String, val color: String): Vehicle()
val kiaCar = Car("KIA", "John", "Blue")
val hyundaiCar = Car("Hyundai", "Britto", "Green")
```

Data Classes

Kotlin's data class construct defines classes whose primary purpose is storing data, similar Java's record types. This construct is similar to normal classes except that the key methods equals, hashCode and toString are automatically generated from the class properties.

In Java, classes are expected to provide implementations for certain standard methods, so that they function properly with methods and classes provided by the standard library.

Java's default implementation—which every class inherits from the base of the class hierarchy, Object—implements these methods only with regard to the identity of the object instance (usually its address in virtual memory). This is a problem, since it is extremely important to

- have information about the object's state in its String representation (toString); and
- detect whether two objects are similar (equals and hashCode). The latter two's implementations should also agree with each other, and therefore be implemented together—meaning when one is changed, the other should also be changed to match. Implementing this functionality also increases the efficiency of standard algorithms which rely on its correct behavior. Conversely, incorrect implementations can even cause errors.

Since implementing these methods manually or with external tools is cumbersome and often leads to repeated or boilerplate code, automatic generation of them as a language feature speeds up development and reduces the potential for errors.

Kotlin Interactive Shell

```
$ kotlinc-jvm
type :help for help; :quit for quit
>>> 2 + 2
4
>>> println("Hello, World!")
Hello, World!
```

Kotlin as a Scripting Language

Kotlin can also be used as a scripting language. A script is a Kotlin source file using the .kts filename extension, with executable source code at the top-level scope:

```
// list_folders.kts
import java.io.File
val folders = File(args[0]).listFiles { file -> file.isDirectory() }
folders?.forEach(::println)
```

Scripts can be run by passing the -script option and the corresponding script file to the compiler.

```
$ kotlinc -script list_folders.kts "path_to_folder_to_inspect"
```

Null Safety

Kotlin makes a distinction between nullable and non-nullable data types. All nullable objects must be declared with a "?" postfix after the type name. Operations on nullable objects need special care from developers: a null-check must be performed before using the value, either explicitly, or with the aid of Kotlin's null-safe operators:

- ?. (the safe navigation operator) can be used to safely access a method or property of a possibly null object. If the object is null, the method will not be called and the expression evaluates to null. Example:

```
// returns null if...
// - foo() returns null,
// - or if foo() is non-null, but bar() returns null,
// - or if foo() and bar() are non-null, but baz() returns null.
// vice versa, return value is non-null if and only if foo(), bar() and baz() are non-null
foo()?.bar()?.baz()
```

- ?: (the null coalescing operator) is a binary operator that returns the first operand, if non-null, else the second operand. It is often referred to as the Elvis operator, due to its resemblance to an emoticon representation of Elvis Presley.

```
fun sayHello(maybe: String?, neverNull: Int) {
   // use of Elvis operator
   val name: String = maybe ?: "stranger"
   println("Hello $name")
}
```

Lambdas

Kotlin provides support for higher-order functions and anonymous functions, or lambdas.

```
// the following function takes a lambda, f, and executes f passing it the string "lambda"
// note that (String) -> Unit indicates a lambda with a String parameter and Unit return type
fun executeLambda(f: (String) -> Unit) {
   f("lambda")
}
```

Lambdas are declared using braces, { }. If a lambda takes parameters, they are declared within the braces and followed by the -> operator.

```
// the following statement defines a lambda that takes a single parameter and passes it to the println function
val l = { c : Any? -> println(c) }
// lambdas with no parameters may simply be defined using { }
val l2 = { print("no parameters") }
```

Tools

- Android Studio (based on IntelliJ IDEA) has official support for Kotlin, starting from Android Studio 3.
- Integration with common Java build tools is supported, including Apache Maven, Apache Ant, and Gradle.
- Emacs has a Kotlin Mode in its MELPA package repository.
- JetBrains also provides a plugin for Eclipse.
- IntelliJ IDEA has plug-in support for Kotlin. IntelliJ IDEA 15 was the first version to bundle the Kotlin plugin in the IntelliJ Installer, and to provide Kotlin support out of the box.
- **Gradle:** Kotlin has seamless integration with Gradle, which is a popular build automation tool. Gradle allows you to build, automate, and manage the lifecycle of your Kotlin projects efficiently

Applications

When Kotlin was announced as an official Android development language at Google I/O in May 2017, it became the third language fully supported for Android, after Java and C++. As of 2020, Kotlin is the most widely used language on Android, with Google estimating that 70% of the top 1,000 apps on the Play Store are written in Kotlin. Google itself has 60 apps written in Kotlin, including Maps and Drive. Many Android apps, such as Google Home, are in the process of being migrated to Kotlin, and therefore use both Kotlin and Java. Kotlin on Android is seen as beneficial for its null-pointer safety, as well as for its features that make for shorter, more readable code.

In addition to its prominent use on Android, Kotlin is gaining traction in server-side development. The Spring Framework officially added Kotlin support with version 5, on 4 January 2017. To further support Kotlin, Spring has translated all its documentation to Kotlin, and added built-in support for many Kotlin-specific features such as coroutines. In addition to Spring, JetBrains has produced a Kotlin-first framework called Ktor for building web applications.

In 2020, JetBrains found in a survey of developers who use Kotlin that 56% were using Kotlin for mobile apps, while 47% were using it for a web back-end. Just over a third of all Kotlin developers said that they were migrating to Kotlin from another language. Most Kotlin users were targeting Android (or otherwise on the JVM), with only 6% using Kotlin Native.

Adoption

In 2018, Kotlin was the fastest growing language on GitHub, with 2.6 times more developers compared to 2017. It is the fourth most loved programming language according to the 2020 Stack Overflow Developer Survey.

Kotlin was also awarded the O'Reilly Open Source Software Conference Breakout Award for 2019. Many companies / organizations have used Kotlin for backend development:

- Allegro
- Amazon
- Atlassian
- Cash App
- Flux
- Google
- Gradle
- JetBrains
- Meshcloud
- Norwegian Tax Administration
- OLX
- Pivotal
- Rocket Travel
- Shazam
- Zalando

Some companies / organizations have used Kotlin for web development:

- Barclay's Bank
- Data2viz
- Fritz2
- JetBrains

A number of companies have publicly stated they were using Kotlin:

- Basecamp
- Corda, a distributed ledger developed by a consortium of well-known banks (such as Goldman Sachs, Wells Fargo, J.P. Morgan, Deutsche Bank, UBS, HSBC, BNP Paribas, and Société Générale), has over 90% Kotlin code in its codebase.
- Coursera

- DripStat
- Duolingo
- Netflix
- Pinterest
- Trello
- Uber

5.1.4 Objective-C

Objective-C is a high-level general-purpose, object-oriented programming language that adds Smalltalk-style messaging to the C programming language. Originally developed by Brad Cox and Tom Love in the early 1980s, it was selected by NeXT for its NeXTSTEP operating system. Due to Apple macOS's direct lineage from NeXTSTEP, Objective-C was the standard programming language used, supported, and promoted by Apple for developing macOS and iOS applications (via their respective APIs, Cocoa and Cocoa Touch) until the introduction of the Swift programming language in 2014.

Objective-C programs developed for non-Apple operating systems or that are not dependent on Apple's APIs may also be compiled for any platform supported by GNU GCC or LLVM/Clang.

Objective-C source code 'messaging/implementation' program files usually have .m filename extensions, while Objective-C 'header/interface' files have .h extensions, the same as C header files. Objective-C++ files are denoted with a .mm file extension.

History

Objective-C was created primarily by Brad Cox and Tom Love in the early 1980s at their company Productivity Products International (PPI). Leading up to the creation of their company, both had been introduced to Smalltalk while at ITT Corporation's Programming Technology Center in 1981. The earliest work on Objective-C traces back to around that time. Cox was intrigued by problems of true reusability in software design and programming. He realized that a language like Smalltalk would be invaluable in building development environments for system developers at ITT. However, he and Tom Love also recognized that backward compatibility with C was critically important in ITT's telecom engineering milieu.

Cox began writing a pre-processor for C to add some of the abilities of Smalltalk. He soon had a working implementation of an object-oriented extension to the C language, which he called "OOPC" for Object-Oriented Pre-Compiler. Love was hired by Schlumberger Research in 1982 and had the opportunity to acquire the first commercial copy of Smalltalk-80, which further influenced the development of their brainchild. In order to demonstrate that real progress could be made, Cox showed that making interchangeable software components really needed only a few practical changes to existing tools. Specifically, they needed to support objects in a flexible manner, come supplied with a usable set of libraries, and allow for the code (and any resources needed by the code) to be bundled into one cross-platform format.

Love and Cox eventually formed PPI to commercialize their product, which coupled an Objective-C compiler with class libraries. In 1986, Cox published the main description of Objective-C in its original form in the book *Object-Oriented Programming, An Evolutionary Approach.* Although he was careful to point out that there is more to the problem of reusability than just what Objective-C provides, the language often found itself compared feature for feature with other languages.

Popularization through NeXT

In 1988, NeXT licensed Objective-C from StepStone (the new name of PPI, the owner of the Objective-C trademark) and extended the GCC compiler to support Objective-C. NeXT developed the AppKit and Foundation Kit libraries on which the NeXTSTEP user interface and Interface Builder were based. While the NeXT workstations failed to make a great impact in the marketplace, the tools were widely lauded in the industry. NeXT dropped hardware production and focused on software tools, selling NeXTSTEP (and OPENSTEP) as a platform for custom programming.

In order to circumvent the terms of the GPL, NeXT had originally intended to ship the Objective-C frontend separately, allowing the user to link it with GCC to produce the compiler executable. Though initially accepted by Richard M. Stallman, this plan was rejected after Stallman consulted with GNU's lawyers and NeXT agreed to make Objective-C part of GCC.

The work to extend GCC was led by Steve Naroff, who joined NeXT from StepStone. The compiler changes were made available as per GPL license terms, but the runtime libraries were not, rendering the open source contribution unusable to the general public.

This led to other parties developing such runtime libraries under open source licenses. Later, Steve Naroff was also principal contributor to work at Apple to build the Objective-C frontend to Clang.

The GNU project started work on its free software implementation of Cocoa, named GNUstep, based on the OpenStep standard. Dennis Glatting wrote the first GNU Objective-C runtime in 1992. The GNU Objective-C runtime, which has been in use since 1993, is the one developed by Kresten Krab Thorup when he was a university student in Denmark. Thorup also worked at NeXT from 1993 to 1996.

Apple Development and Swift

After acquiring NeXT in 1996, Apple Computer used OpenStep in its then-new operating system, Mac OS X. This included Objective-C, NeXT's Objective-C-based developer tool, Project Builder, and its interface design tool, Interface Builder. Both were later merged into one application, Xcode. Most of Apple's current Cocoa API is based on OpenStep interface objects and is the most significant Objective-C environment being used for active development. At WWDC 2014, Apple introduced a new language, Swift, which was characterized as "Objective-C without the C".

Syntax

Objective-C is a thin layer atop C and is a "strict superset" of C, meaning that it is possible to compile any C program with an Objective-C compiler and to freely include C language code within an Objective-C class.

Objective-C derives its object syntax from Smalltalk. All of the syntax for non-object-oriented operations (including primitive variables, pre-processing, expressions, function declarations, and function calls) are identical to those of C, while the syntax for object-oriented features is an implementation of Smalltalk-style messaging.

Messages

The Objective-C model of object-oriented programming is based on message passing to object instances. In Objective-C one does not *call a method*; one *sends a message.* This is unlike the Simula-style programming model used by C++. The difference between these two concepts is in how the code referenced by the method or message name is executed. In a Simula-style language, the method name is in most cases bound to a section of code in the target class by the compiler. In Smalltalk and Objective-C, the target of a message is resolved at runtime, with the receiving object itself interpreting the message.

A method is identified by a *selector* or SEL — a unique identifier for each message name, often just a NUL-terminated string representing its name — and resolved to a C method pointer implementing it: an IMP. A consequence of this is that the message-passing system has no type checking. The object to which the message is directed — the *receiver* — is not guaranteed to respond to a message, and if it does not, it raises an exception.

Sending the message method to the object pointed to by the pointer obj would require the following code in C++:

```
obj->method(argument);
```

In Objective-C, this is written as follows:

```
[obj method:argument];
```

The "method" call is translated by the compiler to the objc_msgSend(id self, SEL op, ...) family of runtime functions. Different implementations handle modern additions like super. In GNU families this function is named objc_msg_sendv, but it has been deprecated in favor of a modern lookup system under objc_msg_lookup.

Both styles of programming have multiple strengths and weaknesses. Object-oriented programming in the Simula (C++) style allows multiple inheritance and faster execution by using compile-time binding whenever possible, but it does not support dynamic binding by default. It also forces all methods to have a corresponding implementation unless they are abstract. The Smalltalk-style programming as used in Objective-C allows messages to go unimplemented, with the method resolved to its implementation at runtime. For example, a message may be sent to a collection of objects, to which only some will be expected to respond, without fear of producing runtime errors. Message passing also does not require that an object be defined at compile time. An implementation is still required for the method to be called in the derived object.

Interfaces and Implementations

Objective-C requires that the interface and implementation of a class be in separately declared code blocks. By convention, developers place the interface in a header file and the implementation in a code file. The header files, normally suffixed .h, are similar to C header files while the implementation (method) files, normally suffixed .m, can be very similar to C code files.

This is analogous to class declarations as used in other object-oriented languages, such as C++ or Python.

The interface of a class is usually defined in a header file. A common convention is to name the header file after the name of the class, e.g. Ball.h would contain the interface for the class Ball.

An interface declaration takes the form:

```
@interface classname : superclassname {
  // instance variables
}
+ classMethod1;
+ (return_type)classMethod2;
+ (return_type)classMethod3:(param1_type)param1_varName;

- (return_type)instanceMethod1With1Parameter:(param1_type)param1_varName;
- (return_type)instanceMethod2With2Parameters:(param1_type)param1_varName
```

```
        param2_callName:(param2_type)param2_varName;
@end
```

In the above, plus signs denote class methods, or methods that can be called on the class itself (not on an instance), and minus signs denote instance methods, which can only be called on a particular instance of the class. Class methods also have no access to instance variables.

The code above is roughly equivalent to the following C++ interface:

```
class classname : public superclassname {
protected:
  // instance variables
public:
  // Class (static) functions
  static void *classMethod1();
  static return_type classMethod2();
  static return_type classMethod3(param1_type param1_varName);
  // Instance (member) functions
  return_type instanceMethod1With1Parameter(param1_type param1_varName);
  return_type
  instanceMethod2With2Parameters(param1_type param1_varName,
                   param2_type param2_varName = default);
};
```

Note that instanceMethod2With2Parameters:param2_callName: demonstrates the interleaving of selector segments with argument expressions, for which there is no direct equivalent in C/C++.

Return types can be any standard C type, a pointer to a generic Objective-C object, a pointer to a specific type of object such as NSArray *, NSImage *, or NSString *, or a pointer to the class to which the method belongs (instancetype). The default return type is the generic Objective-C type id.

Method arguments begin with a name labeling the argument that is part of the method name, followed by a colon followed by the expected argument type in parentheses and the argument name. The label can be omitted.

```
- (void)setRangeStart:(int)start end:(int)end;
- (void)importDocumentWithName:(NSString *)name
```

```
withSpecifiedPreferences:(Preferences *)prefs
        beforePage:(int)insertPage;
```

A derivative of the interface definition is the category, which allows one to add methods to existing classes.

The interface only declares the class interface and not the methods themselves: the actual code is written in the implementation file. Implementation (method) files normally have the file extension .m, which originally signified "messages".

```
@implementation classname
+ (return_type)classMethod {
 // implementation
}
- (return_type)instanceMethod {
 // implementation
}
@end
```

Methods are written using their interface declarations. Comparing Objective-C and C:

```
- (int)method:(int)i {
 return [self square_root:i];
}
int function(int i) {
 return square_root(i);
}
```

The syntax allows pseudo-naming of arguments.

```
- (void)changeColorToRed:(float)red green:(float)green blue:(float)blue {
 //... Implementation ...
}

// Called like so:
[myColor changeColorToRed:5.0 green:2.0 blue:6.0];
```

Internal representations of a method vary between different implementations of Objective-C. If myColor is of the class Color, instance method -changeColorToRed:green:blue: might be internally labeled _i_Color_ changeColorToRed_green_blue. The i is to refer to an instance method, with the class and then method names appended and colons changed to underscores. As the order of parameters is part of the method name, it cannot be changed to suit coding style or expression as with true named parameters.

However, internal names of the function are rarely used directly. Generally, messages are converted to function calls defined in the Objective-C runtime library. It is not necessarily known at link time which method will be called because the class of the receiver (the object being sent the message) need not be known until runtime.

Once an Objective-C class is written, it can be instantiated. This is done by first allocating an uninitialized instance of the class (an object) and then by initializing it. An object is not fully functional until both steps have been completed. These steps should be accomplished with one line of code so that there is never an allocated object that hasn't undergone initialization (and because it is unwise to keep the intermediate result since -init can return a different object than that on which it is called).

Instantiation with the default, no-parameter initializer:

```
MyObject *foo = [[MyObject alloc] init];
```

Instantiation with a custom initializer:

```
MyObject *foo = [[MyObject alloc] initWithString:myString];
```

In the case where no custom initialization is being performed, the "new" method can often be used in place of the alloc-init messages:

```
MyObject *foo = [MyObject new];
```

Also, some classes implement class method initializers. Like +new, they combine +alloc and -init, but unlike +new, they return an autoreleased instance.

The *alloc* message allocates enough memory to hold all the instance variables for an object, sets all the instance variables to zero values, and turns the memory into an instance of the class; at no point during the initialization is the memory an instance of the superclass.

The *init* message performs the set-up of the instance upon creation. The *init* method is often written as follows:

```
- (id)init {
    self = [super init];
    if (self) {
        // perform initialization of object here
```

```
    }
    return self;
}
```

In the above example, notice the `id` return type. This type stands for "pointer to any object" in Objective-C. The initializer pattern is used to assure that the object is properly initialized by its superclass before the init method performs its initialization. It performs the following actions:

- Line 2: Sends the superclass instance an *init* message and assigns the result to *self* (pointer to the current object).
- Line 3: Checks if the returned object pointer is valid before performing any initialization.
- Line 6: Returns the value of self to the caller.

A non-valid object pointer has the value nil; conditional statements like "if" treat nil like a null pointer, so the initialization code will not be executed if [super init] returned nil. If there is an error in initialization the init method should perform any necessary cleanup, including sending a "release" message to self, and return nil to indicate that initialization failed. Any checking for such errors must only be performed after having called the superclass initialization to ensure that destroying the object will be done correctly.

If a class has more than one initialization method, only one of them (the "designated initializer") needs to follow this pattern; others should call the designated initializer instead of the superclass initializer.

Protocols

In other programming languages, these are called "interfaces". Objective-C was extended at NeXT to introduce the concept of multiple inheritance of specification, but not implementation, through the introduction of protocols. This is a pattern achievable either as an abstract multiple inherited base class in C++, or as an "interface" (as in Java and C#). Objective-C makes use of ad hoc protocols called *informal protocols* and compiler-enforced protocols called *formal protocols.*

An informal protocol is a list of methods that a class can opt to implement. It is specified in the documentation, since it has no presence in the language. Informal protocols are implemented as a category on NSObject and often include optional methods, which, if implemented, can change the behavior of a class. For example, a text field class might have a delegate that implements an informal protocol with an optional method for performing auto-completion of user-typed text. The text field discovers whether the delegate implements that method (via reflection) and, if so, calls the delegate's method to support the auto-complete feature.

A formal protocol is similar to an interface in Java, C#, and Ada 2005. It is a list of methods that any class can declare itself to implement. Versions of Objective-C before 2.0 required that a class must implement all methods in a protocol it declares itself as adopting; the compiler will emit an error if the class does not implement every method from its declared protocols. Objective-C 2.0 added support for marking certain methods in a protocol optional, and the compiler will not enforce implementation of optional methods.

A class must be declared to implement that protocol to be said to conform to it. This is detectable at runtime. Formal protocols cannot provide any implementations; they simply assure callers that classes that conform to the protocol will provide implementations. In the NeXT/Apple library, protocols are frequently used by the Distributed Objects system to represent the abilities of an object executing on a remote system.

The syntax

```
@protocol NSLocking
- (void)lock;
- (void)unlock;
@end
```

Denotes that there is the abstract idea of locking. By stating in the class definition that the protocol is implemented,

```
@interface NSLock : NSObject <NSLocking>
// ...
@end
```

instances of NSLock claim that they will provide an implementation for the two instance methods.

Dynamic Typing

Objective-C, like Smalltalk, can use dynamic typing: an object can be sent a message that is not specified in its interface. This can allow for increased flexibility, as it allows an object to "capture" a message and send the message to a different object that can respond to the message appropriately, or likewise send the message on to another object. This behavior is known as *message forwarding* or *delegation*. Alternatively, an error handler can be used in case the message cannot be forwarded. If an object does not forward a message, respond to it, or handle an error, then the system will generate a runtime exception. If messages are sent to *nil* (the null object pointer), they will be silently ignored or raise a generic exception, depending on compiler options.

Static typing information may also optionally be added to variables. This information is then checked at compile time. In the following four statements, increasingly specific type information is provided. The statements are equivalent at runtime, but the extra information allows the compiler to warn the programmer if the passed argument does not match the type specified.

```
- (void)setMyValue:(id)foo;
```

In the above statement, *foo* may be of any class.

```
- (void)setMyValue:(id<NSCopying>)foo;
```

In the above statement, foo may be an instance of any class that conforms to the NSCopying protocol.

```
- (void)setMyValue:(NSNumber *)foo;
```

In the above statement, *foo* must be an instance of the *NSNumber* class.

```
- (void)setMyValue:(NSNumber<NSCopying> *)foo;
```

In the above statement, foo must be an instance of the NSNumber class, and it must conform to the NSCopying protocol.

In Objective-C, all objects are represented as pointers, and static initialization is not allowed. The simplest object is the type that id (objc_obj *) points to, which only has an isa pointer describing its class. Other types from C, like values and structs, are unchanged because they are not part of the object system. This decision differs from the C++ object model, where structs and classes are united.

Forwarding

Objective-C permits the sending of a message to an object that may not respond. Rather than responding or simply dropping the message, an object can forward the message to an object that can respond. Forwarding can be used to simplify implementation of certain design patterns, such as the observer pattern or the proxy pattern.

The Objective-C runtime specifies a pair of methods in Object

- **Forwarding Methods:**
  - (retval_t)forward:(SEL)sel args:(arglist_t)args; // with GCC
  - (id)forward:(SEL)sel args:(marg_list)args; // with NeXT/Apple systems
- **Action Methods:**
  - (retval_t)performv:(SEL)sel args:(arglist_t)args; // with GCC
  - (id)performv:(SEL)sel args:(marg_list)args; // with NeXT/Apple systems

An object wishing to implement forwarding needs only to override the forwarding method with a new method to define the forwarding behavior. The action method performv:: need not be overridden, as this method merely performs an action based on the selector and arguments. Notice the SEL type, which is the type of messages in Objective-C.

Note:inOpenStep,Cocoa,andGNUstep,thecommonlyusedframeworksofObjective-C, one does not use the Object class. The - (void)forwardInvocation:(NSInvocation *) anInvocation method of the NSObject class is used to do forwarding.

Categories

During the design of Objective-C, one of the main concerns was the maintainability of large code bases. Experience from the structured programming world had shown that one of the main ways to improve code was to break it down into smaller pieces. Objective-C borrowed and extended the concept of *categories* from Smalltalk implementations to help with this process.

Furthermore, the methods within a category are added to a class at run-time. Thus, categories permit the programmer to add methods to an existing class - an open class - without the need to recompile that class or even have access to its source code. For example, if a system does not contain a spell checker in its String implementation, it could be added without modifying the String source code.

Methods within categories become indistinguishable from the methods in a class when the program is run. A category has full access to all of the instance variables within the class, including private variables.

If a category declares a method with the same method signature as an existing method in a class, the category's method is adopted. Thus categories can not only add methods to a class, but also replace existing methods. This feature can be used to fix bugs in other classes by rewriting their methods, or to cause a global change to a class's behavior within a program. If two categories have methods with the same name but different method signatures, it is undefined which category's method is adopted.

Other languages have attempted to add this feature in a variety of ways. TOM took the Objective-C system a step further and allowed for the addition of variables also. Other languages have used prototype-based solutions instead, the most notable being Self.

The C# and Visual Basic.NET languages implement superficially similar functionality in the form of extension methods, but these lack access to the private variables of the class. Ruby and several other dynamic programming languages refer to the technique as "monkey patching". Logtalk implements a concept of categories (as first-class entities) that subsumes Objective-C categories functionality (Logtalk categories can also be used as fine-grained units of composition when defining e.g. new classes or prototypes; in particular, a Logtalk category can be virtually imported by any number of classes and prototypes).

Posing

Objective-C permits a class to wholly replace another class within a program. The replacing class is said to "pose as" the target class.

Class posing was declared deprecated with Mac OS X v10.5, and is unavailable in the 64-bit runtime. Similar functionality can be achieved by using method swizzling in categories, that swaps one method's implementation with another's that have the same signature. For the versions still supporting posing, all messages sent to the target class are instead received by the posing class. There are several restrictions:

- A class may only pose as one of its direct or indirect superclasses.
- The posing class must not define any new instance variables that are absent from the target class (though it may define or override methods).
- The target class may not have received any messages prior to the posing.

Posing, similarly with categories, allows global augmentation of existing classes. Posing permits two features absent from categories:

- A posing class can call overridden methods through super, thus incorporating the implementation of the target class.
- A posing class can override methods defined in categories.

For example,

```
@interface CustomNSApplication : NSApplication

@end

@implementation CustomNSApplication

- (void) setMainMenu: (NSMenu*) menu {

 // do something with menu

}

@end

class_poseAs ([CustomNSApplication class], [NSApplication class]);
```

This intercepts every invocation of setMainMenu to NSApplication.

#import

In the C language, the #include pre-compile directive always causes a file's contents to be inserted into the source at that point. Objective-C has the #import directive, equivalent except that each file is included only once per compilation unit, obviating the need for include guards.

Linux gcc Compilation

```
// FILE: hello.m
```

```
#import <Foundation/Foundation.h>
int main (int argc, const char * argv[])
{
   /* my first program in Objective-C */
   NSLog(@"Hello, World! \n");
   return 0;
}
$ # Compile Command Line for gcc and MinGW Compiler:
$ gcc \
   $(gnustep-config --objc-flags) \
   -o hello \
   hello.m \
   -L /GNUstep/System/Library/Libraries \
   -lobjc \
   -lgnustep-base
$ ./hello
```

Other Features

Objective-C's features often allow for flexible, and often easy, solutions to programming issues.

- Delegating methods to other objects and remote invocation can be easily implemented using categories and message forwarding.
- Swizzling of the *isa* pointer allows for classes to change at runtime. Typically used for debugging where freed objects are swizzled into zombie objects whose only purpose is to report an error when someone calls them. Swizzling was also used in Enterprise Objects Framework to create database faults. Swizzling is used today by Apple's Foundation Framework to implement Key-Value Observing.

Language Variants

Objective-C++

Objective-C++ is a language variant accepted by the front-end to the GNU Compiler Collection and Clang, which can compile source files that use a combination of C++ and Objective-C syntax. Objective-C++ adds to C++ the extensions that Objective-C adds to C. As nothing is done to unify the semantics behind the various language features, certain restrictions apply:

- A C++ class cannot derive from an Objective-C class and vice versa.
- C++ namespaces cannot be declared inside an Objective-C declaration.
- Objective-C declarations may appear only in global scope, not inside a C++ namespace
- Objective-C classes cannot have instance variables of C++ classes that lack a default constructor or that have one or more virtual methods, but pointers to C++ objects can be used as instance variables without restriction (allocate them with new in the -init method).
- C++ "by value" semantics cannot be applied to Objective-C objects, which are only accessible through pointers.
- An Objective-C declaration cannot be within a C++ template declaration and vice versa. However, Objective-C types (e.g., `Classname *`) can be used as C++ template parameters.
- Objective-C and C++ exception handling is distinct; the handlers of each cannot handle exceptions of the other type. As a result, object destructors are not run. This is mitigated in recent "Objective-C 2.0" runtimes as Objective-C exceptions are either replaced by C++ exceptions completely (Apple runtime), or partly when Objective-C++ library is linked (GNUstep libobjc2).
- Objective-C blocks and C++11 lambdas are distinct entities. However, a block is transparently generated on macOS when passing a lambda where a block is expected.

Objective-C 2.0

At the 2006 Worldwide Developers Conference, Apple announced the release of "Objective-C 2.0," a revision of the Objective-C language to include "modern garbage collection, syntax enhancements, runtime performance improvements, and 64-bit support". Mac OS X v10.5, released in October 2007, included an Objective-C 2.0 compiler. GCC 4.6 supports many new Objective-C features, such as declared and synthesized properties, dot syntax, fast enumeration, optional protocol methods, method/protocol/class attributes, class extensions, and a new GNU Objective-C runtime API.

The naming Objective-C 2.0 represents a break in the versioning system of the language, as the last Objective-C version for NeXT was "objc4". This project name was kept in the last release of legacy Objective-C runtime source code in Mac OS X Leopard (10.5).

Objective-C 2.0 provided an optional conservative, generational garbage collector. When run in backwards-compatible mode, the runtime turned reference counting operations such as "retain" and "release" into no-ops. All objects were subject to garbage collection when garbage collection was enabled. Regular C pointers could be qualified with "__strong" to also trigger the underlying write-barrier compiler intercepts and thus participate in garbage collection. A zero-ing weak subsystem was also provided such that pointers marked as "__weak" are set to zero when the object (or more simply, GC memory) is collected. The garbage collector does not exist on the iOS implementation of Objective-C 2.0. Garbage collection in Objective-C runs on a low-priority background thread, and can halt on user events, with the intention of keeping the user experience responsive.

Garbage collection was deprecated in Mac OS X v10.8 in favor of Automatic Reference Counting (ARC). Objective-C on iOS 7 running on ARM64 uses 19 bits out of a 64-bit word to store the reference count, as a form of tagged pointers.

Objective-C 2.0 introduces a new syntax to declare instance variables as properties, with optional attributes to configure the generation of accessor methods. Properties are, in a sense, public instance variables; that is, declaring an instance variable as a property provides external classes with access (possibly limited, e.g. read only) to that property. A property may be declared as "readonly", and may be provided with storage semantics such as assign, copy or retain. By default, properties are considered atomic, which results in a lock preventing multiple threads from accessing them at the same time. A property can be declared as nonatomic, which removes this lock.

```
@interface Person : NSObject {
@public
  NSString *name;
@private
  int age;
}
@property(copy) NSString *name;
@property(readonly) int age;
- (id)initWithAge:(int)age;
@end
```

Properties are implemented by way of the @synthesize keyword, which generates getter (and setter, if not read-only) methods according to the property declaration. Alternatively, the getter and setter methods must be implemented explicitly, or the @dynamic keyword can be used to indicate that accessor methods will be provided by other means. When compiled using clang 3.1 or higher, all properties which are not explicitly declared with @dynamic, marked readonly or have complete user-implemented getter and setter will be automatically implicitly @synthesize'd.

```
@implementation Person
@synthesize name;
- (id)initWithAge:(int)initAge {
 self = [super init];
 if (self) {
  // NOTE: direct instance variable assignment, not property setter
  age = initAge;
 }
 return self;
}
- (int)age {
 return age;
}
@end
```

Properties can be accessed using the traditional message passing syntax, dot notation, or, in Key-Value Coding, by name via the "valueForKey:"/"setValue:forKey:" methods.

```
Person *aPerson = [[Person alloc] initWithAge:53];
aPerson.name = @"Steve"; // NOTE: dot notation, uses synthesized setter,
                // equivalent to [aPerson setName: @"Steve"];
NSLog(@"Access by message (%@), dot notation(%@), property name(% @) and "
    "direct instance variable access(% @) ",
        [aPerson name],
    aPerson.name, [aPerson valueForKey:@"name"], aPerson -> name);
```

In order to use dot notation to invoke property accessors within an instance method, the "self" keyword should be used:

```
- (void)introduceMyselfWithProperties:(BOOL)useGetter {
 NSLog(@"Hi, my name is %@.", (useGetter ? self.name : name));
 // NOTE: getter vs. ivar access
}
```

A class or protocol's properties may be dynamically introspected.

```
int i;
int propertyCount = 0;
objc_property_t *propertyList =
   class_copyPropertyList([aPerson class], &propertyCount);
for (i = 0; i < propertyCount; i++) {
  objc_property_t *thisProperty = propertyList + i;
  const char *propertyName = property_getName(*thisProperty);
  NSLog(@"Person has a property: '%s'", propertyName);
}
```

Objective-C 2.0 provides non-fragile instance variables where supported by the runtime (i.e. when building code for 64-bit macOS, and all iOS). Under the modern runtime, an extra layer of indirection is added to instance variable access, allowing the dynamic linker to adjust instance layout at runtime. This feature allows for two important improvements to Objective-C code:

- It eliminates the fragile binary interface problem; superclasses can change sizes without affecting binary compatibility.
- It allows instance variables that provide the backing for properties to be synthesized at runtime without them being declared in the class's interface.

Instead of using an NSEnumerator object or indices to iterate through a collection, Objective-C 2.0 offers the fast enumeration syntax. In Objective-C 2.0, the following loops are functionally equivalent, but have different performance traits.

```
// Using NSEnumerator
NSEnumerator *enumerator = [thePeople objectEnumerator];
Person *p;
while ((p = [enumerator nextObject]) != nil) {
  NSLog(@"%@ is %i years old.", [p name], [p age]);
}
// Using indexes
for (int i = 0; i < [thePeople count]; i++) {
  Person *p = [thePeople objectAtIndex:i];
  NSLog(@"%@ is %i years old.", [p name], [p age]);
```

```
}
// Using fast enumeration
for (Person *p in thePeople) {
  NSLog(@"%@ is %i years old.", [p name], [p age]);
}
```

Fast enumeration generates more efficient code than standard enumeration because method calls to enumerate over objects are replaced by pointer arithmetic using the NSFastEnumeration protocol.

A class extension has the same syntax as a category declaration with no category name, and the methods and properties declared in it are added directly to the main class. It is mostly used as an alternative to a category to add methods to a class without advertising them in the public headers, with the advantage that for class extensions the compiler checks that all the privately declared methods are actually implemented.

All Objective-C applications developed for macOS that make use of the above improvements for Objective-C 2.0 are incompatible with all operating systems prior to 10.5 (Leopard). Since fast enumeration does not generate exactly the same binaries as standard enumeration, its use will cause an application to crash on Mac OS X version 10.4 or earlier.

Blocks

Blocks is a nonstandard extension for Objective-C (and C and C++) that uses special syntax to create closures. Blocks are only supported in Mac OS X 10.6 "Snow Leopard" or later, iOS 4 or later, and GNUstep with libobjc2 1.7 and compiling with clang 3.1 or later.

```
#include <stdio.h>
#include <Block.h>
typedef int (^IntBlock)();
IntBlock MakeCounter(int start, int increment) {
  __block int i = start;
  return Block_copy( ^ {
    int ret = i;
    i += increment;
    return ret;
  });
```

```
}
int main(void) {
 IntBlock mycounter = MakeCounter(5, 2);
 printf("First call: %d\n", mycounter());
 printf("Second call: %d\n", mycounter());
 printf("Third call: %d\n", mycounter());
 /* because it was copied, it must also be released */
 Block_release(mycounter);
 return 0;
}
/* Output:
 First call: 5
 Second call: 7
 Third call: 9
*/
```

Modern Objective-C

Apple has added some additional features to Objective 2.0 over time. The additions only apply to the "Apple LLVM compiler", i.e. clang frontend of the language. Confusingly, the versioning used by Apple differs from that of the LLVM upstream; refer to Xcode § Toolchain versions for a translation to open-source LLVM version numbers.

Automatic Reference Counting (ARC) is a compile-time feature that eliminates the need for programmers to manually manage retain counts using retain and release.

Unlike garbage collection, which occurs at run time, ARC eliminates the overhead of a separate process managing retain counts. ARC and manual memory management are not mutually exclusive; programmers can continue to use non-ARC code in ARC-enabled projects by disabling ARC for individual code files. Xcode can also attempt to automatically upgrade a project to ARC. ARC was introduced in LLVM 3.0. This translates to Xcode 4.2 (2011), or Apple LLVM compiler 3.0.

NeXT and Apple Obj-C runtimes have long included a short-form way to create new strings, using the literal syntax @"a new string", or drop to CoreFoundation constants kCFBooleanTrue and kCFBooleanFalse for NSNumber with Boolean values. Using this format saves the programmer from having to use the longer initWithString or similar methods when doing certain operations.

When using Apple LLVM compiler 4.0 (Xcode 4.4) or later, arrays, dictionaries, and numbers (NSArray, NSDictionary, NSNumber classes) can also be created using literal syntax instead of methods. (Apple LLVM compiler 4.0 translates to open source LLVM and Clang 3.1.)

Example without literals:

```
NSArray *myArray = [NSArray arrayWithObjects:object1,object2,object3,nil];
NSDictionary *myDictionary1 = [NSDictionary dictionaryWithObject:someObject forKey:@"key"];
NSDictionary *myDictionary2 = [NSDictionary dictionaryWithObjectsAndKeys:object1, key1, object2, key2, nil];
NSNumber *myNumber = [NSNumber numberWithInt:myInt];
NSNumber *mySumNumber= [NSNumber numberWithInt:(2 + 3)];
NSNumber *myBoolNumber = [NSNumber numberWithBool:YES];
```

Example with literals:

```
NSArray *myArray = @[ object1, object2, object3 ];
NSDictionary *myDictionary1 = @{ @"key" : someObject };
NSDictionary *myDictionary2 = @{ key1: object1, key2: object2 };
NSNumber *myNumber = @(myInt);
NSNumber *mySumNumber = @(2+3);
NSNumber *myBoolNumber = @YES;
NSNumber *myIntegerNumber = @8;
```

However, different from string literals, which compile to constants in the executable, these literals compile to code equivalent to the above method calls. In particular, under manually reference-counted memory management, these objects are autoreleased, which requires added care when e.g., used with function-static variables or other kinds of globals.

When using Apple LLVM compiler 4.0 or later, arrays and dictionaries (NSArray and NSDictionary classes) can be manipulated using subscripting. Subscripting can be used to retrieve values from indexes (array) or keys (dictionary), and with mutable objects, can also be used to set objects to indexes or keys. In code, subscripting is represented using brackets [ ].

Example without subscripting:

```
id object1 = [someArray objectAtIndex:0];
id object2 = [someDictionary objectForKey:@"key"];
[someMutableArray replaceObjectAtIndex:0 withObject:object3];
```

```
[someMutableDictionary setObject:object4 forKey:@"key"];
```

Example with subscripting:

```
id object1 = someArray[0];
id object2 = someDictionary[@"key"];
someMutableArray[0] = object3;
someMutableDictionary[@"key"] = object4;
```

"Modern" Objective-C syntax (1997)

After the purchase of NeXT by Apple, attempts were made to make the language more acceptable to programmers more familiar with Java than Smalltalk. One of these attempts was introducing what was dubbed "Modern Syntax" for Objective-C at the time (as opposed to the current, "classic" syntax). There was no change in behaviour, this was merely an alternative syntax. Instead of writing a method invocation like

```
object = [[MyClass alloc] init];
[object firstLabel: param1 secondLabel: param2];
```

It was instead written as

```
object = (MyClass.alloc).init;
object.labels ( param1, param2 );
```

Similarly, declarations went from the form

```
-(void) firstLabel: (int)param1 secondLabel: (int)param2;
```

to

```
-(void) labels ( int param1, int param2 );
```

This "modern" syntax is no longer supported in current dialects of the Objective-C language.

Mulle-Objc

The mulle-objc project is another re-implementation of Objective-C. It supports GCC or Clang/LLVM compilers as backends. It diverges from other runtimes in terms of syntax, semantics and ABI compatibility. It supports Linux, FreeBSD, and Windows.

Portable Object Compiler

Besides the GCC/NeXT/Apple implementation, which added several extensions to the original Stepstone implementation, another free, open-source Objective-C implementation called the Portable Object Compiler also exists. The set of extensions implemented by the Portable Object Compiler differs from the GCC/

NeXT/Apple implementation; in particular, it includes Smalltalk-like blocks for Objective-C, while it lacks protocols and categories, two features used extensively in OpenStep and its derivatives and relatives. Overall, POC represents an older, pre-NeXT stage in the language's evolution, roughly conformant to Brad Cox's 1991 book. It also includes a runtime library called ObjectPak, which is based on Cox's original ICPak101 library (which in turn derives from the Smalltalk-80 class library), and is quite radically different from the OpenStep FoundationKit.

GEOS Objective-C

The PC GEOS system used a programming language known as GEOS Objective-C or goc; despite the name similarity, the two languages are similar only in overall concept and the use of keywords prefixed with an @ sign.

Clang

The Clang compiler suite, part of the LLVM project, implements Objective-C and other languages. After GCC 4.3 (2008) switched to GPLv3, Apple abandoned it in favor of clang, a compiler it has more legal power to modify. As a result, many of the modern Objective-C language features are supported only by Clang. Apple's versioning scheme for its clang-based "LLVM compiler" differs from the LLVM's open-source versioning.

GNU, GNUstep, and WinObjC

The GNU project has, for a long time, been interested in a platform to port NeXT and Obj-C programs to. The ChangeLog for the libobjc directory in GCC suggests that it existed before 1998 (GCC 2.95), and its README further points at a rewrite in 1993 (GCC 2.4).

The NeXT frontend source code was released since it was made as part of GCC, released GNU General Public License which forces ones making derivative works to do so. Apple continued this tradition in releasing its fork of GCC up to 4.2.1, after which they abandoned the compiler. GCC maintainers took in the changes, but did not invest much in supporting newer features such as the Objective-C 2.0 language.

The GNUstep developers, interested in the new language, forked the GCC libobjc to a project independent of GCC called libobjc2 in 2009. They also arranged for the runtime to be used with Clang to take advantage of the new language syntax. GCC moved slowly at the same time, but at GCC 4.6.0 (2011) they have moved on to Objective-C 2.0 in their libobjc as well. GNUstep documentation suggest that the GCC implementation still lacks support for blocks, non-fragile variables, and the newer ARC.

Microsoft forked libobjc2 into a part of WinObjC, the iOS bridge for Universal Windows Platform, in 2015. Combined with its own implementation of Cocoa Touch and underlying APIs, the project allows the reuse of iOS Application code inside of UWP apps.

On Windows, Objective-C Development tools are provided for download on GNUStep's website. The GNUStep Development System consists of the following packages: GNUstep MSYS System, GNUstep Core, GNUstep Devel, GNUstep Cairo, ProjectCenter IDE (Like Xcode, but not as complex), Gorm (Interface Builder Like Xcode NIB builder). These binary installers have not been updated since 2016, so it could be a better idea to just install by building under Cygwin or MSYS2 instead.

Library Use

Objective-C today is often used in tandem with a fixed library of standard objects (often known as a "kit" or "framework"), such as Cocoa, GNUstep or ObjFW. These libraries often come with the operating system: the GNUstep libraries often come with Linux-based distributions and Cocoa comes with macOS. The programmer is not forced to inherit functionality from the existing base class (NSObject / OFObject). Objective-C allows for the declaration of new root classes that do not inherit any existing functionality. Originally, Objective-C-based programming environments typically offered an Object class as the base class from which almost all other classes inherited. With the introduction of OpenStep, NeXT created a new base class named NSObject, which offered additional features over Object (an emphasis on using object references and reference counting instead of raw pointers, for example). Almost all classes in Cocoa inherit from NSObject.

Not only did the renaming serve to differentiate the new default behavior of classes within the OpenStep API, but it allowed code that used Object—the original base class used on NeXTSTEP (and, more or less, other Objective-C class libraries)—to co-exist in the same runtime with code that used NSObject (with some limitations). The introduction of the two letter prefix also became a simplistic form of namespaces, which Objective-C lacks. Using a prefix to create an informal packaging identifier became an informal coding standard in the Objective-C community, and continues to this day.

More recently, package managers have started appearing, such as CocoaPods, which aims to be both a package manager and a repository of packages. A lot of open-source Objective-C code that was written in the last few years can now be installed using CocoaPods.

Analysis of the Language

Objective-C implementations use a thin runtime system written in C, which adds little to the size of the application. In contrast, most object-oriented systems at the time that it was created used large virtual machine runtimes. Programs written in Objective-C tend to be not much larger than the size of their code and that of the libraries (which generally do not need to be included in the software distribution), in contrast to Smalltalk systems where a large amount of memory was used just to open a window. Objective-C applications tend to be larger than similar C or C++ applications because Objective-C dynamic typing does not allow methods to be stripped or inlined. Since the programmer has such freedom to delegate, forward calls, build selectors on the fly, and pass them to the runtime system, the Objective-C compiler cannot assume it is safe to remove unused methods or to inline calls.

Likewise, the language can be implemented atop extant C compilers (in GCC, first as a preprocessor, then as a module) rather than as a new compiler. This allows Objective-C to leverage the huge existing collection of C code, libraries, tools, etc. Existing C libraries can be wrapped in Objective-C wrappers to provide an OO-style interface. In this aspect, it is similar to GObject library and Vala language, which are widely used in development of GTK applications.

All of these practical changes lowered the barrier to entry, likely the biggest problem for the widespread acceptance of Smalltalk in the 1980s.

A common criticism is that Objective-C does not have language support for namespaces. Instead, programmers are forced to add prefixes to their class names, which are traditionally shorter than namespace names and thus more prone to collisions. As of 2007, all macOS classes and functions in the Cocoa programming environment are prefixed with "NS" (e.g. NSObject, NSButton) to identify them as belonging to the macOS or iOS core; the "NS" derives from the names of the classes as defined during the development of NeXTSTEP.

Since Objective-C is a strict superset of C, it does not treat C primitive types as first-class objects.

Unlike C++, Objective-C does not support operator overloading. Also unlike C++, Objective-C allows an object to directly inherit only from one class (forbidding multiple inheritance). However, in most cases, categories and protocols may be used as alternative ways to achieve the same results.

Because Objective-C uses dynamic runtime typing and because all method calls are function calls (or, in some cases, syscalls), many common performance optimizations cannot be applied to Objective-C methods (for example: inlining, constant propagation, interprocedural optimizations, and scalar replacement of aggregates). This limits the performance of Objective-C abstractions relative to similar abstractions in languages such as C++ where such optimizations are possible.

Memory Management

The first versions of Objective-C did not support garbage collection. At the time this decision was a matter of some debate, and many people considered long "dead times" (when Smalltalk performed collection) to render the entire system unusable. Some 3rd party implementations have added this feature (most notably GNUstep using Boehm), and Apple has implemented it as of Mac OS X v10.5. However, in more recent versions of macOS and iOS, garbage collection has been deprecated in favor of Automatic Reference Counting (ARC), introduced in 2011.

With ARC, the compiler inserts retain and release calls automatically into Objective-C code based on static code analysis. The automation relieves the programmer of having to write in memory management code. ARC also adds weak references to the Objective-C language.

Philosophical Differences between Objective-C and C++

The design and implementation of C++ and Objective-C represent fundamentally different approaches to extending C. In addition to C's style of procedural programming, C++ directly supports certain forms of object-oriented programming, generic programming, and metaprogramming. C++ also comes with a large standard library that includes several container classes.

Similarly, Objective-C adds object-oriented programming, dynamic typing, and reflection to C. Objective-C does not provide a standard library *per se*, but in most places where Objective-C is used, it is used with an OpenStep-like library such as OPENSTEP, Cocoa, or GNUstep, which provides functionality similar to C++'s standard library.

One notable difference is that Objective-C provides runtime support for reflective features, whereas C++ adds only a small amount of runtime support to C. In Objective-C, an object can be queried about its own properties, e.g., whether it will respond to a certain message. In C++, this is not possible without the use of external libraries.

The use of reflection is part of the wider distinction between dynamic (run-time) features and static (compile-time) features of a language. Although Objective-C and C++ each employ a mix of both features, Objective-C is decidedly geared toward run-time decisions while C++ is geared toward compile-time decisions. The tension between dynamic and static programming involves many of the classic trade-offs in programming: dynamic features add flexibility, static features add speed and type checking.

Generic programming and metaprogramming can be implemented in both languages using runtime polymorphism. In C++ this takes the form of virtual functions and runtime type identification, while Objective-C offers dynamic typing and reflection.

Both Objective-C and C++ support compile-time polymorphism (generic functions), with Objective-C only adding this feature in 2015.

5.1.5 JavaScript

JavaScript often abbreviated as JS, is a programming language and core technology of the Web, alongside HTML and CSS. 99% of websites use JavaScript on the client side for webpage behavior. Web browsers have a dedicated JavaScript engine that executes the client code. These engines are also utilized in some servers and a variety of apps. The most popular runtime system for non-browser usage is Node.js. JavaScript is a high-level, often just-in-time compiled language that conforms to the ECMAScript standard. It has dynamic typing, prototype-based object-orientation, and first-class functions. It is multi-paradigm, supporting event-driven, functional, and imperative programming styles. It has application programming interfaces (APIs) for working with text, dates, regular expressions, standard data structures, and the Document Object Model (DOM).

The ECMAScript standard does not include any input/output (I/O), such as networking, storage, or graphics facilities. In practice, the web browser or other runtime system provides JavaScript APIs for I/O. Although Java and JavaScript are similar in name, syntax, and respective standard libraries, the two languages are distinct and differ greatly in design.

5.1.6 TypeScript

TypeScript is a free and open-source high-level programming language developed by Microsoft that adds static typing with optional type annotations to JavaScript. It is designed for the development of large applications and transpiles to JavaScript. Because TypeScript is a superset of JavaScript, all JavaScript programs are syntactically valid TypeScript, but they can fail to type-check for safety reasons.

TypeScript may be used to develop JavaScript applications for both client-side and server-side execution (as with Node.js, Deno or Bun). Multiple options are available for transpilation. The default TypeScript Compiler can be used, or the Babel compiler can be invoked to convert TypeScript to JavaScript.

TypeScript supports definition files that can contain type information of existing JavaScript libraries, much like C++ header files can describe the structure of existing object files. This enables other programs to use the values defined in the files as if they were statically typed TypeScript entities. There are third-party header files for popular libraries such as jQuery, MongoDB, and D3.js. TypeScript headers for the Node.js library modules are also available, allowing development of Node.js programs within TypeScript.

The TypeScript compiler is itself written in TypeScript and compiled to JavaScript. It is licensed under the Apache License 2.0. Anders Hejlsberg, lead architect of C# and creator of Delphi and Turbo Pascal, has worked on the development of TypeScript.

5.1.7 Dart

Dart is a programming language designed by Lars Bak and Kasper Lund and developed by Google. It can be used to develop web and mobile apps as well as server and desktop applications. Dart is an object-oriented, class-based, garbage-collected language with C-style syntax. It can compile to machine code, JavaScript, or WebAssembly. It supports interfaces, mixins, abstract classes, reified generics and type inference.

5.1.8 C#

C# is a general-purpose high-level programming language supporting multiple paradigms. C# encompasses static typing, strong typing, lexically scoped, imperative, declarative, functional, generic, object-oriented (class-based), and component-oriented programming disciplines.

The C# programming language was designed by Anders Hejlsberg from Microsoft in 2000 and was later approved as an international standard by Ecma (ECMA-334) in 2002 and ISO/IEC (ISO/IEC 23270 and 20619) in 2003. Microsoft introduced C# along with .NET Framework and Visual Studio, both of which were closed-source. At the time, Microsoft had no open-source products. Four years later, in 2004, a free and open-source project called Mono began, providing a cross-platform compiler and runtime environment for the C# programming language. A decade later, Microsoft released Visual Studio Code (code editor), Roslyn (compiler), and the unified .NET platform (software framework), all of which support C# and are free, open-source, and cross-platform. Mono also joined Microsoft but was not merged into .NET. As of November 2023, the most recent stable version of the language is C# 12.0, which was released in 2023 in .NET 8.0.

5.2 CROSS-PLATFORM DEVELOPMENT WITH REACT NATIVE AND FLUTTER

Cross-platform development has become a popular approach in mobile app development, enabling developers to build applications for multiple operating systems from a single codebase. Two of the most prominent frameworks facilitating this are React Native and Flutter.

Cross-platform development with React Native and Flutter offers significant benefits, including reduced development time, cost-efficiency, and the ability to reach a broader audience. React Native, with its JavaScript and React foundation, provides a flexible and well-supported environment for rapid development. Flutter, with its Dart language and innovative widget-based architecture, delivers high performance and consistent UIs.

Choosing the right framework depends on various factors, including team expertise, project requirements, performance needs, and long-term maintenance considerations. Both frameworks continue to evolve, driven by strong community support and ongoing enhancements from their respective developers, ensuring they remain viable choices for cross-platform mobile app development in the years to come.

5.2.1 Introduction to Cross-Platform Development

Cross-platform development allows developers to write code once and deploy it across multiple platforms, primarily iOS and Android. This approach offers significant benefits, including reduced development time, lower costs, and easier maintenance compared to developing separate native applications for each platform.

5.2.2 React Native: Overview and Features

React Native, developed by Facebook, is a widely used framework for building cross-platform mobile applications using JavaScript and React.

- **History and Evolution:** React Native was introduced by Facebook in 2015 to address the need for efficient mobile app development across different platforms. It leverages the popular React library for building user interfaces.
- **Key Features:**
  - *JavaScript and React:* Utilizes JavaScript, one of the most widely used programming languages, and React, a popular library for building user interfaces.
  - *Native Components:* Bridges JavaScript and native code, allowing the use of native components and delivering near-native performance.
  - *Hot Reloading:* Enables developers to see changes in real-time without restarting the entire application, enhancing development efficiency.
  - *Extensive Libraries and Tools:* A vast ecosystem of libraries and tools supports a wide range of functionalities, from UI components to state management.

5.2.3 Advantages of React Native

React Native offers several benefits that make it a popular choice for cross-platform development:

- **Code Reusability:** Write once, run anywhere. A single codebase can be used for both iOS and Android, significantly reducing development time and effort.
- **Community Support:** A large and active community provides extensive resources, plugins, and third-party libraries, facilitating rapid development.

- **Performance:** While not entirely native, React Native delivers near-native performance through the use of native components and optimized code execution.
- **Flexibility:** React Native's architecture allows integration with native code, enabling developers to leverage platform-specific functionalities when necessary.

5.2.4 Challenges with React Native

Despite its advantages, React Native also has some challenges:

- **Performance Overheads:** For very complex and resource-intensive applications, React Native might not match the performance of fully native apps.
- **Learning Curve:** Developers need to be proficient in JavaScript and React, and may also need to understand native development for advanced features.
- **Fragmentation:** With continuous updates and changes, keeping up with the latest React Native versions and maintaining compatibility can be challenging.

5.2.5 Flutter: Overview and Features

Flutter, developed by Google, is another leading framework for building cross-platform mobile applications, using the Dart programming language.

- **History and Evolution:** Flutter was introduced by Google in 2017. It has quickly gained popularity due to its innovative approach to cross-platform development.
- **Key Features:**
  - *Dart Programming Language:* Uses Dart, a language designed for fast and efficient mobile app development with a focus on front-end development.
  - *Widgets:* Provides a rich set of customizable widgets that form the building blocks of the app's UI, ensuring a consistent look and feel across platforms.
  - *Hot Reload:* Similar to React Native, Flutter offers hot reload, enabling developers to see changes instantly.
  - *Native Performance:* Compiles to native ARM code for both iOS and Android, delivering high performance and smooth animations.

5.2.6 Advantages of Flutter

Flutter has several strengths that make it an attractive option for cross-platform development:

- **Single Codebase:** Like React Native, Flutter allows developers to write one codebase for both iOS and Android, reducing development time and cost.
- **High Performance:** Flutter's architecture and compilation to native code provide excellent performance and fluid animations.
- **Consistent UI:** The widget-based approach ensures a consistent and customizable user interface across different devices and screen sizes.
- **Strong Community and Support:** Backed by Google and supported by a growing community, Flutter offers robust resources, plugins, and third-party libraries.

5.2.7 Challenges with Flutter

Flutter also faces certain challenges:

- **Learning Curve:** Dart is not as widely known as JavaScript, so developers may need to invest time in learning a new language.
- **App Size:** Flutter apps can have larger file sizes compared to native apps due to the inclusion of the Flutter engine and widgets.
- **Ecosystem Maturity:** While rapidly growing, Flutter's ecosystem is not as mature as React Native's, potentially limiting available libraries and integrations.

5.2.8 Comparing React Native and Flutter

When deciding between React Native and Flutter, several factors should be considered:

- **Language:** React Native uses JavaScript, a widely known language, whereas Flutter uses Dart, which may require additional learning.
- **Performance:** Both frameworks offer good performance, but Flutter's native compilation can provide an edge in performance-critical applications.
- **UI Customization:** Flutter's widget-based approach offers extensive customization and consistency, while React Native relies on native components.
- **Community and Ecosystem:** React Native has a more mature ecosystem with a vast array of libraries and tools, while Flutter's ecosystem is rapidly growing but still catching up.

5.2.9 Use Cases for React Native and Flutter

Both frameworks are suitable for various applications, but certain scenarios may favor one over the other:

- **React Native:**
  - *Existing Web Apps:* If you have a web application built with React, React Native allows for code reuse and familiarity.
  - *Rapid Development:* Extensive libraries and community support make it ideal for projects requiring quick turnaround times.
  - Integration with Native Code: Projects needing frequent native code integration might benefit from React Native's flexibility.
- **Flutter:**
  - *High Performance and Complex UIs:* If your application requires high performance and complex, custom UIs, Flutter's capabilities shine.
  - *Consistent Design:* For applications needing a uniform look across platforms, Flutter's widget approach ensures consistency.
  - *Google Ecosystem Integration:* If your project involves integrating with Google's ecosystem, Flutter offers strong support and alignment.

CHAPTER 6

USER INTERFACE (UI) AND USER EXPERIENCE (UX) IN MOBILE APPS

6.1 PRINCIPLES OF MOBILE UI/UX DESIGN

Mobile UI/UX design is crucial for creating intuitive, engaging, and effective mobile applications. The principles of UI (User Interface) and UX (User Experience) design guide the process of making apps that not only look good but also function seamlessly and provide an enjoyable user experience.

Mobile UI/UX design is a dynamic and user-centric discipline that requires a deep understanding of user behavior, preferences, and context. By adhering to principles such as user-centered design, simplicity, consistency, accessibility, and performance optimization, designers can create mobile apps that are not only functional and efficient but also delightful and engaging for users. The goal is to strike a balance between aesthetics and usability, ensuring that the app meets user needs while providing an enjoyable experience. Through continuous iteration and user feedback, designers can refine their apps to achieve excellence in mobile UI/UX design.

6.1.1 User-Centered Design

User-centered design is a foundational principle of UI/UX. It focuses on the needs, preferences, and limitations of the end-users at every stage of the design process.

- **User Research:** Conducting thorough user research helps in understanding the target audience. This includes demographic data, user behaviors, pain points, and preferences.
- **Personas and User Stories:** Creating personas and user stories ensures that the design caters to the specific needs and scenarios of different user types.
- **Usability Testing:** Regular testing with real users helps in identifying usability issues and gathering feedback to refine the design.

6.1.2 Simplicity and Clarity

Simplicity and clarity are critical for ensuring that users can navigate the app effortlessly and accomplish their goals without confusion.

- **Minimalist Design:** Use a minimalist approach to reduce clutter. Include only essential elements on each screen.
- **Clear Navigation:** Ensure that navigation is straightforward and intuitive. Use familiar icons and labels to guide users.
- **Visual Hierarchy:** Employ visual hierarchy to prioritize content. Use size, color, and spacing to draw attention to important elements.

6.1.3 Consistency

Consistency in design creates a sense of familiarity and predictability, making it easier for users to interact with the app.

- **Uniform Elements:** Use consistent design elements such as buttons, fonts, and colors across the app.
- **Design Guidelines:** Adhere to platform-specific design guidelines (e.g., Apple's Human Interface Guidelines, Google's Material Design) to maintain consistency and familiarity.
- **Reusable Components:** Develop reusable UI components to ensure uniformity and streamline the design process.

6.1.4 Accessibility

Designing for accessibility ensures that the app is usable by everyone, including people with disabilities.

- **Inclusive Design:** Consider the needs of users with visual, auditory, motor, and cognitive impairments.
- **Contrast and Readability:** Use high-contrast color schemes and readable fonts to make text easily readable for users with visual impairments.
- **Keyboard and Voice Navigation:** Ensure that the app can be navigated using a keyboard or voice commands for users with motor impairments.
- **Alt Text:** Provide alternative text for images and icons to support screen readers.

6.1.5 Feedback and Responsiveness

Providing feedback and ensuring responsiveness are vital for enhancing user interaction and preventing frustration.

- **Immediate Feedback:** Offer immediate feedback for user actions, such as button presses, form submissions, and loading indicators.
- **Error Messages:** Display clear and constructive error messages that help users understand and correct their mistakes.
- **Responsive Design:** Ensure that the app performs well across different

devices and screen sizes. Responsive design adapts the layout and content to fit various resolutions.

6.1.6 Performance Optimization

Optimizing performance is essential for delivering a smooth and responsive user experience.

- **Fast Loading Times:** Minimize loading times by optimizing images, leveraging caching, and reducing unnecessary elements.
- **Smooth Transitions:** Ensure that animations and transitions are smooth and do not hinder performance.
- **Efficient Code:** Write efficient and clean code to enhance the app's performance and reduce the risk of crashes.

6.1.7 Touch-Friendly Interfaces

Designing touch-friendly interfaces ensures that the app is easy to use on touchscreens.

- **Touchable Targets:** Make interactive elements large enough to be easily tappable. The recommended minimum size for touch targets is around 44x44 pixels.
- **Gestures:** Utilize intuitive gestures (e.g., swipe, pinch, tap) for navigation and interaction. Ensure that these gestures are consistent and predictable.
- **Spacing:** Provide adequate spacing between touchable elements to prevent accidental taps.

6.1.8 Visual Design and Aesthetics

The visual design and aesthetics of an app significantly influence the user's first impression and overall experience.

- **Brand Identity:** Incorporate the brand's identity through colors, typography, and imagery to create a cohesive and recognizable design.
- **Consistent Theme:** Maintain a consistent visual theme throughout the app to ensure a harmonious and professional look.
- **Aesthetic Appeal:** Use aesthetically pleasing elements and layouts that attract and retain users. Balance aesthetics with functionality to ensure that beauty does not compromise usability.

6.1.9 Content Prioritization

Prioritizing content ensures that the most important information is readily accessible to users.

- **Primary and Secondary Actions:** Highlight primary actions (e.g., submit, save) and de-emphasize secondary actions (e.g., cancel) to guide user behavior.
- **Progressive Disclosure:** Use progressive disclosure to show only relevant information initially, revealing more details as needed.
- **Readability:** Ensure that content is easy to read and understand. Use short paragraphs, bullet points, and subheadings to break up text.

6.1.10 Contextual Design

Contextual design takes into account the context in which the app will be used, ensuring relevance and convenience for the user.

- **Location-Based Services:** Utilize location-based services to provide contextually relevant information and features (e.g., maps, local recommendations).
- **Personalization:** Personalize the user experience based on user preferences and behavior. Tailor content and features to individual users.
- **Situational Awareness:** Consider the situational context, such as whether the user is in a hurry or has ample time to interact with the app. Design accordingly to cater to different use cases.

6.1.11 Iterative Design Process

An iterative design process involves continuous refinement based on user feedback and testing.

- **Prototyping:** Develop prototypes to test design ideas and gather user feedback early in the process.
- **User Testing:** Conduct regular usability tests to identify issues and areas for improvement. Use A/B testing to compare different design approaches.
- **Feedback Loops:** Establish feedback loops to incorporate user feedback into design revisions, ensuring that the app evolves to meet user needs.

6.2 RESPONSIVE DESIGN AND ADAPTIVE LAYOUTS

In the realm of mobile app development, creating interfaces that provide a seamless user experience across a variety of devices is paramount. This necessity has led to the adoption of responsive design and adaptive layouts, two approaches that ensure mobile apps look and function well on different screen sizes and orientations. Responsive design and adaptive layouts are essential strategies in mobile app development, ensuring that apps deliver a seamless user experience across various devices. Responsive design focuses on creating flexible layouts that adapt fluidly to different screen sizes, while adaptive layouts involve creating distinct layouts for specific device categories. By understanding and implementing these approaches, designers and developers can create mobile apps that are both functional and visually appealing, providing users with an optimal experience regardless of their device. Combining these techniques with best practices such as a mobile-first approach, strategic use of breakpoints, and thorough testing can lead to successful, user-friendly mobile applications.

6.2.1 Introduction to Responsive Design

Responsive design is an approach that aims to make a single app layout adaptable to multiple screen sizes and orientations. It involves the use of flexible grids, images, and CSS media queries to ensure the app's content adjusts smoothly across various devices.

- **Fluid Grids:** Fluid grids use relative units like percentages rather than fixed units like pixels. This allows the layout to resize proportionally to the screen size.
- **Flexible Images:** Images are made responsive by setting their maximum width to 100%, ensuring they scale with their containing elements.
- **Media Queries:** CSS media queries apply different styles based on device characteristics such as screen width, height, and orientation. They enable the creation of breakpoints where the app's layout can change to provide a better user experience.

6.2.2 Principles of Responsive Design

The core principles of responsive design ensure that the app maintains usability and aesthetics regardless of the device it's viewed on.

- **Consistency:** Provide a consistent experience across different devices. While the layout may adjust, the core functionality and aesthetic should remain uniform.
- **Flexibility:** Design with flexibility in mind. Use flexible grids, images, and text that can adapt to various screen sizes without breaking the layout.
- **User-Centric Approach:** Focus on the user's needs and context. Ensure that content is accessible and usable whether the user is on a smartphone, tablet, or desktop.

6.2.3 Techniques for Implementing Responsive Design

Implementing responsive design in mobile apps involves several techniques to ensure smooth adaptability across devices.

- **Viewport Meta Tag:** For web-based mobile apps, the viewport meta tag controls the layout on mobile browsers. Setting the viewport to match the device's width ensures proper scaling.
- **Breakpoints:** Define breakpoints where the layout changes to accommodate different screen sizes. Common breakpoints include small (phones), medium (tablets), and large (desktops).
- **CSS Flexbox and Grid:** Use CSS Flexbox and Grid for creating flexible layouts that adapt to different screen sizes. These tools provide powerful ways to control the placement and sizing of elements.
- **Scalable Vector Graphics (SVG):** Use SVGs for icons and images. SVGs are resolution-independent, ensuring they look sharp on all devices without additional scaling.

6.2.4 Introduction to Adaptive Layouts

Adaptive layouts, unlike responsive design, involve creating multiple fixed layouts tailored to specific screen sizes.

The app detects the device's screen size and loads the appropriate layout.

- **Predefined Layouts:** Develop distinct layouts for different device categories, such as smartphones, tablets, and desktops.
- **Device Detection:** Use device detection techniques to serve the appropriate layout. This can be done through user agent strings or device capabilities.
- **Separate Stylesheets:** Maintain separate CSS stylesheets for each layout. This approach allows for precise control over each layout but increases the complexity of managing multiple stylesheets.

6.2.5 Principles of Adaptive Layouts

Adaptive layouts focus on optimizing the app's design for specific devices rather than scaling a single layout across all devices.

- **Specificity:** Design layouts that cater specifically to the capabilities and limitations of each device category. This ensures optimal performance and user experience.
- **Efficiency:** Load only the necessary resources for each device. This reduces loading times and improves performance.
- **Customization:** Tailor the user experience to each device. For example, a tablet layout might include additional features or a different navigation structure compared to a smartphone layout.

6.2.6 Techniques for Implementing Adaptive Layouts

Implementing adaptive layouts requires a strategic approach to design and development, ensuring each layout is optimized for its target devices.

- **User Agent Detection:** Use server-side or client-side scripts to detect the user agent and load the corresponding layout.
- **Conditional Loading:** Load different CSS and JavaScript files based on the detected device type. This can be managed through conditional statements in the code.
- **Component-Based Design:** Design components that can be reused across different layouts, ensuring consistency and reducing redundancy.

6.2.7 Comparing Responsive Design and Adaptive Layouts

While both responsive design and adaptive layouts aim to enhance the user experience across devices, they have distinct differences.

- **Flexibility vs. Specificity:** Responsive design offers greater flexibility, adapting a single layout to various screens. Adaptive layouts provide specificity, with distinct designs for each device type.
- **Development Complexity:** Responsive design can be simpler to manage as it involves a single layout with flexible elements. Adaptive layouts can become complex due to the need to maintain multiple fixed layouts.
- **Performance:** Adaptive layouts can offer better performance by loading only the necessary resources for each device. Responsive design might involve loading additional resources to accommodate different screen sizes.

6.2.8 Best Practices for Mobile UI/UX Design

Combining responsive design and adaptive layouts can create a robust user experience. Here are some best practices to consider:

- **Start with a Mobile-First Approach:** Design for the smallest screen size first and then scale up. This ensures that the essential features are prioritized and work well on mobile devices.
- **Use Breakpoints Strategically:** Define breakpoints based on the app's content and functionality rather than arbitrary screen sizes. This ensures a more logical and user-friendly layout.
- **Optimize Images and Media:** Use responsive images and media queries to load appropriately sized images for each device, reducing load times and improving performance.

- **Test on Real Devices:** Emulate different devices and screen sizes during development, but also test on real devices to ensure the app works well in actual usage scenarios.
- **Embrace Progressive Enhancement:** Start with a basic level of functionality and add enhancements for devices that can support them. This ensures that the app remains accessible to a wide audience.

6.2.9 Case Studies and Examples

Analyzing successful implementations of responsive design and adaptive layouts can provide valuable insights.

- **Twitter:** Twitter uses responsive design to provide a consistent user experience across different devices. The layout adjusts fluidly to fit the screen size while maintaining core functionality and aesthetic.
- **Airbnb:** Airbnb employs adaptive layouts, serving different layouts for mobile and desktop users. This ensures that the user experience is optimized for the specific device in use, enhancing usability and engagement.
- **BBC News:** The BBC News website combines responsive and adaptive techniques. It uses responsive design for most content but adapts specific elements like the navigation bar to suit different devices.

PART III

MOBILE APP DESIGN PATTERNS

CHAPTER 7

NAVIGATION PATTERNS IN MOBILE APPS

7.1 TAB BARS, NAVIGATION DRAWERS, AND BOTTOM NAVIGATION

7.1.1 Tab Bars

Navigation is a crucial aspect of mobile app design, directly impacting the usability and overall user experience. Among various navigation patterns, tab bars are one of the most popular and effective methods for organizing and accessing different sections of an app. Tab bars are a vital navigation pattern in mobile app design, offering a simple, consistent, and accessible way for users to switch between different sections of an app. By adhering to principles of simplicity, consistency, and accessibility, and by implementing best practices and advanced features, designers can create effective tab bars that enhance the overall user experience. Continuous testing and iteration ensure that the tab bar design remains user-centric and adaptable to evolving user needs and preferences. Whether used in social media, e-commerce, or productivity apps, well-designed tab bars contribute significantly to an app's usability and success.

Introduction to Tab Bars

Tab bars provide a navigation structure that allows users to quickly switch between different sections of an app. Typically located at the bottom of the screen, tab bars consist of multiple tabs, each representing a distinct section or functionality.

- **Visual Structure:** Tab bars are usually horizontal bars containing icons and text labels. They are often fixed at the bottom of the screen for easy access.
- **Usage Context:** Ideal for apps with 3-5 primary sections that users need to access frequently. Examples include social media apps, e-commerce platforms, and productivity tools.

Principles of Effective Tab Bar Design

Designing an effective tab bar involves adhering to several key principles to ensure it enhances the user experience.

- **Simplicity:** Keep the tab bar simple and uncluttered. Limit the number of tabs to 3-5 to avoid overwhelming the user.
- **Consistency:** Use consistent icons and labels that clearly represent the content or functionality of each tab.
- **Accessibility:** Ensure that the tab bar is accessible and easy to interact with, regardless of the device size or user's dexterity.

Design Considerations for Tab Bars

When designing tab bars, consider the following aspects to create an intuitive and user-friendly navigation experience.

- **Iconography:** Choose icons that are easily recognizable and convey the purpose of each tab. Use standard icons where possible to leverage user familiarity.
- **Labels:** Accompany icons with text labels to provide additional clarity. The labels should be concise and descriptive.
- **Visual Feedback:** Provide visual feedback to indicate the active tab. This can be achieved through color changes, highlights, or underlines.
- **Hierarchy and Order:** Arrange tabs in a logical order based on their importance and frequency of use. The most frequently used tabs should be placed in easy-to-reach positions, typically towards the center.

Best Practices for Implementing Tab Bars

Adopting best practices in tab bar design ensures that the navigation is both effective and user-friendly.

- **Responsive Design:** Ensure that the tab bar adjusts seamlessly to different screen sizes and orientations. This includes making touch targets large enough for easy tapping.
- **Visibility:** Keep the tab bar visible and fixed at the bottom of the screen to provide consistent access to navigation options.
- **State Management:** Maintain the state of each tab so that users can easily return to their previous position within a tab.
- **Animations:** Use subtle animations to provide feedback when switching tabs, enhancing the user experience without causing distraction.

Use Cases and Examples of Tab Bars

Tab bars are widely used across various types of apps due to their simplicity and effectiveness in organizing content.

- **Social Media Apps:** Apps like Instagram and Twitter use tab bars to provide quick access to core sections such as the home feed, search, notifications, and user profile.

- **E-Commerce Apps:** Platforms like Amazon and eBay utilize tab bars to navigate between home, categories, cart, and account settings.
- **Productivity Apps:** Applications like Trello and Asana employ tab bars to switch between boards, tasks, notifications, and user settings.

Advanced Tab Bar Features

Enhancing the basic functionality of tab bars with advanced features can further improve the user experience.

- **Badge Notifications:** Display badges on tabs to indicate new messages, notifications, or updates, prompting users to check specific sections.
- **Customizable Tabs:** Allow users to customize the order and visibility of tabs based on their preferences and usage patterns.
- **Contextual Actions:** Integrate contextual actions within tabs, such as long-press menus, to provide quick access to secondary functions without cluttering the main interface.

Comparing Tab Bars with Other Navigation Patterns

Understanding the strengths and weaknesses of tab bars compared to other navigation patterns can help in choosing the right method for a given app.

- **Tab Bars vs. Navigation Drawers:** Navigation drawers (or side menus) can handle more items but are less visible and require additional taps to access. Tab bars, being always visible, offer quicker access to core sections.
- **Tab Bars vs. Bottom Navigation Bars:** Bottom navigation bars are similar to tab bars but often have more flexibility in design and can include floating action buttons for key actions.
- **Tab Bars vs. Top Tabs:** Top tabs can be useful in certain contexts but might be less ergonomic, especially on larger screens where reaching the top of the screen is less convenient.

Testing and Iteration

Iterative testing and refinement are crucial for creating an effective tab bar design.

- **User Testing:** Conduct usability tests with real users to gather feedback on the tab bar's intuitiveness, ease of use, and effectiveness.
- **A/B Testing:** Experiment with different icon sets, label placements, and tab arrangements to determine the most user-friendly design.

- **Analytics:** Use analytics to track user interactions with the tab bar, identifying which tabs are most frequently used and where users might be encountering difficulties.

7.1.2 Navigation Drawers

Navigation drawers, also known as side menus or slide-out menus, are a popular navigation pattern in mobile app design. They provide an effective way to organize and access various sections of an app without overwhelming the main interface.

Navigation drawers are a vital navigation pattern in mobile app design, offering a clean and organized way for users to access different sections of an app. By adhering to principles of accessibility, simplicity, and consistency, and by implementing best practices and advanced features, designers can create effective navigation drawers that enhance the overall user experience. Continuous testing and iteration ensure that the navigation drawer design remains user-centric and adaptable to evolving user needs and preferences. Whether used in news apps, e-commerce platforms, or utility applications, well-designed navigation drawers contribute significantly to an app's usability and success.

Introduction to Navigation Drawers

Navigation drawers are hidden menus that slide out from the side of the screen, typically the left side, when triggered by a swipe gesture or a tap on a menu icon. They allow users to access different sections of an app while keeping the main interface clean and uncluttered.

- **Visual Structure:** Navigation drawers are usually hidden by default and slide in from the side of the screen. They contain a list of menu items, each representing a different section or functionality of the app.
- **Usage Context:** Ideal for apps with multiple sections or features that users need to access but don't require constant visibility. Examples include news apps, e-commerce platforms, and utility apps.

Principles of Effective Navigation Drawer Design

Designing an effective navigation drawer involves following key principles to ensure it enhances the user experience.

- **Accessibility:** Ensure that the navigation drawer is easily accessible through intuitive gestures or icons. The menu icon (often a "hamburger" icon) should be prominently placed, usually in the top-left corner.
- **Simplicity:** Keep the menu items simple and organized. Avoid overcrowding the drawer with too many options, which can overwhelm users.

- **Consistency:** Maintain consistency in the design and placement of menu items to provide a predictable navigation experience.

Design Considerations for Navigation Drawers

When designing navigation drawers, consider the following aspects to create an intuitive and user-friendly navigation experience.

- **Menu Hierarchy:** Organize menu items logically. Use groupings and separators to distinguish between different sections or functionalities.
- **Visual Feedback:** Provide visual feedback to indicate the active menu item. This can be achieved through highlights, bold text, or different colors.
- **Customization:** Allow users to customize their navigation drawer, such as reordering menu items or adding shortcuts to frequently accessed sections.

Best Practices for Implementing Navigation Drawers

Adopting best practices in navigation drawer design ensures that the navigation is both effective and user-friendly.

- **Responsive Design:** Ensure that the navigation drawer works seamlessly across different screen sizes and orientations. The drawer should be easily accessible and usable on both small and large devices.
- **Visibility and Intuitiveness:** While the drawer is hidden by default, make sure the method to reveal it is intuitive. Use standard icons and gestures to make the interaction predictable.
- **State Management:** Maintain the state of the navigation drawer so that users can easily return to their previous position within a menu item.

Use Cases and Examples of Navigation Drawers

Navigation drawers are widely used across various types of apps due to their ability to organize complex menus without cluttering the main interface.

- **News Apps:** Apps like Google News and BBC News use navigation drawers to allow users to switch between different news categories, such as world news, sports, and technology.
- **E-Commerce Apps:** Platforms like Amazon and eBay utilize navigation drawers to navigate between home, categories, orders, and account settings.
- **Utility Apps:** Applications like Google Maps employ navigation drawers to access settings, saved locations, and other utilities.

Challenges and Solutions in Navigation Drawer Design

Despite their benefits, designing navigation drawers can present certain challenges that need to be addressed to ensure optimal usability.

- **Discoverability:** Users might not immediately recognize how to access the navigation drawer. Use clear icons and tutorial overlays to educate users.
- **Overcrowding:** Avoid overcrowding the drawer with too many items. Prioritize essential items and use submenus or other navigation patterns for secondary options.
- **Usability:** Ensure that the drawer is usable with one hand, especially on larger devices. Place frequently accessed items within easy reach.

Advanced Features in Navigation Drawers

Enhancing the basic functionality of navigation drawers with advanced features can further improve the user experience.

- **Dynamic Content:** Update the content of the navigation drawer dynamically based on user behavior or context. For example, show recently accessed items or suggestions based on usage patterns.
- **Badge Notifications:** Display badges on menu items to indicate new messages, notifications, or updates, prompting users to check specific sections.
- **Customizable Layouts:** Allow users to customize the layout of the navigation drawer, such as changing the order of menu items or adding shortcuts.

Comparing Navigation Drawers with Other Navigation Patterns

Understanding the strengths and weaknesses of navigation drawers compared to other navigation patterns can help in choosing the right method for a given app.

- **Navigation Drawers vs. Tab Bars:** Tab bars provide quicker access to core sections but can become cluttered with too many items. Navigation drawers can handle more items and keep the main interface clean but are less immediately visible.
- **Navigation Drawers vs. Bottom Navigation Bars:** Bottom navigation bars are always visible and offer quick access to main sections, while navigation drawers are better for organizing a larger number of options without taking up screen space.
- **Navigation Drawers vs. Top Tabs:** Top tabs are visible and provide easy access to different sections, but can be less ergonomic, especially on

larger screens. Navigation drawers offer a cleaner interface but require additional gestures to access.

Testing and Iteration

Iterative testing and refinement are crucial for creating an effective navigation drawer design.

- **User Testing:** Conduct usability tests with real users to gather feedback on the drawer's intuitiveness, ease of use, and effectiveness.
- **A/B Testing:** Experiment with different icon designs, menu layouts, and interaction methods to determine the most user-friendly approach.
- **Analytics:** Use analytics to track user interactions with the navigation drawer, identifying which items are most frequently used and where users might be encountering difficulties.

7.1.3 Bottom Navigation

Bottom navigation bars are a common navigation pattern in mobile app design, providing users with a simple and intuitive way to access key sections of an app. Positioned at the bottom of the screen, these navigation bars are easily accessible, particularly on larger devices.

Bottom navigation bars are a vital navigation pattern in mobile app design, offering a simple, consistent, and accessible way for users to switch between different sections of an app. By adhering to principles of simplicity, clarity, and feedback, and by implementing best practices and advanced features, designers can create effective bottom navigation bars that enhance the overall user experience. Continuous testing and iteration ensure that the bottom navigation design remains user-centric and adaptable to evolving user needs and preferences. Whether used in social media, messaging, or e-commerce apps, well-designed bottom navigation bars contribute significantly to an app's usability and success.

Introduction to Bottom Navigation

Bottom navigation bars, also known as bottom nav bars, are horizontal menus located at the bottom of the screen. They typically contain 3-5 primary navigation options, represented by icons and sometimes accompanied by labels. This placement ensures that the most important sections of an app are always within easy reach of the user's thumb.

- **Visual Structure:** Bottom navigation bars feature icons and optional text labels, arranged horizontally. The bar is fixed at the bottom of the screen, making it consistently accessible.
- **Usage Context:** Ideal for apps with a few primary sections that users

need to switch between frequently. Common in social media, messaging, and e-commerce apps.

Principles of Effective Bottom Navigation Design

To create an effective bottom navigation bar, designers should follow several key principles that enhance usability and user experience.

- **Simplicity:** Limit the number of tabs to 3-5 to avoid overcrowding and ensure each option is easily tappable.
- **Clarity:** Use clear and recognizable icons. If space allows, include text labels to provide additional context.
- **Feedback:** Provide visual feedback to indicate the active tab, such as color changes, highlighting, or underlines.

Design Considerations for Bottom Navigation

When designing bottom navigation bars, consider the following aspects to ensure an intuitive and user-friendly experience.

- **Iconography:** Choose icons that are easily recognizable and represent their respective sections accurately. Use widely understood symbols to leverage user familiarity.
- **Labels:** If space permits, accompany icons with short, descriptive text labels. This helps clarify the purpose of each tab, especially for less obvious icons.
- **Touch Targets:** Ensure that touch targets are large enough to be easily tapped. The recommended minimum size is 48x48 dp to accommodate varying finger sizes.
- **Hierarchy:** Arrange tabs in a logical order based on importance and frequency of use. Typically, the most important or frequently accessed tab is placed in the center or the far-left position.

Best Practices for Implementing Bottom Navigation

Implementing bottom navigation effectively requires adherence to best practices that enhance usability and performance.

- **Responsive Design:** Ensure that the bottom navigation bar adapts to different screen sizes and orientations. The bar should remain fixed at the bottom of the screen and maintain its usability on both small and large devices.
- **Visibility:** Keep the bottom navigation bar visible at all times. This provides consistent access to primary navigation options, reducing the need for users to search for navigation controls.

- **State Management:** Maintain the state of each tab, allowing users to return to their previous position within a section seamlessly.

Use Cases and Examples of Bottom Navigation

Bottom navigation is widely used in various types of apps due to its simplicity and ease of access.

- **Social Media Apps:** Apps like Instagram and TikTok use bottom navigation to provide quick access to home, search, notifications, and profile sections.
- **Messaging Apps:** Platforms like WhatsApp and Facebook Messenger employ bottom navigation for easy switching between chats, calls, and settings.
- **E-Commerce Apps:** Apps such as Shopify and Wish utilize bottom navigation to navigate between home, categories, cart, and account settings.

Challenges and Solutions in Bottom Navigation Design

Despite its benefits, designing bottom navigation bars can present certain challenges that need to be addressed to ensure optimal usability.

- **Limited Space:** The limited space in bottom navigation bars restricts the number of tabs. Prioritize essential tabs and consider using secondary navigation methods, such as drawers or overflow menus, for additional options.
- **Icon Misinterpretation:** Users might misinterpret icons if they are not universally recognizable. Conduct user testing to ensure that the chosen icons effectively communicate their purpose.
- **Overcrowding:** Avoid overcrowding the bar with too many items or complex designs. Stick to a minimalist approach to maintain clarity and ease of use.

Comparing Bottom Navigation with Other Navigation Patterns

Understanding the strengths and weaknesses of bottom navigation compared to other navigation patterns can help in choosing the right method for a given app.

- **Bottom Navigation vs. Tab Bars:** Both are similar but bottom navigation is typically fixed at the bottom, whereas tab bars can be placed at the top or bottom. Bottom navigation offers better reachability on larger screens.
- **Bottom Navigation vs. Navigation Drawers:** Navigation drawers can handle more items but are less visible and require additional taps to access. Bottom navigation provides quicker access to core sections.

- **Bottom Navigation vs. Top Tabs:** Top tabs are visible and provide easy access to different sections but can be less ergonomic on larger screens where reaching the top of the screen is less convenient. Bottom navigation offers a cleaner interface and easier reach.

7.2 CREATING INTUITIVE NAVIGATION EXPERIENCES

Navigation is a fundamental aspect of mobile app design that directly influences user experience and usability. Creating intuitive navigation experiences involves selecting and implementing the right navigation patterns, ensuring ease of use, and enhancing the overall interaction with the app.

Creating intuitive navigation experiences in mobile apps is crucial for user satisfaction and engagement. By understanding and implementing effective navigation patterns, such as bottom navigation bars, navigation drawers, tab bars, and hamburger menus, designers can enhance the usability and overall experience of their apps. Adhering to principles of consistency, visibility, and feedback, and incorporating best practices and advanced features, ensures that navigation remains user-centric and adaptable to evolving user needs. Continuous testing and iteration are essential for refining navigation designs, ultimately leading to successful and user-friendly mobile applications.

7.2.1 Intuitive Navigation

Intuitive navigation ensures that users can easily find and access different sections and features within an app without confusion or excessive effort. Good navigation design leads to a positive user experience, encouraging engagement and retention.

- **User-Centered Design:** Focus on the needs, behaviors, and preferences of users to create navigation structures that feel natural and easy to use.
- **Clarity and Simplicity:** Navigation should be straightforward, with clear labels and easily recognizable icons to guide users.

7.2.2 Principles of Intuitive Navigation Design

Effective navigation design is rooted in several key principles that enhance usability and user satisfaction.

- **Consistency:** Maintain consistent navigation structures and patterns throughout the app to provide a predictable experience.
- **Visibility:** Ensure that navigation elements are visible and accessible, allowing users to understand their options at a glance.
- **Feedback:** Provide immediate feedback for user actions, such as highlighting the active tab or displaying a confirmation message.

7.2.3 Common Navigation Patterns

Various navigation patterns can be employed to create intuitive navigation experiences in mobile apps. Each pattern has its own strengths and use cases.

- **Bottom Navigation Bars:** Positioned at the bottom of the screen, these bars provide quick access to key sections of the app. They are ideal for apps with a few primary sections that users need to switch between frequently.
- **Navigation Drawers:** Also known as side menus, these are hidden menus that slide out from the side of the screen. They are suitable for apps with multiple sections or features that don't require constant visibility.
- **Tab Bars:** Horizontal bars typically located at the top or bottom of the screen, used to switch between different views or sections within the app.
- **Hamburger Menus:** Represented by a three-line icon, these menus provide access to additional navigation options. They are useful for apps with extensive menus or less frequently accessed features.

7.2.4 Design Considerations for Navigation Patterns

When designing navigation patterns, consider the following aspects to ensure an intuitive and user-friendly experience.

- **Iconography and Labels:** Use clear, easily recognizable icons and concise labels to describe each navigation option. This helps users quickly understand the purpose of each element.
- **Hierarchy and Order:** Organize navigation options logically, prioritizing the most important and frequently accessed sections. Place these options in easily reachable positions.
- **Touch Targets:** Ensure that touch targets are large enough to be easily tappable. This is particularly important for users with larger fingers or those using small-screen devices.

7.2.5 Best Practices for Implementing Navigation Patterns

Adopting best practices in navigation design ensures that the navigation is both effective and user-friendly.

- **Responsive Design:** Ensure that navigation elements adapt seamlessly to different screen sizes and orientations. Navigation should remain usable on both small and large devices.
- **Accessibility:** Design navigation elements to be accessible to all users, including those with disabilities. This includes providing alternative text for icons and ensuring sufficient contrast.

- **Testing and Iteration:** Conduct usability testing with real users to gather feedback and identify areas for improvement. Iterate on the design based on this feedback to enhance usability.

7.2.6 Use Cases and Examples of Navigation Patterns

Navigation patterns are widely used across various types of apps, each catering to different user needs and contexts.

- **Social Media Apps:** Apps like Facebook and Instagram use bottom navigation bars and tab bars to provide quick access to home, search, notifications, and profile sections.
- **E-Commerce Apps:** Platforms like Amazon and eBay utilize navigation drawers and bottom navigation bars to navigate between home, categories, cart, and account settings.
- **Utility Apps:** Applications like Google Maps and Evernote employ a combination of bottom navigation bars, tab bars, and navigation drawers to access maps, saved locations, and notes.

7.2.7 Challenges and Solutions in Navigation Design

Despite the benefits, designing navigation patterns can present certain challenges that need to be addressed to ensure optimal usability.

- **Discoverability:** Users might not immediately recognize how to access certain navigation elements, such as hidden drawers. Use clear icons and tutorial overlays to educate users.
- **Overcrowding:** Avoid overcrowding navigation bars and menus with too many options. Prioritize essential items and use secondary navigation methods, such as overflow menus, for additional options.
- **Contextual Navigation:** Ensure that navigation options are relevant to the current context and user task. Dynamic menus that update based on user behavior can enhance relevance.

7.2.8 Advanced Features in Navigation Patterns

Enhancing basic navigation patterns with advanced features can further improve the user experience.

- **Badge Notifications:** Display badges on navigation icons to indicate new messages, notifications, or updates, prompting users to check specific sections.
- **Customizable Navigation:** Allow users to customize the order and visibility of navigation options based on their preferences and usage patterns.

- **Contextual Actions:** Integrate contextual actions within navigation elements, such as long-press menus, to provide quick access to secondary functions without cluttering the main interface.

7.2.9 Comparing Navigation Patterns

Understanding the strengths and weaknesses of different navigation patterns can help in choosing the right method for a given app.

- **Bottom Navigation Bars vs. Tab Bars:** Both offer quick access to key sections, but bottom navigation bars are more ergonomic on larger screens. Tab bars can be placed at the top or bottom and are often used for switching between views within the same section.
- **Navigation Drawers vs. Bottom Navigation Bars:** Navigation drawers can handle more items and keep the main interface clean, but require additional gestures to access. Bottom navigation bars provide quicker access to core sections but are limited in the number of items they can display.
- **Hamburger Menus vs. Bottom Navigation Bars:** Hamburger menus can accommodate more options but are less visible and require additional taps. Bottom navigation bars offer better visibility and quicker access but are limited to fewer options.

CHAPTER 8

INPUT AND DATA ENTRY PATTERNS

8.1 FORM DESIGN BEST PRACTICES

Form design is a crucial aspect of user experience (UX) in mobile and web applications. Poorly designed forms can frustrate users and lead to high abandonment rates, while well-designed forms facilitate smooth data entry, improving overall user satisfaction. Creating effective and user-friendly forms is essential for collecting accurate data and providing a positive user experience. By adhering to principles of simplicity, clarity, and consistency, and by optimizing input fields, data entry patterns, and error handling, designers can craft intuitive forms that facilitate smooth interactions. Incorporating accessibility considerations and ensuring mobile-friendliness further enhance usability for all users. Continuous testing and iteration are vital for refining form design, ultimately leading to higher completion rates and improved user satisfaction.

8.1.1 Introduction to Form Design

Forms are used to collect user input and data, making them an essential element in many applications. Whether signing up for a service, entering payment information, or providing feedback, forms are often the primary interaction point between users and the application.

- **Purpose:** Ensure that each form serves a clear purpose, helping users understand why they are providing their information and how it will be used.
- **User-Centric Design:** Prioritize the needs and behaviors of users, designing forms that are easy to complete and submit.

8.1.2 Principles of Effective Form Design

Effective form design is grounded in several key principles that enhance usability and user experience.

- **Simplicity:** Keep forms as simple as possible, asking for only the necessary information. Reduce the number of fields to minimize user effort.

- **Clarity:** Use clear and concise labels, instructions, and error messages. Avoid jargon and ensure that all text is easily understandable.
- **Consistency:** Maintain consistent design patterns, such as field sizes, label positions, and button styles, to provide a predictable experience.

8.1.3 Structuring Forms for Usability

The structure and layout of forms significantly impact their usability. A well-structured form guides users through the data entry process efficiently.

- **Logical Grouping:** Organize related fields into logical groups or sections. Use visual cues like borders or background shading to distinguish different sections.
- **Progressive Disclosure:** For lengthy forms, consider breaking them into multiple steps or pages. Display only the necessary fields initially, revealing additional fields as needed.
- **Top-Aligned Labels:** Place labels above the input fields for easy readability and to avoid alignment issues. This layout works well on both mobile and desktop screens.

8.1.4 Input Field Design

Designing input fields to be user-friendly and accessible is crucial for smooth data entry.

- **Field Sizes:** Adjust field sizes based on expected input. For example, use shorter fields for zip codes and longer fields for addresses.
- **Placeholder Text:** Use placeholder text to provide examples of the required input. However, ensure that placeholders disappear when users start typing to avoid confusion.
- **Auto-Complete and Suggestions:** Implement auto-complete and suggestion features to help users fill out fields more quickly and accurately.

8.1.5 Optimizing Data Entry Patterns

Optimizing data entry patterns can reduce user effort and improve the overall experience.

- **Inline Validation:** Provide real-time validation as users enter data. This helps those correct errors immediately rather than waiting until form submission.
- **Pre-Filled Fields:** Pre-fill fields with known information to save users time and effort. For example, use geolocation to auto-fill city and state fields.

- **Keyboard Optimization:** On mobile devices, customize the keyboard type based on the input field (e.g., numeric keypad for phone numbers, email keyboard for email addresses).

8.1.6 Error Handling and Feedback

Effective error handling and feedback mechanisms are essential for guiding users through the form submission process.

- **Clear Error Messages:** Display clear and specific error messages near the relevant fields. Avoid generic messages like "Invalid input" and instead specify what needs to be corrected.
- **Inline Error Indication:** Highlight fields with errors using colors, icons, or both. Ensure that the error indication is easily noticeable without being overly distracting.
- **Real-Time Feedback:** Provide feedback as soon as users make errors, rather than after they submit the form. This immediate feedback helps users' correct mistakes quickly.

8.1.7 Accessibility Considerations

Designing forms with accessibility in mind ensures that all users, including those with disabilities, can interact with the form effectively.

- **Label Association:** Ensure that labels are programmatically associated with their corresponding input fields, making them accessible to screen readers.
- **Keyboard Navigation:** Design forms that can be fully navigated and completed using a keyboard. This includes using the "tab" key to move between fields and the "enter" key to submit the form.
- **Contrast and Readability:** Use high-contrast colors for text and background to ensure readability for users with visual impairments.

8.1.8 Mobile-Friendly Form Design

Mobile-friendly forms are essential for providing a seamless experience on small screens.

- **Responsive Layouts:** Design forms to be responsive, adjusting to different screen sizes and orientations. Use flexible grids and breakpoints to ensure readability and usability on mobile devices.
- **Touch-Friendly Controls:** Optimize controls for touch input. Ensure that buttons and input fields are large enough to be easily tappable.
- **Minimalist Design:** Simplify the form design for mobile devices,

minimizing the number of fields and using features like auto-fill and smart defaults to reduce user effort.

8.1.9 Testing and Iteration

Continuous testing and iteration are crucial for refining form design and improving user experience.

- **Usability Testing:** Conduct usability tests with real users to gather feedback on the form's design, usability, and performance. Identify pain points and areas for improvement.
- **A/B Testing:** Experiment with different form designs, layouts, and features to determine the most effective approach. Compare completion rates, error rates, and user satisfaction.
- **Analytics:** Use analytics to track form interactions, identifying where users drop off or encounter issues. This data can inform design improvements and optimizations.

8.2 LEVERAGING MOBILE-SPECIFIC INPUT METHODS

Mobile-specific input methods significantly impact user experience by making data entry faster, more intuitive, and less error-prone. Leveraging these methods effectively can improve user satisfaction and engagement in mobile applications.

Leveraging mobile-specific input methods can significantly enhance the data entry experience in mobile applications. By optimizing virtual keyboards, implementing voice and camera inputs, utilizing touch gestures, and auto-filling location data, designers can create intuitive and efficient input patterns.

Adhering to best practices and considering design aspects such as contextual relevance, user control, and accessibility ensures that these input methods are user-friendly and effective. Continuous testing and iteration are crucial for refining input methods, ultimately leading to improved user satisfaction and engagement.

8.2.1 Introduction to Mobile-Specific Input Methods

Mobile devices offer unique input methods that are not typically available on desktop platforms. These methods are designed to optimize the data entry process for touchscreens and smaller form factors.

- **Touch-Based Interaction:** Mobile input methods rely heavily on touch interactions, which are intuitive and natural for users.
- **Context-Aware Inputs:** Mobile devices can provide context-aware input options, such as location data and voice input, to streamline data entry.

8.2.2 Types of Mobile-Specific Input Methods

There are several mobile-specific input methods that designers can leverage to enhance data entry experiences.

- **Virtual Keyboards:** Customizable keyboards tailored to specific data types (e.g., numeric, email, phone).
- **Voice Input:** Allows users to dictate text or commands, useful for hands-free operation.
- **Camera Input:** Enables users to capture images or scan barcodes and QR codes.
- **Touch Gestures:** Swipe, tap, and long-press gestures for navigating and entering data.
- **Location Services:** Automatically fill in location-based data using GPS.

8.2.3 Virtual Keyboards

Virtual keyboards are a fundamental input method on mobile devices. Optimizing these keyboards for different types of data can enhance user experience.

- **Keyboard Customization:** Automatically switch to appropriate keyboards based on the input field type. For example, use a numeric keypad for phone numbers and a specialized email keyboard for email addresses.
- **Input Masks:** Use input masks to format data as users type, reducing errors and guiding input. For instance, format phone numbers and credit card entries automatically.

8.2.4 Voice Input

Voice input is increasingly popular due to advancements in speech recognition technology. It offers a hands-free data entry option that can be faster and more convenient.

- **Speech Recognition:** Implement speech-to-text functionality for text fields. Ensure accurate transcription and provide real-time feedback to users.
- **Voice Commands:** Allow users to perform actions through voice commands. This is particularly useful for accessibility and for users who prefer voice interaction.

8.2.5 Camera Input

The camera on mobile devices can be utilized for various input methods, enhancing user convenience and accuracy.

- **Barcode and QR Code Scanning:** Implement barcode and QR code scanning to allow users to quickly enter information by scanning codes. This is useful for product information, ticketing, and payments.
- **Document Scanning:** Enable users to capture and upload documents using the camera. Use optical character recognition (OCR) to extract text from scanned documents for automatic data entry.

8.2.6 Touch Gestures

Touch gestures are a natural and intuitive way for users to interact with mobile applications. They can be used to enhance navigation and data entry.

- **Swipe Gestures:** Implement swipe gestures for navigation and for revealing additional options, such as deleting items or accessing secondary menus.
- **Tap and Long-Press:** Use tap and long-press gestures to enable quick actions and contextual menus. Ensure that these gestures are responsive and consistent throughout the app.

8.2.7 Location Services

Mobile devices equipped with GPS can automatically fill in location-based data, reducing the need for manual entry.

- **Auto-Fill Location Data:** Use location services to auto-fill address fields, city, state, and country information. This is particularly useful for forms requiring location details.
- **Geofencing:** Implement geofencing to trigger actions based on user location, such as check-ins or notifications when entering or leaving a specified area.

8.2.8 Design Considerations for Mobile Input Methods

When leveraging mobile-specific input methods, consider the following design aspects to ensure a smooth and efficient user experience.

- **Contextual Relevance:** Ensure that the input method is relevant to the context of the data being entered. For example, use voice input for text-heavy fields and camera input for scanning tasks.
- **User Control:** Provide users with control over input methods. Allow them to switch between different input options easily and offer alternative methods when needed.
- **Feedback and Validation:** Provide real-time feedback and validation to help users correct errors immediately. Highlight errors clearly and offer suggestions for correction.

8.2.9 Best Practices for Implementing Mobile Input Methods

Adopting best practices in implementing mobile-specific input methods enhances usability and user satisfaction.

- **Optimize for Touch:** Design input fields and buttons to be touch-friendly. Ensure that touch targets are large enough and spaced appropriately to prevent accidental taps.
- **Minimize Typing:** Reduce the need for typing by using auto-fill, predictive text, and smart defaults. Pre-fill known information whenever possible.
- **Test for Accessibility:** Ensure that input methods are accessible to all users, including those with disabilities. Implement voice input and screen reader compatibility to cater to diverse user needs.

8.2.10 Use Cases and Examples

Mobile-specific input methods are widely used across various types of applications to improve user experience.

- **E-Commerce Apps:** Use barcode scanning for product searches, auto-fill address fields with location data, and implement voice search for hands-free browsing.
- **Travel Apps:** Enable users to scan travel documents, use location services to auto-fill booking forms, and provide voice commands for booking and navigation.
- **Healthcare Apps:** Implement document scanning for medical records, use voice input for entering symptoms or medication details, and leverage location services for finding nearby healthcare providers.

8.2.11 Challenges and Solutions

Implementing mobile-specific input methods can present challenges that need to be addressed to ensure optimal usability.

- **Accuracy and Reliability:** Ensure that input methods, such as voice recognition and OCR, are accurate and reliable. Use machine learning and AI to improve accuracy over time.
- **Privacy and Security:** Protect user data when using input methods that involve personal information, such as location data and document scanning. Implement strong encryption and secure data handling practices.
- **User Training:** Educate users on how to use advanced input methods effectively. Provide tutorials, tooltips, and help guides to assist users in adopting new input methods.

CHAPTER 9

NOTIFICATION AND FEEDBACK PATTERNS

9.1 PUSH NOTIFICATIONS AND IN-APP MESSAGING

9.1.1 Push Notifications

Push notifications are a powerful tool for engaging users, driving retention, and enhancing the overall user experience in mobile and web applications. When implemented correctly, they provide timely and relevant information, encouraging users to interact with the app.

Push notifications are a powerful tool for enhancing user engagement and retention in mobile and web applications. By adhering to best practices, such as personalization, relevance, and optimal timing, and by leveraging segmentation, targeting, and A/B testing, developers can create effective notification strategies that resonate with users. Respecting user consent and preferences, addressing challenges, and staying abreast of future trends ensure that push notifications continue to deliver value and enhance the overall user experience.

Introduction to Push Notifications

Push notifications are messages sent from an application to a user's device, alerting them to new information, updates, or actions that need their attention. They can appear on the lock screen or in the notification center of the device, providing a direct line of communication with the user.

- **Purpose:** To deliver timely and relevant information that encourages user interaction with the app.
- **Benefits:** Enhance user engagement, drive retention, improve user experience, and provide a channel for personalized communication.

Types of Push Notifications

There are various types of push notifications, each serving different purposes and providing unique benefits.

- **Transactional Notifications:** Inform users about transactions, such as purchase confirmations, payment receipts, and shipping updates.

- **Promotional Notifications:** Promote special offers, discounts, and new products or features.
- **Engagement Notifications:** Encourage users to engage with the app through reminders, updates, and activity alerts.
- **System Notifications:** Provide information about system updates, maintenance, and app-related issues.

Best Practices for Push Notifications

Implementing push notifications effectively requires adherence to best practices that ensure they are timely, relevant, and user-friendly.

- **Personalization:** Tailor notifications to individual user preferences and behaviors. Use the user's name, recommend products based on past purchases, and send alerts related to their interests.
- **Timing:** Send notifications at appropriate times to maximize their impact. Avoid sending messages during late hours or at times when users are likely to be busy.
- **Relevance:** Ensure that notifications are relevant to the user. Irrelevant notifications can lead to user annoyance and increased opt-out rates.

Crafting Effective Push Notification Messages

The content of push notifications plays a crucial role in their effectiveness. Crafting compelling and concise messages is essential for capturing user attention.

- **Clear and Concise:** Keep messages short and to the point. Clearly state the purpose of the notification and include a call to action.
- **Actionable:** Encourage users to take immediate action by including a clear call to action (CTA). Use action-oriented language to prompt user interaction.
- **Urgency and Scarcity:** Create a sense of urgency or scarcity to motivate users to act quickly. Phrases like "Limited time offer" or "Act now" can drive immediate engagement.

Segmentation and Targeting

Segmentation and targeting are critical for delivering relevant push notifications that resonate with users.

- **User Segmentation:** Divide users into segments based on demographics, behavior, preferences, and past interactions. This allows for more precise targeting and personalization.
- **Behavioral Targeting:** Send notifications based on user behavior,

such as app usage patterns, purchase history, and browsing activity. Behavioral targeting increases the relevance of notifications.

- **Geolocation Targeting:** Use geolocation data to send location-specific notifications. This is particularly useful for promoting in-store offers and local events.

Frequency and Timing

The frequency and timing of push notifications can significantly impact their effectiveness and user reception.

- **Optimal Frequency:** Avoid overwhelming users with too many notifications. Determine the optimal frequency based on user engagement and feedback. Balance between staying top-of-mind and avoiding annoyance.
- **Time of Day:** Consider the time of day when sending notifications. Schedule messages when users are most likely to engage, such as during lunch breaks or in the evening.

A/B Testing and Analytics

A/B testing and analytics are essential for optimizing push notification strategies and improving their effectiveness.

- **A/B Testing:** Experiment with different message formats, CTAs, timing, and frequency. Compare the performance of different variations to identify the most effective approach.
- **Performance Metrics:** Track key performance metrics, such as open rates, click-through rates, conversion rates, and opt-out rates. Use these insights to refine and improve notification strategies.
- **User Feedback:** Collect and analyze user feedback to understand their preferences and pain points. Use this information to tailor notifications and enhance user satisfaction.

Consent and User Preferences

Respecting user consent and preferences is crucial for maintaining a positive relationship with users and complying with regulations.

- **Opt-In Mechanisms:** Use clear and transparent opt-in mechanisms to obtain user consent for receiving push notifications. Explain the benefits and provide users with control over their notification settings.
- **Preference Management:** Allow users to customize their notification preferences, such as the types of notifications they want to receive and the frequency. Provide easy access to notification settings within the app.

- **Compliance:** Ensure compliance with regulations, such as the General Data Protection Regulation (GDPR) and the California Consumer Privacy Act (CCPA), regarding user consent and data privacy.

Examples of Effective Push Notification Strategies

Examining successful push notification strategies can provide valuable insights and inspiration for your own implementation.

- **E-Commerce:** Retail apps use push notifications to alert users about flash sales, abandoned cart reminders, and personalized product recommendations.
- **Social Media:** Social media apps send notifications about new messages, comments, likes, and friend requests to keep users engaged with their networks.
- **Travel:** Travel apps provide real-time updates on flight status, gate changes, and booking confirmations, enhancing the travel experience.
- **Finance:** Financial apps notify users about account activities, transaction alerts, and budget updates, helping them stay informed about their finances.

Challenges and Solutions in Push Notification Implementation

Implementing push notifications effectively can present certain challenges. Addressing these challenges is key to maximizing their benefits.

- **User Annoyance:** Overloading users with frequent or irrelevant notifications can lead to annoyance and opt-outs. Solution: Prioritize relevance, personalize messages, and allow users to customize their notification preferences.
- **Technical Issues:** Ensuring reliable delivery and handling varying device and OS requirements can be challenging. Solution: Use robust push notification services and regularly test across different devices and platforms.
- **Privacy Concerns:** Users may have concerns about privacy and data security. Solution: Clearly communicate how user data is used, ensure compliance with privacy regulations, and implement strong security measures.

Future Trends in Push Notifications

The landscape of push notifications is continually evolving, with emerging trends shaping their future.

- **AI and Machine Learning:** Leveraging AI and machine learning to analyze user behavior and predict the best times to send notifications, enhancing personalization and relevance.

- **Rich Media Notifications:** Incorporating rich media elements, such as images, videos, and interactive buttons, to create more engaging and visually appealing notifications.
- **Cross-Platform Integration:** Ensuring seamless integration of push notifications across different platforms and devices, providing a consistent user experience.

9.1.2 In-App Messaging

In-app messaging refers to the messages and notifications that users receive while they are actively using an application. This form of communication is integral for app developers and businesses, offering a direct and immediate way to engage with users, provide updates, offer support, and drive user retention and satisfaction. Unlike push notifications that appear outside the app, in-app messages are seen by users when they are already engaged with the application.

In-app messaging is a powerful tool for engaging users, enhancing their experience, and driving retention. By understanding the different types of in-app messages and implementing best practices, businesses can effectively communicate with their users and achieve their goals. As technology advances, in-app messaging will continue to evolve, offering even more sophisticated and personalized ways to connect with users.

Types of In-App Messaging

Pop-up Messages

Pop-up messages are dialog boxes that appear in the center of the app screen, requiring users to take action before proceeding. These are often used for important alerts, updates, or announcements that need immediate attention. They can include buttons for users to accept, dismiss, or learn more about the content of the message.

Banners

Banners are non-intrusive messages that appear at the top or bottom of the app interface. They provide information without disrupting the user's activity. Banners are suitable for less critical updates, such as new features, promotions, or general notifications.

Tooltips

Tooltips are small, contextual messages that appear next to a user interface element. They provide additional information or guidance about that specific element, helping users understand how to use the app more effectively. Tooltips are commonly used during onboarding or when introducing new features.

In-App Chats

In-app chats allow real-time communication between users and support teams. This feature is particularly valuable for customer service, enabling users to get help without leaving the app.

In-app chats can also be used for user-to-user communication, enhancing the social aspect of an app.

Full-Screen Takeovers

Full-screen takeovers are messages that occupy the entire screen, providing a highly immersive and engaging experience. These are typically used for major announcements, onboarding tutorials, or important updates that require undivided user attention.

Benefits of In-App Messaging

Improved User Engagement

In-app messaging provides a direct line of communication with users, which can significantly enhance engagement. By delivering relevant and timely messages, apps can keep users informed and involved, reducing the likelihood of abandonment.

Enhanced User Experience

In-app messages can guide users through complex processes, offer tips and tricks, and highlight new features. This support can lead to a smoother and more enjoyable user experience, helping users get the most out of the app.

Increased Retention Rates

Effective in-app messaging strategies can boost user retention by keeping users informed and engaged. Regular updates, personalized messages, and timely support can encourage users to return to the app frequently.

Personalization

In-app messaging can be highly personalized based on user behavior, preferences, and demographics. Personalized messages are more likely to resonate with users, increasing the chances of positive interactions and actions.

Real-Time Feedback

In-app messaging allows businesses to gather real-time feedback from users. By prompting users to provide feedback or rate their experience, apps can quickly identify issues and areas for improvement, leading to better user satisfaction.

Best Practices for In-App Messaging

Relevance and Timing

Ensure that in-app messages are relevant to the user's current activity and context. Timing is crucial; messages should be delivered when they are most likely to be useful and welcome. For example, a tutorial message should appear when a user first encounters a new feature, not after they have already struggled with it.

Clear and Concise Content

In-app messages should be clear, concise, and to the point. Users are less likely to engage with lengthy or complicated messages. The content should be easy to understand and should convey the intended message quickly.

Non-Intrusive

While in-app messages are meant to be noticed, they should not disrupt the user's experience. Avoid excessive or repetitive messages that can lead to frustration and app abandonment. The frequency and placement of messages should be carefully considered to maintain a balance between engagement and annoyance.

Call to Action

Each in-app message should have a clear call to action (CTA). Whether it's to update the app, explore a new feature, provide feedback, or complete a purchase, the CTA should be prominently displayed and easy to follow.

Personalization

Leverage user data to personalize in-app messages. Personalized messages based on user behavior, preferences, and history are more likely to be effective. Personalization can increase user satisfaction and drive desired actions.

A/B Testing

Regularly test different in-app messaging strategies to determine what works best for your audience. A/B testing allows you to compare different messages, timings, and formats to find the most effective approach. Continuous testing and optimization are key to improving engagement and retention.

Challenges and Solutions

User Overload

One of the main challenges of in-app messaging is avoiding user overload. Bombarding users with too many messages can lead to message fatigue and app abandonment. To mitigate this, prioritize the most important messages and space them out appropriately. Use analytics to track user responses and adjust your messaging frequency accordingly.

Maintaining Relevance

Keeping messages relevant can be challenging, especially as user behavior and preferences change over time. Regularly update your messaging content and strategies based on user feedback and analytics. Use segmentation to target specific user groups with tailored messages.

Technical Integration

Implementing in-app messaging can be technically challenging, requiring integration with the app's infrastructure and user data. Collaborate with developers and use robust messaging platforms that offer easy integration and comprehensive features. Regularly test and update your messaging system to ensure it functions smoothly.

Case Studies

E-Commerce Apps

E-commerce apps frequently use in-app messaging to promote sales, offer discounts, and remind users of abandoned carts. By sending personalized product recommendations and time-sensitive offers, these apps can drive conversions and increase sales.

Mobile Games

Mobile games use in-app messaging to engage players, provide tips and tricks, and announce new levels or events. By creating a sense of community and excitement, in-app messages help retain players and encourage them to spend more time in the game.

Social Media Apps

Social media apps utilize in-app messaging to keep users informed about new friend requests, messages, and activity on their posts. By keeping users engaged with timely updates, these apps maintain high levels of user interaction and satisfaction.

Future Trends in In-App Messaging

AI and Machine Learning

Artificial intelligence (AI) and machine learning are set to revolutionize in-app messaging. These technologies can analyze vast amounts of user data to deliver highly personalized and predictive messages. AI-powered chatbots can provide instant support and improve user experience.

Rich Media Messages

Future in-app messages will likely incorporate more rich media elements, such as images, videos, and interactive content. Rich media can make messages more engaging and informative, enhancing user interaction.

Cross-Platform Messaging

As users interact with apps across multiple devices, cross-platform messaging will become increasingly important. Ensuring a seamless messaging experience across smartphones, tablets, and desktops will be crucial for maintaining user engagement and satisfaction.

9.2 PROVIDING USER FEEDBACK EFFECTIVELY

Providing user feedback effectively is crucial for businesses and organizations aiming to improve products, services, and user experiences. Feedback serves as a valuable source of insights into customer satisfaction, preferences, and areas needing improvement. When gathered and utilized properly, feedback can lead to enhanced products, increased customer loyalty, and overall business growth. Effective user feedback collection and utilization are essential for businesses aiming to enhance products, services, and user experiences. By implementing clear feedback channels, analyzing insights comprehensively, and prioritizing actionable improvements, businesses can align with customer expectations and drive sustainable growth. As technology evolves, leveraging AI, predictive analytics, and immersive feedback mechanisms will further optimize feedback strategies, ensuring continuous innovation and customer-centricity.

9.2.1 Importance of User Feedback

User feedback plays a pivotal role in understanding customer needs and expectations. It provides direct insights into what users like, dislike, and wish to see improved. By listening to feedback, businesses can align their strategies with customer preferences, ultimately boosting satisfaction and loyalty.

Driving Product Improvement

Feedback serves as a compass for product development. It highlights features that resonate with users and areas that require enhancement. This iterative process of gathering and implementing feedback leads to products that better meet user expectations and deliver superior value.

Enhancing User Experience

Feedback helps identify pain points in the user journey, allowing businesses to streamline processes and create a smoother experience. Addressing these issues can reduce friction, increase usability, and ultimately enhance overall satisfaction.

Fostering Customer Loyalty

When users feel heard and see their feedback implemented, it fosters a sense of loyalty and partnership with the brand. This emotional connection can lead to repeat business, positive word-of-mouth referrals, and advocacy within their networks.

9.2.2 Types of User Feedback

Surveys and Questionnaires

Surveys and questionnaires are structured tools for gathering quantitative and qualitative feedback. They can be distributed via email, within apps, or on websites. Surveys help capture broad sentiments and preferences, while open-ended questions provide deeper insights into specific issues.

Reviews and Ratings

Online reviews and ratings on platforms like Google, Yelp, or app stores offer public feedback that influences potential customers. Monitoring and responding to reviews can not only manage reputation but also show responsiveness to user concerns.

In-App Feedback

In-app feedback mechanisms, such as feedback forms or prompts within the application, allow users to share their thoughts while using the product. These are effective for capturing real-time insights and improving user experience.

Social Media Listening

Monitoring social media channels for mentions, tags, and comments provides organic feedback on user experiences. Engaging with users directly on these platforms demonstrates responsiveness and builds community trust.

9.2.3 Strategies for Effective User Feedback Collection

- **Clear and Accessible Channels:** Make feedback channels easily accessible through multiple touchpoints, such as websites, apps, and social media. Clear instructions and user-friendly interfaces encourage participation and ensure feedback is readily available.
- **Timing and Context:** Request feedback at appropriate times in the user journey, such as after completing a purchase or using a feature. Contextual requests enhance relevance and encourage more accurate responses.
- **Incentives and Rewards:** Offer incentives, such as discounts or entries into contests, to encourage feedback participation. Rewards acknowledge users' time and effort while boosting engagement with feedback initiatives.

- **Anonymous Options:** Provide anonymous feedback options to encourage honest and unbiased responses. Assuring anonymity can lead to more candid feedback, especially when addressing sensitive topics or negative experiences.
- **Personalized Outreach:** Tailor feedback requests based on user behavior and preferences. Personalization increases relevance and shows users that their opinions are valued, leading to higher response rates.

9.2.4 Best Practices for Analyzing and Utilizing Feedback

- **Quantitative Analysis:** Use data analytics tools to quantify feedback trends, such as sentiment analysis or Net Promoter Score (NPS). Quantitative data provides statistical insights into overall satisfaction levels and identifies areas for improvement.
- **Qualitative Insights:** Analyze qualitative feedback for detailed insights into user experiences, preferences, and suggestions. Themes and recurring issues can inform strategic decisions and guide product development priorities.
- **Prioritization and Actionable Insights:** Prioritize feedback based on impact and feasibility of implementation. Focus on actionable insights that align with business goals and user needs, ensuring efficient use of resources.
- **Continuous Improvement:** Feedback collection and analysis should be an ongoing process. Regularly review and update feedback strategies to reflect evolving user expectations and market dynamics.

9.2.5 Challenges in Collecting and Using Feedback

- **Response Bias:** Users who choose to provide feedback may not represent the broader user base, leading to response bias. To mitigate bias, encourage diverse participation and analyze feedback across different user segments.
- **Interpretation of Feedback:** Interpreting feedback accurately requires context and understanding of user perspectives. Misinterpretation can lead to misguided decisions or overlooking critical insights. Use multiple sources and tools for comprehensive analysis.
- **Actionable vs. Noise:** Not all feedback is actionable or aligned with strategic objectives. Distinguishing between constructive feedback and noise requires careful evaluation and prioritization to focus on impactful improvements.

- **Managing Volume:** High volumes of feedback can overwhelm teams and delay response times. Implementing scalable systems and automation tools can streamline feedback management while ensuring timely responses.

9.2.6 Case Studies in Effective Feedback Utilization

- **Amazon:** Amazon utilizes user reviews and ratings extensively to influence purchasing decisions. The platform's review system helps users make informed choices while providing valuable feedback to sellers and manufacturers.
- **Airbnb:** Airbnb gathers feedback through guest reviews and host ratings, which are crucial for maintaining trust and improving service quality. Feedback helps Airbnb refine its platform, enhance user experiences, and address emerging trends.
- **Spotify:** Spotify uses personalized recommendations based on user listening habits and feedback. This approach enhances user satisfaction by delivering relevant content and improving music discovery.

9.2.7 Emerging Trends in User Feedback

- **Artificial Intelligence (AI) and Machine Learning:** AI-powered sentiment analysis and chatbots are transforming feedback collection and analysis. These technologies automate responses, detect sentiment patterns, and provide real-time insights for proactive improvements.
- **Predictive Analytics:** Predictive analytics forecast future trends based on historical feedback data. By anticipating user preferences and behavior, businesses can preemptively address issues and innovate proactively.
- **Augmented Reality (AR) Feedback:** AR enables users to provide feedback directly within immersive experiences. AR-driven feedback mechanisms enhance engagement and gather real-time insights during interactive sessions.

PART IV

MOBILE SECURITY AND PRIVACY

CHAPTER 10
MOBILE APP SECURITY

10.1 SECURING DATA TRANSMISSION AND STORAGE

Securing data transmission and storage in mobile apps is critical to protect user privacy, prevent unauthorized access, and comply with data protection regulations. Mobile apps often handle sensitive information such as personal data, financial details, and credentials, making them potential targets for cyberattacks. Effective security measures ensure that data remains confidential, integral, and available only to authorized users and systems. Securing data transmission and storage in mobile apps is imperative to protect user privacy, maintain trust, and comply with regulatory requirements.

By implementing robust encryption, secure authentication mechanisms, and best practices for data handling, businesses can mitigate security risks and safeguard sensitive information. Continuous monitoring, regular updates, and collaboration with cybersecurity experts are essential to adapt to evolving threats and maintain effective data security strategies in mobile app development. Embracing emerging technologies and adhering to stringent security standards will ensure that mobile apps remain resilient against cyber threats and provide users with a secure digital experience.

10.1.1 Importance of Data Security in Mobile Apps

Ensuring robust data security in mobile apps is essential for several reasons:

- **Protection of Sensitive Information:** Mobile apps frequently collect and store sensitive user information, including personal identifiers, payment details, and health records. Securing this data prevents unauthorized access and safeguards user privacy.
- **Trust and Reputation:** A secure app instills trust among users, reassuring them that their data is safe from breaches and misuse. Protecting user information enhances the app's reputation and encourages continued usage and positive reviews.
- **Compliance with Regulations:** Regulatory frameworks such as GDPR (General Data Protection Regulation) and CCPA (California Consumer Privacy Act) mandate stringent data protection measures. Compliance with these regulations is crucial to avoid penalties and legal liabilities.

10.1.2 Securing Data Transmission

Encryption

Encrypting data during transmission prevents interception by unauthorized parties. Transport Layer Security (TLS) protocols, such as HTTPS, encrypt data exchanged between mobile apps and servers. Implementing strong encryption algorithms ensures data confidentiality and integrity.

Certificate Pinning

Certificate pinning enhances security by validating server certificates against predefined trusted certificates. This mitigates risks of man-in-the-middle attacks where attackers intercept and manipulate data transmissions.

Secure APIs

APIs (Application Programming Interfaces) facilitate data exchange between mobile apps and backend servers. Securing APIs with authentication mechanisms (e.g., OAuth) and rate limiting prevents unauthorized access and ensures data integrity.

VPN (Virtual Private Network)

Using VPNs for data transmission adds an extra layer of security by creating encrypted tunnels between the mobile device and the server. VPNs protect data from interception when users access public Wi-Fi networks or unsecured connections.

10.1.3 Securing Data Storage

Data Encryption

Encrypting data at rest ensures that stored information remains unreadable to unauthorized users or applications. Use strong encryption algorithms and securely manage encryption keys to protect sensitive data stored locally on mobile devices or servers.

Secure Data Handling Practices

Adopt secure coding practices to mitigate vulnerabilities such as SQL injection or insecure data storage. Implement data minimization strategies to collect only essential information and securely delete unnecessary data.

Secure Authentication and Authorization

Implement strong authentication methods (e.g., biometrics, multi-factor authentication) to control access to sensitive data within the app. Use authorization mechanisms to restrict user permissions based on roles and privileges.

Regular Security Audits and Updates

Conduct regular security audits and vulnerability assessments to identify and remediate potential threats.

Promptly apply security patches and updates to mobile apps and backend systems to mitigate newly discovered vulnerabilities.

10.1.4 Best Practices for Data Security in Mobile Apps

- **User Education:** Educate users about data security best practices, such as avoiding public Wi-Fi for sensitive transactions and recognizing phishing attempts. Empowering users with knowledge reduces the risk of inadvertent data exposure.
- **Data Privacy Policy:** Maintain transparent data privacy policies that clearly outline how user data is collected, used, and protected. Obtain explicit consent from users before accessing or processing their personal information.
- **Secure Development Lifecycle (SDLC):** Incorporate security into every phase of the app development lifecycle, from design and coding to testing and deployment. Conduct security reviews and assessments at regular intervals to address potential vulnerabilities proactively.
- **Data Breach Response Plan:** Develop and maintain a data breach response plan outlining procedures for detecting, containing, and notifying affected users in the event of a security incident. Prompt and transparent communication mitigates reputational damage and legal consequences.
- **Collaboration with Security Experts:** Collaborate with cybersecurity experts and consultants to stay informed about emerging threats and industry best practices. Engage in knowledge sharing and continuous learning to strengthen data security measures.

10.1.5 Challenges in Data Security for Mobile Apps

Device Fragmentation

The diversity of mobile devices and operating systems complicates security management and compatibility testing. Implementing consistent security measures across various platforms requires comprehensive testing and adaptation.

User Behavior

User behaviors such as device rooting/jailbreaking or downloading apps from unofficial sources increase vulnerability to malware and unauthorized access. Educating users about risks and promoting safe practices mitigates security threats.

Regulatory Compliance

Navigating complex and evolving data protection regulations (e.g., GDPR, HIPAA) requires ongoing compliance efforts and proactive adjustments to security practices. Non-compliance can result in severe penalties and legal repercussions.

Emerging Threat Landscape

The rapid evolution of cybersecurity threats, including ransomware, phishing attacks, and zero-day exploits, necessitates continuous monitoring and adaptation of security strategies. Proactive threat detection and response are essential to safeguard data.

10.1.6 Case Studies in Effective Data Security Implementation

- **WhatsApp:** WhatsApp uses end-to-end encryption to secure user communications, ensuring that only the sender and recipient can read messages. This approach protects user privacy and prevents unauthorized interception of messages.
- **Signal:** Signal employs open-source encryption protocols and minimal data collection practices to prioritize user privacy and security. Transparency about data handling practices builds trust among users concerned about data security.
- **Microsoft Teams:** Microsoft Teams integrates advanced security features such as data encryption, multi-factor authentication, and compliance with regulatory standards (e.g., GDPR). These measures secure sensitive communications and data shared within the platform.

10.1.7 Future Trends in Mobile App Data Security

- **Blockchain Technology:** Blockchain offers decentralized and immutable data storage solutions, enhancing transparency and security for mobile app transactions and data exchanges.
- **AI-driven Security Solutions:** Artificial intelligence and machine learning enable predictive analytics and anomaly detection to identify and mitigate emerging security threats in real-time.
- **Quantum Cryptography:** Quantum-resistant encryption algorithms are being developed to withstand future advancements in quantum computing, ensuring long-term data security.

10.2 AUTHENTICATION AND AUTHORIZATION BEST PRACTICES

10.2.1 Authentication

Authentication in mobile apps is a critical aspect of security that ensures only authorized users gain access to the application and its data. It involves verifying the identity of users before allowing them to use the app's features or access sensitive information. Effective authentication mechanisms are crucial to protect user data, maintain privacy, and prevent unauthorized access. Authentication in mobile apps is a crucial aspect of security, protecting user data and preventing unauthorized access. Implementing strong authentication methods, such as biometrics, MFA, and secure password policies, enhances security and user trust. Balancing security and usability, staying updated on emerging threats, and adopting future trends in authentication will ensure mobile apps remain secure and resilient against cyber threats. By prioritizing authentication, businesses can safeguard sensitive information and provide a secure digital experience for users.

Importance of Authentication in Mobile Apps

Protecting User Data

Mobile apps often handle sensitive information such as personal details, financial data, and health records. Robust authentication mechanisms protect this data from unauthorized access and breaches, ensuring user privacy and security.

Preventing Unauthorized Access

Authentication prevents unauthorized users from accessing the app and its data. This is particularly important for apps dealing with sensitive information or financial transactions, where unauthorized access can lead to significant security risks.

Compliance with Regulations

Many regulatory frameworks, such as GDPR, HIPAA, and CCPA, mandate strong authentication measures to protect user data. Compliance with these regulations is essential to avoid legal penalties and build user trust.

Enhancing User Trust

Users are more likely to trust and use apps that offer robust security features. Effective authentication mechanisms enhance user trust by ensuring their data is protected and only accessible to authorized individuals.

Types of Authentication Methods

Password Authentication Protocol

Password Authentication Protocol (PAP) is a password-based authentication protocol used by Point-to-Point Protocol (PPP) to validate users. PAP is specified in RFC 1334.

Almost all network operating systems support PPP with PAP, as do most network access servers. PAP is also used in PPPoE, for authenticating DSL users.

As the Point-to-Point Protocol (PPP) sends data unencrypted and "in the clear", PAP is vulnerable to any attacker who can observe the PPP session. An attacker can see the users name, password, and any other information associated with the PPP session. Some additional security can be gained on the PPP link by using CHAP or EAP. However, there are always tradeoffs when choosing an authentication method, and there is no single answer for which is more secure.

When PAP is used in PPP, it is considered a weak authentication scheme. Weak schemes are simpler and have lighter computational overhead than more complex schemes such as Transport Layer Security (TLS), but they are much more vulnerable to attack. While weak schemes are used where the transport layer is expected to be physically secure, such as a home DSL link. Where the transport layer is not physically secure a system such as Transport Layer Security (TLS) or Internet Protocol Security (IPsec) is used instead.

PAP is also used to describe password authentication in other protocols such as RADIUS and Diameter. However, those protocols provide for transport or network layer security, and therefore that usage of PAP does not have the security issues seen when PAP is used with PPP.

When the client sends a clear-text password, the authentication server will receive it, and compare it to a "known good" password. Since the authentication server has received the password in clear-text, the format of the stored password can be chosen to be secure "at rest". If an attacker were to steal the entire database of passwords, it is computationally infeasible to reverse the function to recover a plaintext password.

As a result, while PAP passwords are less secure when sent over a PPP link, they allow for more secure storage "at rest" than with other methods such as CHAP.

PAP authentication is only done at the time of the initial link establishment, and verifies the identity of the client using a two-way handshake.

- Client sends username and password. This is sent repeatedly until a response is received from the server.
- Server sends authentication-ack (if credentials are OK) or authentication-nak (otherwise)

Biometric Authentication

Biometrics are body measurements and calculations related to human characteristics and features. Biometric authentication (or realistic authentication) is used in computer science as a form of identification and access control. It is also used to identify individuals in groups that are under surveillance. Biometric identifiers are the distinctive, measurable characteristics used to label and describe individuals.

Biometric identifiers are often categorized as physiological characteristics which are related to the shape of the body. Examples include, but are not limited to fingerprint, palm veins, face recognition, DNA, palm print, hand geometry, iris recognition, retina, odor/scent, voice, shape of ears and gait. Behavioral characteristics are related to the pattern of behavior of a person, including but not limited to mouse movement, typing rhythm, gait, signature, behavioral profiling, and voice. Some researchers have coined the term behaviometrics to describe the latter class of biometrics.

More traditional means of access control include token-based identification systems, such as a driver's license or passport, and knowledge-based identification systems, such as a password or personal identification number. Since biometric identifiers are unique to individuals, they are more reliable in verifying identity than token and knowledge-based methods; however, the collection of biometric identifiers raises privacy concerns about the ultimate use of this information.

Many different aspects of human physiology, chemistry or behavior can be used for biometric authentication. The selection of a particular biometric for use in a specific application involves a weighting of several factors. Jain *et al.* (1999) identified seven such factors to be used when assessing the suitability of any trait for use in biometric authentication. Biometric authentication is based upon biometric recognition which is an advanced method of recognising biological and behavioural characteristics of an Individual.

- Universality means that every person using a system should possess the trait.
- Uniqueness means the trait should be sufficiently different for individuals in the relevant population such that they can be distinguished from one another.
- Permanence relates to the manner in which a trait varies over time. More specifically, a trait with *good* permanence will be reasonably invariant over time with respect to the specific matching algorithm.
- Measurability (collectability) relates to the ease of acquisition or measurement of the trait. In addition, acquired data should be in a form that permits subsequent processing and extraction of the relevant feature sets.
- Performance relates to the accuracy, speed, and robustness of technology used.
- Acceptability relates to how well individuals in the relevant population accept the technology such that they are willing to have their biometric trait captured and assessed.

- Circumvention relates to the ease with which a trait might be imitated using an artifact or substitute.

Proper biometric use is very application dependent. Certain biometrics will be better than others based on the required levels of convenience and security. No single biometric will meet all the requirements of every possible application.

Second, in identification mode the system performs a one-to-many comparison against a biometric database in an attempt to establish the identity of an unknown individual. The system will succeed in identifying the individual if the comparison of the biometric sample to a template in the database falls within a previously set threshold. Identification mode can be used either for *positive recognition* (so that the user does not have to provide any information about the template to be used) or for *negative recognition* of the person "where the system establishes whether the person is who she (implicitly or explicitly) denies to be". The latter function can only be achieved through biometrics since other methods of personal recognition, such as passwords, PINs, or keys, are ineffective.

The first time an individual uses a biometric system is called *enrollment*. During enrollment, biometric information from an individual is captured and stored. In subsequent uses, biometric information is detected and compared with the information stored at the time of enrollment. Note that it is crucial that storage and retrieval of such systems themselves be secure if the biometric system is to be robust. The first block (sensor) is the interface between the real world and the system; it has to acquire all the necessary data. Most of the times it is an image acquisition system, but it can change according to the characteristics desired. The second block performs all the necessary pre-processing: it has to remove artifacts from the sensor, to enhance the input (e.g. removing background noise), to use some kind of normalization, etc. In the third block, necessary features are extracted. This step is an important step as the correct features need to be extracted in an optimal way. A vector of numbers or an image with particular properties is used to create a *template*. A template is a synthesis of the relevant characteristics extracted from the source. Elements of the biometric measurement that are not used in the comparison algorithm are discarded in the template to reduce the file size and to protect the identity of the enrollee. However, depending on the scope of the biometric system, original biometric image sources may be retained, such as the PIV-cards used in the Federal Information Processing Standard Personal Identity Verification (PIV) of Federal Employees and Contractors (FIPS 201).

During the enrollment phase, the template is simply stored somewhere (on a card or within a database or both). During the matching phase, the obtained template is passed to a matcher that compares it with other existing templates, estimating the distance between them using any algorithm (e.g. Hamming distance). The matching program will analyze the template with the input. This will then be output for a specified use or purpose (e.g. entrance in a restricted area), though it is a fear that the use of biometric data may face mission creep. Selection of biometrics in any practical application depending upon the characteristic measurements and user requirements. In selecting a particular biometric, factors to consider include, performance, social acceptability, ease of circumvention and/or spoofing, robustness, population coverage, size of equipment needed and identity theft deterrence. The selection of a biometric is based on user requirements and considers sensor and device availability, computational time and reliability, cost, sensor size, and power consumption.

Multimodal biometric systems use multiple sensors or biometrics to overcome the limitations of unimodal biometric systems. For instance iris recognition systems can be compromised by aging irises and electronic fingerprint recognition can be worsened by worn-out or cut fingerprints. While unimodal biometric systems are limited by the integrity of their identifier, it is unlikely that several unimodal systems will suffer from identical limitations. Multimodal biometric systems can obtain sets of information from the same marker (i.e., multiple images of an iris, or scans of the same finger) or information from different biometrics (requiring fingerprint scans and, using voice recognition, a spoken passcode).

Multimodal biometric systems can fuse these unimodal systems sequentially, simultaneously, a combination thereof, or in series, which refer to sequential, parallel, hierarchical and serial integration modes, respectively. Fusion of the biometrics information can occur at different stages of a recognition system. In case of feature level fusion, the data itself or the features extracted from multiple biometrics are fused. Matching-score level fusion consolidates the scores generated by multiple classifiers pertaining to different modalities. Finally, in case of decision level fusion the final results of multiple classifiers are combined via techniques such as majority voting. Feature level fusion is believed to be more effective than the other levels of fusion because the feature set contains richer information about the input biometric data than the matching score or the output decision of a classifier. Therefore, fusion at the feature level is expected to provide better recognition results.

Furthermore, the evolving biometric market trends underscore the importance of technological integration, showcasing a shift towards combining multiple biometric modalities for enhanced security and identity verification, aligning with the advancements in multimodal biometric systems.

Spoof attacks consist in submitting fake biometric traits to biometric systems, and are a major threat that can curtail their security. Multi-modal biometric systems are commonly believed to be intrinsically more robust to spoof attacks, but recent studies have shown that they can be evaded by spoofing even a single biometric trait.

The discriminating powers of all biometric technologies depend on the amount of entropy they are able to encode and use in matching. The following are used as performance metrics for biometric systems:

- **False Match Rate (FMR, also called FAR = False Accept Rate):** The probability that the system incorrectly matches the input pattern to a non-matching template in the database. It measures the percent of invalid inputs that are incorrectly accepted. In case of similarity scale, if the person is an imposter in reality, but the matching score is higher than the threshold, then he is treated as genuine. This increases the FMR, which thus also depends upon the threshold value.
- **False Non-Match Rate (FNMR, also called FRR = False Reject Rate):** The probability that the system fails to detect a match between the input pattern and a matching template in the database. It measures the percent of valid inputs that are incorrectly rejected.
- **Receiver Operating Characteristic or Relative Operating Characteristic (ROC):** The ROC plot is a visual characterization of the trade-off between the FMR and the FNMR. In general, the matching algorithm performs a decision based on a threshold that determines how close to a template the input needs to be for it to be considered a match. If the threshold is reduced, there will be fewer false non-matches but more false accepts. Conversely, a higher threshold will reduce the FMR but increase the FNMR. A common variation is the *Detection error trade-off (DET)*, which is obtained using normal deviation scales on both axes. This more linear graph illuminates the differences for higher performances (rarer errors).
- **Equal Error Rate or Crossover Error Rate (EER or CER):** The rate at which both acceptance and rejection errors are equal. The value of the EER can be easily obtained from the ROC curve. The EER is a quick way to compare the accuracy of devices with different ROC curves. In general, the device with the lowest EER is the most accurate.
- **Failure to Enroll Rate (FTE or FER):** The rate at which attempts to create a template from an input is unsuccessful. This is most commonly caused by low-quality inputs.
- **Failure to Capture Rate (FTC):** Within automatic systems, the probability that the system fails to detect a biometric input when presented correctly.

- **Template Capacity:** The maximum number of sets of data that can be stored in the system.

Adaptive biometric systems aim to auto-update the templates or model to the intra-class variation of the operational data. The two-fold advantages of these systems are solving the problem of limited training data and tracking the temporal variations of the input data through adaptation. Recently, adaptive biometrics have received a significant attention from the research community. This research direction is expected to gain momentum because of their key promulgated advantages. First, with an adaptive biometric system, one no longer needs to collect a large number of biometric samples during the enrollment process. Second, it is no longer necessary to enroll again or retrain the system from scratch in order to cope with the changing environment. This convenience can significantly reduce the cost of maintaining a biometric system.

Despite these advantages, there are several open issues involved with these systems. For mis-classification error (false acceptance) by the biometric system, cause adaptation using impostor sample. However, continuous research efforts are directed to resolve the open issues associated to the field of adaptive biometrics. More information about adaptive biometric systems can be found in the critical review by Rattani *et al.*

In recent times, biometrics based on brain (electroencephalogram) and heart (electrocardiogram) signals have emerged. An example is finger vein recognition, using pattern-recognition techniques, based on images of human vascular patterns. The advantage of this newer technology is that it is more fraud resistant compared to conventional biometrics like fingerprints. However, such technology is generally more cumbersome and still has issues such as lower accuracy and poor reproducibility over time.

On the portability side of biometric products, more and more vendors are embracing significantly miniaturized biometric authentication systems (BAS) thereby driving elaborate cost savings, especially for large-scale deployments.

An operator signature is a biometric mode where the manner in which a person using a device or complex system is recorded as a verification template. One potential use for this type of biometric signature is to distinguish among remote users of telerobotic surgery systems that utilize public networks for communication.

John Michael (Mike) McConnell, a former vice admiral in the United States Navy, a former Director of U.S. National Intelligence, and Senior Vice President of Booz Allen Hamilton promoted the development of a future capability to require biometric authentication to access certain public networks in his keynote speech at the 2009 Biometric Consortium Conference.

A basic premise in the above proposal is that the person that has uniquely authenticated themselves using biometrics with the computer is in fact also the agent performing potentially malicious actions from that computer. However, if control of the computer has been subverted, for example in which the computer is part of a botnet controlled by a hacker, then knowledge of the identity of the user at the terminal does not materially improve network security or aid law enforcement activities.

Rather than tags or tattoos, biometric techniques may be used to identify individual animals: zebra stripes, blood vessel patterns in rodent ears, muzzle prints, bat wing patterns, primate facial recognition and koala spots have all been tried.

Biometrics have been considered also instrumental to the development of state authority (to put it in Foucauldian terms, of discipline and biopower). By turning the human subject into a collection of biometric parameters, biometrics would dehumanize the person, infringe bodily integrity, and, ultimately, offend human dignity.

In a well-known case, Italian philosopher Giorgio Agamben refused to enter the United States in protest at the United States Visitor and Immigrant Status Indicator (US-VISIT) program's requirement for visitors to be fingerprinted and photographed. Agamben argued that gathering of biometric data is a form of bio-political tattooing, akin to the tattooing of Jews during the Holocaust. According to Agamben, biometrics turn the human persona into a bare body. Agamben refers to the two words used by Ancient Greeks for indicating "life", *zoe*, which is the life common to animals and humans, just life; and *bios*, which is life in the human context, with meanings and purposes. Agamben envisages the reduction to bare bodies for the whole humanity. For him, a new bio-political relationship between citizens and the state is turning citizens into pure biological life (*zoe*) depriving them from their humanity (*bios*); and biometrics would herald this new world.

In Dark Matters: On the Surveillance of Blackness, surveillance scholar Simone Browne formulates a similar critique as Agamben, citing a recent study relating to biometrics R&D that found that the gender classification system being researched "is inclined to classify Africans as males and Mongoloids as females." Consequently, Browne argues that the conception of an objective biometric technology is difficult if such systems are subjectively designed, and are vulnerable to cause errors as described in the study above. The stark expansion of biometric technologies in both the public and private sector magnifies this concern. The increasing commodification of biometrics by the private sector adds to this danger of loss of human value. Indeed, corporations value the biometric characteristics more than the individuals value them. Browne goes on to suggest that modern society should incorporate a "biometric consciousness" that "entails informed public debate around these technologies and their application, and accountability by the state and the private sector, where the ownership of and access to one's own body data and other intellectual property that is generated from one's body data must be understood as a right."

Other scholars have emphasized, however, that the globalized world is confronted with a huge mass of people with weak or absent civil identities. Most developing countries have weak and unreliable documents and the poorer people in these countries do not have even those unreliable documents. Without certified personal identities, there is no certainty of right, no civil liberty. One can claim his rights, including the right to refuse to be identified, only if he is an identifiable subject, if he has a public identity. In such a sense, biometrics could play a pivotal role in supporting and promoting respect for human dignity and fundamental rights.

It is possible that data obtained during biometric enrollment may be used in ways for which the enrolled individual has not consented. For example, most biometric features could disclose physiological and/or pathological medical conditions (e.g., some fingerprint patterns are related to chromosomal diseases, iris patterns could reveal sex, hand vein patterns could reveal vascular diseases, most behavioral biometrics could reveal neurological diseases, etc.). Moreover, second generation biometrics, notably behavioral and electro-physiologic biometrics (e.g., based on electrocardiography, electroencephalography, electromyography), could be also used for emotion detection.

There are three categories of privacy concerns:

- **Unintended Functional Scope:** The authentication goes further than authentication, such as finding a tumor.
- **Unintended Application Scope:** The authentication process correctly identifies the subject when the subject did not wish to be identified.
- **Covert Identification:** The subject is identified without seeking identification or authentication, i.e. a subject's face is identified in a crowd.

When thieves cannot get access to secure properties, there is a chance that the thieves will stalk and assault the property owner to gain access. If the item is secured with a biometric device, the damage to the owner could be irreversible, and potentially cost more than the secured property. For example, in 2005, Malaysian car thieves cut off a man's finger when attempting to steal his Mercedes-Benz S-Class.

In the context of biometric systems, presentation attacks may also be called "spoofing attacks". As per the recent ISO/IEC 30107 standard, presentation attacks are defined as "presentation to the biometric capture subsystem with the goal of interfering with the operation of the biometric system". These attacks can be either impersonation or obfuscation attacks. Impersonation attacks try to gain access by pretending to be someone else. Obfuscation attacks may, for example, try to evade face detection and face recognition systems. Several methods have been proposed to counteract presentation attacks.

Biometrics are employed by many aid programs in times of crisis in order to prevent fraud and ensure that resources are properly available to those in need. Humanitarian efforts are motivated by promoting the welfare of individuals in need, however the use of biometrics as a form of surveillance humanitarianism can create conflict due to varying interests of the groups involved in the particular situation. Disputes over the use of biometrics between aid programs and party officials stalls the distribution of resources to people that need help the most. In July 2019, the United Nations World Food Program and Houthi Rebels were involved in a large dispute over the use of biometrics to ensure resources are provided to the hundreds of thousands of civilians in Yemen whose lives are threatened. The refusal to cooperate with the interests of the United Nations World Food Program resulted in the suspension of food aid to the Yemen population. The use of biometrics may provide aid programs with valuable information, however its potential solutions may not be best suited for chaotic times of crisis. Conflicts that are caused by deep-rooted political problems, in which the implementation of biometrics may not provide a long-term solution.

One advantage of passwords over biometrics is that they can be re-issued. If a token or a password is lost or stolen, it can be cancelled and replaced by a newer version. This is not naturally available in biometrics. If someone's face is compromised from a database, they cannot cancel or reissue it. If the electronic biometric identifier is stolen, it is nearly impossible to change a biometric feature. This renders the person's biometric feature questionable for future use in authentication, such as the case with the hacking of security-clearance-related background information from the Office of Personnel Management (OPM) in the United States.

Cancelable biometrics is a way in which to incorporate protection and the replacement features into biometrics to create a more secure system. It was first proposed by Ratha *et al.*

"Cancelable biometrics refers to the intentional and systematically repeatable distortion of biometric features in order to protect sensitive user-specific data. If a cancelable feature is compromised, the distortion characteristics are changed, and the same biometrics is mapped to a new template, which is used subsequently. Cancelable biometrics is one of the major categories for biometric template protection purpose besides biometric cryptosystem." In biometric cryptosystem, "the error-correcting coding techniques are employed to handle intraclass variations." This ensures a high level of security but has limitations such as specific input format of only small intraclass variations.

Several methods for generating new exclusive biometrics have been proposed. The first fingerprint-based cancelable biometric system was designed and developed by Tulyakov *et al.* Essentially, cancelable biometrics perform a distortion of the biometric image or features before matching. The variability in the distortion parameters provides the cancelable nature of the scheme. Some of the proposed techniques operate using their own recognition engines, such as Teoh *et al.* and Savvides *et al.*, whereas other methods, such as Dabbah *et al.*, take the advantage of the advancement of the well-established biometric research for their recognition front-end to conduct recognition. Although this increases the restrictions on the protection system, it makes the cancellable templates more accessible for available biometric technologies

Soft biometrics are understood as not strict biometrical recognition practices that are proposed in favour of identity cheaters and stealers.

Traits are physical, behavioral or adhered human characteristics that have been derived from the way human beings normally distinguish their peers (e.g. height, gender, hair color). They are used to complement the identity information provided by the primary biometric identifiers. Although soft biometric characteristics lack the distinctiveness and permanence to recognize an individual uniquely and reliably, and can be easily faked, they provide some evidence about the users identity that could be beneficial. In other words, despite the fact they are unable to individualize a subject, they are effective in distinguishing between people. Combinations of personal attributes like gender, race, eye color, height and other visible identification marks can be used to improve the performance of traditional biometric systems. Most soft biometrics can be easily collected and are actually collected during enrollment. Two main ethical issues are raised by soft biometrics. First, some of soft biometric traits are strongly cultural based; e.g., skin colors for determining ethnicity risk to support racist approaches, biometric sex recognition at the best recognizes gender from tertiary sexual characters, being unable to determine genetic and chromosomal sexes; soft biometrics for aging recognition are often deeply influenced by ageist stereotypes, etc. Second, soft biometrics have strong potential for categorizing and profiling people, so risking of supporting processes of stigmatization and exclusion.

Many countries, including the United States, are planning to share biometric data with other nations. In testimony before the US House Appropriations Committee, Subcommittee on Homeland Security on "biometric identification" in 2009, Kathleen Kraninger and Robert A Mocny commented on international cooperation and collaboration with respect to biometric data, as follows:

- To ensure we can shut down terrorist networks before they ever get to the United States, we must also take the lead in driving international biometric standards. By developing compatible systems, we will be able to securely share terrorist information internationally to bolster our defenses. Just as we are improving the way we collaborate within the U.S. Government to identify and weed out terrorists and other dangerous people, we have the same obligation to work with our partners abroad to prevent terrorists from making any move undetected. Biometrics provide a new way to bring terrorists' true identities to light, stripping them of their greatest advantage—remaining unknown.

According to an article written in 2009 by S. Magnuson in the National Defense Magazine entitled "Defense Department Under Pressure to Share Biometric Data" the United States has bilateral agreements with other nations aimed at sharing biometric data. To quote that article:

- Miller [a consultant to the Office of Homeland Defense and America's security affairs] said the United States has bilateral agreements to share biometric data with about 25 countries. Every time a foreign leader has visited Washington during the last few years, the State Department has made sure they sign such an agreement.

Certain members of the civilian community are worried about how biometric data is used but full disclosure may not be forthcoming. In particular, the Unclassified Report of the United States' Defense Science Board Task Force on Defense Biometrics states that it is wise to protect, and sometimes even to disguise, the true and total extent of national capabilities in areas related directly to the conduct of security-related activities. This also potentially applies to Biometrics. It goes on to say that this is a classic feature of intelligence and military operations. In short, the goal is to preserve the security of 'sources and methods'.

Multi-Factor Authentication (MFA)

Multi-factor authentication (MFA; two-factor authentication, or 2FA, along with similar terms) is an electronic authentication method in which a user is granted access to a website or application only after successfully presenting two or more pieces of evidence (or factors) to an authentication mechanism. MFA protects personal data—which may include personal identification or financial assets—from being accessed by an unauthorized third party that may have been able to discover, for example, a single password.

Usage of MFA has increased in recent years, however, there are numerous threats that consistently makes it hard to ensure MFA is entirely secure. Authentication takes place when someone tries to log into a computer resource (such as a computer network, device, or application). The resource requires the user to supply the identity by which the user is known to the resource, along with evidence of the authenticity of the user's claim to that identity. Simple authentication requires only one such piece of evidence (factor), typically a password. For additional security, the resource may require more than one factor—multi-factor authentication, or two-factor authentication in cases where exactly two pieces of evidence are to be supplied.

The use of multiple authentication factors to prove one's identity is based on the premise that an unauthorized actor is unlikely to be able to supply the factors required for access. If, in an authentication attempt, at least one of the components is missing or supplied incorrectly, the user's identity is not established with sufficient certainty and access to the asset (e.g., a building, or data) being protected by multi-factor authentication then remains blocked. The authentication factors of a multi-factor authentication scheme may include:

- **Something the User Has:** Any physical object in the possession of the user, such as a security token (USB stick), a bank card, a key, etc.
- **Something the User Knows:** Certain knowledge only known to the user, such as a password, PIN, PUK, etc.
- **Something the User Is:** Some physical characteristic of the user (biometrics), such as a fingerprint, eye iris, voice, typing speed, pattern in key press intervals, etc.

An example of two-factor authentication is the withdrawing of money from an ATM; only the correct combination of a bank card (something the user possesses) and a PIN (something the user knows) allows the transaction to be carried out. Two other examples are to supplement a user-controlled password with a one-time password (OTP) or code generated or received by an authenticator (e.g. a security token or smartphone) that only the user possesses.

A third-party authenticator app enables two-factor authentication in a different way, usually by showing a randomly generated and constantly refreshing code which the user can use, rather than sending an SMS or using another method.

Knowledge factors are a form of authentication. In this form, the user is required to prove knowledge of a secret in order to authenticate.

A password is a secret word or string of characters that is used for user authentication. This is the most commonly used mechanism of authentication. Many multi-factor authentication techniques rely on passwords as one factor of authentication. Variations include both longer ones formed from multiple words (a passphrase) and the shorter, purely numeric, PIN commonly used for ATM access. Traditionally, passwords are expected to be memorized, but can also be written down on a hidden paper or text file. Possession factors ("something only the user has") have been used for authentication for centuries, in the form of a key to a lock. The basic principle is that the key embodies a secret that is shared between the lock and the key, and the same principle underlies possession factor authentication in computer systems. A security token is an example of a possession factor.

Disconnected tokens have no connections to the client computer. They typically use a built-in screen to display the generated authentication data, which is manually typed in by the user. This type of token mostly uses a OTP that can only be used for that specific session.

Connected tokens are devices that are *physically* connected to the computer to be used. Those devices transmit data automatically. There are a number of different types, including USB tokens, smart cards and wireless tags. Increasingly, FIDO2 capable tokens, supported by the FIDO Alliance and the World Wide Web Consortium (W3C), have become popular with mainstream browser support beginning in 2015.

A software token (a.k.a. *soft token*) is a type of two-factor authentication security device that may be used to authorize the use of computer services. Software tokens are stored on a general-purpose electronic device such as a desktop computer, laptop, PDA, or mobile phone and can be duplicated. (Contrast hardware tokens, where the credentials are stored on a dedicated hardware device and therefore cannot be duplicated, absent physical invasion of the device). A soft token may not be a device the user interacts with. Typically an X.509v3 certificate is loaded onto the device and stored securely to serve this purpose.

Multi-factor authentication can also be applied in physical security systems. These physical security systems are known and commonly referred to as access control. Multi-factor authentication is typically deployed in access control systems through the use, firstly, of a physical possession (such as a fob, keycard, or QR-code displayed on a device) which acts as the identification credential, and secondly, a validation of one's identity such as facial biometrics or retinal scan. This form of multi-factor authentication is commonly referred to as facial verification or facial authentication.

These are factors associated with the user, and are usually biometric methods, including fingerprint, face, voice, or iris recognition. Behavioral biometrics such as keystroke dynamics can also be used.

Increasingly, a fourth factor is coming into play involving the physical location of the user. While hard wired to the corporate network, a user could be allowed to login using only a pin code. Whereas if the user was off the network, entering a code from a soft token as well could be required. This could be seen as an acceptable standard where access into the office is controlled.

Systems for network admission control work in similar ways where the level of network access can be contingent on the specific network a device is connected to, such as Wi-Fi vs wired connectivity. This also allows a user to move between offices and dynamically receive the same level of network access in each.

Two-factor authentication over text message was developed as early as 1996, when AT&T described a system for authorizing transactions based on an exchange of codes over two-way pagers.

Many multi-factor authentication vendors offer mobile phone-based authentication. Some methods include push-based authentication, QR code-based authentication, one-time password authentication (event-based and time-based), and SMS-based verification. SMS-based verification suffers from some security concerns. Phones can be cloned, apps can run on several phones and cell-phone maintenance personnel can read SMS texts. Not least, cell phones can be compromised in general, meaning the phone is no longer something only the user has.

The major drawback of authentication including something the user possesses is that the user must carry around the physical token (the USB stick, the bank card, the key or similar), practically at all times. Loss and theft are risks. Many organizations forbid carrying USB and electronic devices in or out of premises owing to malware and data theft risks, and most important machines do not have USB ports for the same reason. Physical tokens usually do not scale, typically requiring a new token for each new account and system. Procuring and subsequently replacing tokens of this kind involves costs. In addition, there are inherent conflicts and unavoidable trade-offs between usability and security.

Two-step authentication involving mobile phones and smartphones provides an alternative to dedicated physical devices. To authenticate, people can use their personal access codes to the device (i.e. something that only the individual user knows) plus a one-time-valid, dynamic passcode, typically consisting of 4 to 6 digits. The passcode can be sent to their mobile device by SMS or can be generated by a one-time passcode-generator app. In both cases, the advantage of using a mobile phone is that there is no need for an additional dedicated token, as users tend to carry their mobile devices around at all times.

Notwithstanding the popularity of SMS verification, security advocates have publicly criticized SMS verification, and in July 2016, a United States NIST draft guideline proposed deprecating it as a form of authentication. A year later NIST reinstated SMS verification as a valid authentication channel in the finalized guideline.

In 2016 and 2017 respectively, both Google and Apple started offering user two-step authentication with push notifications as an alternative method. Security of mobile-delivered security tokens fully depends on the mobile operator's operational security and can be easily breached by wiretapping or SIM cloning by national security agencies.

According to proponents, multi-factor authentication could drastically reduce the incidence of online identity theft and other online fraud, because the victim's password would no longer be enough to give a thief permanent access to their information. However, many multi-factor authentication approaches remain vulnerable to phishing, man-in-the-browser, and man-in-the-middle attacks. Two-factor authentication in web applications are especially susceptible to phishing attacks, particularly in SMS and e-mails, and, as a response, many experts advise users not to share their verification codes with anyone, and many web application providers will place an advisory in an e-mail or SMS containing a code.

Multi-factor authentication may be ineffective against modern threats, like ATM skimming, phishing, and malware.

In May 2017, O2 Telefónica, a German mobile service provider, confirmed that cybercriminals had exploited SS7 vulnerabilities to bypass SMS based two-step authentication to do unauthorized withdrawals from users' bank accounts. The criminals first infected the account holder's computers in an attempt to steal their bank account credentials and phone numbers.

Then the attackers purchased access to a fake telecom provider and set up a redirect for the victim's phone number to a handset controlled by them. Finally, the attackers logged into victims' online bank accounts and requested for the money on the accounts to be withdrawn to accounts owned by the criminals. SMS passcodes were routed to phone numbers controlled by the attackers and the criminals transferred the money out.

An increasingly common approach to defeating MFA is to bombard the user with many requests to accept a log-in, until the user eventually succumbs to the volume of requests and accepts one.

Many multi-factor authentication products require users to deploy client software to make multi-factor authentication systems work. Some vendors have created separate installation packages for network login, Web access credentials, and VPN connection credentials. For such products, there may be four or five different software packages to push down to the client PC in order to make use of the token or smart card. This translates to four or five packages on which version control has to be performed, and four or five packages to check for conflicts with business applications. If access can be operated using web pages, it is possible to limit the overheads outlined above to a single application. With other multi-factor authentication technology such as hardware token products, no software must be installed by end-users.

There are drawbacks to multi-factor authentication that are keeping many approaches from becoming widespread. Some users have difficulty keeping track of a hardware token or USB plug. Many users do not have the technical skills needed to install a client-side software certificate by themselves. Generally, multi-factor solutions require additional investment for implementation and costs for maintenance.

Most hardware token-based systems are proprietary, and some vendors charge an annual fee per user. Deployment of hardware tokens is logistically challenging. Hardware tokens may get damaged or lost, and issuance of tokens in large industries such as banking or even within large enterprises needs to be managed. In addition to deployment costs, multi-factor authentication often carries significant additional support costs. A 2008 survey of over 120 U.S. credit unions by the *Credit Union Journal* reported on the support costs associated with two-factor authentication. In their report, software certificates and software toolbar approaches were reported to have the highest support costs.

Research into deployments of multi-factor authentication schemes has shown that one of the elements that tend to impact the adoption of such systems is the line of business of the organization that deploys the multi-factor authentication system. Examples cited include the U.S. government, which employs an elaborate system of physical tokens (which themselves are backed by robust Public Key Infrastructure), as well as private banks, which tend to prefer multi-factor authentication schemes for their customers that involve more accessible, less expensive means of identity verification, such as an app installed onto a customer-owned smartphone. Despite the variations that exist among available systems that organizations may have to choose from, once a multi-factor authentication system is deployed within an organization, it tends to remain in place, as users invariably acclimate to the presence and use of the system and embrace it over time as a normalized element of their daily process of interaction with their relevant information system.

While the perception is that multi-factor authentication is within the realm of perfect security, Roger Grimes writes that if not properly implemented and configured, multi-factor authentication can in fact be easily defeated.

- **Advantages:**
  - No additional tokens are necessary because it uses mobile devices that are (usually) carried all the time.
  - As they are constantly changed, dynamically generated passcodes are safer to use than fixed (static) log-in information.
  - Depending on the solution, passcodes that have been used are automatically replaced in order to ensure that a valid code is always available, transmission/reception problems do not, therefore, prevent logins.

- **Disadvantages:**
  - Users may still be susceptible to phishing attacks. An attacker can send a text message that links to a spoofed website that looks identical to the actual website. The attacker can then get the authentication code, user name and password.
  - A mobile phone is not always available—it can be lost, stolen, have a dead battery, or otherwise not work.
  - Despite their growing popularity, some users may not even own a mobile device, and take umbrage at being required to own one as a condition of using some service on their home PC.
  - Mobile phone reception is not always available—large areas, particularly outside of towns, lack coverage.
  - SIM cloning gives hackers access to mobile phone connections. Social-engineering attacks against mobile-operator companies have resulted in the handing over of duplicate SIM cards to criminals.
  - Text messages to mobile phones using SMS are insecure and can be intercepted by IMSI-catchers. Thus third parties can steal and use the token.
  - Account recovery typically bypasses mobile-phone two-factor authentication.
  - Modern smartphones are used both for receiving email and SMS. So if the phone is lost or stolen and is not protected by a password or biometric, all accounts for which the email is the key can be hacked as the phone can receive the second factor.
  - Mobile carriers may charge the user messaging fees.

Token-Based Authentication

Token-based authentication involves issuing a token, usually in the form of a time-limited code, that users must provide along with their credentials. Tokens are typically delivered via SMS, email, or authentication apps, adding an extra layer of security.

OAuth

OAuth (short for "Open Authorization") is an open standard for access delegation, commonly used as a way for internet users to grant websites or applications access to their information on other websites but without giving them the passwords. This mechanism is used by companies such as Amazon, Google, Meta Platforms, Microsoft, and Twitter to permit users to share information about their accounts with third-party applications or websites.

Generally, the OAuth protocol provides a way for resource owners to provide a client [application] with secure delegated access to server resources. It specifies a process for resource owners to authorize third-party access to their server resources without providing credentials. Designed specifically to work with Hypertext Transfer Protocol (HTTP), OAuth essentially allows access tokens to be issued to third-party clients by an authorization server, with the approval of the resource owner. The third party then uses the access token to access the protected resources hosted by the resource server.

OAuth began in November 2006 when Blaine Cook was developing the Twitter OpenID implementation. Meanwhile, Ma.gnolia needed a solution to allow its members with OpenIDs to authorize Dashboard Widgets to access their service. Cook, Chris Messina and Larry Halff from Magnolia met with David Recordon to discuss using OpenID with the Twitter and Magnolia APIs to delegate authentication. They concluded that there were no open standards for API access delegation.

The OAuth discussion group was created in April 2007, for a small group of implementers to write the draft proposal for an open protocol. DeWitt Clinton from Google learned of the OAuth project, and expressed his interest in supporting the effort. In July 2007, the team drafted an initial specification. Eran Hammer joined and coordinated the many OAuth contributions creating a more formal specification. On 4 December 2007, the OAuth Core 1.0 final draft was released.

At the 73rd Internet Engineering Task Force (IETF) meeting in Minneapolis in November 2008, an OAuth BoF was held to discuss bringing the protocol into the IETF for further standardization work. The event was well attended and there was wide support for formally chartering an OAuth working group within the IETF.

The OAuth 1.0 protocol was published as RFC 5849, an informational Request for Comments, in April 2010. Since 31 August 2010, all third party Twitter applications have been required to use OAuth.

The OAuth 2.0 framework was published considering additional use cases and extensibility requirements gathered from the wider IETF community. Albeit being built on the OAuth 1.0 deployment experience, OAuth 2.0 is not backwards compatible with OAuth 1.0. OAuth 2.0 was published as RFC 6749 and the Bearer Token Usage as RFC 6750, both standards track Requests for Comments, in October 2012.

The OAuth 2.1 Authorization Framework is in draft stage and consolidates the functionality in the RFCs OAuth 2.0, OAuth 2.0 for Native Apps, Proof Key for Code Exchange, OAuth 2.0 for Browser-Based Apps, OAuth Security Best Current and Bearer Token Usage.

On 23 April 2009, a session fixation security flaw in the 1.0 protocol was announced. It affects the OAuth authorization flow (also known as "3-legged OAuth") in OAuth Core 1.0 Section 6. Version 1.0a of the OAuth Core protocol was issued to address this issue.

In January 2013, the Internet Engineering Task Force published a threat model for OAuth 2.0. Among the threats outlined is one called "Open Redirector"; in early 2014, a variant of this was described under the name "Covert Redirect" by Wang Jing.

OAuth 2.0 has been analyzed using formal web protocol analysis. This analysis revealed that in setups with multiple authorization servers, one of which is behaving maliciously, clients can become confused about the authorization server to use and may forward secrets to the malicious authorization server (AS Mix-Up Attack). This prompted the creation of a new best current practice internet draft that sets out to define a new security standard for OAuth 2.0. Assuming a fix against the AS Mix-Up Attack in place, the security of OAuth 2.0 has been proven under strong attacker models using formal analysis.

One implementation of OAuth 2.0 with numerous security flaws has been exposed.

In April and May 2017, about one million users of Gmail (less than 0.1% of users as of May 2017) were targeted by an OAuth-based phishing attack, receiving an email purporting to be from a colleague, employer or friend wanting to share a document on Google Docs. Those who clicked on the link within the email were directed to sign in and allow a potentially malicious third-party program called "Google Apps" to access their "email account, contacts and online documents". Within "approximately one hour", the phishing attack was stopped by Google, who advised those who had given "Google Apps" access to their email to revoke such access and change their passwords.

In the draft of OAuth 2.1 the use of the PKCE extension for native apps has been recommended to all kinds of OAuth clients, including web applications and other confidential clients in order to prevent malicious browser extensions from performing OAuth 2.0 code injection attacks.

OAuth framework specifies several grant types for different use cases. Some of the most common OAuth grant types are:

- Authorization Code.
- PKCE.
- Client Credentials.
- Device Code.
- Refresh Token.

Facebook's Graph API only supports OAuth 2.0. Google supports OAuth 2.0 as the recommended authorization mechanism for all of its APIs. Microsoft also supports OAuth 2.0 for various APIs and its Azure Active Directory service, which is used to secure many Microsoft and third party APIs.

OAuth can be used as an authorizing mechanism to access secured RSS/Atom feeds. Access to RSS/ATOM feeds that require authentication has always been an issue. For example, an RSS feed from a secured Google Site could not have been accessed using Google Reader. Instead, three-legged OAuth would have been used to authorize that RSS client to access the feed from the Google Site.

OAuth is a service that is complementary to and distinct from OpenID. OAuth is unrelated to OATH, which is a reference architecture for authentication, not a standard for authorization.

However, OAuth is directly related to OpenID Connect (OIDC), since OIDC is an authentication layer built on top of OAuth 2.0. OAuth is also unrelated to XACML, which is an authorization policy standard. OAuth can be used in conjunction with XACML, where OAuth is used for ownership consent and access delegation whereas XACML is used to define the authorization policies (e.g., managers can view documents in their region).

OAuth is an *authorization* protocol, rather than an *authentication* protocol. Using OAuth on its own as an authentication method may be referred to as pseudo-authentication. The following diagrams highlight the differences between using OpenID (specifically designed as an authentication protocol) and OAuth for authorization.

The communication flow in both processes is similar:

- The user requests a resource or site login from the application.
- The site sees that the user is not authenticated. It formulates a request for the identity provider, encodes it, and sends it to the user as part of a redirect URL.
- The user's browser makes a request to the redirect URL for the identity provider, including the application's request
- If necessary, the identity provider authenticates the user (perhaps by asking them for their username and password)
- Once the identity provider is satisfied that the user is sufficiently authenticated, it processes the application's request, formulates a response, and sends that back to the user along with a redirect URL back to the application.
- The user's browser requests the redirect URL that goes back to the application, including the identity provider's response
- The application decodes the identity provider's response, and carries on accordingly.

- (OAuth only) The response includes an access token which the application can use to gain direct access to the identity provider's services on the user's behalf.

The crucial difference is that in the OpenID *authentication* use case, the response from the identity provider is an assertion of identity; while in the OAuth *authorization* use case, the identity provider is also an API provider, and the response from the identity provider is an access token that may grant the application ongoing access to some of the identity provider's APIs, on the user's behalf. The access token acts as a kind of "valet key" that the application can include with its requests to the identity provider, which prove that it has permission from the user to access those APIs.

Because the identity provider typically (but not always) authenticates the user as part of the process of granting an OAuth access token, it is tempting to view a successful OAuth access token request as an authentication method itself. However, because OAuth was not designed with this use case in mind, making this assumption can lead to major security flaws.

XACML is a policy-based, attribute-based access control authorization framework. It provides:

- An access control architecture.
- A policy language with which to express a wide range of access control policies including policies that can use consents handled / defined via OAuth.
- A request / response scheme to send and receive authorization requests.

XACML and OAuth can be combined to deliver a more comprehensive approach to authorization. OAuth does not provide a policy language with which to define access control policies. XACML can be used for its policy language.

Where OAuth focuses on delegated access (I, the user, grant Twitter access to my Facebook wall), and identity-centric authorization, XACML takes an attribute-based approach which can consider attributes of the user, the action, the resource, and the context (who, what, where, when, how). With XACML it is possible to define policies such as

- Managers can view documents in their department
- Managers can edit documents they own in draft mode

XACML provides more fine-grained access control than OAuth does. OAuth is limited in granularity to the coarse functionality (the scopes) exposed by the target service. As a result, it often makes sense to combine OAuth and XACML together where OAuth will provide the delegated access use case and consent management and XACML will provide the authorization policies that work on the applications, processes, and data.

Lastly, XACML can work transparently across multiple stacks (APIs, web SSO, ESBs, home-grown apps, databases...). OAuth focuses exclusively on HTTP-based apps.

Eran Hammer resigned from his role of lead author for the OAuth 2.0 project, withdrew from the IETF working group, and removed his name from the specification in July 2012. Hammer cited a conflict between web and enterprise cultures as his reason for leaving, noting that IETF is a community that is "all about enterprise use cases" and "not capable of simple". "What is now offered is a blueprint for an authorization protocol", he noted, "that is the enterprise way", providing a "whole new frontier to sell consulting services and integration solutions". In comparing OAuth 2.0 with OAuth 1.0, Hammer points out that it has become "more complex, less interoperable, less useful, more incomplete, and most importantly, less secure". He explains how architectural changes for 2.0 unbound tokens from clients, removed all signatures and cryptography at a protocol level and added expiring tokens (because tokens could not be revoked) while complicating the processing of authorization. Numerous items were left unspecified or unlimited in the specification because "as has been the nature of this working group, no issue is too small to get stuck on or leave open for each implementation to decide."

David Recordon later also removed his name from the specifications for unspecified reasons. Dick Hardt took over the editor role, and the framework was published in October 2012.

David Harris, author of the email client Pegasus Mail, has criticised OAuth 2.0 as "an absolute dog's breakfast", requiring developers to write custom modules specific to each service (Gmail, Microsoft Mail services, etc.), and to register specifically with them.

OpenID Connect

OpenID is an open standard and decentralized authentication protocol promoted by the non-profit OpenID Foundation. It allows users to be authenticated by co-operating sites (known as relying parties, or RP) using a third-party identity provider (IDP) service, eliminating the need for webmasters to provide their own *ad hoc* login systems, and allowing users to log in to multiple unrelated websites without having to have a separate identity and password for each. Users create accounts by selecting an OpenID identity provider, and then use those accounts to sign on to any website that accepts OpenID authentication. Several large organizations either issue or accept OpenIDs on their websites.

The OpenID standard provides a framework for the communication that must take place between the identity provider and the OpenID acceptor (the "relying party"). An extension to the standard (the OpenID Attribute Exchange) facilitates the transfer of user attributes, such as name and gender, from the OpenID identity provider to the relying party (each relying party may request a different set of attributes, depending on its requirements). The OpenID protocol does not rely on a central authority to authenticate a user's identity. Moreover, neither services nor the OpenID standard may mandate a specific means by which to authenticate users, allowing for approaches ranging from the common (such as passwords) to the novel (such as smart cards or biometrics).

The final version of OpenID is OpenID 2.0, finalized and published in December 2007. The term *OpenID* may also refer to an identifier as specified in the OpenID standard; these identifiers take the form of a unique Uniform Resource Identifier (URI), and are managed by some "OpenID provider" that handles authentication.

The original OpenID authentication protocol was developed in May 2005 by Brad Fitzpatrick, creator of popular community website LiveJournal, while working at Six Apart. Initially referred to as Yadis (an acronym for "Yet another distributed identity system"), it was named OpenID after the openid.net domain name was given to Six Apart to use for the project. OpenID support was soon implemented on LiveJournal and fellow LiveJournal engine community DeadJournal for blog post comments and quickly gained attention in the digital identity community. Web developer JanRain was an early supporter of OpenID, providing OpenID software libraries and expanding its business around OpenID-based services.

In late June, discussions started between OpenID users and developers from enterprise software company NetMesh, leading to collaboration on interoperability between OpenID and NetMesh's similar Light-weight Identity (LID) protocol. The direct result of the collaboration was the Yadis discovery protocol, adopting the name originally used for OpenID. The new Yadis was announced on October 24, 2005. After a discussion at the 2005 Internet Identity Workshop a few days later, XRI/i-names developers joined the Yadis project, contributing their Extensible Resource Descriptor Sequence (XRDS) format for utilization in the protocol.

In December, developers at Sxip Identity began discussions with the OpenID/Yadis community after announcing a shift in the development of version 2.0 of its Simple Extensible Identity Protocol (SXIP) to URL-based identities like LID and OpenID. In March 2006, JanRain developed a Simple Registration (SREG) extension for OpenID enabling primitive profile-exchange and in April submitted a proposal to formalize extensions to OpenID. The same month, work had also begun on incorporating full XRI support into OpenID. Around early May, key OpenID developer David Recordon left Six Apart, joining VeriSign to focus more on digital identity and guidance for the OpenID spec. By early June, the major differences between the SXIP 2.0 and OpenID projects were resolved with the agreement to support multiple personas in OpenID by submission of an identity provider URL rather than a full identity URL. With this, as well as the addition of extensions and XRI support underway, OpenID was evolving into a full-fledged digital identity framework, with Recordon proclaiming "We see OpenID as being an umbrella for the framework that encompasses the layers for identifiers, discovery, authentication and a messaging services layer that sits atop and this entire thing has sort of been dubbed 'OpenID 2.0'. " In late July, Sxip began to merge its Digital Identity Exchange (DIX) protocol into OpenID, submitting initial drafts of the OpenID Attribute Exchange (AX) extension in August. Late in 2006, a ZDNet opinion piece made the case for OpenID to users, web site operators and entrepreneurs.

On January 31, 2007, Symantec announced support for OpenID in its Identity Initiative products and services. A week later, on February 6 Microsoft made a joint announcement with JanRain, Sxip, and VeriSign to collaborate on interoperability between OpenID and Microsoft's Windows CardSpace digital identity platform, with particular focus on developing a phishing-resistant authentication solution for OpenID. As part of the collaboration, Microsoft pledged to support OpenID in its future identity server products and JanRain, Sxip, and VeriSign pledged to add support for Microsoft's Information Card profile to their future identity solutions. In mid-February, AOL announced that an experimental OpenID provider service was functional for all AOL and AOL Instant Messenger (AIM) accounts.

In May, Sun Microsystems began working with the OpenID community, announcing an OpenID program, as well as entering a non-assertion covenant with the OpenID community, pledging not to assert any of its patents against implementations of OpenID. In June, OpenID leadership formed the OpenID Foundation, an Oregon-based public benefit corporation for managing the OpenID brand and property. The same month, an independent OpenID Europe Foundation was formed in Belgium by Snorri Giorgetti. By early December, non-assertion agreements were collected by the major contributors to the protocol and the final OpenID Authentication 2.0 and OpenID Attribute Exchange 1.0 specifications were ratified on December 5.

In mid-January 2008, Yahoo! announced initial OpenID 2.0 support, both as a provider and as a relying party, releasing the provider service by the end of the month. In early February, Google, IBM, Microsoft, VeriSign and Yahoo! joined the OpenID Foundation as corporate board members. Around early May, SourceForge, Inc. introduced OpenID provider and relying party support to leading open source software development website SourceForge.net. In late July, popular social network service MySpace announced support for OpenID as a provider. In late October, Google launched support as an OpenID provider and Microsoft announced that Windows Live ID would support OpenID. In November, JanRain announced a free hosted service, RPX Basic, that allows websites to begin accepting OpenIDs for registration and login without having to install, integrate and configure the OpenID open source libraries.

In January 2009, PayPal joined the OpenID Foundation as a corporate member, followed shortly by Facebook in February. The OpenID Foundation formed an executive committee and appointed Don Thibeau as executive director. In March, MySpace launched their previously announced OpenID provider service, enabling all MySpace users to use their MySpace URL as an OpenID. In May, Facebook launched their relying party functionality, letting users use an automatic login-enabled OpenID account (e.g. Google) to log into Facebook.

In September 2013, Janrain announced that MyOpenID.com would be shut down on February 1, 2014; a pie chart showed Facebook and Google dominate the social login space as of Q2 2013. Facebook has since left OpenID; it is no longer a sponsor, represented on the board, or permitting OpenID logins.

In May 2016, Symantec announced that they would be discontinuing their pip.verisignlabs.com OpenID personal identity portal service.

In March 2018, Stack Overflow announced an end to OpenID support, citing insufficient usage to justify the cost. In the announcement, it was stated that based on activity, users strongly preferred Facebook, Google, and e-mail/password based account authentication.

As of March 2016, there are over 1 billion OpenID-enabled accounts on the Internet and approximately 1,100,934 sites have integrated OpenID consumer support: AOL, Flickr, Google, Amazon.com, Canonical (provider name Ubuntu One), LiveJournal, Microsoft (provider name Microsoft account), Mixi, Myspace, Novell, OpenStreetMap, Orange, Sears, Sun, Telecom Italia, Universal Music Group, VeriSign, WordPress, Yahoo!, the BBC, IBM, PayPal, and Steam, although some of those organizations also have their own authentication management.

Many if not all of the larger organizations require users to provide authentication in the form of an existing email account or mobile phone number in order to sign up for an account (which then can be used as an OpenID identity). There are several smaller entities that accept sign-ups with no extra identity details required.

Facebook did use OpenID in the past, but moved to Facebook Connect. Blogger also used OpenID, but since May 2018 no longer supports it.

OpenID is a decentralized authentication protocol that allows users to authenticate with multiple websites using a single set of credentials, eliminating the need for separate usernames and passwords for each website. OpenID authenticates with user with an identity provider (IDP), who then provides the user with a unique identifier (called an OpenID). This identifier can then be used to authenticate the user with any website that supports OpenID.

When a user visits a website that supports OpenID authentication, the website will redirect the user to their chosen IDP. The IDP will then prompt the user to authenticate themselves (e.g., by entering a username and password). Once the user is authenticated, the IDP will generate an OpenID and send it back to the website. The website can then use this OpenID to authenticate the user without needing to know their actual credentials.

OpenID is built on top of several existing standards, including HTTP, HTML, and XML. OpenID relies on a number of technologies, including a discovery mechanism that allows websites to find the IDP associated with a particular OpenID, as well as security mechanisms to protect against phishing and other attacks.

One of the key benefits of OpenID is that it allows users to control their own identity information, rather than relying on individual websites to store and manage their login credentials. This can be particularly important in cases where websites are vulnerable to security breaches or where users are concerned about the privacy of their personal information.

OpenID has been widely adopted by a number of large websites and service providers, including Google, Yahoo!, and PayPal. The protocol is also used by a number of open source projects and frameworks, including Ruby on Rails and Django.

The end user interacts with a relying party (such as a website) that provides an option to specify an OpenID for the purposes of authentication; an end user typically has previously registered an OpenID (e.g. alice.openid.example.org) with an OpenID provider (e.g. openid.example.org).

The relying party typically transforms the OpenID into a canonical URL form (e.g. http://alice.openid.example.org/).

- With OpenID 1.0, the relying party then requests the HTML resource identified by the URL and reads an HTML link tag to discover the OpenID provider's URL (e.g. http://openid.example.org/openid-auth.php). The relying party also discovers whether to use a *delegated identity*.
- With OpenID 2.0, the relying party discovers the OpenID provider URL by requesting the *XRDS document* (also called the *Yadis document*) with the content type application/xrds+xml; this document may be available at the target URL and is always available for a target XRI.

There are two modes in which the relying party may communicate with the OpenID provider:

- checkid_immediate, in which the relying party requests that the OpenID provider not interact with the end user. All communication is relayed through the end user's user-agent without explicitly notifying the end user.

- checkid_setup, in which the end user communicates with the OpenID provider via the same user-agent used to access the relying party.

The checkid_immediate mode can fall back to the checkid_setup mode if the operation cannot be automated.

First, the relying party and the OpenID provider (optionally) establish a shared secret, referenced by an *associate handle*, which the relying party then stores. If using the checkid_setup mode, the relying party redirects the end user's user-agent to the OpenID provider so the end user can authenticate directly with the OpenID provider.

The method of authentication may vary, but typically, an OpenID provider prompts the end user for a password or some cryptographic token, and then asks whether the end user trusts the relying party to receive the necessary identity details.

If the end user declines the OpenID provider's request to trust the relying party, then the user-agent is redirected back to the relying party with a message indicating that authentication was rejected; the relying party in turn refuses to authenticate the end user.

If the end user accepts the OpenID provider's request to trust the relying party, then the user-agent is redirected back to the relying party along with the end user's credentials. That relying party must then confirm that the credentials really came from the OpenID provider. If the relying party and OpenID provider had previously established a shared secret, then the relying party can validate the identity of the OpenID provider by comparing its copy of the shared secret against the one received along with the end user's credentials; such a relying party is called *stateful* because it stores the shared secret between sessions. In contrast, a *stateless* or *dumb* relying party must make one more background request (`check_authentication`) to ensure that the data indeed came from the OpenID provider.

After the OpenID has been verified, authentication is considered successful and the end user is considered logged into the relying party under the identity specified by the given OpenID (e.g. `alice.openid.example.org`). The relying party typically then stores the end user's OpenID along with the end user's other session information.

To obtain an OpenID-enabled URL that can be used to log into OpenID-enabled websites, a user registers an OpenID identifier with an identity provider. Identity providers offer the ability to register a URL (typically a third-level domain, e.g. username.example.com) that will automatically be configured with OpenID authentication service.

Once they have registered an OpenID, a user can also use an existing URL under their own control (such as a blog or home page) as an alias or "delegated identity". They simply insert the appropriate OpenID tags in the HTML or serve a Yadis document.

Starting with OpenID Authentication 2.0 (and some 1.1 implementations), there are two types of identifiers that can be used with OpenID: URLs and XRIs.

XRIs are a new form of Internet identifier designed specifically for cross-domain digital identity. For example, XRIs come in two forms—i-names and i-numbers—that are usually registered simultaneously as synonyms. I-names are reassignable (like domain names), while i-numbers are never reassigned. When an XRI i-name is used as an OpenID identifier, it is immediately resolved to the synonymous i-number (the CanonicalID element of the XRDS document). This i-number is the OpenID identifier stored by the relying party. In this way, both the user and the relying party are protected from the end user's OpenID identity ever being taken over by another party as can happen with a URL based on a reassignable DNS name.

The OpenID Foundation (OIDF) promotes and enhances the OpenID community and technologies. The OIDF is a non-profit international standards development organization of individual developers, government agencies and companies who wish to promote and protect OpenID. The OpenID Foundation was formed in June 2007 and serves as a public trust organization representing an open community of developers, vendors and users. OIDF assists the community by providing needed infrastructure and help in promoting and supporting adoption of OpenID. This includes managing intellectual property and trade marks as well a fostering viral growth and global participation in OpenID.

The OIDF ensures that OpenID specifications are freely implementable therefore the OIDF requires all contributors to sign a contribution agreement. This agreement both grants a copyright license to the Foundation to publish the collective specifications and includes a patent non-assertion agreement. The non-assertion agreement states that the contributor will not sue someone for implementing OpenID specifications.

The OpenID trademark in the United States was assigned to the OpenID Foundation in March 2008. It had been registered by NetMesh Inc. before the OpenID Foundation was operational. In Europe, as of August 31, 2007, the OpenID trademark is registered to the OpenID Europe Foundation.

The OpenID logo was designed by Randy "ydnar" Reddig, who in 2005 had expressed plans to transfer the rights to an OpenID organization.

Since the original announcement of OpenID, the official site has stated:

- Nobody should own this. Nobody's planning on making any money

> from this. The goal is to release every part of this under the most liberal licenses possible, so there's no money or licensing or registering required to play. It benefits the community as a whole if something like this exists, and we're all a part of the community.

Sun Microsystems, VeriSign and a number of smaller companies involved in OpenID have issued patent non-assertion covenants covering OpenID 1.1 specifications. The covenants state that the companies will not assert any of their patents against OpenID implementations and will revoke their promises from anyone who threatens, or asserts, patents against OpenID implementors.

In March, 2012, a research paper reported two generic security issues in OpenID. Both issues allow an attacker to sign in to a victim's relying party accounts. For the first issue, OpenID and Google (an Identity Provider of OpenID) both published security advisories to address it. Google's advisory says "An attacker could forge an OpenID request that doesn't ask for the user's email address, and then insert an unsigned email address into the IDPs response. If the attacker relays this response to a website that doesn't notice that this attribute is unsigned, the website may be tricked into logging the attacker in to any local account." The research paper claims that many popular websites have been confirmed vulnerable, including Yahoo! Mail, smartsheet.com, Zoho, manymoon.com, diigo.com. The researchers have notified the affected parties, who have then fixed their vulnerable code.

For the second issue, the paper called it "Data Type Confusion Logic Flaw", which also allows attackers to sign in to victims' RP accounts. Google and PayPal were initially confirmed vulnerable. OpenID published a vulnerability report on the flaw. The report says Google and PayPal have applied fixes, and suggest other OpenID vendors to check their implementations.

Some observers have suggested that OpenID has security weaknesses and may prove vulnerable to phishing attacks. For example, a malicious relaying party may forward the end user to a bogus identity provider authentication page asking that end user to input their credentials. On completion of this, the malicious party (who in this case also controls the bogus authentication page) could then have access to the end user's account with the identity provider, and then use that end user's OpenID to log into other services.

In an attempt to combat possible phishing attacks, some OpenID providers mandate that the end user needs to be authenticated with them prior to an attempt to authenticate with the relying party.

This relies on the end user knowing the policy of the identity provider. In December 2008, the OpenID Foundation approved version 1.0 of the Provider Authentication Policy Extension (PAPE), which "enables Relying Parties to request that OpenID Providers employ specified authentication policies when authenticating users and for OpenID Providers to inform the Relying Parties which policies were actually used."

Other security issues identified with OpenID involve lack of privacy and failure to address the trust problem. However, this problem is not unique to OpenID and is simply the state of the Internet as commonly used.

The Identity Provider does, however, get a log of your OpenID logins; they know when you logged into what website, making cross-site tracking much easier. A compromised OpenID account is also likely to be a more serious breach of privacy than a compromised account on a single site.

Another important vulnerability is present in the last step in the authentication scheme when TLS/SSL are not used: the redirect-URL from the identity provider to the relying party. The problem with this redirect is the fact that anyone who can obtain this URL (e.g. by sniffing the wire) can replay it and get logged into the site as the victim user. Some of the identity providers use nonces (a number used just once) to allow a user to log into the site once and fail all the consecutive attempts. The nonce solution works if the user is the first one to use the URL. However, a fast attacker who is sniffing the wire can obtain the URL and immediately reset a user's TCP connection (as an attacker is sniffing the wire and knows the required TCP sequence numbers) and then execute the replay attack as described above. Thus nonces only protect against passive attackers, but cannot prevent active attackers from executing the replay attack. Use of TLS/SSL in the authentication process can significantly reduce this risk.

This can be restated as:

IF (Both RP1 and RP2 have Bob as a client) AND // a common case

(Bob uses the same IDP with both RP1 and RP2) AND // a common case

(RP1 does not use VPN/SSL/TLS to secure their connection with the client) // preventable!

THEN

RP2 could obtain credentials sufficient to impersonate Bob with RP1

END-IF

On May 1, 2014, a bug dubbed "Covert Redirect related to OAuth 2.0 and OpenID" was disclosed. It was discovered by mathematics doctoral student Wang Jing at the School of Physical and Mathematical Sciences, Nanyang Technological University, Singapore.

The announcement of OpenID is: "'Covert Redirect', publicized in May 2014, is an instance of attackers using open redirectors – a well-known threat, with well-known means of prevention. The OpenID Connect protocol mandates strict measures that preclude open redirectors to prevent this vulnerability."

"The general consensus, so far, is that Covert Redirect is not as bad, but still a threat. Understanding what makes it dangerous requires a basic understanding of Open Redirect, and how it can be exploited." A patch was not immediately made available. Ori Eisen, founder, chairman and chief innovation officer at 41st Parameter told Sue Marquette Poremba, "In any distributed system, we are counting of the good nature of the participants to do the right thing. In cases like OAuth and OpenID, the distribution is so vast that it is unreasonable to expect each and every website to patch up in the near future".

Published in February 2014 by the OpenID Foundation, OpenID Connect is the third generation of OpenID technology. It is an authentication layer on top of the OAuth 2.0 authorization framework.

It allows computing clients to verify the identity of an end user based on the authentication performed by an authorization server, as well as to obtain the basic profile information about the end user in an interoperable and REST-like manner. In technical terms, OpenID Connect specifies a RESTful HTTP API, using JSON as a data format.

OpenID Connect allows a range of parties, including web-based, mobile and JavaScript clients, to request and receive information about authenticated sessions and end users. The OpenID Connect specification is extensible, supporting optional features such as encryption of identity data, discovery of OpenID providers, and session management.

Certificate-Based Authentication

Certificate-based authentication uses digital certificates issued by a trusted authority to verify a user's identity. This method is highly secure and is often used in enterprise environments to protect sensitive data.

Best Practices for Implementing Authentication

- **Strong Password Policies:** Implementing strong password policies, such as requiring a mix of letters, numbers, and special characters, can enhance security. Encourage users to create unique passwords and avoid common or easily guessable ones.
- **Secure Storage of Credentials:** Store user credentials securely using encryption and hashing techniques. Avoid storing plain text passwords and use strong hashing algorithms, such as bcrypt or Argon2, to protect against breaches.
- **Use of Biometric Authentication:** Incorporate biometric authentication methods, such as fingerprint or facial recognition, to provide a higher level of security. Biometric data should be stored securely and handled

with care to protect user privacy.

- **Implementing MFA:** Enable multi-factor authentication to add an extra layer of security. This can include SMS-based verification, authentication apps, or hardware tokens. MFA significantly reduces the risk of unauthorized access.
- **Regular Security Audits:** Conduct regular security audits and vulnerability assessments to identify and address potential weaknesses in the authentication system. Stay updated on emerging threats and best practices to ensure ongoing security.
- **User Education:** Educate users on the importance of security and best practices for protecting their accounts. This includes creating strong passwords, recognizing phishing attempts, and enabling MFA.

Challenges in Authentication

Balancing Security and Usability

Finding the right balance between security and usability is a challenge. While strong authentication methods enhance security, they can also add friction to the user experience. Striking a balance that maintains security without compromising usability is essential.

Device Fragmentation

The diversity of mobile devices and operating systems can complicate the implementation of consistent authentication mechanisms. Ensuring compatibility and security across various platforms requires comprehensive testing and adaptation.

Managing Authentication Data

Storing and managing authentication data securely is a challenge. Proper encryption, secure key management, and regular audits are necessary to protect authentication data from breaches and unauthorized access.

Emerging Threats

The evolving threat landscape, including phishing attacks, malware, and zero-day exploits, requires continuous monitoring and adaptation of authentication strategies. Proactive threat detection and response are essential to maintaining security.

Case Studies in Effective Authentication Implementation

- **Google:** Google implements multi-factor authentication and offers advanced security features such as security keys and Google

Authenticator. These measures enhance account security and protect user data from unauthorized access.

- **Apple:** Apple uses biometric authentication methods such as Touch ID and Face ID to secure its devices and apps. These methods provide a high level of security and convenience, enhancing user trust and experience.
- **Microsoft:** Microsoft incorporates Azure Active Directory for secure authentication across its services. Features such as conditional access, MFA, and identity protection ensure robust security for enterprise users.

Future Trends in Authentication

- **Passwordless Authentication:** Passwordless authentication methods, such as biometric verification and magic links, are gaining popularity. These methods enhance security and improve user experience by eliminating the need for passwords.
- **Decentralized Identity:** Decentralized identity solutions, based on blockchain technology, offer greater user control over personal information. Users can manage their identities securely without relying on centralized authorities.
- **Adaptive Authentication:** Adaptive authentication uses machine learning and behavioral analytics to assess risk levels and adjust authentication requirements accordingly. This approach enhances security while maintaining a seamless user experience.
- **Quantum-Resistant Authentication:** As quantum computing advances, developing quantum-resistant authentication algorithms will be essential to protect against future threats. Research in this area is ongoing to ensure long-term security.

10.2.2 Authorization Best Practices

Authorization in mobile apps is the process of determining what an authenticated user is allowed to do within the application. It involves granting or denying permissions to access resources, perform actions, or view specific content based on the user's identity and roles. Implementing robust authorization mechanisms is crucial for ensuring that users can only access the data and functionalities they are permitted to, thereby protecting sensitive information and maintaining the app's integrity.

Implementing robust authorization mechanisms in mobile apps is essential for ensuring data security, maintaining application integrity, and enhancing user trust. By adopting best practices such as the principle of least privilege, role-based and attribute-based access control, and regular audits, developers can create secure and efficient authorization systems. Staying informed about emerging trends and challenges in authorization will help ensure that mobile apps remain resilient against evolving security threats and provide a secure experience for users.

Importance of Authorization in Mobile Apps

Ensuring Data Security

Proper authorization ensures that sensitive data is only accessible to authorized users. This is particularly important for apps that handle personal information, financial data, or proprietary business information, as unauthorized access could lead to data breaches and significant harm.

Maintaining Application Integrity

Authorization mechanisms help maintain the integrity of the application by ensuring that users can only perform actions within their permissions. This prevents unauthorized modifications, deletions, or access to critical functionalities that could disrupt the app's operations.

Enhancing User Experience

Effective authorization ensures that users have a seamless experience by providing access to the resources they need while restricting access to unnecessary features. This not only improves usability but also helps in preventing accidental misuse of functionalities.

Compliance with Regulations

Regulatory frameworks such as GDPR, HIPAA, and CCPA require strict access controls to protect user data. Implementing robust authorization practices helps in complying with these regulations, thereby avoiding legal penalties and building trust with users.

Authorization Models

Role-Based Access Control (RBAC)

Role-based access control (RBAC) or role-based security is an approach to restricting system access to authorized users, and to implementing mandatory access control (MAC) or discretionary access control (DAC).

Role-based access control is a policy-neutral access control mechanism defined around roles and privileges. The components of RBAC such as role-permissions, user-role and role-role relationships make it simple to perform user assignments. A study by NIST has demonstrated that RBAC addresses many needs of commercial and government organizations. RBAC can be used to facilitate administration of security in large organizations with hundreds of users and thousands of permissions.

Although RBAC is different from MAC and DAC access control frameworks, it can enforce these policies without any complication.

Within an organization, roles are created for various job functions. The permissions to perform certain operations are assigned to specific roles. Since users are not assigned permissions directly, but only acquire them through their role (or roles), management of individual user rights becomes a matter of simply assigning appropriate roles to the user's account; this simplifies common operations, such as adding a user, or changing a user's department.

Three primary rules are defined for RBAC:

- **Role Assignment:** A subject can exercise a permission only if the subject has selected or been assigned a role.
- **Role Authorization:** A subject's active role must be authorized for the subject. With rule 1 above, this rule ensures that users can take on only roles for which they are authorized.
- **Permission Authorization:** A subject can exercise a permission only if the permission is authorized for the subject's active role. With rules 1 and 2, this rule ensures that users can exercise only permissions for which they are authorized.

Additional constraints may be applied as well, and roles can be combined in a hierarchy where higher-level roles subsume permissions owned by sub-roles.

With the concepts of role hierarchy and constraints, one can control RBAC to create or simulate lattice-based access control (LBAC). Thus RBAC can be considered to be a superset of LBAC.

When defining an RBAC model, the following conventions are useful:

- S = Subject = A person or automated agent
- R = Role = Job function or title which defines an authority level
- P = Permissions = An approval of a mode of access to a resource
- SE = Session = A mapping involving S, R and/or P
- SA = Subject Assignment
- PA = Permission Assignment
- RH = Partially ordered Role Hierarchy. RH can also be written: ≥ (The notation: $x \geq y$ means that x inherits the permissions of y.)
  - A subject can have multiple roles.
  - A role can have multiple subjects.
  - A role can have many permissions.
  - A permission can be assigned to many roles.

- An operation can be assigned to many permissions.
- A permission can be assigned to many operations.

The NIST/ANSI/INCITS RBAC standard (2004) recognizes three levels of RBAC:

- Core RBAC.
- Hierarchical RBAC, which adds support for inheritance between roles.
- Constrained RBAC, which adds separation of duties.

RBAC is a flexible access control technology whose flexibility allows it to implement DAC or MAC. DAC with groups (e.g., as implemented in POSIX file systems) can emulate RBAC. MAC can simulate RBAC if the role graph is restricted to a tree rather than a partially ordered set.

Prior to the development of RBAC, the Bell-LaPadula (BLP) model was synonymous with MAC and file system permissions were synonymous with DAC. These were considered to be the only known models for access control: if a model was not BLP, it was considered to be a DAC model, and vice versa. Research in the late 1990s demonstrated that RBAC falls in neither category. Unlike context-based access control (CBAC), RBAC does not look at the message context (such as a connection's source). RBAC has also been criticized for leading to role explosion, a problem in large enterprise systems which require access control of finer granularity than what RBAC can provide as roles are inherently assigned to operations and data types. In resemblance to CBAC, an Entity-Relationship Based Access Control (ERBAC, although the same acronym is also used for modified RBAC systems, such as Extended Role-Based Access Control) system is able to secure instances of data by considering their association to the executing subject.

Access control lists (ACLs) are used in traditional discretionary access-control (DAC) systems to affect low-level data-objects. RBAC differs from ACL in assigning permissions to operations which change the direct-relations between several entities. For example, an ACL could be used for granting or denying write access to a particular system file, but it wouldn't dictate how that file could be changed. In an RBAC-based system, an operation might be to 'create a credit account' transaction in a financial application or to 'populate a blood sugar level test' record in a medical application. A Role is thus a sequence of operations within a larger activity. RBAC has been shown to be particularly well suited to separation of duties (SoD) requirements, which ensure that two or more people must be involved in authorizing critical operations. Necessary and sufficient conditions for safety of SoD in RBAC have been analyzed. An underlying principle of SoD is that no individual should be able to effect a breach of security through dual privilege. By extension, no person may hold a role that exercises audit, control or review authority over another, concurrently held role.

Then again, a "minimal RBAC Model", *RBACm*, can be compared with an ACL mechanism, *ACLg*, where only groups are permitted as entries in the ACL. Barkley (1997) showed that *RBACm* and *ACLg* are equivalent. In modern SQL implementations, like ACL of the CakePHP framework, ACLs also manage groups and inheritance in a hierarchy of groups. Under this aspect, specific "modern ACL" implementations can be compared with specific "modern RBAC" implementations, better than "old (file system) implementations".

For data interchange, and for "high level comparisons", ACL data can be translated to XACML.

Attribute-based access control or ABAC is a model which evolves from RBAC to consider additional attributes in addition to roles and groups. In ABAC, it is possible to use attributes of:

- the user, e.g., citizenship, clearance,
- the resource, e.g., classification, department, owner,
- the action, and
- the context, e.g., time, location, IP.

ABAC is policy-based in the sense that it uses policies rather than static permissions to define what is allowed or what is not allowed.

Relationship-based access control or ReBAC is a model which evolves from RBAC. In ReBAC, a subject's permission to access a resource is defined by the presence of relationships between those subjects and resources.

The advantage of this model is that allows for fine-grained permissions; for example, in a social network where users can share posts with other specific users.

The use of RBAC to manage user privileges (computer permissions) within a single system or application is widely accepted as a best practice. A 2010 report prepared for NIST by the Research Triangle Institute analyzed the economic value of RBAC for enterprises, and estimated benefits per employee from reduced employee downtime, more efficient provisioning, and more efficient access control policy administration.

In an organization with a heterogeneous IT infrastructure and requirements that span dozens or hundreds of systems and applications, using RBAC to manage sufficient roles and assign adequate role memberships becomes extremely complex without hierarchical creation of roles and privilege assignments. Newer systems extend the older NIST RBAC model to address the limitations of RBAC for enterprise-wide deployments. The NIST model was adopted as a standard by INCITS as ANSI/INCITS 359-2004.

Role based access control interference is a relatively new issue in security applications, where multiple user accounts with dynamic access levels may lead to encryption key instability, allowing an outside user to exploit the weakness for unauthorized access. Key sharing applications within dynamic virtualized environments have shown some success in addressing this problem.

Attribute-Based Access Control (ABAC)

Attribute-based access control (ABAC), also known as policy-based access control for IAM, defines an access control paradigm whereby a subject's authorization to perform a set of operations is determined by evaluating attributes associated with the subject, object, requested operations, and, in some cases, environment attributes.

ABAC is a method of implementing access control policies that is highly adaptable and can be customized using a wide range of attributes, making it suitable for use in distributed or rapidly changing environments. The only limitations on the policies that can be implemented with ABAC are the capabilities of the computational language and the availability of relevant attributes. ABAC policy rules are generated as Boolean functions of the subject's attributes, the object's attributes, and the environment attributes.

Unlike role-based access control (RBAC), which defines roles that carry a specific set of privileges associated with them and to which subjects are assigned, ABAC can express complex rule sets that can evaluate many different attributes. Through defining consistent subject and object attributes into security policies, ABAC eliminates the need for explicit authorizations to individuals' subjects needed in a non-ABAC access method, reducing the complexity of managing access lists and groups.

Attribute values can be set-valued or atomic-valued. Set-valued attributes contain more than one atomic value. Examples are *role* and *project.* Atomic-valued attributes contain only one atomic value. Examples are *clearance* and *sensitivity.* Attributes can be compared to static values or to one another, thus enabling relation-based access control.

Although the concept itself existed for many years, ABAC is considered a "next generation" authorization model because it provides dynamic, context-aware and risk-intelligent access control to resources allowing access control policies that include specific attributes from many different information systems to be defined to resolve an authorization and achieve an efficient regulatory compliance, allowing enterprises flexibility in their implementations based on their existing infrastructures.

Attribute-based access control is sometimes referred to as policy-based access control (PBAC) or claims-based access control (CBAC), which is a Microsoft-specific term. The key standards that implement ABAC are XACML and ALFA (XACML). ABAC comes with a recommended architecture which is as follows:

- **The PEP or Policy Enforcement Point:** It is responsible for protecting the apps & data you want to apply ABAC to. The PEP inspects the request and generates an authorization request from which it sends to the PDP.
- **The PDP or Policy Decision Point is the Brain of the Architecture:** This is the piece which evaluates incoming requests against policies it has been configured with. The PDP returns a Permit/ Deny decision. The PDP may also use PIPs to retrieve missing metadata
- The PIP or Policy Information Point bridges the PDP to external sources of attributes, e.g., LDAP or databases.

Attributes can be about anything and anyone. They tend to fall into 4 different categories:

- **Subject Attributes:** Attributes that describe the user attempting the access e.g. age, clearance, department, role, job title
- **Action Attributes:** Attributes that describe the action being attempted e.g. read, delete, view, approve
- **Object Attributes:** Attributes that describe the object (or resource) being accessed e.g. the object type (medical record, bank account), the department, the classification or sensitivity, the location
- **Contextual (Environment) Attributes:** Attributes that deal with time, location or dynamic aspects of the access control scenario.

Policies are statements that bring together attributes to express what can happen and is not allowed. Policies in ABAC can be granting or denying policies. Policies can also be local or global and can be written in a way that they override other policies. Examples include:

- A user can view a document if the document is in the same department as the user
- A user can edit a document if they are the owner and if the document is in draft mode
- Deny access before 9 AM

With ABAC you can have as many policies as you like that cater to many different scenarios and technologies.

Historically, access control models have included mandatory access control (MAC), discretionary access control (DAC), and more recently role-based access control (RBAC). These access control models are user-centric and do not take into account additional parameters such as resource information, the relationship between the user (the requesting entity) and the resource, and dynamic information, e.g. time of the day or user IP. ABAC tries to address this by defining access control based on attributes which describe the requesting entity (the user), the targeted object or resource, the desired action (view, edit, delete), and environmental or contextual information. This is why access control is said to be attribute-based.

There are three main implementations of ABAC:

- OASIS XACML.
- Abbreviated Language for Authorization (ALFA).
- NIST's Next-generation Access Control (NGAC).

XACML, the eXtensible Access Control Markup Language, defines an architecture (shared with ALFA and NGAC), a policy language, and a request/response scheme. It does not handle attribute management (user attribute assignment, object attribute assignment, environment attribute assignment) which is left to traditional IAM tools, databases, and directories.

Companies, including every branch in the United States military, have started using ABAC. At a basic level, ABAC protects data with 'IF/THEN/AND' rules rather than assign data to users. The US Department of Commerce has made this a mandatory practice and the adoption is spreading throughout several governmental and military agencies.

The concept of ABAC can be applied at any level of the technology stack and an enterprise infrastructure. For example, ABAC can be used at the firewall, server, application, database, and data layer. The use of attributes bring additional context to evaluate the legitimacy of any request for access and inform the decision to grant or deny access.

An important consideration when evaluating ABAC solutions is to understand its potential overhead on performance and its impact on the user experience. It is expected that the more granular the controls, the higher the overhead.

ABAC can be used to apply attribute-based, fine-grained authorization to the API methods or functions. For instance, a banking API may expose an approveTransaction(transId) method. ABAC can be used to secure the call. With ABAC, a policy author can write the following:

- **Policy:** Managers can approve transactions up to their approval limit
- **Attributes Used:** Role, action ID, object type, amount, approval limit.

The flow would be as follows:

- The user, Alice, calls the API method approveTransaction(123)
- The API receives the call and authenticates the user.
- An interceptor in the API calls out to the authorization engine (typically called a Policy Decision Point or PDP) and asks: *Can Alice approve transaction 123?*
- The PDP retrieves the ABAC policy and necessary attributes.
- The PDP reaches a decision e.g. Permit or Deny and returns it to the API interceptor
- If the decision is Permit, the underlying API business logic is called. Otherwise the API returns an error or access denied.

One of the key benefits to ABAC is that the authorization policies and attributes can be defined in a technology neutral way. This means policies defined for APIs or databases can be reused in the application space. Common applications that can benefit from ABAC are:

- Content Management Systems
- ERPs
- Home-grown Applications
- Web Applications

The same process and flow as the one described in the API section applies here too. Security for databases has long been specific to the database vendors: Oracle VPD, IBM FGAC, and Microsoft RLS are all means to achieve fine-grained ABAC-like security.

An example would be:

- **Policy:** Managers can view transactions in their region
- **Reworked Policy in a Data-Centric Way:** Users with role == manager can do the action SELECT on table == TRANSACTIONS if user.region == transaction.region

Data security typically goes one step further than database security and applies control directly to the data element. This is often referred to as data-centric security. On traditional relational databases, ABAC policies can control access to data at the table, column, field, cell and sub-cell using logical controls with filtering conditions and masking based on attributes. Attributes can be data, user, session or tools based to deliver the greatest level of flexibility in dynamically granting/ denying access to a specific data element. On big data, and distributed file systems such as Hadoop, ABAC applied at the data layer control access to folder, sub-folder, file, sub-file and other granular.

Attribute-based access control can also be applied to Big Data systems like Hadoop. Policies similar to those used previously can be applied when retrieving data from data lakes.

As of Windows Server 2012, Microsoft has implemented an ABAC approach to controlling access to files and folders. This is achieved through dynamic access control (DAC) and Security Descriptor Definition Language (SDDL). SDDL can be seen as an ABAC language as it uses metadata of the user (claims) and of the file/folder to control access.

Discretionary Access Control (DAC)

Discretionary access control (DAC) is a type of access control defined by the Trusted Computer System Evaluation Criteria (TCSEC) as a means of restricting access to objects based on the identity of subjects and/or groups to which they belong. The controls are discretionary in the sense that a subject with a certain access permission is capable of passing that permission (perhaps indirectly) on to any other subject (unless restrained by mandatory access control).

Discretionary access control is commonly discussed in contrast to mandatory access control (MAC). Occasionally, a system as a whole is said to have "discretionary" or "purely discretionary" access control when that system lacks mandatory access control. On the other hand, systems can implement both MAC and DAC simultaneously, where DAC refers to one category of access controls that subjects can transfer among each other, and MAC refers to a second category of access controls that imposes constraints upon the first.

The meaning of the term in practice is not as clear-cut as the definition given in the TCSEC standard, because the TCSEC definition of DAC does not impose any implementation. There are at least two implementations: with owner (as a widespread example) and with capabilities.

The term DAC is commonly used in contexts that assume that every object has an *owner* that controls the permissions to access the object, probably because many systems do implement DAC using the concept of an owner. But the TCSEC definition does not say anything about owners, so technically an access control system doesn't have to have a concept of ownership to meet the TCSEC definition of DAC.

Users (owners) have under this DAC implementation the ability to make policy decisions and/or assign security attributes. A straightforward example is the Unix file mode which represent write, read, and execute in each of the 3 bits for each of

User, Group and Others. (It is prepended by another bit that indicates additional characteristics).

As another example, capability systems are sometimes described as providing discretionary controls because they permit subjects to transfer their access to other subjects, even though capability-based security is fundamentally not about restricting access "based on the identity of subjects". In general, capability systems do not allow permissions to be passed "to any other subject"; the subject wanting to pass its permissions must first have access to the receiving subject, and subjects generally only have access to a strictly limited set of subjects consistent with the principle of least privilege.

Mandatory Access Control (MAC)

Mandatory access control (MAC) refers to a type of access control by which a secured environment (e.g., an operating system or a database) constrains the ability of a *subject* or *initiator* to access or modify on an *object* or *target*. In the case of operating systems, the subject is a process or thread, while objects are files, directories, TCP/UDP ports, shared memory segments, or IO devices. Subjects and objects each have a set of security attributes. Whenever a subject attempts to access an object, the operating system kernel examines these security attributes, examines the authorization rules (aka *policy*) in place, and decides whether to grant access. A database management system, in its access control mechanism, can also apply mandatory access control; in this case, the objects are tables, views, procedures, etc.

In mandatory access control, the security policy is centrally controlled by a policy administrator and is guaranteed (in principle) to be enforced for all users. Users cannot override the policy and, for example, grant access to files that would otherwise be restricted. By contrast, discretionary access control (DAC), which also governs the ability of subjects to access objects, allows users the ability to make policy decisions or assign security attributes.

Historically and traditionally, MAC has been closely associated with multilevel security (MLS) and specialized military systems. In this context, MAC implies a high degree of rigor to satisfy the constraints of MLS systems. More recently, however, MAC has deviated out of the MLS niche and has started to become more mainstream. The more recent MAC implementations, such as SELinux and AppArmor for Linux and Mandatory Integrity Control for Windows, allow administrators to focus on issues such as network attacks and malware without the rigor or constraints of MLS.

Historically, MAC was strongly associated with multilevel security (MLS) as a means of protecting classified information of the United States. The Trusted Computer System Evaluation Criteria (TCSEC), the seminal work on the subject and often known as the Orange Book, provided the original definition of MAC as "a means of restricting access to objects based on the sensitivity (as represented by a label) of the information contained in the objects and the formal authorization (i.e., clearance) of subjects to access information of such sensitivity". Early implementations of MAC such as Honeywell's SCOMP, USAF's SACDIN, NSA's Blacker, and Boeing's MLS LAN focused on MLS to protect military-oriented security classification levels with robust enforcement.

The word "mandatory" in MAC has acquired a special meaning derived from its use with military systems. In this context, MAC implies an extremely high degree of robustness that assures that the control mechanisms can resist any type of subversion, thereby enabling them to enforce access controls that are mandated by the order of a government such as the Executive Order 12958. Enforcement is supposed to be more imperative than for commercial applications. This precludes enforcement by best-effort mechanisms. Only mechanisms that can provide absolute or near-absolute enforcement of the mandate are acceptable for MAC. This is a tall order and sometimes assumed unrealistic by those unfamiliar with high assurance strategies, and very difficult for those who are.

In some systems, users have the authority to decide whether to grant access to any other user. To allow that, all users have clearances for all data. This is not necessarily true of an MLS system. If individuals or processes exist that may be denied access to any of the data in the system environment, then the system must be trusted to enforce MAC. Since there can be various levels of data classification and user clearances, this implies a quantified scale for robustness. For example, more robustness is indicated for system environments containing classified "Top Secret" information and uncleared users than for one with "Secret" information and users cleared to at least "Confidential." To promote consistency and eliminate subjectivity in degrees of robustness, an extensive scientific analysis and risk assessment of the topic produced a landmark benchmark standardization quantifying security robustness capabilities of systems and mapping them to the degrees of trust warranted for various security environments. The result was documented in CSC-STD-004-85. Two relatively independent components of robustness were defined: Assurance level and functionality. Both were specified with a degree of precision that warranted significant confidence in certifications based on these criteria.

The Common Criteria standard is based on this science and it intended to preserve the assurance level as EAL levels and the functionality specifications as Protection Profiles. Of these two essential components of objective robustness benchmarks, only EAL levels were faithfully preserved. In one case, TCSEC level C2 (not a MAC-capable category) was fairly faithfully preserved in the Common Criteria, as the Controlled Access Protection Profile (CAPP). MLS Protection Profiles (such as

MLSOSPP similar to B2) is more general than B2. They are pursuant to MLS, but lack the detailed implementation requirements of their Orange Book predecessors, focusing more on objectives. This gives certifiers more subjective flexibility in deciding whether the evaluated product's technical features adequately achieve the objective, potentially eroding consistency of evaluated products and making it easier to attain certification for less trustworthy products. For these reasons, the importance of the technical details of the Protection Profile is critical to determining the suitability of a product.

Such an architecture prevents an authenticated user or process at a specific classification or trust-level from accessing information, processes, or devices in a different level. This provides a containment mechanism of users and processes, both known and unknown. An unknown program might comprise an untrusted application where the system should monitor or control accesses to devices and files.

A few MAC implementations, such as Unisys' Blacker project, were certified robust enough to separate Top Secret from Unclassified late in the last millennium. Their underlying technology became obsolete and they were not refreshed. Today there are no current implementations certified by TCSEC to that level of robust implementation. However, some less robust products exist.

Starting with Windows Vista and Server 2008, Microsoft has incorporated Mandatory Integrity Control (MIC) in the Windows operating system, which adds integrity levels (IL) to running processes. The goal is to restrict access of less trustworthy processes to sensitive info. MIC defines five integrity levels: Low, medium, high, system, and trusted installer. By default, processes started at medium IL. Elevated processes receive high IL. Child processes, by default, inherit their parent's integrity, although the parent process can launch them with a lower IL. For example, Internet Explorer 7 launches its subprocesses with low IL. Windows controls access to objects based on ILs. Named objects, including files, registry keys or other processes and threads, have an entry in their ACL indicating the minimum IL of the process that can use the object. MIC enforces that a process can write to or delete an object only when its IL is equal to or higher than the object's IL. Furthermore, to prevent access to sensitive data in memory, processes can't open processes with a higher IL for read access.

Apple Inc. has incorporated an implementation of the TrustedBSD framework in its iOS and macOS operating systems. (The word "mac" in "macOS" is short for "Macintosh" and has nothing to do with the abbreviation of "mandatory access control.") The command-line function sandbox_init provides a limited high-level sandboxing interface.

Version 5.0 and later of the Android operating system, developed by Google, use SELinux to enforce a MAC security model on top of its original UID-based DAC approach.

Linux and many other Unix distributions have MAC for CPU (multi-ring), disk, and memory. While OS software may not manage privileges well, Linux became famous during the 1990s as being more secure and far more stable than non-Unix alternatives.

Amon Ott's RSBAC (Rule Set Based Access Control) provides a framework for Linux kernels that allows several different security policy / decision modules. One of the models implemented is Mandatory Access Control model. A general goal of RSBAC design was to try to reach (obsolete) Orange Book (TCSEC) B1 level. The model of mandatory access control used in RSBAC is mostly the same as in Unix System V/MLS, Version 1.2.1 (developed in 1989 by the National Computer Security Center of the USA with classification B1/TCSEC). RSBAC requires a set of patches to the stock kernel, which are maintained quite well by the project owner.

Smack (Simplified Mandatory Access Control Kernel) is a Linux kernel security module that protects data and process interaction from malicious manipulation using a set of custom mandatory access control rules, with simplicity as its main design goal. It has been officially merged since the Linux 2.6.25 release.

TOMOYO Linux is a lightweight MAC implementation for Linux and Embedded Linux, developed by NTT Data Corporation. It has been merged in Linux Kernel mainline version 2.6.30 in June 2009. Differently from the label-based approach used by SELinux, TOMOYO Linux performs a pathname-based Mandatory Access Control, separating security domains according to process invocation history, which describes the system behavior. Policy are described in terms of pathnames. A security domain is simply defined by a process call chain, and represented by a string. There are 4 modes: disabled, learning, permissive, enforcing. Administrators can assign different modes for different domains. TOMOYO Linux introduced the "learning" mode, in which the accesses occurred in the kernel are automatically analyzed and stored to generate MAC policy: this mode could then be the first step of policy writing, making it easy to customize later.

SUSE Linux and Ubuntu 7.10 have added a MAC implementation called AppArmor, which utilizes the Linux Security Modules (LSM) interface of Linux 2.6. LSM provides a kernel API that allows modules of kernel code to govern ACL (DAC ACL, access-control lists). AppArmor is not capable of restricting all programs and is optionally in the Linux kernel as of version 2.6.36.

GRsecurity is a patch for the Linux kernel providing a MAC implementation (precisely, it is an RBAC implementation). grsecurity is not implemented via the LSM API.

Astra Linux OS developed for Russian Army has its own mandatory access control.

FreeBSD supports Mandatory Access Control, implemented as part of the TrustedBSD project. It was introduced in FreeBSD 5.0. Since FreeBSD 7.2, MAC support is enabled by default. The framework is extensible; various MAC modules implement policies such as Biba and multilevel security. Sun's Trusted Solaris uses a mandatory and system-enforced access control mechanism (MAC), where clearances and labels are used to enforce a security policy. However note that the capability to manage labels does not imply the kernel strength to operate in multilevel security mode. Access to the labels and control mechanisms are not robustly protected from corruption in protected domain maintained by a kernel. The applications a user runs are combined with the security label at which the user works in the session. Access to information, programs and devices are only weakly controlled.

Best Practices for Implementing Authorization

- **Principle of Least Privilege:** Grant users the minimum level of access necessary to perform their tasks. This reduces the risk of unauthorized access to sensitive data and minimizes the potential impact of compromised accounts.
- **Role-Based Access Control:** Implement RBAC to simplify the management of permissions. Define clear roles and assign permissions based on the responsibilities associated with each role. Regularly review and update roles to ensure they reflect current organizational needs.
- **Attribute-Based Access Control:** Use ABAC to provide fine-grained control over access decisions. Define policies that consider user attributes, resource attributes, and environmental conditions to dynamically determine access permissions.
- **Multi-Factor Authorization:** Combine multiple factors, such as user roles, attributes, and context, to make authorization decisions. This approach enhances security by considering various aspects before granting access.
- **Token-Based Authorization:** Use secure tokens (e.g., OAuth tokens, JWT) to manage user sessions and authorization. Tokens should be signed, encrypted, and have a limited lifespan to prevent unauthorized use. Implement mechanisms to refresh tokens securely.
- **Regular Audits and Monitoring:** Conduct regular audits of access controls and authorization mechanisms to identify and rectify any discrepancies. Implement continuous monitoring to detect and respond to unauthorized access attempts in real time.

- **Dynamic Permission Management:** Implement mechanisms to dynamically adjust permissions based on changing user roles, attributes, and context. This ensures that access controls remain relevant and effective as the user's status or environment changes.
- **Secure API Gateways:** Use secure API gateways to manage and enforce authorization policies for API calls. This centralizes authorization logic and ensures consistent application of access controls across all API endpoints.

Common Challenges in Authorization

- **Complexity of Managing Permissions:** As applications grow, managing permissions becomes increasingly complex. Implementing a scalable and manageable authorization model, such as RBAC or ABAC, can help simplify this complexity.
- **Balancing Security and Usability:** Ensuring robust security while maintaining a seamless user experience is challenging. Striking the right balance requires careful planning and consideration of both security needs and user convenience.
- **Keeping Authorization Policies Up-to-Date:** Authorization policies must evolve with changing user roles, responsibilities, and organizational needs. Regular reviews and updates are necessary to ensure that policies remain relevant and effective.
- **Ensuring Consistency Across Platforms:** Mobile apps often interact with web applications and backend services. Ensuring consistent authorization policies across all platforms is crucial to maintaining security and user experience.

Case Studies in Effective Authorization Implementation

- **Google Drive:** Google Drive uses RBAC to manage access to files and folders. Users can share documents with specific roles (viewer, commenter, editor), ensuring that only authorized users can view or modify the content.
- **AWS Identity and Access Management (IAM):** AWS IAM implements a combination of RBAC and ABAC to manage access to AWS resources. Policies can be defined based on user roles, attributes, and conditions, providing granular control over permissions.
- **Slack:** Slack uses a combination of RBAC and token-based authorization to manage access to workspaces, channels, and messages. Permissions

are assigned based on user roles (admin, member, guest), and secure tokens are used for session management.

Future Trends in Authorization

- **Zero Trust Architecture:** Zero Trust Architecture (ZTA) emphasizes continuous verification of user identity and access permissions, regardless of location. This approach enhances security by assuming that threats can come from inside and outside the network.
- **Machine Learning for Adaptive Authorization:** Machine learning can be used to analyze user behavior and adapt authorization policies dynamically. This approach enhances security by identifying and responding to unusual access patterns in real time.
- **Decentralized Identity and Access Management:** Decentralized identity solutions leverage blockchain technology to provide users with control over their identities. This approach can enhance security and privacy by reducing reliance on centralized authorities.
- **Context-Aware Authorization:** Context-aware authorization considers the context of access requests, such as location, time, and device, to make more informed decisions. This dynamic approach enhances security by adapting to changing conditions.

CHAPTER 11

PRIVACY CONSIDERATIONS IN MOBILE APPS

11.1 GDPR AND PRIVACY COMPLIANCE

The General Data Protection Regulation (GDPR) represents a significant evolution in the realm of data protection and privacy compliance. Adopted by the European Union (EU) in 2016 and enforceable from May 25, 2018, GDPR has fundamentally changed how organizations around the world approach data privacy.

GDPR has set a new standard for data protection and privacy compliance, compelling organizations to adopt rigorous data protection practices. While achieving compliance can be challenging, the benefits of GDPR extend beyond avoiding fines. By prioritizing data protection, organizations can build trust with their customers, enhance their reputation, and gain a competitive advantage in today's data-driven world. As data privacy continues to evolve, staying informed about regulatory changes and implementing best practices will be crucial for maintaining compliance and protecting individuals' rights.

11.1.1 Understanding GDPR: Core Principles

Lawfulness, Fairness, and Transparency

GDPR mandates that personal data must be processed lawfully, fairly, and in a transparent manner. Organizations are required to provide clear and accessible information to individuals about how their data is being used. This ensures that data subjects are fully informed about the purposes for data processing and the legal basis for doing so.

Purpose Limitation

Data must be collected for specified, explicit, and legitimate purposes and not further processed in a manner incompatible with those purposes. This principle ensures that organizations collect data only for clearly defined objectives and do not use it for unrelated activities.

Data Minimization

Organizations are required to collect only the data that is necessary for the intended purpose. This principle, known as data minimization, helps reduce the risk of data breaches and protects individuals' privacy by limiting the amount of personal information held by organizations.

Accuracy

GDPR emphasizes the importance of maintaining accurate and up-to-date personal data. Organizations must take reasonable steps to ensure the accuracy of the data they hold and correct any inaccuracies without delay.

Storage Limitation

Personal data must be kept in a form that permits identification of data subjects for no longer than necessary for the purposes for which it is processed. This principle helps mitigate the risks associated with long-term data storage and ensures that data is deleted when it is no longer needed.

Integrity and Confidentiality

Organizations must ensure the security of personal data through appropriate technical and organizational measures. This includes protecting data against unauthorized access, accidental loss, destruction, or damage.

Accountability

GDPR places a strong emphasis on accountability, requiring organizations to demonstrate compliance with its principles. This involves maintaining detailed records of data processing activities, conducting impact assessments, and implementing data protection policies.

11.1.2 Key Requirements of GDPR

Data Subject Rights

GDPR grants individuals a set of robust rights regarding their personal data. These rights include the right to access, rectify, erase, and restrict the processing of their data. Additionally, individuals have the right to data portability and the right to object to data processing in certain circumstances.

Consent

Obtaining valid consent is a cornerstone of GDPR compliance. Consent must be freely given, specific, informed, and unambiguous. Organizations must provide clear information about the data processing activities and ensure that consent is obtained through an affirmative action, such as checking a box or clicking a button.

Data Protection Officer (DPO)

Organizations that process large volumes of personal data or handle sensitive data are required to appoint a Data Protection Officer (DPO). The DPO is responsible for overseeing data protection strategies, ensuring compliance with GDPR, and acting as a point of contact for data subjects and supervisory authorities.

Data Breach Notification

In the event of a data breach, GDPR requires organizations to notify the relevant supervisory authority within 72 hours of becoming aware of the breach.

If the breach poses a high risk to individuals' rights and freedoms, the affected data subjects must also be informed without undue delay.

Data Protection Impact Assessments (DPIAs)

DPIAs are required for processing activities that are likely to result in a high risk to individuals' rights and freedoms.

These assessments help organizations identify and mitigate risks associated with data processing, ensuring compliance with GDPR and protecting individuals' privacy.

11.1.3 Challenges of GDPR Compliance

Global Reach and Jurisdiction

One of the most significant challenges of GDPR is its extraterritorial reach. Any organization, regardless of location, that processes the personal data of EU citizens must comply with GDPR. This poses challenges for multinational companies and requires a thorough understanding of the regulation's requirements.

Balancing Privacy and Innovation

Organizations must strike a balance between protecting individuals' privacy and fostering innovation. GDPR compliance can sometimes hinder data-driven projects and technological advancements. Companies need to find ways to innovate while adhering to strict data protection standards.

Complex and Evolving Regulation

GDPR is a complex regulation with numerous requirements and guidelines. Keeping up with the evolving regulatory landscape and ensuring ongoing compliance can be challenging, especially for organizations with limited resources or expertise in data protection.

High Costs of Non-Compliance

Non-compliance with GDPR can result in severe financial penalties, with fines of up to 20 million euros or 4% of the organization's global annual revenue, whichever is higher. The high costs of non-compliance underscore the importance of investing in robust data protection measures.

11.1.4 Best Practices for GDPR Compliance

Conduct Regular Audits

Regular audits of data processing activities are essential for ensuring ongoing GDPR compliance. These audits help identify potential gaps in data protection practices and provide opportunities to implement corrective measures.

Implement Data Protection Policies

Organizations should develop and implement comprehensive data protection policies that outline how personal data is collected, processed, stored, and deleted. These policies should be regularly reviewed and updated to reflect changes in data protection laws and organizational practices.

Train Employees

Employee training is critical for fostering a culture of data protection within an organization. Regular training sessions on GDPR requirements and data protection best practices can help employees understand their responsibilities and reduce the risk of data breaches.

Use Privacy by Design and Default

Privacy by design and default is a key principle of GDPR, requiring organizations to incorporate data protection measures into their systems and processes from the outset. This includes implementing strong security measures, minimizing data collection, and ensuring that privacy settings are set to the highest level by default.

Appoint a Data Protection Officer

Appointing a dedicated Data Protection Officer (DPO) can help organizations navigate the complexities of GDPR compliance. The DPO can provide expert guidance, oversee data protection strategies, and ensure that the organization meets its regulatory obligations.

Leverage Technology Solutions

Technology can play a crucial role in achieving GDPR compliance. Data protection management tools, encryption, and anonymization techniques can help organizations safeguard personal data and streamline compliance efforts.

11.2 BALANCING PERSONALIZATION WITH USER PRIVACY

In today's digital age, personalization has become a significant aspect of the user experience. Businesses and service providers strive to offer tailored experiences to their users by leveraging vast amounts of data. However, the collection and use of personal data raise substantial privacy concerns. Balancing personalization with user privacy is a delicate act that requires thoughtful strategies and robust frameworks.

Balancing personalization with user privacy is a complex but essential endeavor in the digital age. Companies must adopt transparent, ethical, and user-centric approaches to data collection and usage. By implementing robust security measures, empowering users with control over their data, and leveraging privacy-preserving technologies, businesses can achieve a balance that enhances user experience while safeguarding privacy. The path forward involves continuous adaptation to evolving privacy standards, technological advancements, and user expectations, ensuring that the benefits of personalization are realized without compromising user trust and privacy.

11.2.1 The Importance of Personalization

Personalization enhances user experience by delivering content, recommendations, and services that are specifically tailored to individual preferences and behaviors. It can drive customer satisfaction, engagement, and loyalty. For instance, streaming services like Netflix use personalization algorithms to suggest shows and movies, improving user engagement. E-commerce platforms utilize similar techniques to recommend products based on previous purchases and browsing history, thereby increasing sales and customer retention.

11.2.2 Privacy Concerns in the Digital Era

With the benefits of personalization come significant privacy concerns. Users are increasingly aware of the data being collected about them and are concerned about how it is used, stored, and shared. High-profile data breaches and misuse of personal information have heightened these concerns. Privacy is not just a legal issue but a trust issue; when users feel their privacy is compromised, it can damage a company's reputation and erode user trust.

11.2.3 Legal and Regulatory Landscape

Various laws and regulations have been enacted worldwide to address privacy concerns. The General Data Protection Regulation (GDPR) in Europe, the California Consumer Privacy Act (CCPA) in the United States, and other similar regulations aim to give users more control over their personal data. These laws require companies to be transparent about data collection practices, obtain explicit consent from users, and provide options for users to access, correct, or delete their data.

11.2.4 Strategies for Balancing Personalization and Privacy

Achieving a balance between personalization and privacy involves several key strategies:

Transparency and Consent

Transparency is crucial in building trust. Companies should clearly communicate what data is being collected, how it will be used, and with whom it will be shared.

Obtaining explicit consent from users before collecting their data is not only a regulatory requirement but also a best practice. Providing users with clear choices about their data can help mitigate privacy concerns while still enabling personalization.

Data Minimization and Anonymization

Data minimization involves collecting only the data that is necessary for the intended purpose. By limiting data collection to essential information, companies can reduce the risk of data breaches and misuse. Anonymization techniques, where personally identifiable information is removed or masked, can also help in using data for personalization without compromising user privacy.

Robust Security Measures

Ensuring robust security measures is essential to protect user data. Encryption, secure access controls, and regular security audits can help prevent unauthorized access and data breaches. Companies should also have incident response plans in place to address any security breaches promptly and effectively.

User Control and Empowerment

Empowering users with control over their data is a key aspect of balancing personalization and privacy. Providing easy-to-use tools for users to manage their data, including options to view, edit, and delete their information, can enhance user trust. Allowing users to set their privacy preferences and providing clear information on how these settings affect their experience can also help balance personalization and privacy.

11.2.5 Ethical Considerations

Beyond legal compliance, ethical considerations play a crucial role in balancing personalization and privacy. Companies should adopt ethical data practices that respect user autonomy and privacy. This includes being mindful of the potential impacts of data collection and personalization on different user groups and avoiding practices that may be perceived as intrusive or manipulative.

11.2.6 Case Studies and Examples

Several companies have successfully navigated the balance between personalization and privacy:

Apple

Apple has positioned itself as a privacy-focused company, emphasizing that privacy is a fundamental human right. The company's approach to personalization involves on-device processing, where data is processed locally on the user's device rather than being sent to servers. This method enhances personalization while minimizing data exposure.

Mozilla Firefox

Mozilla Firefox offers robust privacy features, including enhanced tracking protection and tools for users to manage their data. The browser also provides clear explanations about data collection and usage, ensuring transparency and user control.

11.2.7 Future Trends and Technologies

Emerging technologies such as artificial intelligence (AI) and machine learning (ML) present both opportunities and challenges for personalization and privacy. AI and ML can drive more sophisticated and accurate personalization, but they also require access to large datasets. Privacy-preserving technologies, such as federated learning and differential privacy, are being developed to enable AI and ML while protecting user privacy. These technologies allow models to be trained on decentralized data sources without exposing individual data points.

CHAPTER 12
MOBILE PAYMENT SECURITY

12.1 IMPLEMENTING SECURE MOBILE PAYMENT SOLUTIONS

In recent years, mobile payment solutions have revolutionized the way consumers transact, offering convenience and speed. However, as the adoption of mobile payments grows, so do the concerns about security. Implementing secure mobile payment solutions is critical to protect sensitive financial data and maintain user trust.

Implementing secure mobile payment solutions is crucial in today's digital economy. By incorporating robust security features such as encryption, tokenization, and multi-factor authentication, and adhering to best practices, service providers can protect sensitive financial data and maintain user trust. As technology continues to evolve, staying vigilant and proactive in addressing security challenges will be essential to ensure the continued growth and success of mobile payment systems. Balancing security with user experience and staying ahead of emerging threats will define the future of secure mobile payments.

12.1.1 The Rise of Mobile Payments

Mobile payments have gained immense popularity due to their convenience and the proliferation of smartphones. Services like Apple Pay, Google Wallet, and Samsung Pay allow users to make purchases with just a tap of their device. Additionally, mobile payment apps such as Venmo and PayPal facilitate peer-to-peer transactions. This shift towards mobile payments has made financial transactions more accessible, but it has also introduced new security challenges.

12.1.2 Security Challenges in Mobile Payments

The security of mobile payment solutions is paramount as they handle sensitive financial information. Some of the primary security challenges include:

- **Data Breaches:** Mobile payment systems are attractive targets for cybercriminals seeking to steal financial data. Data breaches can lead to significant financial losses and damage to the service provider's reputation.
- **Malware and Phishing Attacks:** Mobile devices are susceptible to malware and phishing attacks, which can compromise payment

information. Cybercriminals use these methods to gain unauthorized access to users' financial data.

- **Device Theft:** The theft or loss of a mobile device can lead to unauthorized transactions if the payment information is not adequately secured.

12.1.3 Essential Security Features for Mobile Payment Solutions

To address these challenges, mobile payment solutions must incorporate robust security features:

- **Encryption:** Encryption is a fundamental security measure that ensures data is protected during transmission and storage. Advanced encryption standards (AES) should be used to secure payment data, making it unreadable to unauthorized parties.
- **Tokenization:** Tokenization replaces sensitive payment information, such as credit card numbers, with unique tokens. These tokens can be used to process payments without exposing the actual data, reducing the risk of data breaches.
- **Multi-Factor Authentication (MFA):** MFA adds an extra layer of security by requiring users to provide multiple forms of identification, such as a password and a biometric verification (e.g., fingerprint or facial recognition). This makes it more difficult for unauthorized users to access the payment system.
- **Secure Payment Gateways:** Payment gateways should be PCI DSS (Payment Card Industry Data Security Standard) compliant, ensuring they adhere to stringent security standards for handling payment information.

12.1.4 Best Practices for Implementing Secure Mobile Payments

Implementing secure mobile payment solutions involves adopting best practices that address both technological and user-centric aspects:

- **Regular Security Audits:** Conducting regular security audits and vulnerability assessments helps identify and address potential weaknesses in the mobile payment system. This proactive approach ensures that security measures are up-to-date and effective.
- **User Education:** Educating users about security best practices is crucial. Users should be informed about the importance of keeping their devices secure, recognizing phishing attempts, and using strong, unique passwords.
- **Secure App Development:** Developers should follow secure coding practices to minimize vulnerabilities in the mobile payment app. This

includes input validation, secure data storage, and regular updates to address security patches.

- **Compliance with Regulations:** Mobile payment providers must comply with relevant regulations and standards, such as PCI DSS, GDPR, and CCPA. Compliance ensures that the solution meets industry standards for data protection and user privacy.

12.1.5 Case Studies: Secure Mobile Payment Solutions

Several companies have successfully implemented secure mobile payment solutions, setting benchmarks for the industry:

- **Apple Pay:** Apple Pay uses a combination of tokenization and biometric authentication to secure transactions. Each transaction is authorized with a one-time dynamic security code, ensuring that payment information is not stored or shared.
- **PayPal:** PayPal employs advanced encryption and tokenization to protect user data. The platform also offers MFA and regular security monitoring to detect and prevent fraudulent activities.

12.1.6 Future Trends in Mobile Payment Security

The landscape of mobile payment security is continually evolving, with new technologies and trends emerging:

- **Biometric Authentication:** Biometric authentication methods, such as fingerprint scanning, facial recognition, and voice recognition, are becoming more prevalent. These methods provide a higher level of security compared to traditional passwords.
- **Blockchain Technology:** Blockchain technology offers a decentralized and transparent way to secure transactions. By using cryptographic techniques and distributed ledgers, blockchain can enhance the security and integrity of mobile payments.
- **Artificial Intelligence (AI) and Machine Learning (ML):** AI and ML can be used to detect and prevent fraudulent activities in real-time. These technologies analyze transaction patterns and user behaviors to identify anomalies and potential threats.

12.1.7 Challenges and Considerations

Despite advancements in technology, there are still challenges in implementing secure mobile payment solutions:

- **Balancing Security and User Experience:** Ensuring robust security without compromising user experience is a delicate balance. Overly stringent security measures can lead to user frustration and decreased adoption.

- **Interoperability:** Ensuring that mobile payment solutions are interoperable with various devices and platforms is essential for widespread adoption. However, this can also introduce security vulnerabilities if not managed properly.
- **Constantly Evolving Threat Landscape:** Cyber threats are constantly evolving, requiring continuous updates and improvements to security measures. Staying ahead of potential threats is a significant challenge for mobile payment providers.

12.2 ADDRESSING RISKS IN MOBILE TRANSACTIONS

Mobile transactions have revolutionized the way we conduct financial activities, offering convenience and efficiency. However, this innovation brings a range of risks that need to be addressed to ensure secure and trustworthy financial interactions. Addressing the risks associated with mobile transactions requires a multifaceted approach that involves enhancing device and network security, protecting user privacy, preventing fraud, and ensuring regulatory compliance. By implementing these strategies, businesses can provide a secure and trustworthy environment for mobile transactions, thereby gaining the confidence and trust of their users.

12.2.1 Introduction to Mobile Transaction Risks

Mobile transactions encompass a wide array of activities, including online shopping, banking, and peer-to-peer payments. With the increasing reliance on smartphones for these activities, understanding the associated risks is crucial for both consumers and businesses. The primary risks in mobile transactions include security vulnerabilities, privacy concerns, fraud, and regulatory compliance issues.

12.2.2 Security Vulnerabilities

Device Security

Mobile devices are susceptible to various security threats, such as malware, phishing attacks, and unauthorized access. Many users fail to implement basic security measures, like using strong passwords or enabling biometric authentication, making their devices easy targets for cybercriminals.

Network Security

Public Wi-Fi networks pose significant risks to mobile transactions. These networks are often unsecured, allowing hackers to intercept data transmitted between the user and the service provider. This interception can lead to unauthorized access to sensitive information, such as login credentials and financial data.

App Security

Not all mobile apps follow stringent security protocols. Some may have vulnerabilities that can be exploited by hackers to gain access to user data. Additionally, malicious apps can disguise themselves as legitimate ones, tricking users into downloading them and compromising their devices.

12.2.3 Privacy Concerns

Data Collection and Usage

Mobile transactions often require the collection of personal information, including names, addresses, and payment details. Users may not always be aware of how this data is used or stored. Companies may share or sell this data to third parties, leading to privacy breaches.

Location Tracking

Many mobile apps track users' locations to provide personalized services. However, this information can be misused if it falls into the wrong hands. Unauthorized access to location data can lead to stalking or targeted attacks.

12.2.4 Fraud

Phishing and Social Engineering

Phishing attacks are prevalent in the mobile space, where attackers send deceptive messages to trick users into revealing their personal and financial information. These messages often appear to be from legitimate sources, making it difficult for users to identify them as fraudulent.

SIM Swapping

SIM swapping is a form of identity theft where fraudsters transfer a victim's phone number to a new SIM card. This allows them to intercept calls and messages, including two-factor authentication codes, enabling them to gain access to the victim's financial accounts.

Unauthorized Transactions

Unauthorized transactions can occur when cybercriminals gain access to a user's mobile device or account credentials. These transactions can result in significant financial losses and can be challenging to resolve.

12.2.5 Regulatory Compliance

Data Protection Regulations

Compliance with data protection regulations, such as the General Data Protection Regulation (GDPR) and the California Consumer Privacy Act (CCPA), is essential for businesses handling mobile transactions. These regulations require businesses to implement robust data protection measures and to inform users about how their data is collected, used, and stored.

Payment Card Industry Data Security Standard (PCI DSS)

The PCI DSS is a set of security standards designed to protect card information during and after a financial transaction.

Businesses involved in mobile transactions must comply with these standards to ensure the secure processing of payment card data.

12.2.6 Mitigation Strategies

Enhancing Device Security

- **Strong Authentication:** Implementing strong authentication methods, such as biometric authentication (fingerprint or facial recognition) and two-factor authentication (2FA), can significantly enhance device security. These measures make it more difficult for unauthorized users to access the device and conduct transactions.
- **Regular Updates:** Keeping mobile devices and apps updated with the latest security patches is crucial in protecting against known vulnerabilities. Regular updates ensure that security weaknesses are addressed promptly.

Securing Networks

- **Use of VPNs:** Encouraging the use of Virtual Private Networks (VPNs) can help secure data transmitted over public Wi-Fi networks. VPNs encrypt the data, making it more difficult for hackers to intercept and read.
- **Avoiding Public Wi-Fi for Transactions:** Users should be advised to avoid conducting sensitive transactions over public Wi-Fi networks. Instead, they should use cellular data or secured Wi-Fi connections.

App Security Measures

- **Vetting and Monitoring:** Businesses should vet mobile apps rigorously before approving them for use. Continuous monitoring for security threats and vulnerabilities is also essential to maintain a secure app environment.
- **Educating Users:** Educating users about the risks of downloading apps from untrusted sources and encouraging them to download apps only from official app stores can reduce the likelihood of malware infections.

Protecting Privacy

- **Transparency in Data Collection:** Businesses should be transparent about their data collection practices and obtain explicit consent from users before collecting personal information. Clear privacy policies can help users understand how their data is used and stored.
- **Minimizing Data Collection:** Collecting only the necessary data required for a transaction can minimize the risk of privacy breaches. Businesses should avoid collecting excessive personal information that is not essential for the service provided.

Preventing Fraud

- **Phishing Awareness:** Raising awareness about phishing scams and educating users on how to recognize and avoid them is crucial. Users should be encouraged to verify the authenticity of messages and links before clicking on them.
- **Monitoring for Suspicious Activity:** Implementing systems to monitor transactions for suspicious activity can help detect and prevent fraud. Unusual transaction patterns should trigger alerts and prompt further investigation.

Compliance with Regulations

Implementing Data Protection Measures

Businesses must implement robust data protection measures to comply with regulations like GDPR and CCPA. This includes encrypting sensitive data, conducting regular security audits, and ensuring that third-party service providers also comply with these regulations.

Adhering to PCI DSS

Ensuring compliance with PCI DSS involves implementing measures such as encryption of cardholder data, maintaining secure systems and networks, and regularly monitoring and testing security systems. Compliance with these standards is essential for protecting payment card data during mobile transactions.

PART V

MOBILE CONNECTIVITY AND NETWORKING

CHAPTER 13

MOBILE NETWORKS AND COMMUNICATION PROTOCOLS

13.1 3G, 4G AND 5G NETWORKS

13.1.1 3G

The advent of 3G mobile connectivity marked a significant milestone in the evolution of telecommunications. Offering enhanced data transfer rates and improved network reliability, 3G networks facilitated the widespread adoption of mobile internet and revolutionized the way people communicate, access information, and perform everyday tasks. 3G mobile connectivity and networking have had a profound impact on the telecommunications landscape, driving the mobile internet revolution and transforming the way people live, work, and communicate. Despite its limitations, the benefits of 3G connectivity—enhanced data speeds, improved network capacity, and global roaming—have left an indelible mark on society. As the world moves towards 4G, 5G, and beyond, the legacy of 3G serves as a testament to the remarkable progress in mobile technology and its potential to shape the future.

Technological Foundation of 3G

Evolution from 2G to 3G

The transition from 2G to 3G represented a major leap in mobile technology. While 2G networks primarily supported voice calls and limited text messaging, 3G introduced high-speed data services. This advancement was made possible through the implementation of new radio technologies and protocols, such as Wideband Code Division Multiple Access (W-CDMA) and Universal Mobile Telecommunications System (UMTS).

W-CDMA and UMTS

W-CDMA, a key component of 3G networks, allows multiple users to share the same frequency band by assigning unique codes to each user. This technique significantly enhances spectral efficiency and supports higher data rates. UMTS, on the other hand, is the 3G standard developed by the 3rd Generation Partnership Project (3GPP). It encompasses W-CDMA and various other technologies, providing a comprehensive framework for 3G mobile communication.

Network Architecture

The architecture of 3G networks consists of several key components, including the User Equipment (UE), Radio Access Network (RAN), and Core Network (CN). The UE, typically a mobile phone or modem, communicates with the RAN, which handles radio signal transmission and reception. The RAN connects to the CN, which manages data routing, switching, and service delivery. This layered architecture ensures efficient data flow and robust connectivity.

Benefits of 3G Connectivity

Enhanced Data Speeds

One of the most significant benefits of 3G connectivity is the substantial increase in data transfer speeds compared to 2G networks. 3G networks support data rates of up to 2 Mbps for stationary or walking users and 384 kbps for users in a moving vehicle. This improvement enabled the seamless streaming of multimedia content, faster web browsing, and more efficient data transfer.

Improved Network Capacity

3G networks offer improved capacity to handle a larger number of simultaneous connections. This is particularly important in densely populated urban areas, where network congestion can degrade service quality. By efficiently managing network resources, 3G technology provides a more reliable and consistent user experience.

Global Roaming

The standardization of 3G technologies facilitated global roaming capabilities. Users could travel internationally and maintain connectivity, as 3G networks were widely adopted across various regions. This global compatibility was a significant advantage for business travelers and tourists, ensuring they could stay connected regardless of their location.

Limitations of 3G Networks

Infrastructure Costs

Deploying 3G infrastructure required significant investment from telecom operators. The need to upgrade existing 2G infrastructure to support 3G technologies, such as W-CDMA and UMTS, posed financial challenges. Additionally, maintaining and optimizing 3G networks demanded ongoing expenditure.

Power Consumption

3G devices typically consume more power than their 2G counterparts. The higher data transfer rates and increased processing demands of 3G technology lead to faster battery depletion. This was a notable concern for mobile users, as it impacted the usability and convenience of their devices.

Limited Coverage

While 3G networks offered improved performance, their coverage was initially limited compared to the widespread availability of 2G networks. Rural and remote areas often lacked 3G infrastructure, restricting the benefits of high-speed mobile internet to urban and suburban regions.

Impact on Society

Mobile Internet Revolution

3G connectivity played a pivotal role in the mobile internet revolution. The ability to access high-speed internet on mobile devices transformed various aspects of daily life, including communication, entertainment, education, and commerce. Social media platforms, video streaming services, and mobile applications flourished, creating new opportunities for businesses and individuals alike.

Economic Growth

The widespread adoption of 3G technology contributed to economic growth by enabling new business models and services. Mobile banking, e-commerce, and remote work became more viable with reliable mobile internet access. Furthermore, the telecommunications industry experienced growth as demand for 3G-enabled devices and services increased.

Bridging the Digital Divide

3G connectivity helped bridge the digital divide by providing internet access to previously underserved populations. In many developing countries, 3G networks were the first introduction to the internet for millions of people. This access facilitated educational opportunities, healthcare improvements, and socio-economic development.

Transition to 4G and Beyond

Evolution to 4G LTE

The evolution from 3G to 4G LTE (Long-Term Evolution) brought further advancements in mobile connectivity. 4G networks offer significantly higher data rates, lower latency, and improved network efficiency compared to 3G. This transition enabled the proliferation of data-intensive applications, such as high-definition video streaming, online gaming, and real-time communication.

Legacy of 3G

Despite the advent of 4G and the ongoing deployment of 5G networks, 3G remains a foundational technology in the history of mobile communication. Its introduction paved the way for subsequent generations of mobile connectivity, setting the stage for the rapid technological advancements that followed. Understanding the legacy of 3G is essential for appreciating the current and future landscape of mobile networking.

Challenges and Opportunities

The phase-out of 3G networks presents challenges and opportunities for the telecommunications industry. Operators must balance the need to maintain 3G services for legacy devices and applications with the imperative to allocate resources towards more advanced technologies. Transitioning users to newer networks while ensuring uninterrupted service requires careful planning and execution.

13.1.2 4G

Fourth-generation mobile networks, commonly known as 4G, represent a significant evolution in wireless communication technology. 4G succeeded the third-generation (3G) networks, offering enhanced data transfer speeds, better reliability, and more efficient connectivity.

4G mobile connectivity has transformed the landscape of wireless communication, providing the high-speed, reliable connectivity needed to support a wide range of applications and services. From mobile internet and video streaming to real-time gaming and IoT, 4G technology has enabled unprecedented levels of connectivity and convenience. As we look to the future, the advancements made with 4G will serve as the foundation for the next generation of mobile networks, paving the way for a more connected and innovative world.

Evolution from 3G to 4G

The transition from 3G to 4G was driven by the increasing demand for high-speed internet and the growing number of internet-enabled devices. While 3G networks provided a significant improvement over the previous 2G systems, they were not equipped to handle the explosion of mobile data usage and the diverse range of applications that emerged in the late 2000s and early 2010s. 4G networks were designed to meet these demands, offering faster data rates, lower latency, and greater capacity.

Key Features of 4G Technology

- **Enhanced Data Speeds:** One of the most notable features of 4G technology is its superior data transfer speeds. 4G networks can offer peak download speeds of up to 1 Gbps and upload speeds of up to 500 Mbps. These speeds are significantly higher than those provided by 3G networks, enabling users to download large files, stream high-definition videos, and use data-intensive applications without experiencing lag or buffering.

- **Lower Latency:** Latency refers to the time it takes for data to travel from the source to the destination. 4G networks have significantly reduced latency compared to 3G, with typical values ranging from 20 to 30 milliseconds. This reduction in latency is crucial for applications that require real-time communication, such as online gaming, video conferencing, and VoIP (Voice over Internet Protocol) services.
- **Increased Capacity:** With the proliferation of smartphones, tablets, and other connected devices, network capacity has become a critical issue. 4G networks use advanced technologies such as Orthogonal Frequency-Division Multiplexing (OFDM) and Multiple Input Multiple Output (MIMO) to increase network capacity and efficiently manage the growing volume of data traffic.

Technical Aspects of 4G Networks

OFDM and MIMO

- **Orthogonal Frequency-Division Multiplexing (OFDM):** OFDM is a digital modulation technique used in 4G networks to improve spectral efficiency and reduce interference. It works by dividing a single data stream into multiple smaller sub-streams, which are transmitted simultaneously over different frequencies. This method allows for more efficient use of the available bandwidth and enhances the overall performance of the network.
- **Multiple Input Multiple Output (MIMO):** MIMO technology uses multiple antennas at both the transmitter and receiver ends to improve communication performance. By leveraging multiple signal paths, MIMO can increase data throughput and reliability. This technology is particularly effective in urban environments where signal reflections and obstructions are common.

LTE and LTE-Advanced

- **Long-Term Evolution (LTE):** LTE is the standard for 4G networks, designed to provide high-speed data communication and improve the overall user experience. LTE networks use advanced techniques like OFDM and MIMO to deliver faster data rates, lower latency, and increased capacity.
- **LTE-Advanced:** LTE-Advanced is an enhancement of the original LTE standard, offering even higher data rates and improved performance. It introduces features like carrier aggregation, which combines multiple frequency bands to increase bandwidth, and advanced MIMO

configurations, which further enhance data throughput and network reliability.

Applications of 4G Technology

Mobile Internet

One of the primary uses of 4G technology is mobile internet access. With its high-speed connectivity and low latency, 4G networks have transformed the way people use their mobile devices. Users can now browse the web, stream videos, and download content at speeds comparable to those of many fixed-line broadband connections.

Video Streaming

The advent of 4G has revolutionized video streaming, making it possible to watch high-definition videos on the go without buffering. Services like YouTube, Netflix, and other streaming platforms have benefited immensely from the increased bandwidth and improved performance of 4G networks.

Real-Time Gaming

Real-time gaming on mobile devices has become increasingly popular with the introduction of 4G. The low latency and high data speeds provided by 4G networks ensure a seamless gaming experience, even for data-intensive multiplayer games.

Internet of Things (IoT)

The Internet of Things (IoT) encompasses a wide range of connected devices, from smart home appliances to industrial sensors. 4G technology has played a crucial role in the growth of IoT by providing reliable, high-speed connectivity for these devices. This connectivity enables real-time data collection, remote monitoring, and control of IoT devices, driving innovation across various industries.

Challenges and Limitations of 4G

Network Coverage

While 4G networks offer impressive performance, achieving comprehensive coverage can be challenging, especially in rural and remote areas. Deploying 4G infrastructure requires significant investment in network equipment and base stations, which can be a barrier to widespread adoption in less densely populated regions.

Spectrum Availability

The availability of radio spectrum is a critical factor in the deployment and performance of 4G networks. Spectrum is a finite resource, and competition for it is intense among various communication services. Efficient spectrum management and allocation are essential to ensure the optimal performance of 4G networks.

Interference and Congestion

As the number of connected devices continues to grow, interference and network congestion can become significant issues. Managing these challenges requires ongoing advancements in network technology and infrastructure, as well as effective spectrum management.

The Future: Transition to 5G

The next generation of mobile networks, 5G, is poised to build on the foundation established by 4G. 5G promises even higher data speeds, lower latency, and greater capacity, enabling new applications and services that were previously unimaginable. While 4G will continue to play a vital role in mobile connectivity for the foreseeable future, the transition to 5G will usher in a new era of innovation and connectivity.

13.1.3 5G Networks

Fifth-generation mobile networks, commonly known as 5G, represent the latest and most advanced stage in the evolution of wireless communication technology. Designed to supersede 4G, 5G aims to deliver significantly faster data transfer speeds, ultra-low latency, and massive connectivity to support a wide range of applications and services. This next-generation technology is set to revolutionize industries, enhance user experiences, and enable innovative use cases that were previously unimaginable.

5G mobile connectivity represents a transformative leap in wireless communication, offering unprecedented data speeds, ultra-low latency, and massive device connectivity. These advancements will enable a wide range of applications and services, from enhanced mobile broadband and real-time communications to the vast IoT ecosystem and immersive AR/VR experiences. While challenges remain in infrastructure deployment, spectrum management, and security, the potential benefits of 5G are immense. As we move toward the future, 5G will pave the way for new innovations and more connected, intelligent systems, driving progress across various industries and improving the overall quality of life.

Evolution from 4G to 5G

The leap from 4G to 5G is driven by the need to accommodate the exponential growth in data traffic and the increasing demand for more connected devices. While 4G networks have enabled significant advancements in mobile internet and applications, they are reaching their limits in terms of capacity and performance. 5G addresses these limitations by offering enhanced capabilities that support emerging technologies like the Internet of Things (IoT), augmented reality (AR), and autonomous vehicles.

Key Features of 5G Technology

- **Enhanced Data Speeds:** 5G networks are designed to deliver peak data speeds of up to 10 Gbps, which is ten times faster than the maximum speeds offered by 4G networks. This substantial increase in speed allows for instantaneous downloads, seamless high-definition video streaming, and the efficient handling of large data sets, making 5G suitable for data-intensive applications.
- **Ultra-Low Latency:** One of the most significant advantages of 5G is its ultra-low latency, with response times as low as 1 millisecond. This near-instantaneous communication is crucial for applications that require real-time interaction, such as remote surgery, autonomous driving, and immersive virtual reality experiences. The reduction in latency will enable more responsive and reliable connections.
- **Massive Device Connectivity:** 5G is designed to connect a massive number of devices simultaneously, supporting up to one million devices per square kilometer. This capability is essential for the IoT ecosystem, where a multitude of sensors, devices, and machines need to communicate efficiently and reliably. The increased connectivity will facilitate smart cities, industrial automation, and other IoT applications.

Technical Aspects of 5G Networks

New Radio (NR) and Spectrum

- **5G New Radio (NR):** 5G New Radio (NR) is the global standard for the air interface of 5G networks. NR is designed to deliver improved performance and efficiency through advanced technologies such as beamforming, massive MIMO, and millimeter-wave (mmWave) frequencies. These technologies enhance the capacity, coverage, and reliability of 5G networks.
- **Spectrum Bands:** 5G operates across a broader range of spectrum bands compared to previous generations. These include low-band, mid-band, and high-band (mmWave) frequencies. Low-band frequencies offer wide coverage and good penetration, making them suitable for rural and suburban areas. Mid-band frequencies provide a balance between coverage and capacity, while high-band frequencies deliver ultra-high speeds and capacity, ideal for densely populated urban areas.

Network Slicing

Network slicing is a key feature of 5G that allows operators to create multiple virtual networks within a single physical 5G infrastructure. Each slice can be customized to meet the specific requirements of different applications or services, such as enhanced mobile broadband, ultra-reliable low-latency communications, or massive IoT. This flexibility enables more efficient use of network resources and tailored services for various use cases.

Edge Computing

Edge computing is a crucial component of 5G architecture, bringing data processing closer to the end-users and devices. By processing data at the network edge, rather than in centralized data centers, edge computing reduces latency and bandwidth usage, enabling real-time applications and improving overall network performance. This capability is essential for applications like autonomous driving, industrial automation, and smart cities.

Applications of 5G Technology

Enhanced Mobile Broadband (eMBB)

Enhanced mobile broadband is one of the primary use cases of 5G, offering users faster and more reliable internet access on their mobile devices. With 5G, users can experience seamless high-definition video streaming, faster downloads, and improved performance for data-intensive applications. This enhanced connectivity will drive the growth of mobile entertainment, gaming, and other digital services.

Ultra-Reliable Low-Latency Communications (URLLC)

URLLC is designed to support applications that require extremely low latency and high reliability. This capability is critical for mission-critical applications such as remote surgery, autonomous vehicles, and industrial automation. The ultra-low latency and high reliability of 5G will enable new levels of precision and safety in these applications.

Massive Machine-Type Communications (mMTC)

Massive machine-type communications (mMTC) is focused on connecting a vast number of IoT devices. 5G's ability to support up to one million devices per square kilometer makes it ideal for IoT applications such as smart cities, environmental monitoring, and smart agriculture. The extensive connectivity and efficient data handling of 5G will drive the growth of IoT ecosystems and enable more intelligent and responsive systems.

Augmented Reality (AR) and Virtual Reality (VR)

The high-speed, low-latency, and high-capacity features of 5G make it ideal for augmented reality (AR) and virtual reality (VR) applications. These immersive technologies require real-time data processing and high bandwidth to deliver seamless and interactive experiences. With 5G, users can enjoy more realistic and responsive AR and VR applications, enhancing entertainment, education, training, and other sectors.

Challenges and Limitations of 5G

Infrastructure Deployment

The deployment of 5G infrastructure is a significant challenge due to the need for a dense network of small cells and base stations, especially for mmWave frequencies. This extensive infrastructure requires substantial investment and coordination, posing challenges for network operators and governments.

Spectrum Management

Effective spectrum management is crucial for the successful deployment and operation of 5G networks. The allocation and regulation of spectrum bands must be carefully managed to avoid interference and ensure optimal performance. Additionally, the limited availability of certain spectrum bands can create challenges for network operators.

Security and Privacy

The increased connectivity and complexity of 5G networks introduce new security and privacy challenges. The vast number of connected devices and the critical nature of some 5G applications require robust security measures to protect against cyber threats and ensure data privacy. Addressing these challenges will be essential to maintaining trust and reliability in 5G networks.

The Future: Beyond 5G

While 5G is still in the early stages of deployment, research and development are already underway for the next generation of mobile networks, often referred to as 6G. These future networks aim to build on the capabilities of 5G, offering even higher data speeds, lower latency, and more advanced applications. The development of 6G will likely focus on integrating artificial intelligence, advanced network automation, and more sophisticated IoT ecosystems.

13.2 BLUETOOTH, WI-FI AND NFC COMMUNICATION

13.2.1 Bluetooth

Bluetooth is a wireless technology standard used for exchanging data over short distances from fixed and mobile devices, creating personal area networks (PANs). Initially developed as a cable replacement technology, Bluetooth has evolved to support a wide range of applications, including audio streaming, data transfer, and device control. It operates on the globally available 2.4 GHz ISM band, which is shared with other technologies like Wi-Fi and microwave ovens.

Bluetooth communication has evolved from a simple cable replacement technology to a versatile and ubiquitous wireless standard. Its wide range of applications, from audio streaming and data transfer to IoT and device control, demonstrates its adaptability and importance in the modern technological landscape. While challenges remain, continuous improvements and innovations promise to keep Bluetooth at the forefront of wireless communication for years to come.

Evolution of Bluetooth Technology

Since its inception in the late 1990s, Bluetooth has undergone several iterations, each bringing improvements in speed, range, and functionality. The technology's evolution can be categorized into different versions, each with distinct features and enhancements.

Bluetooth 1.0 and 1.1

The initial versions of Bluetooth, 1.0 and 1.1, introduced basic wireless communication capabilities. They supported data rates of up to 721 kbps and had a range of approximately 10 meters. However, these early versions faced issues with interoperability and security.

Bluetooth 2.0 and 2.1 + EDR

Bluetooth 2.0, introduced in 2004, brought Enhanced Data Rate (EDR) technology, which increased data transfer speeds to 3 Mbps. Bluetooth 2.1 + EDR further improved the technology by enhancing pairing processes with Secure Simple Pairing (SSP), making connections more secure and user-friendly.

Bluetooth 3.0 + HS

Bluetooth 3.0 + High Speed (HS) was launched in 2009, offering data transfer speeds of up to 24 Mbps by using an alternative Wi-Fi radio. This version was particularly beneficial for applications requiring rapid data transfer, such as file sharing and multimedia streaming.

Bluetooth 4.0, 4.1, and 4.2

The introduction of Bluetooth 4.0 in 2010 marked a significant milestone with the inclusion of Bluetooth Low Energy (BLE), also known as Bluetooth Smart. BLE was designed for applications that require low power consumption, such as health monitors and wearable devices. Subsequent versions, 4.1 and 4.2, improved co-existence with LTE networks, enhanced data transfer capabilities, and added security features.

Bluetooth 5.0 and Beyond

Bluetooth 5.0, released in 2016, brought substantial improvements in range, speed, and broadcasting capacity. It supports data rates of up to 2 Mbps, extends the range up to 200 meters, and allows for larger broadcast message capacity. These advancements make Bluetooth 5.0 suitable for IoT applications, smart home devices, and advanced audio solutions. Subsequent versions like Bluetooth 5.1 and 5.2 have introduced features like direction finding and improved audio capabilities with LE Audio.

Technical Aspects of Bluetooth

Frequency and Channels

Bluetooth operates in the 2.4 GHz ISM band, divided into 79 channels, each 1 MHz wide. For BLE, there are 40 channels, each 2 MHz wide. The technology uses frequency hopping spread spectrum (FHSS) to minimize interference and ensure reliable communication. Devices rapidly switch between channels, reducing the likelihood of interference from other wireless technologies.

Pairing and Security

Pairing is the process of establishing a trusted connection between Bluetooth devices. Different pairing methods are used depending on the Bluetooth version and application, including Legacy Pairing, Secure Simple Pairing (SSP), and LE Secure Connections for BLE devices. Security measures include encryption, authentication, and key management to protect data from unauthorized access and ensure secure communication.

Profiles and Services

Bluetooth profiles define standard functionalities for specific applications, ensuring interoperability between devices from different manufacturers. Common profiles include:

- **Advanced Audio Distribution Profile (A2DP):** For streaming high-quality audio.
- **Hands-Free Profile (HFP):** For hands-free calling in car kits and headsets.
- **Human Interface Device Profile (HID):** For input devices like keyboards, mice, and game controllers.
- **Health Device Profile (HDP):** For transmitting medical data from health devices to computers or smartphones.

Applications of Bluetooth Technology

Audio Streaming

One of the most popular uses of Bluetooth is wireless audio streaming. Bluetooth audio devices, such as headphones, speakers, and car stereo systems, use profiles like A2DP and HFP to deliver high-quality audio. The introduction of aptX and

LDAC codecs has further improved audio fidelity, making Bluetooth a viable option for audiophiles.

Data Transfer

Bluetooth facilitates easy and quick data transfer between devices without the need for cables. This includes file sharing between smartphones, syncing data between wearable devices and computers, and transferring contact information between phones.

Internet of Things (IoT)

Bluetooth is a key enabler of the Internet of Things (IoT), providing connectivity for a wide range of smart devices. Bluetooth Low Energy (BLE) is particularly well-suited for IoT applications due to its low power consumption and extended battery life. Common IoT applications include smart home devices, fitness trackers, and environmental sensors.

Device Control and Automation

Bluetooth technology is used for controlling and automating devices, such as smart home systems, lighting, and appliances. Through mobile apps or voice assistants, users can remotely control their Bluetooth-enabled devices, enhancing convenience and efficiency.

Health and Fitness

Bluetooth plays a crucial role in health and fitness applications by enabling connectivity for wearable devices like fitness trackers, smartwatches, and medical devices. These devices can monitor vital signs, track physical activity, and transmit data to health apps or cloud services for analysis and monitoring.

Challenges and Limitations of Bluetooth

Range and Interference

While Bluetooth has made significant strides in extending its range, it is still limited compared to other wireless technologies like Wi-Fi. Interference from other devices operating in the 2.4 GHz band can also impact performance, especially in crowded environments.

Data Transfer Speed

Although Bluetooth 5.0 and later versions have improved data transfer speeds, they are still lower compared to Wi-Fi and other wireless technologies. This limitation can be a bottleneck for applications requiring high-speed data transfer.

Security Concerns

Despite various security measures, Bluetooth is not immune to vulnerabilities.

Issues like BlueBorne and other attack vectors have highlighted the need for robust security practices, such as regular software updates and secure pairing methods.

The Future of Bluetooth

As technology continues to advance, Bluetooth is poised to play an even more significant role in wireless communication. Future developments may focus on further enhancing data transfer speeds, improving range and reliability, and introducing new features to support emerging applications. Areas like Bluetooth Mesh, which enables many-to-many device communication for large-scale networks, and LE Audio, which offers improved audio quality and new capabilities, are examples of ongoing advancements in Bluetooth technology.

13.2.2 Wi-Fi

Wi-Fi, short for Wireless Fidelity, is a technology that allows electronic devices to connect to a wireless LAN (Local Area Network) primarily using the 2.4 GHz and 5 GHz radio bands. Developed in the late 1990s, Wi-Fi has become a ubiquitous feature in homes, businesses, and public spaces, enabling seamless internet access and communication for billions of devices worldwide. The technology has evolved through multiple generations, each bringing enhancements in speed, capacity, and reliability.

Wi-Fi has revolutionized the way we connect and communicate, providing wireless internet access for billions of devices worldwide. Its evolution through various generations has brought significant improvements in speed, range, and performance, making it a critical technology for homes, businesses, and public spaces.

While challenges such as interference, range limitations, and security concerns remain, ongoing advancements and innovations promise to keep Wi-Fi at the forefront of wireless communication, driving connectivity and enabling new applications for years to come.

Evolution of Wi-Fi Technology

Wi-Fi technology has gone through several iterations, each marked by improvements in data transfer rates, range, and overall performance. These advancements have been standardized by the Institute of Electrical and Electronics Engineers (IEEE) under the 802.11 family.

Wi-Fi 1 (802.11b)

Introduced in 1999, Wi-Fi 1, based on the 802.11b standard, was the first widely adopted version of Wi-Fi. It operated in the 2.4 GHz band and offered maximum data rates of up to 11 Mbps. Despite its relatively low speeds by today's standards, it laid the foundation for wireless networking.

Wi-Fi 2 (802.11a)

Released concurrently with 802.11b, Wi-Fi 2 (802.11a) operated in the 5 GHz band and provided higher data rates of up to 54 Mbps. However, its adoption was limited due to higher costs and shorter range compared to 802.11b.

Wi-Fi 3 (802.11g)

Wi-Fi 3 (802.11g), introduced in 2003, combined the best features of its predecessors by operating in the 2.4 GHz band like 802.11b but offering higher data rates of up to 54 Mbps similar to 802.11a. This version saw widespread adoption due to its improved performance and compatibility with existing devices.

Wi-Fi 4 (802.11n)

Launched in 2009, Wi-Fi 4 (802.11n) brought significant advancements, including support for both 2.4 GHz and 5 GHz bands, MIMO (Multiple Input Multiple Output) technology, and data rates up to 600 Mbps. These improvements made Wi-Fi 4 suitable for bandwidth-intensive applications like video streaming and online gaming.

Wi-Fi 5 (802.11ac)

Wi-Fi 5 (802.11ac), released in 2013, further enhanced performance by operating exclusively in the 5 GHz band, offering data rates of up to several gigabits per second, and incorporating advanced technologies such as MU-MIMO (Multi-User MIMO) and beamforming. This version became the standard for high-speed wireless communication.

Wi-Fi 6 (802.11ax)

Wi-Fi 6 (802.11ax), introduced in 2019, represents the latest generation of Wi-Fi technology. It operates in both 2.4 GHz and 5 GHz bands and introduces OFDMA (Orthogonal Frequency-Division Multiple Access) for more efficient spectrum use, improved data rates, lower latency, and better performance in dense environments. Wi-Fi 6 can achieve speeds up to 9.6 Gbps, making it ideal for modern applications such as 4K streaming, virtual reality, and IoT devices.

Technical Aspects of Wi-Fi

Frequency Bands

Wi-Fi primarily operates in the 2.4 GHz and 5 GHz frequency bands. The 2.4 GHz band offers broader coverage and better penetration through walls, making it suitable for larger areas. However, it is also more susceptible to interference from other devices such as microwaves and cordless phones. The 5 GHz band, on the other hand, provides higher data rates and less interference, but with a shorter range compared to 2.4 GHz.

Channels and Bandwidth

Wi-Fi networks operate on different channels within the 2.4 GHz and 5 GHz bands. Each channel represents a specific frequency range that devices use to communicate. The 2.4 GHz band has 14 channels, each 20 MHz wide, but with significant overlap, leading to potential interference. The 5 GHz band has more channels, many of which are non-overlapping, allowing for better performance and reduced interference. Modern Wi-Fi standards also support wider channel bandwidths (40 MHz, 80 MHz, and 160 MHz), which increase data transfer rates but require cleaner, less crowded spectrum.

Security Protocols

Wi-Fi security is essential to protect data and prevent unauthorized access. Over the years, several security protocols have been developed:

- **WEP (Wired Equivalent Privacy):** The earliest Wi-Fi security protocol, now considered insecure due to its vulnerabilities.
- **WPA (Wi-Fi Protected Access):** Introduced as an interim solution to improve security over WEP.
- **WPA2 (Wi-Fi Protected Access II):** A significant improvement over WPA, using AES (Advanced Encryption Standard) for stronger encryption.
- **WPA3 (Wi-Fi Protected Access III):** The latest security protocol, providing enhanced encryption, improved protection against brute-force attacks, and more secure public Wi-Fi networks.

Mesh Networking

Mesh networking is a recent development in Wi-Fi technology that provides better coverage and reliability. In a mesh network, multiple Wi-Fi nodes work together to create a single, seamless network. This setup allows for more consistent performance, especially in large areas or environments with many obstacles. Mesh networks automatically route traffic through the most efficient path, improving overall network efficiency and reducing dead zones.

Applications of Wi-Fi

Home Networking

Wi-Fi has become an integral part of modern homes, enabling wireless internet access for various devices such as smartphones, tablets, laptops, smart TVs, and IoT devices. With the advent of smart home technology, Wi-Fi is crucial for connecting and controlling devices like smart thermostats, lights, security cameras, and voice assistants.

Business and Enterprise

In business environments, Wi-Fi provides flexible and efficient networking solutions. It enables employees to connect to corporate networks, access resources, and collaborate wirelessly. Wi-Fi is also essential for guest access, allowing customers and clients to stay connected while on-site. Advanced Wi-Fi solutions for enterprises include features like network segmentation, access control, and enhanced security to protect sensitive data.

Public Wi-Fi

Public Wi-Fi networks, available in places like cafes, airports, hotels, and shopping centers, provide internet access to the general public. These networks are essential for keeping people connected while on the go. However, they also pose security risks, making it important for users to use VPNs and other protective measures when accessing public Wi-Fi.

Education and Healthcare

Wi-Fi has transformed education and healthcare by enabling wireless connectivity in schools, universities, hospitals, and clinics. In educational settings, Wi-Fi supports digital learning, online resources, and collaboration tools. In healthcare, Wi-Fi facilitates access to electronic medical records, telemedicine, and wireless medical devices, improving patient care and operational efficiency.

Industrial and IoT

Wi-Fi is increasingly used in industrial environments and IoT applications. It supports the connectivity of sensors, machinery, and control systems, enabling real-time monitoring, data collection, and automation. In IoT, Wi-Fi connects a wide range of devices, from smart appliances to industrial equipment, driving the growth of smart cities, smart homes, and smart manufacturing.

Challenges and Limitations of Wi-Fi

Interference and Congestion

Wi-Fi networks can suffer from interference and congestion, particularly in densely populated areas where many devices compete for the same spectrum. Interference from other electronic devices and overlapping Wi-Fi networks can degrade performance and reliability.

Range and Coverage

The range of Wi-Fi networks is limited, particularly for higher frequency bands like 5 GHz. Physical obstacles such as walls and floors can further reduce coverage, leading to dead zones where the signal is weak or unavailable. Solutions like mesh networking and Wi-Fi extenders can help mitigate these issues.

Security Concerns

Despite advancements in security protocols, Wi-Fi networks remain vulnerable to various threats, including hacking, eavesdropping, and unauthorized access. Ensuring robust security measures, such as strong passwords, encryption, and regular updates, is essential to protect Wi-Fi networks and connected devices.

The Future of Wi-Fi

The future of Wi-Fi promises further enhancements in speed, capacity, and reliability. Wi-Fi 6E, an extension of Wi-Fi 6, operates in the 6 GHz band, offering more spectrum, reduced congestion, and improved performance. Wi-Fi 7, currently in development, aims to deliver even higher data rates, lower latency, and better support for emerging applications such as augmented reality, virtual reality, and advanced IoT.

13.2.3 NFC Communication

Near Field Communication (NFC) is a wireless technology that enables short-range communication between compatible devices. Operating at a frequency of 13.56 MHz, NFC allows data to be exchanged over distances of up to 10 centimeters. This technology is widely used for contactless payments, access control, data sharing, and various other applications that require secure and convenient communication.

NFC communication has emerged as a powerful and versatile technology, enabling secure and convenient wireless interactions across various domains. Its evolution from RFID technology, combined with robust security features and ease of use, has made NFC a popular choice for contactless payments, access control, data sharing, and more. While challenges like limited range and data transfer speed remain, ongoing advancements and new applications promise to drive the growth and adoption of NFC technology. As NFC continues to integrate with emerging technologies and industries, it will play an increasingly vital role in shaping the future of wireless communication.

Evolution and Development of NFC

NFC technology emerged from the convergence of existing contactless technologies, including radio-frequency identification (RFID). The development of NFC began in the early 2000s, and it quickly gained momentum as a versatile and secure means of wireless communication. The NFC Forum, an industry association founded in 2004, has played a crucial role in standardizing and promoting NFC technology.

Early Beginnings

NFC's roots can be traced back to RFID, which was first used for tracking and identifying objects via radio waves. The idea of enhancing RFID to support two-way communication led to the development of NFC. The first NFC-enabled devices were introduced in the mid-2000s, paving the way for widespread adoption.

Standardization and Adoption

The NFC Forum, comprising leading companies like Sony, Nokia, and Philips, established the initial standards and protocols for NFC.

These standards ensured interoperability between devices and promoted the development of a robust ecosystem. By the early 2010s, NFC was integrated into a variety of smartphones, making it accessible to a broad audience.

Technical Aspects of NFC

Operating Principles

NFC operates in the 13.56 MHz ISM band and uses magnetic field induction to enable communication between devices.

It supports three modes of operation: reader/writer mode, peer-to-peer mode, and card emulation mode.

- **Reader/Writer Mode**: In this mode, an NFC-enabled device can read data from or write data to an NFC tag or card. This is commonly used in applications like smart posters and data exchange.
- **Peer-to-Peer Mode**: This mode allows two NFC-enabled devices to communicate directly, enabling data sharing, such as contact information or media files.
- **Card Emulation Mode**: In this mode, an NFC device emulates a contactless smart card, enabling it to be used for payments, access control, and ticketing.

Communication Range and Speed

NFC operates over very short distances, typically up to 10 centimeters. This limited range enhances security by reducing the likelihood of unauthorized access. The data transfer rate for NFC is relatively low compared to other wireless technologies, ranging from 106 kbps to 424 kbps. However, this is sufficient for the small data payloads typically exchanged in NFC applications.

Security Features

Security is a critical aspect of NFC technology, especially for applications involving sensitive data like payments and access control. NFC incorporates several security measures, including encryption, secure channels, and mutual authentication. These features help protect against eavesdropping, data corruption, and unauthorized access.

Applications of NFC Technology

Contactless Payments

One of the most prominent applications of NFC is in contactless payment systems. Services like Apple Pay, Google Wallet, and Samsung Pay leverage NFC to enable secure and convenient transactions.

By simply tapping their NFC-enabled smartphone or card on a payment terminal, users can complete transactions quickly and securely.

Access Control and Identification

NFC is widely used in access control systems for securing buildings, offices, and restricted areas. NFC-enabled access cards and smartphones can be used to grant entry to authorized individuals.

Additionally, NFC technology is employed in identification applications, such as electronic passports and identity cards, to store and retrieve personal information securely.

Data Sharing and Exchange

NFC facilitates easy and quick data sharing between devices. Users can exchange contact information, photos, videos, and other files by bringing their NFC-enabled devices close together.

This peer-to-peer communication is often faster and more convenient than traditional methods like Bluetooth pairing.

Public Transport and Ticketing

NFC is extensively used in public transportation systems for ticketing and fare collection. NFC-enabled smart cards and smartphones can be used to access public transport services, eliminating the need for physical tickets. This streamlines the process and reduces the need for cash transactions.

Smart Marketing and Information Sharing

NFC technology is employed in smart marketing campaigns and information sharing through the use of NFC tags embedded in posters, brochures, and other promotional materials. By tapping their NFC-enabled devices on these tags, users can access additional information, websites, or special offers.

Healthcare and Wellness

NFC technology is making significant inroads into the healthcare sector. It is used for patient identification, medication tracking, and health monitoring. NFC-enabled devices can store and transmit patient data securely, improving the accuracy and efficiency of healthcare services.

Advantages of NFC

Ease of Use

One of the primary advantages of NFC is its simplicity and ease of use. Users can initiate communication or transactions by simply bringing their devices close together. This intuitive process enhances user experience and encourages adoption.

Security

NFC offers robust security features, making it suitable for applications that require secure communication. The short communication range, encryption, and authentication mechanisms help protect against unauthorized access and data breaches.

Versatility

NFC is a versatile technology that supports a wide range of applications across various industries. From payments and access control to data sharing and healthcare, NFC can be adapted to meet diverse needs.

Interoperability

Standardization by the NFC Forum ensures that NFC-enabled devices and services are interoperable. This means that devices from different manufacturers can work seamlessly together, fostering a cohesive ecosystem.

Challenges and Limitations of NFC

- **Limited Range:** The short communication range of NFC, while beneficial for security, can be a limitation in some applications. It requires users to bring devices very close together, which may not always be convenient.
- **Data Transfer Speed:** NFC's data transfer speed is relatively low compared to other wireless technologies like Bluetooth and Wi-Fi. This limits its use to applications that require the exchange of small data payloads.
- **Adoption and Infrastructure:** While NFC is widely used, its adoption is not universal. Some regions and industries have been slower to adopt NFC technology, and the necessary infrastructure, such as NFC-enabled payment terminals, is not yet ubiquitous.

Future of NFC

The future of NFC technology looks promising, with continued advancements and new applications emerging. Developments in fields like IoT, smart cities, and augmented reality are expected to drive the growth of NFC. Enhanced security features, increased interoperability, and expanded use cases will further solidify NFC's role in the wireless communication landscape.

Integration with IoT

NFC is poised to play a significant role in the Internet of Things (IoT) ecosystem. Its ability to facilitate secure, short-range communication makes it ideal for connecting and managing IoT devices. NFC can enable seamless interactions between smart objects, enhancing the functionality and user experience of IoT systems.

Expansion in Wearable Technology

Wearable devices, such as smartwatches and fitness trackers, are increasingly incorporating NFC technology. This enables functionalities like contactless payments, access control, and health monitoring directly from the wearable device, enhancing convenience and utility.

Augmented Reality and Marketing

NFC technology is expected to be integrated with augmented reality (AR) to create interactive and immersive marketing experiences. By tapping NFC-enabled devices on tagged objects, users can access AR content, enhancing engagement and information delivery.

CHAPTER 14
OFFLINE FUNCTIONALITY IN MOBILE APPS

14.1 STRATEGIES FOR OFFLINE DATA ACCESS

Offline data access is crucial for mobile applications to ensure functionality and usability even when users are not connected to the internet. Implementing effective strategies for offline data access enhances user experience by allowing seamless operation, data availability, and performance optimization.

Effective implementation of offline data access strategies is essential for ensuring reliable and responsive mobile applications. By leveraging techniques such as data caching, synchronization, pre-fetching, and error handling, developers can enhance app usability and performance in offline scenarios.

Understanding the importance of offline data access, addressing implementation challenges, and embracing future trends will empower developers to create robust, user-centric mobile experiences that seamlessly integrate offline capabilities with online functionality.

14.1.1 Importance of Offline Data Access

Mobile apps often rely on continuous internet connectivity to retrieve and update data. However, users may experience connectivity issues due to network outages, limited coverage, or data restrictions.

Offline data access ensures that users can still access essential functionalities and information, regardless of their network status. This improves app reliability, user satisfaction, and overall usability, making it a critical consideration for app development.

14.1.2 Strategies for Implementing Offline Data Access

Data Caching

Data caching involves storing frequently accessed data locally on the device. When the app is online, it fetches data from the server and stores a copy in the local cache. Subsequent requests for the same data can be fulfilled from the cache, reducing the need for frequent network requests. This approach improves app responsiveness and reduces data consumption. Developers can implement caching using libraries like Room (for Android) or CoreData (for iOS) for relational databases or simple key-value stores for other types of data.

Synchronization

Synchronization ensures that data stored locally on the device remains consistent with the server's data when the app is online. Changes made offline are queued and synchronized with the server once connectivity is restored. This bi-directional syncing process requires careful handling of conflicts and resolutions to maintain data integrity. Techniques such as differential sync, where only changed data is synchronized, can optimize synchronization processes and reduce bandwidth usage.

Pre-fetching and Background Sync

Pre-fetching involves fetching data in anticipation of user actions based on usage patterns or predictive algorithms. By prefetching data when the app is online, developers can ensure that relevant content is available offline, enhancing user experience and responsiveness. Background sync processes periodically synchronize data in the background, ensuring that the app remains up-to-date even when not actively used. This approach minimizes user intervention and maintains data freshness.

Offline Mode Design

Designing specific offline modes within the app allows users to continue using certain functionalities even without internet connectivity. Offline mode can provide access to cached data, basic features, and limited functionality that do not depend on real-time data updates. Clear communication of offline capabilities and restrictions ensures a seamless transition between online and offline modes, optimizing user experience.

Error Handling and Resilience

Effective error handling is crucial for managing offline scenarios gracefully. Apps should provide informative error messages, retry mechanisms, and offline indicators to notify users of connectivity issues. Implementing resilience patterns like exponential backoff, where retries are delayed and progressively spaced out, helps mitigate network congestion and server load during connectivity restoration attempts.

14.1.3 Implementing Offline Data Access in Practice

Case Study: Evernote

Evernote, a note-taking app, implements robust offline data access strategies to ensure continuous usability. Users can create, edit, and access notes offline, with changes synchronized when connectivity is restored. Evernote employs local caching for frequently accessed notes, background synchronization for updates, and clear indicators of offline mode to manage user expectations effectively.

Best Practices and Considerations

- **Data Partitioning:** Divide data into critical and non-critical segments to prioritize caching and synchronization efforts.
- **Conflict Resolution:** Implement conflict resolution strategies to handle data conflicts during synchronization, ensuring data consistency.
- **User Control:** Provide users with control over offline settings, such as data storage limits, sync frequency, and offline mode preferences.
- **Testing and Optimization:** Conduct thorough testing of offline scenarios, including network simulation and edge cases, to identify and resolve potential issues. Optimize data storage and synchronization algorithms for performance and efficiency.

14.1.4 Challenges in Implementing Offline Data Access

- **Data Consistency:** Ensuring data consistency between the local device and the server, especially in scenarios with frequent updates or concurrent access, requires careful synchronization and conflict resolution strategies.
- **Storage Management:** Managing local storage constraints and optimizing data caching strategies to balance performance with storage efficiency can be challenging, particularly on devices with limited storage capacity.
- **Security and Privacy:** Safeguarding locally stored data against unauthorized access and ensuring compliance with data protection regulations, such as GDPR, requires robust encryption and access control measures.

14.1.5 Future Trends in Offline Data Access

As mobile technology continues to evolve, future trends in offline data access are expected to focus on enhancing synchronization efficiency, improving user control over offline settings, and integrating with emerging technologies like edge computing and AI-driven predictive caching.

These advancements aim to further optimize app performance, reduce dependency on continuous connectivity, and enhance user experience across diverse mobile environments.

14.2 SYNCHRONIZATION AND CONFLICT RESOLUTION

Synchronization and conflict resolution are critical aspects of mobile app development, especially in scenarios where multiple devices or users access and modify shared data. These processes ensure that data remains consistent across devices and platforms, regardless of network connectivity or concurrent updates.

Synchronization and conflict resolution are fundamental aspects of mobile app development, ensuring seamless data access, consistency, and collaboration across devices and platforms. By employing strategies like data replication, real-time synchronization, and conflict resolution techniques such as timestamps, automatic resolution, or user-driven resolution, developers can enhance app reliability, user experience, and scalability. Addressing challenges like concurrency control, data consistency, and scalability requires robust architecture design, performance optimization, and adherence to best practices. As mobile technology continues to evolve, embracing future trends in synchronization and conflict resolution will enable developers to create innovative, responsive, and collaborative mobile applications that meet evolving user expectations and business needs.

14.2.1 Importance of Synchronization and Conflict Resolution

In mobile app development, synchronization refers to the process of harmonizing data between a local device and a remote server or between multiple devices. This ensures that users have access to up-to-date information and that changes made on one device are reflected on others. Conflict resolution addresses situations where conflicting updates occur, ensuring data consistency and preventing data loss or corruption. Effective synchronization and conflict resolution mechanisms are essential for maintaining data integrity, enhancing user experience, and enabling collaborative functionalities in mobile applications.

14.2.2 Strategies for Synchronization in Mobile Apps

Data Replication

Data replication involves copying data from a central server to multiple devices or databases. In mobile apps, replication ensures that each device has a local copy of relevant data, reducing reliance on continuous network connectivity. Techniques like push and pull mechanisms allow devices to receive updates automatically or on-demand, optimizing data synchronization based on usage patterns and network conditions.

Real-Time Synchronization

Real-time synchronization enables immediate updates between devices and servers as changes occur. This approach is crucial for applications requiring instant data availability, such as messaging apps or collaborative editing tools. Technologies like WebSockets or MQTT (Message Queuing Telemetry Transport) facilitate real-time communication, minimizing latency and enabling seamless user interactions across devices.

Batch Synchronization

Batch synchronization involves collecting and transmitting data updates in batches rather than individually. This approach reduces network overhead and conserves battery life on mobile devices by minimizing the frequency of network requests. Batch synchronization is suitable for applications handling large volumes of data or operating in environments with limited network bandwidth.

Conflict Detection and Resolution

Conflict detection identifies discrepancies between multiple versions of the same data, often resulting from concurrent updates on different devices. Conflict resolution strategies aim to resolve conflicts automatically or with user intervention while maintaining data integrity. Techniques such as timestamp-based conflict resolution or operational transformation (OT) algorithms help reconcile conflicting changes based on predefined rules or user preferences.

14.2.3 Techniques for Conflict Resolution in Mobile Apps

Timestamps and Versioning

Timestamps and versioning mechanisms track the timeline of data modifications across devices. By comparing timestamps or version numbers, apps can prioritize newer updates or prompt users to resolve conflicts manually. This approach ensures chronological order and consistency in data synchronization, mitigating conflicts arising from simultaneous edits.

Automatic Conflict Resolution

Automatic conflict resolution uses predefined rules or algorithms to resolve conflicts without user intervention. Common strategies include "last write wins," where the most recent update overrides conflicting changes, or merging changes based on specific criteria. While efficient for straightforward conflicts, automatic resolution may require careful consideration to avoid unintended data loss or inconsistency.

User-Driven Conflict Resolution

User-driven conflict resolution empowers users to review and resolve conflicts manually through intuitive interfaces. Apps present conflicting changes and relevant context to users, allowing them to choose preferred versions or merge modifications selectively. This approach enhances transparency and user control over data integrity, particularly in collaborative environments or critical applications.

Conflict Avoidance

Conflict avoidance strategies aim to minimize the occurrence of conflicts through proactive measures. Techniques like locking mechanisms or session-based edits restrict simultaneous access to shared data, reducing the likelihood of conflicting updates. By enforcing sequential access or exclusive editing rights, apps promote data consistency and simplify conflict resolution processes.

14.2.4 Implementing Synchronization and Conflict Resolution in Practice

Case Study: Google Docs

Google Docs exemplifies effective synchronization and conflict resolution in collaborative document editing. Multiple users can edit the same document simultaneously, with changes synchronized in real-time.

Google Docs employs operational transformation (OT) algorithms to manage concurrent edits, ensuring that conflicting changes are resolved seamlessly while preserving document integrity and consistency.

Best Practices and Considerations

- **Data Partitioning:** Divide data into manageable segments to optimize synchronization and minimize conflicts, especially in large-scale applications or distributed systems.
- **Error Handling:** Implement robust error handling mechanisms to manage synchronization failures, network interruptions, and data inconsistencies effectively.
- **Performance Optimization:** Optimize synchronization processes by minimizing network overhead, prioritizing critical updates, and leveraging caching or prefetching strategies.
- **Security and Privacy:** Ensure secure transmission and storage of synchronized data, adhering to encryption standards and data protection regulations to safeguard user information.

14.2.5 Challenges in Synchronization and Conflict Resolution

Concurrency Control

Managing concurrent access to shared data poses challenges in synchronization, requiring effective concurrency control mechanisms to prevent data corruption or inconsistent states. Techniques like locking, optimistic concurrency control, or distributed transactions address these challenges but require careful implementation and performance considerations.

Data Consistency

Ensuring consistent data across multiple devices or platforms is essential for maintaining application reliability and user trust. Synchronization processes must handle data conflicts, inconsistencies, and synchronization delays while preserving data integrity and coherence.

Complexity and Scalability

Scalability issues arise when synchronizing large datasets or supporting a growing user base. Complex synchronization logic, network latency, and server-side processing constraints can impact performance and scalability, requiring scalable architecture design and optimization strategies.

14.2.6 Future Trends in Synchronization and Conflict Resolution

As mobile technology evolves, future trends in synchronization and conflict resolution focus on enhancing real-time capabilities, integrating with edge computing and IoT devices, and leveraging AI-driven algorithms for predictive synchronization and conflict detection. These advancements aim to improve synchronization efficiency, reduce dependency on continuous connectivity, and enhance collaborative functionalities across diverse mobile environments.

CHAPTER 15
MOBILE CLOUD COMPUTING

15.1 CLOUD INTEGRATION IN MOBILE APPLICATIONS

Cloud integration plays a pivotal role in modern mobile application development, enabling seamless access to data, services, and computing resources hosted on remote servers via the internet. Cloud integration empowers mobile app developers to leverage scalable computing resources, real-time data synchronization, and flexible backend services hosted in the cloud. By adopting strategies like BaaS, API integration, and serverless computing, developers can enhance app scalability, performance, and user engagement while addressing challenges like data security, integration complexity, and network dependency. Embracing best practices, monitoring app performance, and anticipating future trends in cloud technology will enable developers to create innovative, resilient, and competitive mobile applications that meet evolving user expectations and business objectives in a cloud-first era.

15.1.1 Importance of Cloud Integration

Cloud integration allows mobile apps to leverage the scalability, flexibility, and accessibility of cloud computing resources. By offloading data storage, processing, and backend functionalities to the cloud, mobile apps can enhance performance, reduce infrastructure costs, and support advanced features that require real-time data synchronization and collaboration across devices.

15.1.2 Strategies for Cloud Integration

Backend as a Service (BaaS)

Backend as a Service platforms provide pre-built backend infrastructure and services, such as databases, user authentication, file storage, and push notifications. BaaS solutions abstract backend complexities, allowing developers to focus on app functionality and user experience without managing server infrastructure. Popular BaaS providers include Firebase, AWS Amplify, and Microsoft Azure Mobile Apps.

API Integration

API integration enables mobile apps to interact with external services, databases, and third-party APIs hosted in the cloud. APIs facilitate data retrieval, updates, and communication between mobile apps and backend systems, ensuring seamless integration of functionalities like social media login, payment gateways, and location-based services.

Data Synchronization

Cloud integration supports real-time data synchronization between mobile devices and cloud servers, ensuring consistency and accessibility of shared data. Techniques like delta synchronization and conflict resolution mechanisms manage data updates efficiently, enabling offline access, collaborative editing, and seamless user experiences across devices.

Serverless Computing

Serverless computing platforms, such as AWS Lambda and Google Cloud Functions, enable developers to deploy event-driven backend functions without managing server infrastructure. Serverless architectures scale automatically based on demand, optimize resource utilization, and reduce operational overhead, making them ideal for executing lightweight tasks and microservices in mobile apps.

15.1.3 Benefits of Cloud Integration in Mobile Applications

Scalability and Flexibility

Cloud integration enables mobile apps to scale dynamically based on user demand and business growth. Cloud platforms offer elastic computing resources, allowing apps to handle fluctuating workloads, accommodate user traffic spikes, and scale backend services seamlessly without upfront investment in infrastructure.

Cost Efficiency

Cloud-based solutions eliminate the need for maintaining and upgrading on-premises servers, reducing capital expenditures and operational costs associated with hardware provisioning, maintenance, and energy consumption. Pay-as-you-go pricing models enable cost-effective resource utilization, aligning expenses with app usage and scalability requirements.

Enhanced Performance and Reliability

Cloud environments provide robust infrastructure, global data centers, and high-speed network connectivity, ensuring superior performance, low latency, and reliable data access for mobile apps. Content delivery networks (CDNs) and edge computing technologies optimize data delivery and minimize response times, enhancing user experience and app responsiveness.

Cross-Platform Compatibility

Cloud integration supports cross-platform development frameworks and tools, enabling developers to build and deploy mobile apps across multiple operating systems (iOS, Android) and devices (smartphones, tablets). Cloud-based services facilitate platform-agnostic development, code reusability, and consistent user experiences across diverse mobile ecosystems.

15.1.4 Challenges of Cloud Integration in Mobile Applications

Data Security and Compliance

Ensuring data privacy, encryption, and compliance with regulatory requirements (e.g., GDPR, HIPAA) are critical challenges in cloud integration. Mobile apps must implement robust security measures, authentication mechanisms, and data encryption techniques to protect sensitive information transmitted and stored in the cloud.

Network Dependency and Connectivity

Mobile apps reliant on cloud services are susceptible to network outages, latency issues, and variable internet connectivity, affecting app performance and user experience. Implementing offline capabilities, caching strategies, and error handling mechanisms mitigate dependency on continuous network connectivity and ensure seamless app functionality.

Integration Complexity

Integrating diverse cloud services, APIs, and backend components introduces complexity in app development, configuration, and maintenance. Developers must navigate compatibility issues, versioning challenges, and API dependencies while ensuring interoperability and consistency across integrated cloud platforms.

Vendor Lock-in and Migration

Vendor lock-in risks associated with proprietary cloud services and platforms may limit app scalability, flexibility, and migration options. Adopting open standards, modular architectures, and cloud-agnostic solutions mitigate vendor dependencies, enabling seamless migration and interoperability across different cloud providers.

15.1.5 Implementing Cloud Integration in Practice

Case Study: Spotify

Spotify utilizes cloud integration to deliver personalized music streaming services across global markets. The app leverages cloud-based storage, content delivery networks (CDNs), and scalable backend infrastructure to manage vast music libraries, user playlists, and real-time music recommendations. Cloud integration supports seamless content delivery, offline access, and continuous app updates, enhancing user engagement and retention.

Best Practices and Considerations

- **Performance Optimization**: Implement caching strategies, content delivery networks (CDNs), and edge computing technologies to optimize data delivery and minimize latency in mobile apps.
- **Security and Compliance**: Adhere to industry best practices for data encryption, access control, and regulatory compliance to protect sensitive information stored and transmitted in the cloud.
- **Monitoring and Analytics**: Implement monitoring tools, performance metrics, and analytics dashboards to monitor app performance, user behavior, and cloud service utilization, enabling proactive troubleshooting and optimization.

15.1.6 Future Trends in Cloud Integration

As mobile technology evolves, future trends in cloud integration focus on enhancing AI-driven analytics, integrating with IoT devices, adopting serverless architectures, and leveraging blockchain technology for enhanced security and transparency. These advancements aim to optimize app performance, data governance, and user experience in increasingly interconnected and data-driven mobile ecosystems.

15.2 LEVERAGING CLOUD SERVICES FOR SCALABILITY

Cloud services offer mobile applications scalable computing resources, storage, and functionalities without the need for on-premises infrastructure. Leveraging cloud services for scalability empowers mobile app developers to enhance performance, reliability, and user experience while optimizing operational efficiency and reducing costs. By adopting strategies like elastic computing, load balancing, serverless architectures, and scalable databases, developers can accommodate growing user bases, fluctuating workloads, and evolving business demands without upfront investments in infrastructure. Addressing challenges such as performance monitoring, data security, vendor lock-in, and network dependency requires robust planning, proactive management, and adherence to best practices in cloud integration. Embracing future trends in cloud technology will enable developers to innovate, differentiate, and deliver scalable, competitive, and resilient mobile applications that meet evolving user expectations and business objectives in a dynamic digital landscape.

15.2.1 Importance of Scalability in Mobile Applications

Scalability is crucial for mobile applications to accommodate growing user bases, fluctuating workloads, and evolving business requirements. Cloud-based scalability enables apps to expand or contract computing resources dynamically based on demand, ensuring optimal performance, responsiveness, and user experience. By leveraging cloud services, mobile apps can scale seamlessly to meet increasing user traffic, maintain reliability, and support new features without upfront investment in hardware infrastructure.

15.2.2 Strategies for Leveraging Cloud Services for Scalability

Elastic Computing Resources

Cloud platforms provide elastic computing capabilities, allowing mobile apps to scale resources (CPU, memory, storage) automatically in response to workload fluctuations. Auto-scaling features monitor app performance metrics, such as CPU utilization or incoming requests, and adjust resource allocation dynamically to maintain performance levels and optimize cost-efficiency.

Load Balancing

Load balancing distributes incoming app traffic across multiple cloud instances or servers, optimizing resource utilization and preventing overloading of individual components. Cloud-based load balancers, such as AWS Elastic Load Balancing (ELB) or Google Cloud Load Balancing, enhance app scalability by ensuring even distribution of requests, minimizing latency, and improving fault tolerance.

Serverless Architectures

Serverless computing platforms, like AWS Lambda or Azure Functions, enable developers to deploy event-driven functions and microservices without managing server infrastructure. Serverless architectures scale automatically based on triggered events or incoming requests, optimizing resource utilization and reducing operational overhead associated with provisioning, monitoring, and scaling backend services.

Database Scalability

Cloud databases, such as Amazon RDS (Relational Database Service) or Google Cloud SQL, offer scalable storage and computing capacity to accommodate growing data volumes and transactional workloads. Features like horizontal scaling (sharding) and read/write replicas enable mobile apps to handle increased database traffic, ensure data availability, and maintain performance during peak usage periods.

15.2.3 Benefits of Leveraging Cloud Services for Scalability

Improved Performance and Reliability

Cloud-based scalability enhances app performance by dynamically allocating computing resources based on demand, minimizing response times, and optimizing data processing. Reliable infrastructure, global data centers, and high-speed network connectivity ensure consistent app availability and uptime, supporting seamless user experiences across diverse geographical regions.

Cost Efficiency

Cloud scalability models, such as pay-as-you-go pricing and auto-scaling capabilities, optimize resource utilization and reduce operational costs associated with idle capacity or over-provisioning. Mobile apps can scale resources flexibly in response to user traffic patterns, seasonal peaks, or promotional events, aligning expenses with app usage and business growth.

Agility and Time-to-Market

Cloud services accelerate app development and deployment cycles by providing pre-built infrastructure, managed services, and developer tools. Agile development practices, continuous integration/continuous deployment (CI/CD) pipelines, and cloud-native architectures enable rapid iteration, feature delivery, and adaptation to market changes, enhancing competitiveness and innovation in mobile app development.

Scalable Backend Services

Cloud integration facilitates scalable backend services, such as authentication, data storage, push notifications, and analytics, essential for modern mobile applications. Managed services, APIs, and SDKs simplify integration with cloud platforms, enabling developers to focus on app functionality, user experience, and business logic without managing underlying infrastructure complexities.

15.2.4 Challenges of Leveraging Cloud Services for Scalability

Performance Monitoring and Optimization

Monitoring app performance, resource utilization, and cost management in cloud environments requires proactive monitoring tools, performance metrics, and optimization strategies. Balancing resource allocation, scaling thresholds, and workload management ensures efficient scalability and optimal app performance under varying conditions.

Data Security and Compliance

Ensuring data privacy, encryption, and regulatory compliance (e.g., GDPR, HIPAA) are critical challenges in cloud-based scalability. Implementing robust security measures, access controls, and encryption standards protect sensitive information stored and transmitted in cloud environments, mitigating risks of data breaches or compliance violations.

Vendor Lock-in and Interoperability

Vendor lock-in risks associated with proprietary cloud services or platform dependencies may limit flexibility, migration options, and interoperability across different cloud providers. Adopting cloud-agnostic solutions, open standards, and modular architectures facilitates seamless integration, scalability, and future-proofing of mobile apps across diverse cloud environments.

Network Dependency and Latency

Mobile apps reliant on cloud services are susceptible to network latency, connectivity issues, and variable internet conditions, impacting app responsiveness and user experience. Implementing caching strategies, offline capabilities, and edge computing technologies mitigate dependency on continuous network connectivity and ensure consistent app performance in diverse mobile environments.

15.2.5 Implementing Cloud Services for Scalability in Practice

Case Study: Uber

Uber leverages cloud services, including AWS and Google Cloud Platform, to support global scalability, real-time ride matching, and data-intensive operations. Cloud-based architectures enable Uber to scale computing resources dynamically, handle millions of concurrent users and transactions, and optimize driver-passenger interactions through location-based services and real-time data analytics.

Best Practices and Considerations

- **Scalability Planning:** Design scalable architectures, set scaling thresholds, and implement auto-scaling policies based on app performance metrics and user traffic patterns.
- **Performance Testing:** Conduct load testing, stress testing, and performance optimization to validate scalability, identify bottlenecks, and optimize resource allocation in cloud environments.
- **Data Management:** Implement data partitioning, replication strategies, and disaster recovery plans to ensure data availability, integrity, and resilience in scalable cloud infrastructures.

15.2.6 Future Trends in Cloud Services for Scalability

As mobile technology evolves, future trends in cloud services focus on enhancing AI-driven automation, edge computing integration, adopting serverless architectures for microservices, and leveraging blockchain technology for enhanced security and decentralized computing. These advancements aim to optimize app scalability, performance, and agility in increasingly interconnected and data-driven mobile ecosystems.

PART VI

MOBILE ANALYTICS AND PERFORMANCE

CHAPTER 16
MOBILE APP ANALYTICS

16.1 KEY METRICS FOR MOBILE APP PERFORMANCE

Monitoring key metrics is crucial for assessing the performance and success of a mobile app. These metrics provide insights into user behavior, engagement levels, app stability, and overall user satisfaction. By tracking these metrics, developers and businesses can make informed decisions to optimize their app and enhance user experience.

Monitoring key metrics for mobile app performance is essential for optimizing user experience, enhancing engagement, and achieving business goals. By tracking metrics related to installs, retention, engagement, performance, conversions, and user feedback, developers and businesses can identify strengths and weaknesses, implement targeted improvements, and ultimately build a successful and sustainable mobile app.

16.1.1 App Installs and Uninstalls

The number of app installs reflects the initial interest and adoption rate among users. Monitoring installs over time helps gauge the effectiveness of marketing campaigns and user acquisition strategies. Conversely, tracking uninstalls provides insights into user dissatisfaction or issues with the app's functionality or usability. High uninstall rates may indicate a need for improvements in user experience or performance optimization.

16.1.2 Retention Rate

Retention rate measures the percentage of users who continue to use the app over a period of time. It is a critical metric for assessing user satisfaction and the app's ability to retain its audience. Higher retention rates typically indicate that users find value in the app and are more likely to continue using it. Monitoring retention rates helps identify factors that contribute to user churn and allows for targeted improvements to increase user loyalty.

16.1.3 Session Length and Frequency

Session length refers to the amount of time users spend actively using the app during a single session. Tracking session length provides insights into user engagement and app stickiness. Longer sessions generally indicate higher user satisfaction and engagement with the app's content or features. Similarly, monitoring session frequency—the number of times users launch the app—helps assess how frequently users interact with the app and identify trends in usage patterns.

16.1.4 User Engagement Metrics

User engagement metrics encompass a range of indicators that reflect how users interact with the app. Key metrics include:

- **Average Screen Views per Session:** This metric measures the number of screens or pages users navigate through during a single session. It indicates how deeply users engage with the app's content or functionality.
- **Click-Through Rate (CTR):** CTR measures the percentage of users who click on specific elements such as ads, notifications, or calls-to-action within the app. It helps evaluate the effectiveness of app features and promotional campaigns.
- **Social Shares and Referrals:** Tracking how often users share content from the app on social media or refer others to download the app provides insights into user satisfaction and advocacy.

16.1.5 App Performance and Stability

App performance metrics focus on technical aspects such as load times, responsiveness, and crash rates:

- **Load Time:** The time it takes for the app to load and become usable after launch. Longer load times can lead to user frustration and abandonment.
- **Responsiveness:** Measures how quickly the app responds to user interactions such as taps and swipes. A laggy or unresponsive app can negatively impact user experience.
- **Crash Rate:** The frequency at which the app crashes or experiences errors during use. High crash rates indicate stability issues that need to be addressed to prevent user dissatisfaction and churn.

16.1.6 Conversion Rates

Conversion rates track specific actions or goals that users complete within the app, such as making a purchase, subscribing to a service, or upgrading to a premium version. Monitoring conversion rates helps assess the effectiveness of user interface design, onboarding processes, and monetization strategies. Improving conversion rates requires identifying barriers to conversion and optimizing the user journey accordingly.

16.1.7 User Feedback and Ratings

User feedback and ratings provide qualitative insights into user satisfaction, usability issues, and feature requests. Monitoring app store ratings and reviews, as well as soliciting feedback through in-app surveys or feedback forms, helps prioritize improvements and address user concerns promptly. Positive reviews and high ratings can boost app visibility and attract new users, while negative feedback highlights areas for enhancement.

16.2 TOOLS FOR MONITORING USER BEHAVIOUR

Monitoring user behavior is crucial for businesses aiming to understand their customers better, optimize user experiences, and enhance overall performance. Various tools provide insights into how users interact with websites, applications, or products. These tools employ different techniques such as analytics, heatmaps, session recordings, and A/B testing to gather data.

Monitoring user behavior using these tools provides businesses with actionable insights to improve user experiences, optimize conversions, and drive business growth. Each tool offers unique functionalities—from analytics and session recording to A/B testing and heatmaps—that cater to specific aspects of user interaction. By leveraging these tools effectively, businesses can make informed decisions, enhance user satisfaction, and stay competitive in today's digital landscape.

16.2.1 Google Analytics

- **Functionality:** Google Analytics is a robust web analytics service that tracks and reports website traffic, providing valuable insights into user behavior. It helps businesses understand where users come from, how they navigate through the site, and which actions they take.
- **Applications:** Google Analytics is used for conversion rate optimization (CRO), identifying popular pages, tracking marketing campaign effectiveness, and understanding user demographics and interests.

16.2.2 Hotjar

- **Functionality:** Hotjar offers behavior analytics through features like heatmaps, session recordings, and surveys. Heatmaps visually represent user interaction data, showing where users click, scroll, or hover on a webpage. Session recordings provide playback of individual user sessions, offering a deeper understanding of user behavior.
- **Applications:** Hotjar is used for optimizing website usability, identifying friction points in user journeys, improving conversion rates, and validating design changes through user feedback.

16.2.3 Mixpanel

- **Functionality:** Mixpanel focuses on event-based analytics, tracking specific actions users take within an application or website. It allows businesses to create custom events and funnels, analyze user retention, and measure the impact of product changes on user behavior.
- **Applications:** Mixpanel is beneficial for product analytics, understanding user engagement with specific features, improving user onboarding processes, and optimizing product funnels.

16.2.4 Crazy Egg

- **Functionality:** Crazy Egg provides heatmaps, scrollmaps, and confetti reports to visualize user behavior on websites. Heatmaps indicate where users click the most, while scrollmaps show how far users scroll down a page. Confetti reports segment clicks based on various factors like referral sources or search terms.
- **Applications:** Crazy Egg helps in optimizing website layout and design, improving call-to-action (CTA) placement, understanding user engagement patterns, and refining content strategy based on user interaction.

16.2.5 FullStory

- **Functionality:** FullStory captures user interactions through session replay, allowing businesses to watch recordings of user sessions. It also provides heatmaps and analytics to understand user behavior patterns, error tracking, and conversion funnel analysis.
- **Applications:** FullStory is used for troubleshooting UX issues, identifying reasons for cart abandonment, improving customer support interactions, and validating user experience improvements.

16.2.6 Optimizely

- **Functionality:** Optimizely is an experimentation platform that enables A/B testing and personalization. It allows businesses to create and test different versions of web pages or features to determine which performs better based on user behavior metrics.
- **Applications:** Optimizely is used for optimizing conversion rates, improving user engagement, validating design changes through data-driven decisions, and personalizing user experiences based on behavior.

16.2.7 Mouseflow

- **Functionality:** Mouseflow provides session replay, heatmaps, funnels, and form analytics to visualize user behavior on websites. It captures mouse movements, clicks, scrolls, and keystrokes to understand how users interact with forms and pages.

- **Applications:** Mouseflow is beneficial for optimizing form usability, improving checkout processes, identifying usability issues through user behavior analysis, and enhancing overall website performance.

16.2.8 Kissmetrics

- **Functionality:** Kissmetrics focuses on customer behavior analytics, tracking user interactions across different devices and channels. It provides insights into user engagement, conversion rates, customer lifetime value (CLV), and retention metrics.
- **Applications:** Kissmetrics helps in understanding user journeys, improving marketing campaign effectiveness, optimizing sales funnels, and personalizing user experiences based on behavior and engagement history.

16.2.9 Pendo

- **Functionality:** Pendo offers product analytics and user feedback tools to understand how users interact with software applications. It tracks feature adoption, user engagement, and offers in-app surveys to gather qualitative feedback.
- **Applications:** Pendo is used for optimizing product onboarding experiences, prioritizing feature development based on user feedback, improving user retention, and measuring the impact of product changes on user behavior.

CHAPTER 17
MOBILE APP PERFORMANCE OPTIMIZATION

17.1 STRATEGIES FOR SPEED AND RESPONSIVENESS

Optimizing mobile app performance is crucial for delivering a seamless user experience. Users expect fast loading times, smooth interactions, and responsive interfaces. Poor performance can lead to high abandonment rates and negative reviews.

Optimizing mobile app performance for speed and responsiveness requires a holistic approach that addresses coding practices, asset management, network efficiency, UI rendering, memory management, background tasks, testing, and platform-specific optimizations. By implementing these strategies, developers can ensure their apps deliver a seamless user experience, minimize user frustration, and maintain high user engagement and satisfaction levels in an increasingly competitive mobile landscape.

17.1.1 Efficient Code and Architecture

- **Efficient Coding Practices:** Utilize efficient coding practices to minimize memory usage, reduce CPU cycles, and optimize app size. This includes avoiding nested loops, optimizing algorithms, and using efficient data structures.
- **Modular Architecture:** Implement a modular architecture that separates components logically. This allows for better code maintenance, easier debugging, and scalability. Use design patterns like MVC (Model-View-Controller) or MVVM (Model-View-ViewModel) to achieve this separation.

17.1.2 Image and Asset Optimization

- **Image Compression:** Optimize images for mobile screens by compressing them without compromising quality. Use tools like ImageOptim or TinyPNG to reduce file size while maintaining visual integrity.
- **Lazy Loading:** Implement lazy loading for images and assets that are not immediately visible on the screen. This technique reduces initial

load times and improves app responsiveness, especially for content-heavy applications.

17.1.3 Minimize Network Requests

- **API Consolidation:** Reduce the number of API calls by consolidating requests whenever possible. Combine data fetching into single requests or batch requests to minimize network overhead and latency.
- **Caching:** Implement caching mechanisms to store frequently accessed data locally. Use techniques like HTTP caching headers or local storage (e.g., SQLite, UserDefaults) to reduce the need for repeated network requests and improve app responsiveness.

17.1.4 UI and Rendering Optimization

- **UI Thread Management:** Ensure UI operations are performed on the main thread to maintain smooth interactions and responsiveness. Offload heavy tasks, such as image processing or data fetching, to background threads using Grand Central Dispatch (GCD) or Operations.
- **Render Performance:** Optimize UI rendering by reducing the complexity of views and layouts. Use lightweight components, flatten view hierarchies, and leverage techniques like pre-drawing or pre-rendering for complex UI elements.

17.1.5 Memory Management

- **Memory Profiling:** Use tools like Xcode's Instruments or Android Profiler to monitor memory usage and identify memory leaks or excessive memory allocations. Optimize memory usage by releasing unused objects, using weak references, and implementing object pooling where applicable.
- **Resource Cleanup:** Properly manage resources such as file handles, network connections, and database connections. Ensure resources are released promptly after use to prevent memory bloat and improve overall app performance.

17.1.6 Background Tasks and Multitasking

- **Background Execution:** Minimize background execution to conserve battery life and system resources. Use background fetch, silent push notifications, or background processing for critical tasks only, optimizing their frequency and duration.
- **Multitasking Considerations:** Design app workflows to handle interruptions gracefully, such as incoming calls or switching between

apps. Save app state and resume quickly when returning from the background to maintain a seamless user experience.

17.1.7 Performance Monitoring and Testing

- **Real-time Monitoring:** Implement performance monitoring tools (e.g., Firebase Performance Monitoring, New Relic) to track app performance metrics in real-time. Monitor CPU usage, network latency, and user interactions to identify bottlenecks and areas for improvement.
- **Automated Testing:** Conduct performance testing using tools like XCTest for iOS or Espresso for Android to simulate various user scenarios and stress test the app under different conditions. Identify performance regressions early in the development cycle and optimize accordingly.

17.1.8 Optimize App Startup Time

- **Lazy Initialization:** Delay initialization of non-essential components until they are needed to reduce app startup time. Use lazy loading and asynchronous initialization techniques to prioritize essential functionalities during app launch.
- **Pre-fetching Data:** Pre-fetch necessary data and resources in advance during app startup to minimize loading times when users interact with the app. Predict user behavior patterns and preload relevant content to enhance responsiveness.

17.1.9 Platform-specific Optimization

Platform Guidelines

Adhere to platform-specific guidelines and best practices (e.g., iOS Human Interface Guidelines, Android Performance Guidelines) for optimizing app performance. Leverage platform-specific APIs and optimizations to enhance app responsiveness and usability.

Hardware Acceleration

Utilize hardware acceleration features (e.g., GPU rendering, Metal on iOS, Vulkan on Android) to offload graphical and computational tasks from the CPU, improving rendering performance and overall app responsiveness.

17.2 ADDRESSING BATTERY AND RESOURCE CONSUMPTION

Optimizing battery and resource consumption is essential for mobile apps to enhance user satisfaction and device efficiency. Excessive consumption can lead to increased device heating, reduced battery life, and diminished overall performance.

Optimizing battery and resource consumption in mobile apps requires a holistic approach that integrates efficient coding practices, network optimizations, background operations management, UI rendering improvements, power-efficient design strategies, and iterative testing cycles. By implementing these strategies, developers can deliver apps that operate efficiently on mobile devices, enhance user satisfaction, and prolong device battery life in today's competitive mobile landscape.

17.2.1 Efficient Code and Algorithms

Algorithm Optimization

Use efficient algorithms and data structures to minimize CPU usage and reduce computational overhead. Choose algorithms with lower time complexity for operations like sorting, searching, and data processing to conserve CPU resources.

Memory Management

Implement efficient memory management practices, such as releasing unused objects promptly and avoiding memory leaks. Use object pooling, where applicable, to reuse objects and reduce memory allocations, thereby optimizing overall resource usage.

17.2.2 Network Efficiency

Reduce Network Requests

Minimize unnecessary network requests by consolidating data fetching operations and implementing caching mechanisms. Use techniques like HTTP caching, local data storage, and prefetching to reduce reliance on frequent network communication, thereby saving battery and reducing data usage.

Optimize Data Transfer

Optimize data transfer protocols (e.g., HTTP/2, WebSocket) to reduce latency and improve network efficiency. Compress data payloads, prioritize critical data transfers, and implement efficient error handling mechanisms to minimize battery drain associated with network activities.

17.2.3 Background Operations Management

Limit Background Activity

Restrict background operations to essential tasks only, such as syncing critical data or receiving notifications. Use efficient background execution modes provided by mobile platforms (e.g., iOS Background Modes, Android Background Execution Limits) to conserve battery and prioritize user-initiated actions.

Optimize Sync Intervals

Adjust sync intervals dynamically based on user activity and network conditions. Implement smart scheduling algorithms to synchronize data updates during periods of low device activity or when the device is charging to minimize battery impact.

17.2.4 UI and Rendering Optimization

Efficient UI Rendering

Optimize UI rendering to minimize GPU usage and conserve battery. Use lightweight UI components, flatten view hierarchies, and leverage hardware-accelerated rendering techniques (e.g., OpenGL ES, Metal on iOS, Vulkan on Android) to improve rendering performance without compromising visual quality.

Animation Optimization

Limit the use of complex animations and transitions that consume CPU and GPU resources excessively. Use animation libraries optimized for mobile platforms and employ techniques like frame rate throttling to maintain smooth animations while conserving battery power.

17.2.5 Power-efficient Design Practices

Use System APIs

Leverage system APIs provided by mobile platforms for power management and resource optimization. Utilize features like Doze Mode (Android) or App Nap (iOS) to minimize background activity and maximize battery life during periods of inactivity.

Low Power Modes

Support low power modes or battery saver features offered by mobile operating systems. Adjust app behavior dynamically based on the device's power state to reduce CPU frequency, disable non-critical features, and extend battery life during prolonged use.

17.2.6 Performance Monitoring and Optimization

Real-time Monitoring

Implement performance monitoring tools (e.g., Firebase Performance Monitoring, New Relic) to track battery usage, CPU cycles, and memory consumption in real-time.

Monitor resource-intensive operations and optimize code accordingly to reduce overall app footprint and improve efficiency.

Battery Profiling

Use battery profiling tools provided by mobile development environments (e.g., Xcode Energy Diagnostics, Android Battery Historian) to analyze app behavior and identify power-hungry components or processes. Optimize algorithms and workflows based on profiling data to minimize battery impact.

17.2.7 Testing and Optimization Iterations

Battery and Resource Testing

Conduct comprehensive testing across different devices, network conditions, and usage scenarios to evaluate battery and resource consumption. Use automated testing frameworks (e.g., XCTest, Espresso) to simulate real-world conditions and identify areas for optimization.

Iterative Optimization

Implement iterative optimization cycles based on testing feedback and performance metrics. Prioritize improvements that yield significant reductions in battery drain and resource usage, while maintaining app functionality and user experience standards.

17.2.8 User Education and Feedback

Educate Users

Provide transparency regarding app resource consumption through user settings or in-app notifications. Educate users on how to optimize app usage to minimize battery drain, such as adjusting sync settings, managing background activity, or enabling power-saving features.

Collect User Feedback

Gather user feedback regarding battery performance and resource usage through app reviews, surveys, or analytics. Use qualitative insights to identify pain points and prioritize optimizations that align with user expectations and device capabilities.

PART VII

EMERGING TRENDS IN MOBILE TECHNOLOGIES

CHAPTER 18
MOBILE AR AND VR TECHNOLOGIES

18.1 AUGMENTED REALITY (AR) AND VIRTUAL REALITY (VR) IN MOBILE

18.1.1 Augmented Reality (AR) in Mobile

Augmented Reality (AR) has emerged as a transformative technology, blending digital information with the real-world environment through mobile devices. By overlaying virtual elements onto the user's physical surroundings, AR enhances user experience and interaction with digital content. This technology has gained significant traction in various fields, including gaming, education, healthcare, and retail, reshaping how people perceive and interact with digital information on mobile platforms.

Augmented Reality in mobile devices continues to redefine how users interact with digital content and their physical surroundings. From enhancing gaming experiences to revolutionizing education, healthcare, and retail, AR offers limitless possibilities for innovation.

As technology continues to advance, addressing challenges such as hardware limitations and privacy concerns will be crucial in realizing the full potential of AR on mobile platforms. Looking ahead, the integration of AI, 5G, and wearable AR devices promises to further elevate AR experiences, paving the way for a future where digital and physical realities seamlessly converge.

Evolution of Augmented Reality in Mobile Devices

The evolution of AR in mobile devices traces back to the early experiments with marker-based AR applications.

These applications relied on predefined markers or images to trigger virtual overlays, providing users with basic interactions. Over time, advancements in mobile hardware capabilities, such as improved sensors, processors, and cameras, enabled more sophisticated AR experiences. This evolution facilitated the transition towards markerless AR, where digital content could be anchored to real-world objects or environments without the need for specific markers.

Key Components and Technologies Driving AR on Mobile

Sensors and Cameras

Mobile devices integrate various sensors, including accelerometers, gyroscopes, and depth sensors, along with high-resolution cameras. These sensors enable AR applications to accurately track the device's position and orientation in real-time, essential for overlaying virtual content seamlessly onto the user's view of the physical world.

Computer Vision

Computer vision algorithms play a crucial role in AR by interpreting visual data captured through mobile cameras.

These algorithms help identify and track objects, surfaces, and environments, enabling AR applications to place virtual objects accurately and realistically within the user's surroundings.

AR Software Development Kits (SDKs)

AR SDKs provided by tech giants like Apple (ARKit) and Google (ARCore) empower developers to create AR applications for iOS and Android platforms, respectively. These SDKs offer robust frameworks, APIs, and tools that simplify the integration of AR features, such as motion tracking, environmental understanding, and light estimation, into mobile applications.

Applications of Augmented Reality in Mobile

Gaming

AR has revolutionized mobile gaming by blending virtual elements with the player's physical environment. Games like Pokémon GO leverage AR to allow players to capture virtual creatures overlaid onto real-world locations, creating an immersive and interactive gaming experience.

Education and Training

In education, AR enhances learning experiences by providing interactive visualizations and simulations. Mobile AR applications can overlay educational content, such as 3D models of historical artifacts or anatomical structures, onto textbooks or real-world objects, making learning more engaging and memorable.

Retail and Marketing

Retailers utilize AR on mobile devices to offer virtual try-on experiences for clothing and accessories. AR applications allow consumers to visualize how products will look in real-time, using their smartphones or tablets, thereby enhancing purchasing decisions and reducing returns.

Healthcare

AR applications in healthcare assist medical professionals in visualizing patient data, such as MRI scans or anatomical models, overlaid onto the patient's body or medical equipment. This technology aids in surgical planning, medical training, and patient education, improving overall healthcare outcomes.

Challenges and Future Trends

Hardware Limitations

While mobile devices continue to evolve, challenges such as battery life, processing power, and sensor accuracy remain significant hurdles for delivering seamless AR experiences on a large scale.

User Interface and Experience

Designing intuitive user interfaces (UI) and ensuring a smooth user experience (UX) are critical for the widespread adoption of AR applications on mobile devices. Developers must balance functionality with simplicity to create compelling AR experiences that resonate with users.

Privacy and Security

As AR applications collect and process real-time data from the user's environment, concerns about privacy and data security arise. Implementing robust privacy measures and ensuring transparent data handling practices are essential to building trust among users.

Future Trends

The future of AR in mobile devices holds promise with advancements in wearable AR glasses, 5G connectivity, and AI-driven AR experiences. These developments are expected to enhance AR capabilities, enabling more immersive interactions and unlocking new possibilities across various industries.

18.1.2 Virtual Reality (VR) in Mobile

Virtual Reality (VR) represents a transformative technology that immerses users in a simulated environment, creating a sense of presence and interaction. While traditionally associated with dedicated headsets, VR has increasingly made its way into mobile devices, offering portable and accessible VR experiences. This integration leverages the powerful capabilities of smartphones and tablets to deliver immersive content and applications, reshaping entertainment, education, training, and various other industries.

Virtual Reality in mobile devices continues to evolve, offering immersive experiences across entertainment, education, healthcare, and beyond. From gaming and virtual travel to therapeutic applications, mobile VR unlocks new possibilities for user engagement and interaction with digital content. As technology advances and hardware capabilities improve, addressing challenges such as content quality, user comfort, and hardware limitations will be crucial in driving the widespread adoption of VR on mobile platforms.

Looking ahead, innovations in connectivity, device integration, and content development are set to further elevate the role of VR in reshaping how users experience and interact with virtual worlds on their smartphones and tablets.

Evolution of Virtual Reality in Mobile Devices

The evolution of VR in mobile devices began with early experiments in stereoscopic 3D viewing and basic VR applications. Early smartphone-based VR solutions relied on inexpensive headsets, often made of cardboard or plastic, paired with mobile applications to provide immersive experiences.

These solutions laid the groundwork for more advanced VR experiences, driven by improvements in mobile hardware, including display resolutions, processing power, and motion sensors.

Today, smartphones equipped with high-resolution screens, powerful processors, and advanced graphics capabilities can deliver compelling VR content without the need for external sensors or bulky equipment.

Key Components and Technologies Driving VR on Mobile

Display Technology

High-resolution displays with fast refresh rates are essential for delivering immersive VR experiences on mobile devices. OLED and AMOLED screens are preferred for their ability to provide vibrant colors and deep blacks, enhancing the visual fidelity of VR content.

Motion Tracking and Sensors

Mobile VR headsets incorporate gyroscopes, accelerometers, and magnetometers to track the user's head movements accurately. Some devices also include external sensors or use smartphone cameras for positional tracking, enabling users to move within virtual environments and interact with objects.

VR Software Development

VR development kits and platforms, such as Google Cardboard, Google Daydream, and Samsung Gear VR, provide tools and APIs for developers to create VR applications for Android and iOS devices.

These platforms simplify the integration of VR features like stereoscopic rendering, spatial audio, and motion controls into mobile apps.

Applications of Virtual Reality in Mobile

Entertainment and Gaming

Mobile VR offers immersive gaming experiences where players can interact with virtual worlds and characters in 360-degree environments. Games like "Minecraft VR" and "Beat Saber" provide engaging gameplay experiences that leverage the immersive nature of VR to enhance user engagement.

Education and Training

VR applications in education enable students to explore historical landmarks, dive into virtual science labs, or participate in immersive language learning experiences. Mobile VR makes these educational simulations accessible and cost-effective, allowing learners to engage with content in a more interactive and memorable way.

Virtual Tours and Travel

Mobile VR facilitates virtual tours of destinations worldwide, enabling users to explore museums, landmarks, and scenic locations from the comfort of their homes. Applications like "Google Expeditions" provide guided tours with 360-degree panoramic views, enhancing the travel and tourism experience.

Healthcare and Therapy

VR applications on mobile devices support therapeutic interventions, such as exposure therapy for phobias or pain management techniques. Mobile VR headsets can deliver immersive environments that aid in relaxation, distraction, or rehabilitation, complementing traditional medical treatments.

Challenges and Future Trends

Hardware Limitations

Despite advancements, mobile VR experiences may still face limitations in terms of processing power, battery life, and thermal management. These factors can impact the quality and duration of VR sessions on mobile devices, necessitating ongoing improvements in hardware efficiency.

Content Quality and Development

Developing high-quality VR content for mobile platforms requires optimization for performance and user experience. Balancing visual fidelity with device capabilities is crucial for delivering smooth and immersive VR experiences that meet user expectations.

User Comfort and Safety

VR experiences can induce motion sickness or discomfort, especially if latency or motion tracking issues are present. Designing ergonomic and lightweight VR headsets, along with optimizing software for smooth performance, can help mitigate these challenges and enhance user comfort.

Future Trends

The future of VR in mobile devices holds promise with advancements in 5G connectivity, augmented reality (AR) integration, and standalone VR headsets. These developments are expected to expand the capabilities of mobile VR, enabling more interactive experiences, improved content streaming, and enhanced social interactions within virtual environments.

18.2 APPLICATIONS AND CHALLENGES

Mobile technologies have become ubiquitous in modern society, revolutionizing how individuals communicate, work, and access information. From smartphones and tablets to wearable devices and IoT (Internet of Things) gadgets, mobile technologies encompass a wide range of applications that enhance productivity, connectivity, and entertainment. However, along with their transformative benefits, these technologies also present various challenges related to security, privacy, infrastructure, and user experience.

Mobile technologies have become integral to daily life, offering diverse applications across communication, commerce, healthcare, education, entertainment, and beyond. While these technologies enhance convenience, productivity, and connectivity, they also present challenges related to security, infrastructure, compatibility, and user experience. Addressing these challenges requires collaborative efforts from technology developers, policymakers, and stakeholders to ensure the responsible and sustainable evolution of mobile technologies. Looking ahead, embracing emerging trends and technologies will be key to unlocking new potentials and delivering innovative solutions that meet the evolving needs of global mobile users.

18.2.1 Applications of Mobile Technologies

Communication and Social Networking

Mobile technologies have fundamentally transformed communication, enabling instant messaging, voice calls, and video conferencing from anywhere with internet connectivity. Social networking platforms like Facebook, Instagram, and Twitter leverage mobile apps to connect users globally, fostering community engagement and real-time interaction.

E-commerce and Mobile Payments

The rise of mobile e-commerce platforms, such as Amazon and Alibaba, allows consumers to shop online conveniently using their smartphones or tablets. Mobile payment systems like Apple Pay and Google Pay enable secure transactions via NFC (Near Field Communication) technology, reducing the dependence on physical credit cards.

Productivity and Remote Work

Mobile technologies empower professionals to work remotely by accessing emails, documents, and enterprise applications on mobile devices. Collaboration tools like Slack and Microsoft Teams facilitate real-time communication and project management, enabling teams to collaborate efficiently regardless of location.

Healthcare and Telemedicine

Mobile technologies support telemedicine initiatives, allowing healthcare providers to deliver remote consultations, monitor patient health data, and provide medical advice through mobile apps. Wearable health trackers and IoT-enabled devices further enhance patient care by collecting real-time health metrics and facilitating proactive healthcare management.

Education and E-learning

Mobile technologies play a pivotal role in education by enabling access to online courses, digital textbooks, and interactive learning apps. Platforms like Coursera and Khan Academy offer mobile apps that facilitate self-paced learning and skill development, making education more accessible and flexible.

Entertainment and Media Consumption

Mobile devices serve as portable entertainment hubs, offering access to streaming services like Netflix and Spotify for on-the-go media consumption. Mobile gaming apps, such as PUBG Mobile and Candy Crush Saga, provide immersive gaming experiences that leverage the graphical capabilities and touch interface of smartphones.

18.2.2 Challenges in Mobile Technologies

Security and Privacy

Ensuring the security of sensitive data stored and transmitted via mobile devices remains a significant challenge. Issues such as data breaches, malware attacks, and unauthorized access pose risks to user privacy and organizational security, necessitating robust encryption, authentication measures, and mobile security solutions.

Infrastructure and Connectivity

Disparities in mobile network infrastructure and connectivity impact user experience and accessibility, particularly in rural or underserved areas. Issues such as network congestion, coverage gaps, and bandwidth limitations can hinder seamless communication, data transmission, and access to online services.

Device Fragmentation and Compatibility

The diversity of mobile devices, operating systems (iOS, Android, etc.), and screen sizes contributes to fragmentation challenges for app developers. Ensuring compatibility and optimizing performance across multiple devices and OS versions requires thorough testing and adaptation of mobile applications.

User Experience Design

Designing intuitive and responsive user interfaces (UI) for mobile applications is crucial for enhancing user experience (UX). Factors such as navigation complexity, loading times, and accessibility influence user satisfaction and adoption rates, requiring careful UI/UX design principles and usability testing.

Battery Life and Performance

Mobile devices face limitations in battery life and performance, impacting user productivity and application usage. Optimizing software efficiency, managing background processes, and adopting power-saving techniques are essential for extending battery life and ensuring consistent performance.

Regulatory Compliance

Compliance with regulatory requirements, such as data protection laws (GDPR, CCPA) and industry standards, poses compliance challenges for mobile app developers and organizations. Implementing data privacy practices, obtaining user consent, and adhering to legal frameworks are essential for maintaining trust and avoiding penalties.

18.2.3 Future Trends in Mobile Technologies

The future of mobile technologies is poised for continuous innovation and advancement, driven by emerging technologies and evolving user demands. Trends such as 5G connectivity, AI-driven applications, augmented reality (AR), and wearable devices are expected to redefine mobile experiences, offering new opportunities for connectivity, efficiency, and personalization.

CHAPTER 19

ARTIFICIAL INTELLIGENCE (AI) IN MOBILE APPS

19.1 INTEGRATING AI AND MACHINE LEARNING IN MOBILE APPLICATIONS

Artificial Intelligence (AI) and Machine Learning (ML) have revolutionized mobile applications by enabling advanced functionalities that enhance user experience, improve efficiency, and personalize interactions. From intelligent recommendations and predictive analytics to natural language processing and computer vision, AI and ML algorithms empower mobile apps to understand, analyze, and respond to user behavior and data in real-time.

AI and Machine Learning have transformed mobile applications by enabling intelligent features, personalized experiences, and enhanced functionalities that cater to user needs and preferences. From personalized recommendations and virtual assistants to healthcare diagnostics and augmented reality, AI-driven mobile apps offer unprecedented capabilities that enhance productivity, efficiency, and user engagement. Addressing challenges related to data privacy, performance optimization, ethical considerations, and user experience design is crucial for harnessing the full potential of AI in mobile applications. Looking ahead, embracing emerging trends and innovations will shape the future landscape of AI-powered mobile technologies, driving continuous evolution and redefining how users interact with digital services on their smartphones and tablets.

19.1.1 Evolution of AI and Machine Learning in Mobile Applications

The integration of AI and ML in mobile applications has evolved significantly, driven by advancements in algorithm development, computational power, and data availability. Initially, AI capabilities were limited to simple tasks like voice recognition or basic predictive models. However, with the proliferation of smartphones equipped with powerful processors and sensors, developers can now deploy sophisticated AI algorithms directly on mobile devices. This evolution has facilitated the emergence of AI-powered features such as virtual assistants, personalized recommendations, and real-time image recognition, offering seamless and responsive user experiences.

19.1.2 Key Components and Technologies Driving AI in Mobile Applications

Natural Language Processing (NLP)

NLP algorithms enable mobile apps to understand and interpret human language, facilitating voice commands, chatbots, and language translation services. Applications like Siri (Apple), Google Assistant, and chatbots integrated into customer service apps utilize NLP to enhance user interaction and accessibility.

Computer Vision

Mobile apps leverage computer vision algorithms to analyze and interpret visual data captured through smartphone cameras. This technology enables features such as facial recognition, object detection, augmented reality (AR), and image-based search capabilities, enhancing user engagement and interaction with digital content.

Predictive Analytics

Machine learning models embedded in mobile applications analyze user behavior and historical data to predict preferences, trends, and future actions. This capability enables personalized recommendations, targeted marketing campaigns, and proactive customer service, improving user satisfaction and business outcomes.

Edge Computing

Edge computing frameworks allow AI and ML computations to be processed locally on mobile devices, reducing latency and enhancing privacy by minimizing data transfer to cloud servers. This approach enables real-time decision-making and responsiveness in AI-driven mobile applications, particularly in scenarios where network connectivity is limited or unreliable.

19.1.3 Applications of AI and Machine Learning in Mobile Applications

Personalized Recommendations

E-commerce and content streaming apps use AI algorithms to analyze user preferences, purchase history, and browsing behavior to offer personalized product recommendations and content suggestions. This enhances user engagement and increases conversion rates by delivering relevant content tailored to individual interests.

Virtual Assistants

AI-powered virtual assistants like Siri, Google Assistant, and Amazon Alexa provide hands-free interaction and perform tasks based on voice commands. These assistants can schedule appointments, answer queries, control smart home devices, and perform various tasks, enhancing productivity and convenience for users.

Healthcare and Fitness Monitoring

Mobile health apps leverage AI and ML to monitor user health metrics, analyze medical data, and provide personalized health insights and recommendations. AI-powered diagnostics and predictive analytics help in early detection of health conditions, medication adherence, and lifestyle management, promoting proactive healthcare management.

Enhanced Security and Fraud Detection

Mobile banking and finance apps utilize AI algorithms for fraud detection, risk assessment, and biometric authentication. Machine learning models analyze transaction patterns, user behavior, and device characteristics to detect suspicious activities and protect sensitive information from unauthorized access.

Augmented Reality (AR) and Gaming

AR-enabled mobile apps integrate AI and computer vision to overlay virtual objects and information onto the real-world environment. Gaming apps like Pokémon GO and educational apps use AR to create immersive experiences that blend digital content with the user's physical surroundings, enhancing engagement and interactivity.

19.1.4 Challenges and Considerations in Integrating AI in Mobile Applications

Data Privacy and Security

AI-driven mobile apps require access to vast amounts of user data for training and inference, raising concerns about data privacy, security breaches, and compliance with regulatory requirements (e.g., GDPR, CCPA). Implementing robust data encryption, anonymization techniques, and secure data storage practices are essential to protect user privacy and maintain trust.

Performance Optimization

Deploying AI models on resource-constrained mobile devices necessitates optimizing algorithms for efficiency, minimizing computational resources, and reducing power consumption. Techniques such as model compression, quantization, and edge computing enable AI inference to be performed locally on devices, enhancing responsiveness and user experience.

Ethical and Bias Considerations

AI algorithms embedded in mobile applications must mitigate biases in data and decision-making processes to ensure fair and unbiased outcomes for all users. Ethical considerations, transparency in algorithmic decision-making, and continuous monitoring of AI systems are critical to prevent unintended consequences and promote responsible AI usage.

User Experience Design

Designing intuitive user interfaces (UI) and seamless user experiences (UX) for AI-driven features is crucial for adoption and usability. Clear communication of AI capabilities, providing user control over data usage, and integrating AI functionalities seamlessly into existing app workflows contribute to positive user interactions and satisfaction.

19.1.5 Future Trends in AI and Machine Learning in Mobile Applications

The future of AI and ML in mobile applications is poised for continued innovation and expansion, driven by advancements in AI research, mobile hardware capabilities, and user demand for personalized experiences. Emerging trends such as federated learning, AI-driven IoT integration, emotion recognition, and contextual awareness are expected to redefine mobile app development and user engagement across diverse industries.

19.2 PERSONALIZATION AND PREDICTIVE ANALYTICS

Personalization and predictive analytics have become integral components of mobile applications, transforming user experiences by tailoring content, recommendations, and interactions based on individual preferences and behaviors. These technologies leverage data insights and machine learning algorithms to anticipate user needs, deliver relevant content, and enhance engagement across various sectors, including e-commerce, entertainment, healthcare, and finance. By harnessing user data and behavioral patterns, mobile apps can offer personalized experiences that drive user satisfaction, loyalty, and business growth.

Personalization and predictive analytics have revolutionized mobile applications by enabling tailored experiences that anticipate user needs, enhance engagement, and drive business growth. From e-commerce and media streaming to healthcare and financial services, personalized recommendations, content, and services empower users with relevant information and seamless interactions. Addressing challenges related to data privacy, algorithmic fairness, user consent, and scalability is crucial for leveraging the full potential of personalization in mobile applications responsibly. Looking ahead, embracing emerging trends and innovations will enable mobile apps to deliver increasingly personalized and adaptive experiences that meet the evolving expectations and preferences of global users.

19.2.1 Evolution of Personalization and Predictive Analytics in Mobile Applications

The evolution of personalization and predictive analytics in mobile applications has been driven by advancements in data collection, storage, and processing capabilities. Initially, mobile apps relied on basic user preferences and manual customization options. However, with the proliferation of smartphones and the availability of big data analytics tools, developers can now harness vast amounts of user data to create dynamic and adaptive experiences. This evolution has enabled the integration of AI-driven algorithms that analyze user behavior, predict preferences, and automate personalized recommendations in real-time.

19.2.2 Key Components and Technologies Driving Personalization in Mobile Applications

User Data Collection and Profiling

Mobile apps collect user data through interactions, preferences, location information, and social media integrations. This data is aggregated and analyzed to create user profiles that capture demographic information, interests, browsing history, and purchase patterns, enabling personalized recommendations and content delivery.

Machine Learning Algorithms

Machine learning algorithms power predictive analytics in mobile applications by analyzing historical data to identify patterns, trends, and correlations. Algorithms such as collaborative filtering, content-based filtering, and reinforcement learning enable apps to predict user preferences, optimize recommendations, and personalize user interfaces based on real-time interactions.

Real-time Data Processing

Real-time data processing frameworks and technologies, such as Apache Kafka and Apache Spark, enable mobile apps to handle large volumes of data efficiently. These platforms facilitate data streaming, event processing, and real-time decision-making, allowing apps to deliver personalized notifications, updates, and recommendations instantly.

Contextual Awareness

Context-aware computing techniques leverage sensor data, environmental cues, and user context (e.g., time of day, location) to customize interactions and content delivery. Mobile apps use contextual information to adapt interfaces, suggest relevant content, and provide location-based services that enhance user relevance and utility.

19.2.3 Applications of Personalization and Predictive Analytics in Mobile Applications

E-commerce and Retail

E-commerce apps leverage predictive analytics to recommend products based on browsing history, purchase behavior, and demographic data. Personalized product suggestions, discounts, and targeted promotions enhance shopping experiences, increase conversion rates, and drive customer loyalty.

Content Streaming and Media

Media streaming apps like Netflix and Spotify use personalization algorithms to curate content recommendations tailored to user preferences, viewing history, and music preferences. By analyzing user interactions and feedback, these apps optimize content discovery and engagement, fostering a personalized entertainment experience.

Healthcare and Fitness

Mobile health and fitness apps employ predictive analytics to personalize wellness plans, recommend exercise routines, and track health metrics based on user goals and historical data. Personalized health insights, reminders, and adaptive coaching enhance user motivation and support long-term behavior change.

Financial Services

Mobile banking and finance apps utilize predictive analytics to offer personalized financial advice, budgeting tools, and investment recommendations tailored to individual financial goals and risk profiles. Predictive models analyze transaction history, spending patterns, and market trends to optimize financial planning and decision-making.

Travel and Hospitality

Travel apps leverage predictive analytics to offer personalized travel recommendations, hotel suggestions, and itinerary planning based on user preferences, travel history, and destination interests. Dynamic pricing models and real-time updates enhance travel planning efficiency and customer satisfaction.

19.2.4 Challenges and Considerations in Implementing Personalization in Mobile Applications

Data Privacy and Security

Collecting and storing user data for personalization raises concerns about data privacy, security breaches, and compliance with regulatory requirements (e.g., GDPR, CCPA). Implementing robust data protection measures, anonymizing user data, and obtaining explicit consent are critical to safeguarding user privacy and maintaining trust.

Algorithmic Bias and Fairness

Machine learning algorithms used for personalization may inadvertently perpetuate biases based on demographic factors, historical data, or implicit assumptions. Ensuring algorithmic fairness, transparency in decision-making, and continuous monitoring of model performance are essential to mitigate biases and promote equitable user experiences.

User Consent and Control

Providing users with transparency and control over their data usage and personalization preferences is essential for building trust and compliance with privacy regulations. Offering opt-in/opt-out mechanisms, clear data access policies, and user-friendly settings for managing preferences empower users to customize their experience while respecting their privacy rights.

Scalability and Performance

Scaling personalization strategies to accommodate growing user bases and diverse data sources requires robust infrastructure, scalable architectures, and efficient data processing pipelines. Optimizing algorithm performance, minimizing latency, and ensuring responsiveness are crucial for delivering seamless personalized experiences across mobile platforms.

19.2.5 Future Trends in Personalization and Predictive Analytics in Mobile Applications

The future of personalization and predictive analytics in mobile applications is poised for continuous innovation and expansion, driven by advancements in AI technologies, real-time data processing, and user-centric design principles. Emerging trends such as hyper-personalization, AI-driven recommendations, contextual intelligence, and predictive user interfaces are expected to redefine user engagement and elevate personalized experiences across diverse sectors.

APPENDIX A: GLOSSARY OF MOBILE TECHNOLOGY TERMS

Android: An operating system developed by Google for mobile devices, based on the Linux kernel. It is widely used in smartphones, tablets, and other smart devices.

App: Short for application, it refers to software designed to perform specific tasks or provide specific functions on mobile devices.

Bluetooth: A wireless technology standard for exchanging data over short distances between mobile devices, peripherals, and accessories.

Cloud Storage: Storage space provided by remote servers accessed via the internet, allowing users to store and access data from mobile devices.

CPU (Central Processing Unit): The main processing unit of a mobile device responsible for executing instructions and performing calculations.

Device Firmware: Software embedded in hardware devices, such as smartphones and tablets, to control their basic operations and functionalities.

Edge Computing: A distributed computing paradigm where data processing occurs closer to the data source (e.g., mobile device) rather than relying on centralized cloud servers.

Encryption: The process of encoding data to secure it from unauthorized access or interception, commonly used to protect data on mobile devices and during transmission.

Fingerprint Scanner: Biometric authentication technology used in mobile devices to verify users' identities based on their fingerprint patterns.

GPS (Global Positioning System): Satellite-based navigation system that provides location and time information to mobile devices for navigation and location-based services.

Hotspot: A feature on mobile devices that allows them to act as Wi-Fi access points, enabling other devices to connect to the internet through them.

iOS: Apple's mobile operating system used exclusively on iPhone, iPad, and iPod Touch devices.

Mobile Data: Internet connectivity provided by mobile carriers, allowing mobile devices to access the internet without Wi-Fi.

Mobile Payment: Transaction methods using mobile devices, such as NFC (Near Field Communication) or QR code scanning, to make payments electronically.

NFC (Near Field Communication): Short-range wireless technology that enables communication between mobile devices and other NFC-enabled devices, used for contactless payments and data exchange.

Operating System (OS): Software that manages hardware resources and provides services for mobile applications to run, such as Android, iOS, and Windows Phone.

Push Notification: Messages or alerts sent by mobile apps to users' devices, even when the app is not actively in use, to provide updates or reminders.

RAM (Random Access Memory): Temporary storage used by mobile devices to hold data and applications currently in use, providing fast access for processing.

Smartphone: A mobile phone that combines features of a cellular phone with capabilities similar to a computer, such as internet access, touchscreen interface, and apps.

SIM Card (Subscriber Identity Module): A removable smart card used in mobile devices to authenticate users on cellular networks and store user data.

Touchscreen: A display screen that responds to touch input, allowing users to interact directly with mobile devices by tapping, swiping, and pinching.

UI (User Interface): The visual and interactive elements of a mobile application or device through which users interact, including screens, menus, buttons, and icons.

UX (User Experience): The overall experience and usability of a mobile application or device, encompassing ease of use, responsiveness, and satisfaction.

Virtual Assistant: AI-powered software that responds to voice commands or text input to perform tasks and provide information on mobile devices, such as Siri, Google Assistant, and Alexa.

Wi-Fi: Wireless networking technology that allows mobile devices to connect to the internet and other devices within a local area network (LAN) using radio waves.

APPENDIX B: RECOMMENDED READING AND RESOURCES

Handbook of Mobile Ad Hoc Networks for Mobility Models edited by Wenbing Zhao, Auerbach Publications, 2010.

Handbook of Research on Mobile Software Engineering: Design, Implementation, and Emergent Applications by D. B. Lenarduzzi et al., IGI Global, 2017.

Handbook of Research on Mobility and Computing: Evolving Technologies and Ubiquitous Impacts edited by Maria Manuela Cruz-Cunha et al., IGI Global, 2010.

Location-Based Services and Geo-Information Engineering by Allan Brimicombe, CRC Press, 2013.

Mobile Agents and Applications edited by James A. Hendler, Springer, 1998.

Mobile Agents in Networking and Distributed Computing by C. Molina-Jimenez and J. Cabot, Wiley, 2004.

Mobile and Wireless Communications: Key Technologies and Future Applications by Alan Bensky, Wiley, 2006.

Mobile Application Development, Usability, and Security by Sougata Mukherjea, IGI Global, 2016.

Mobile Application Development: Building Applications for the iPhone and Android by Tony Gaitatzis, Wiley, 2010.

Mobile Broadcasting with WiMAX: Principles, Technology, and Applications by Amitabha Ghosh and Rapeepat Ratasuk, Academic Press, 2008.

Mobile Business: Strategies for Mobile and Wireless Companies by Peter Curwen and Jason Whalley, Wiley, 2010.

Mobile Commerce: Technology, Theory and Applications by Turban et al., Prentice Hall, 2002.

Mobile Communication and Society: A Global Perspective edited by Manuel Castells et al., MIT Press, 2006.

Mobile Communications Handbook by Jerry D. Gibson, Academic Press, 2019.

Mobile Computing Deployment and Management: Real World Skills for CompTIA Mobility+ Certification and Beyond by Robert J. Bartz, McGraw-Hill Education, 2015.

Mobile Computing Principles: Designing and Developing Mobile Applications with UML and XML by Reza B'Far, Cambridge University Press, 2004.

Mobile Computing, Applications, and Services: Second International ICST Conference, MobiCASE 2010, Santa Clara, CA, USA, October 25-28, 2010, Revised Selected Papers edited by Sirajum Munir et al., Springer, 2011.

Mobile Computing: A Systems Integrative Approach by Dharma Prakash Agarwal, Oxford University Press, 2007.

Mobile Computing: Concepts, Methodologies, Tools, and Applications edited by David Taniar, IGI Global, 2009.

Mobile Computing: Implementing Pervasive Information and Communications Technologies by Tomasz Imielinski and Hank Korth, Kluwer Academic Publishers, 2013.

Mobile Computing: Securing Your Workforce by Amitabh Mishra, Packt Publishing, 2016.

Mobile Computing: Technology, Applications, and Service Creation by Talukder & Yavagal, McGraw-Hill Education, 2007.

Mobile Design and Development: Practical Concepts and Techniques for Creating Mobile Sites and Web Apps by Brian Fling, O'Reilly Media, 2009.

Mobile Device Security: A Comprehensive Guide to Securing Your Information in a Moving Environment by David D. Coleman and Matthew S. Shoemaker, Wiley, 2012.

Mobile Health: Sensors, Analytic Methods, and Applications edited by Xia Hu, CRC Press, 2017.

Mobile Interface Theory: Embodied Space and Locative Media by Jason Farman, Routledge, 2012.

Mobile IP Technology for M-Business by Mohammad Ilyas and Syed A. Ahson, CRC Press, 2006.

Mobile Learning: A Handbook for Developers, Educators, and Learners by Scott McQuiggan, Routledge, 2016.

Mobile Learning: Transforming the Delivery of Education and Training by Mohamed Ally, Athabasca University Press, 2009.

Mobile Location Services: The Definitive Guide by Andrew Jagoe, Wiley, 2008.

Mobile Messaging Technologies and Services: SMS, EMS and MMS by Gwenaël Le Bodic and Pascal Couderc, Wiley, 2005.

Mobile Payment: Technologien, Strategien, Trends und Fallstudien by Jörg Himmelreich and Jörg Becker, Springer Vieweg, 2013. [In German]

Mobile Platforms and Development Environments edited by Sumi Helal and Michael G. Hinchey, Wiley, 2006.

Mobile Robotics: Solutions and Challenges by J. Norberto Pires, Springer, 2013.

Mobile Service Innovation and Business Models edited by Bouwman et al., Springer, 2008.

Mobile Technologies for Conflict Management: Online Dispute Resolution, Governance, Participation by Marta Poblet, Springer, 2018.

Mobile Technology: Principles and Practice by Ajay R. Mishra, Auerbach Publications, 2016.

Mobile Video with Mobile IPv6 by B. Stiller et al., Springer, 2012.

Mobile Web Development: Building mobile websites, SMS and MMS messaging, mobile payments, and automated voice call systems with XHTML MP, WCSS, and mobile AJAX by Nirav Mehta, Packt Publishing, 2008.

Security for Mobile Networks and Platforms by K. Daniel Wong, Artech House, 2012.

Wireless Communications & Networks by William Stallings, Pearson, 2017.

Wireless Communications and Networks: Recent Advances by Sudhir Warrier, Taylor & Francis Group, 2012.

Wireless LANs and Bluetooth by Gordon Ramsey, Artech House, 2002.

Wireless Personal Communications: Emerging Technologies for Enhanced Communications edited by William H. Tranter et al., Prentice Hall, 2007.

Wireless Sensor Networks: Technology, Protocols, and Applications edited by Kazem Sohraby et al., Wiley, 2007.

APPENDIX C: MOBILE APP DEVELOPMENT TOOLS AND FRAMEWORKS

Mobile app development has evolved significantly with the advent of sophisticated tools and frameworks that streamline the development process, enhance efficiency, and facilitate cross-platform compatibility.

Cross-Platform Development Tools

Cross-platform development tools enable developers to build applications that can run on multiple platforms, reducing development time and effort by leveraging shared codebases.

Flutter

Flutter is an open-source UI toolkit by Google for building natively compiled applications for mobile, web, and desktop from a single codebase.

Features:

- **Hot Reload:** Allows developers to instantly view changes made to the code.
- **Expressive UI:** Offers customizable widgets for creating rich interfaces.
- **Native Performance:** Compiles to native ARM code for high-performance applications.
- **Extensive Widget Library:** Includes Material Design and Cupertino widgets for Android and iOS style interfaces, respectively.
- **Use Case:** Ideal for startups, enterprises, and developers aiming for visually appealing, high-performance applications with a single codebase.

React Native

React Native, developed by Facebook, enables developers to build native mobile apps using JavaScript and React.

Features:

- **Reusable Components:** Components written in React can be reused across iOS and Android.
- **Fast Development Cycles:** Supports hot reloading to view changes instantly.
- **Strong Community Support:** Active community with extensive libraries and components.

Use Case:

- Suited for developers familiar with JavaScript and React, aiming for native-like performance and look while sharing a significant amount of code across platforms.

Xamarin

Xamarin, owned by Microsoft, allows developers to build cross-platform apps using C# and .NET.

Features:

- **Native UI:** Uses native UI controls, resulting in native performance and look.
- **Code Sharing:** Shares up to 90% of code across platforms.
- **Integration with Visual Studio:** Fully integrated with Visual Studio and supports other IDEs.

Use Case:

- Best for enterprises and developers proficient in C#, aiming for native performance with shared code across Android, iOS, and Windows platforms.

Ionic

Ionic is an open-source framework for building hybrid mobile apps using web technologies like HTML, CSS, and JavaScript.

Features:

- **UI Components:** Pre-designed UI components and layouts.
- **Cross-Platform Compatibility:** Runs on iOS, Android, and the web.
- **Integration with Angular or React:** Offers integration with popular frameworks for enhanced functionality.

Use Case:

- Suitable for developers familiar with web technologies, aiming to deploy applications across multiple platforms with a single codebase.

PhoneGap / Apache Cordova

Apache Cordova (formerly PhoneGap) is an open-source framework for building mobile apps using web technologies.

Features:

- **Access to Device APIs:** Utilizes device APIs through JavaScript.
- **Cross-Platform Compatibility:** Supports Android, iOS, Windows, and more.
- **Plugin Ecosystem:** Extensive plugin ecosystem for additional functionality.

Use Case:

- Developers looking to leverage existing web development skills for building mobile apps with access to native device features.

Native Development Tools

Native development tools are platform-specific, offering deep integration with the respective operating systems and providing access to native APIs and performance.

Android Studio

Android Studio is the official IDE for Android app development, based on IntelliJ IDEA.

Features:

- **Android SDK Tools:** Includes tools for building, debugging, and profiling Android apps.
- **Emulator:** Android Emulator for testing apps on virtual devices.
- **Support for Kotlin and Java:** Officially supports both Kotlin and Java programming languages.

Use Case:

- Essential for Android developers looking for a powerful IDE with comprehensive tools for native Android app development.

Xcode

Xcode is Apple's integrated development environment (IDE) for macOS used for developing software for macOS, iOS, iPadOS, watchOS, and tvOS.

Features:

- **Interface Builder:** Design interface elements visually.

- **Swift and Objective-C Support:** Officially supports both Swift and Objective-C languages.
- **iOS Simulator:** Test apps on simulated iOS devices.

Use Case:

- Crucial for iOS and macOS developers looking to build native applications with deep integration into Apple's ecosystem.

Backend Services and APIs

Backend services and APIs provide the infrastructure and functionalities required to power mobile applications, including data storage, user management, and real-time communication.

Firebase

Firebase is Google's platform providing a suite of backend services for mobile and web apps.

Features:

- **Authentication:** Securely authenticate users with email, password, and social logins.
- **Realtime Database:** NoSQL cloud database for storing and syncing data in real time.
- **Analytics and Crash Reporting:** Insights into app usage and performance.
- **Cloud Messaging:** Send notifications and messages to users across platforms.

Use Case:

- Suitable for developers needing a scalable backend infrastructure with real-time data synchronization and analytics capabilities.

AWS Amplify

AWS Amplify is a set of tools and services by Amazon Web Services (AWS) for building scalable mobile and web applications.

Features:

- **Authentication:** Easily add authentication using Amazon Cognito.
- **Data Storage:** Provides a managed backend with features like offline data synchronization.
- **APIs and GraphQL:** Develop APIs and interact with GraphQL endpoints.
- **Analytics and AI/ML:** Integrates with AWS services for analytics, machine learning, and more.

Use Case:

- Ideal for developers looking for a robust backend solution with scalable infrastructure and integration with AWS services.

App Design and Prototyping Tools

App design and prototyping tools help designers and developers create intuitive and visually appealing user interfaces (UI) and user experiences (UX).

Sketch

Sketch is a vector graphics editor for macOS used for designing interfaces and prototypes for mobile and web apps.

Features:

- **Vector Editing:** Create scalable designs with precision.
- **Artboards:** Organize designs for different screen sizes.
- **Plugins:** Extensible with plugins for added functionality.

Use Case:

- Essential for UI/UX designers creating pixel-perfect designs for mobile applications.

Adobe XD

Adobe XD is Adobe's platform for designing and prototyping user experiences for web and mobile apps.

Features:

- **Prototyping:** Create interactive prototypes with transitions and animations.
- **Collaboration:** Share designs for feedback and collaboration.
- **Integration with Adobe Creative Cloud:** Sync assets and workflows across Adobe tools.

Use Case:

- Suited for designers and developers collaborating on UX/UI design and prototyping for mobile applications.

Mobile Testing and Debugging Tools

Testing and debugging tools ensure the quality and performance of mobile applications across different devices and platforms.

Appium

Appium is an open-source tool for automating native, hybrid, and mobile web apps on iOS and Android platforms.

Features:

- **Cross-Platform:** Write tests using any programming language and test framework.
- **Real Devices and Emulators:** Test on real devices, simulators, and emulators.
- **Integration:** Integrates with CI/CD tools for continuous testing.

Use Case:

- Essential for mobile developers and testers automating functional testing across multiple platforms.

Firebase Test Lab

Firebase Test Lab is a cloud-based app-testing infrastructure by Google for testing Android and iOS apps.

Features:

- **Automated and Manual Testing:** Run automated and manual tests on real devices.
- **Robust Test Environment:** Test apps for functionality, performance, and usability.
- **Integration with Firebase:** Seamless integration with other Firebase services.

Use Case:

- Ideal for developers ensuring app quality through automated and manual testing on real devices.

Version Control and Collaboration Tools

Version control and collaboration tools enable teams to manage codebase changes, track versions, and collaborate effectively.

Git

Git is a distributed version control system for tracking changes in source code during software development.

Features:

- **Branching and Merging:** Manage multiple versions of code simultaneously.
- **Collaboration:** Facilitates collaborative development with pull requests and code reviews.
- **Open Source:** Widely adopted and supported by a vast community.

Use Case:

- Essential for teams managing codebase versions, facilitating collaboration, and ensuring code integrity.

GitHub

GitHub is a web-based hosting service for version control using Git, offering collaboration, code review, and issue tracking features.

Features:

- **Repositories:** Host Git repositories and manage projects.
- **Issues and Projects:** Track issues, manage tasks, and organize projects.
- **Community and Collaboration:** Explore open-source projects and collaborate with developers worldwide.

Use Case:

- Crucial for teams working on open-source projects, enabling collaborative development and community engagement.

Continuous Integration and Deployment (CI/CD) Tools

CI/CD tools automate the build, test, and deployment processes, ensuring code quality and accelerating time-to-market.

Jenkins

Jenkins is an open-source automation server for building, testing, and deploying software.

Features:

- **Pipeline:** Define CI/CD pipelines for automating build, test, and deployment processes.
- **Extensibility:** Extensive plugin ecosystem for integrating with other tools and services.
- **Distributed Builds:** Scale automation across multiple machines and environments.

Use Case:

- Essential for teams implementing continuous integration and delivery pipelines for mobile app development.

INDEX

S

T

U

V

Z

www.ingramcontent.com/pod-product-compliance
Lightning Source LLC
LaVergne TN
LVHW062111200926
848484LV00007B/1641